Dismantling Race in Hi

"In this impressive collection, editors Arday and Mirza tackle the perennial status of racism in the academy. Beyond the common refrain that Whites are the center of the problem, the contributors rightfully focus our efforts at dismantling the ideology of whiteness itself. They argue that decolonizing higher education means confronting the white occupation of academic knowledge and unsettling its grip over mundane as well as high stakes decisions. The authors launch a compelling assault on whiteness that not only grabs our attention, it renews our commitment to democracy and simple decency. Their brave response is a welcomed voice during these challenging times."
—Professor Zeus Leonardo, *University of California, Berkeley, USA*

"Arday and Mirza have brought together some of the most exciting and highly respected voices in contemporary anti-racist research. They explore the processes by which a war is being waged to determine the knowledge that universities are allowed to teach and the racialized nature of the staff and student body. This superb collection is a landmark intervention into one of the most important debates of our time. The World's universities are becoming a key battleground in the ongoing struggle for racial justice, equity and respect. From Cape Town to Berkeley, Oxford to Sydney, Harvard to Toronto, a battle is being waged for the soul of Higher Education. Minoritized scholars, students and communities are making their voices heard as never before but the forces of repression have many weapons and shamelessly deploy concepts like 'free speech', 'choice' and 'meritocracy' as loaded devices that camouflage White self-interest behind the hypocrisy of grand-sounding ideas."
—Professor David Gillborn, *University of Birmingham, UK*

"This collection is a long awaited and much needed challenge to institutional racism in UK universities. It insists on the necessity for present/future decolonization for racial equality and social justice transformation within these white spaces."
—Professor Shirley Anne Tate, *Leeds Beckett University, UK*

"*Dismantling Race in Higher Education* is a must read edited volume for those individuals who are really interested in understanding the influences of race within the UK higher education enterprise. Both Dr Jason Arday and Professor

Heidi Safia Mirza assembled an all-star team of UK 'race studies' scholars and researchers to put this book together. In my opinion, it includes important content that may stimulate a new generation of 'race studies' thought leaders in the UK. This edited volume has immense potential to become a classic text for higher education scholars and researchers throughout the UK higher education system and beyond."

—Professor James L. Moore III, *The Ohio State University, USA*

"This collection of essays is a timely intervention given the discussions going on in Whitehall and on campuses about access, equality and the legacy of colonialism and empire in our universities. Whilst of course attention must be paid to who is able to participate in higher education, we must also focus on issues of race within the institutions themselves."

—Rt Hon David Lammy MP, *Higher Education Minister 2007–10, House of Commons, UK Parliament*

"Covering multiple experiences, histories, policies and pedagogies, Dismantling Race is an impressive contribution to scholarship on higher education. Across a set of beautifully curated chapters the imbrication of whiteness in the British Academy is catalogued, reported and explained. Few, having read the book, will doubt that higher education is institutionally racist; and few will doubt the urgency of contemporary decolonizing initiatives."

—Professor Robbie Shilliam, *Johns Hopkins University, USA*

"This landmark publication takes on an ambitious project: fiercely critical analyses intertwined with intersectional visions of hope and tools for a different practice. A new generation of critical voices takes us closer to the tipping point where 'enough =enough' can trigger genuine transformation."

—Professor Philomena Essed, *Antioch University, USA*

Jason Arday · Heidi Safia Mirza
Editors

Dismantling Race in Higher Education

Racism, Whiteness and Decolonising the Academy

Editors
Jason Arday
University of Roehampton
London, UK

Heidi Safia Mirza
Goldsmiths College
University of London
London, UK

ISBN 978-3-319-60260-8   ISBN 978-3-319-60261-5   (eBook)
https://doi.org/10.1007/978-3-319-60261-5

Library of Congress Control Number: 2018938347

This Palgrave Macmillan imprint is published by the registered company Springer International Publishing AG part of Springer Nature
The registered company address is: Gewerbestrasse 11, 6330 Cham, Switzerland

Foreword

Dismantling Racial Inequality Within the Academy

The foreword to this volume argues that in Britain issues of race and racism continue to be viewed as 'outside' academia's domain. The greatest barrier to addressing race equality in higher education is academia's refusal to regard race as a legitimate object of scrutiny, either in scholarship or policy. Consequently, there is little recognition of the role played by universities in (re)producing racial injustice. The contributions to this collection challenge this studied ignorance by drawing attention to academia's racialised culture and practices, detailing experiences and outcomes among those Black and Minority Ethnic (BME) students and academics who have successfully accessed higher education but who still find themselves marginalised.

As a way of explaining why this collection of writing on race and higher education in Britain is important and why it is overdue, let me begin with an everyday story: a story of everyday racism. Some years back, I sat on the equalities committee of an elite university. Since the university's physical environment was a regular agenda item, I raised the issue of graffiti in the changing rooms of the gym. Now, I grew up on 1970s council estates and I am not liable to be shocked by scribble on walls. However, this was not the odd mark but an accretion of racist, sexist, anti-Semitic and homophobic scrawl. Layer upon layer, it must have taken years of deposit. Once I had convinced the committee that I was not mistaken, that the graffiti really did exist and that it was a problem, the university acted: not just painting over the graffiti but resurfacing the walls with a kind of meringue-like woodchip so that they could not be defaced again. At the next committee meeting we congratulated ourselves on having taken practical and immediate action—at which point, an experienced member of the committee piped up, 'Yes, it was terrible. Perhaps it was done by visitors from outside the university'.

From *outside* the university. From *outside* the university. The most powerful block to challenging and dismantling racial inequality in higher education is glossed in those four words. For in British universities, race is rarely considered a legitimate object of scrutiny, either in scholarship or in policy. Race very much remains the 'outside child' and its continuing illegitimacy means that often the most significant discussions about race and racism remain at the level of corridor conversations: rarely surfacing in published papers, unlikely to attract the validation of grant funding. The marginalisation of critical voices is compounded at the institutional level, where equalities committees are too often out of the executive loop, entirely separate from the senior bodies that make decisions about learning and teaching, staffing and funding. Consequently, too much of our energy is spent fending off derision at the very mention of the 'R' word: going over and over the same back-to-square-one arguments about the legitimacy of scholarship on race and the need for institutional action on racism.

In particular, there exists a stubborn refusal to acknowledge that academia itself might be complicit in the (re)production of racial injustices, that it does not just passively 'reflect' disadvantages already existing in society but actively (re)creates inequalities. This current collection suggests ways forward in the struggle to dismantle these inequalities but it does not underestimate the extent of the challenge. The book's starting point is that race and racism are not 'outside' the university; they are not prior entities, carried on to campus like a lunch bag. Academia—like schools, the labour market and the criminal justice system—is one of the social sites in which race as a social relationship is constructed, in a tangle of stratifications, exclusions, privileges and assumptions. Sadly, in British academia Gargi Bhattacharyya's words, written some twenty years ago, still too often hold true:

> The powerful hog the privilege of the norm and the rest of us squeeze in behind, around, wherever there is room. Boys stride and girls cower, light skin preens while dark waits.
>
> (Bhattacharyya 1997: 250).

Remember also that in Britain issues of race in higher education are a belated concern. Early post-war work on race and education in Britain focused, for demographic reasons, on schooling. It was not until the late 1970s that education policymakers, confronted with unemployment figures and deep urban unrest, began to contemplate the fate of BME school-leavers and it was not really until the 1980s that BME access to higher education became a fledgling policy item. One problem of the current century is that the higher education sector got stuck for rather too long on access. In strictly numerical terms, Britain's minority ethnic groups are now solidly represented in higher education. However, it has taken the work of committed researchers, alert practitioners and, crucially, the agitation of BME students to draw attention to the 'inside': to experiences and outcomes among those BME students and academics who have successfully 'accessed' higher education but still find themselves marginalised.

In short, while widening participation is a necessary condition for dismantling racial inequality in higher education (and in wider society), it is not sufficient in itself. It is inadequate to recruit BME students and staff while holding to deficit models, wherein the onus to change, to fit, to come up to snuff lies entirely with those students and staff; transformation in the university population necessitates transformation in policy and practice. As yet, the sector has responded only fitfully to the challenge but the degree to which universities acknowledge the need for change in what they do and how they think has increasingly become a red line. It is apparent in contemporary student movements, such as 'Rhodes Must Fall' and 'Why is My Curriculum White', as well as in mainstream strategies, such as the Race Equality Charter Mark, designed for universities that actively promote race equality.

The contributors to this volume include some of British academia's brightest hopes: new, passionate voices who have helped shaped the current campaigns for racial justice. Other contributors are relative veterans, with long-standing experience of the cycles of interest and disinterest in race equality that have characterised education policy in the UK. While the contributors address race and higher education from different perspectives, drawing on diverse disciplines, they share a sobering recognition that they are writing at a moment when issues of race and racism are no more than a hoarse whisper in the national/nativist conversation—the forgotten inequality. Eighteen years ago, the Macpherson Report impelled universities, like other public institutions, to acknowledge the pervasive nature of institutional racism. Since then race has again slipped from the education policy agenda, and is usually seen only through the prism of black underachievement.

For the most part, higher education has resorted—to borrow a phrase from Nobel Prize winner Paul Beatty—to its old, haughty notions of fair play. Concerns about institutional racism have been displaced by shoulder-shrugging concept of 'unconscious bias'—a voguish term that has little purchase on structural inequality as it is understood by this book's commentators. Today, it seems that race is again 'outside' higher education: outside a current set of interests that seem to be reducible to 'quality', 'standards', 'markets' and 'employability'—terms not nearly so neutral as they sound.

The structural, deeply cultural questions addressed in this book confront many facets of academia's self-reproductive power. How, for instance, can a sector so dependent on the shoulder tap, on buying-in, on headhunting commit itself to principles of equality in its recruitment and promotion of academic staff? How can Britain retain BME academics, for whom academic flight has become a rational response to institutional neglect and to the disparaging of scholarship that dares to treat Dubois, Said and hooks with same seriousness that it treats Foucault? How are BME students to negotiate a sector that has historically preferred to objectify black and brown bodies, rather than to hear black and brown voices? These questions are now seeping through a cracked edifice. For, it is no longer possible to slap on a dash of paint or plaster to disguise the stratification of our higher education system: stratification that so heavily concentrates BME, working class and mature students in one particular fraction of the sector (thirty or so new universities, in the Greater London area or other 'urban' safe spaces). And it is no longer possible to gloss over the racialised disparities in undergraduate attainment or the blocked pipelines to work and post-graduate study in which high-achieving BME graduates can find themselves lodged.

Often times, everyday culture and practice in contemporary British academia feel like a continual rephrasing of the question posed by one of the chapters in this collection: 'Are you supposed to be in here?' Yet that is not the whole story. Within this collection multiple possibilities for transformation are envisaged: possibilities rooted in already burgeoning activism, wherein BME students, scholars and their allies are creating spaces of contestation, challenging academia's business-as-usual forms of mission, leadership, admissions and curriculum. The contributions to this volume share a commitment to educational change; the authors' hopes are embedded in realism about where we currently stand and therefore its prescriptions are as strong as its critiques. This book is about contests that are central to higher education in Britain in the twenty-first century, as told from the inside.

Coventry, UK   Professor Paul Warmington

Paul Warmington is a Professorial Research Fellow in The Centre for Research in Race and Education at the University of Birmingham. He has taught, researched and written extensively on education and social justice, focusing on critical theories of race and class, and on widening participation. Beginning in the late 1980s, he has worked in both further and higher education. His work has included developing pioneering black studies courses and Access programmes. Paul was also one of the founders of Birmingham University's Centre for Research in Race and Education. His most recent book is *Black British Intellectuals and Education: Multiculturalism's Hidden History* (2014).

Acknowledgements

Collating and curating a book on the challenging topic of racism in higher education is a tough task emotionally and intellectually, and working in tandem with each other has been a joy that has lifted our spirits on long cold days with hot cups of tea, accompanied by many WhatsApp exchanges 'to stay strong!' This book would not have been possible without the vision and support and of Dr. Omar Khan, the Director of the Runnymede Trust and Professor Claire Alexander in her role as Chair of Runnymede's Academic and Emerging Scholars Forums, whose landmark seminar series Aiming Higher: Race, Inequality and Diversity in the Academy (2013–2015) inspired this Volume. We wish to thank all the many academic contributors to the series, whose razor-sharp research and generous scholarship fills these pages both as authors and supporters of the book, and who will forever remain our intellectual companions in the wider cause to 'dismantle racism in the Academy'.

In particular, Heidi would like to thank her long-time sisters-in-arms, who share with her the inmost secrets of racism and sexual harassment inside the 'black magic box' of higher education. Sara Ahmed, Diane Reay, Vini Lander, Veena Meetoo, Suki Ali, Veronica Poku, Geetha

Marcus, Jacqui MacDonald. Lucinda Platt, Miriam David, and last but not least, Deborah Gabriel and Shirley Anne Tate and the fabulous women of the historic 'Inside the Ivory Tower' Black Academics group! A special mention must go to Saleem Badat, Director of International Higher Education of the Andrew W. Mellon Foundation for his unstinting personal support and utmost dedication for the quest of *inclusion diversity and difference* in the global Academy. Heidi dedicates this book to her dearest friend and colleague Cynthia Joseph whose spirit lives on in these pages, though she is no longer with us.

Jason Arday would also like to thank the following colleagues and friends who have been instrumental in supporting him throughout this process; Nadena Doharty, Paul Warmington, Robbie Shilliam, Vikki Boliver, Aarti Ratna, Marcia Wilson, Debbie Weekes-Bernard, Jasmine Rhamie, Paul Miller, Christine Callender, David Gillborn and the Runnymede Trust Board of Trustees.

We also wish to thank the Palgrave Macmillan Editorial Team; Eleanor Christie; Rebecca Wyde and in particular Andrew James for the initial vision and opportunity. They believed in us from the beginning, and have been unstinting in their enthusiasm for this important project, and have gently encouraged us onwards throughout the process of pulling this mighty tome together.

Our families are the backbone of this book, and we cannot thank them enough for their love, patience and understanding, especially when we disappear for long hours over the two years it took to produce this book. Heidi Mirza's special thanks go to her gentle and encouraging daughter Aliya Mirza, her supportive brother Gerard, and loving mother Hilda Hosier who never fails to tell her how proud she is of her incomprehensible academic achievements.

Finally, Jason Arday would like to thank his beautiful wife Debbie-Ann and his two amazing children Taylah and Noah. Thanks must also go to his amazing parents Gifty and Joseph Arday and exceptional brothers Joseph and Simon Peter. As always, Jason would also like to extend his appreciation and gratitude to his dearest friend and mentor Sandro Sandri, without him… the dream would not be possible.

We dedicate this book to all the 'dreamers' of the world, who can only dream of a better life through the gift of education if we succeed in dismantling the 'walls' of racism and sexism in our schools and universities.

Contents

xviii   Contents

Notes on Contributors

Lina Abushouk is a Graduate of Sarah Lawrence College, USA. She co-founded Skin Deep magazine, and is now co-editor, while on her junior year abroad at Wadham College, Oxford. She worked as a Research Fellow at Georgetown University in Qatar, and is currently completing a Ph.D. in English at Princeton University.

Sara Ahmed is an Independent Feminist writer, scholar and activist. Her most recent books include *Living a Feminist Life* (2017), *Willful Subjects* (2014), *On Being Included: Racism and Diversity in Institutional Life* (2012) and the award-winning *The Promise of Happiness* (2010). She blogs at www.feministkilljoys.com.

Kehinde Andrews is Associate Professor of Sociology, and has been leading the development of the Black Studies Degree at Birmingham City University. His latest book *Back to Black: Retelling the Story of Black Radicalism for the Twenty-First Century* will be published in July 2018 by Zed Books. He recently co-edited *Blackness in Britain* (2016) and his first book was *Resisting Racism: Race, Inequality and the Black Supplementary School Movement* (2013). Kehinde is director of the Centre for Critical Social Research; founder of the Harambee Organisation of Black Unity; and co-chair of the Black Studies Association.

Jason Arday is a Senior Lecturer in Education Studies at Roehampton University, School of Education, a Visiting Research Fellow at the Ohio State University, USA, in the Office of Diversity and Inclusion and a Trustee of the Runnymede Trust. His research focuses Race, Social Justice, Cultural Studies and Education. He is author of the forthcoming titles: *Considering Racialized Contexts in Education: Using Reflective Practice and Peer-Mentoring to Support Black and Ethnic Minority Educators* (Routledge); *Being Young, Black and Male: Challenging the Dominant Discourse* (Palgrave); *Exploring Cool Britannia and Multi-Ethnic Britain: Uncorking the Champagne Supernova* (Routledge). He is the co-editor of an upcoming book series on *Race and Education* (Palgrave) with Professor Michael Peters (University of Waitako), Professor Paul Warmington (University of Birmingham), Professor Vikki Boliver (Durham University), Professor Zeus Leonardo (University of California) and Professor James Moore III (The Ohio State University).

Kalwant Bhopal is Professor of Education and Social Justice in the Centre for Research for Race and Education, University of Birmingham. Her research focuses on the achievements and experiences of minority ethnic groups in education. Her research specifically explores how processes of racism, exclusion and marginalisation operate in predominantly White spaces with a focus on social justice and inclusion. She is Visiting Professor at Harvard University in the Harvard Graduate School of Education and Visiting Professor at Kings College London (Department of Education and Professional Studies). Her book, *White Privilege: The Myth of a Post-Racial Society* will be published by Policy Press, April 2018.

Vikki Boliver is a Professor of Sociology in the Department of Sociology at Durham University. Her research interests centre on ethnic and social class inequalities of access to higher education, with a particular focus on admission to highly selective universities. She is also interested in patterns and processes of social mobility over multiple generations. Vikki's current research examines the use of contextual data to widening participation at the point of admission to university, and explores competing conceptions of fairness in access to higher education.

Hazel Brown is the Head of Department of Sport, Exercise and Health at the University of Winchester. Her research investigates equality and diversity issues in academia. Previous research has looked into the undergraduate student experience in the UK as compared with that in New Zealand. Current research focuses on career ambitions and career planning of BME students, and career planning of students planning to enter teaching careers. She has also undertaken research on the contribution of sailing to wellbeing, and on the state of play of coaching in Europe.

Penny Jane Burke is Global Innovation Chair of Equity and Director of the Centre of Excellence for Equity in Higher Education at the University of Newcastle, Australia. She is Editor of the international journal Teaching in Higher Education and has published extensively in the field of the sociology of higher education, with a focus on challenging inequalities. Penny is passionately dedicated to developing methodological, theoretical and pedagogical frameworks that support critical understanding and practice of equity and social justice in higher education.

Kate D'Arcy is acting Principal Lecturer at the University of Bedfordshire. Having worked in education and with marginalised communities for many years, she has extensive knowledge and professional experience of working with vulnerable young people and their communities. She is committed to educational inclusion, social justice and equity. Her research into Travellers' experiences of home education made an original contribution to a neglected area of research.

Adam Elliott-Cooper is a Research Associate at Kings College, University of London researching gentrification and urban displacement. He received his doctorate from the School of Geography and the Environment, University of Oxford. His research focuses on state power, race, policing, resistance movements and post-colonialism. He has previously worked as a teaching fellow in the Department of Sociology, University of Warwick, a research associate in the Department of Philosophy, University College London, the Sociology

Department at Goldsmith's and the School of Politics and International Relations, University of Nottingham.

Lisa Galloway is a Programme Leader for Society, Health and Childhood studies at Blackpool and the Fylde College University Centre. She has worked across the Further and Higher Education sector for over 19 years. Lisa is currently undertaking research on Gypsy, Roma and Traveller communities as part of a Doctorate study. She is currently completing a book entitled; *Let Me Tell You: Experiences of Gypsy and Traveller Families of Education in Contemporary Society.*

Anuradha Henriques is a Graduate of Wadham College, Oxford. She founded Race Matters, co-founded Skin Deep magazine, and is now co-editor of the London-based multimedia platform. She currently works in film and television production in London and hopes to see Skin Deep continue to grow as a transnational race and culture platform.

Michael Hobson is a Lecturer in Physical and Sport Education, at St Mary's University. His interests lie in within the sociology of sport and education. In particular how social stratification impacts upon students experience of privilege and inequality in higher education. He is currently completing his Doctorate at Loughborough University, exploring the relationships between social class, body pedagogies and students' educational trajectories prior to and during undergraduate study.

June Jackson (1954–2017) worked in the Centre for Ethnic Minority Studies at Royal Holloway and subsequently set up a university spin-out company, Equality and Research and Consulting. She worked on many projects for the British Council. Her work included consulting with staff to identify areas of discrimination or disadvantage, and she contributed to the development of organisational diversity schemes to address these issues. She has assisted on projects exploring experiences of minority ethnic academics and career progression. June will be remembered for her smile, which brought light into every room she entered.

Azeezat Johnson is a Lecturer in Geography at Queen Mary University of London. She recently completed her Ph.D. at University of Sheffield where her research was focused on the experiences and clothing practices of Black Muslim women in Britain. She is also a co-editor for *The Fire Now*, a collection that explores new directions in anti-racist scholarship as a response to racist developments across the West.

Remi Joseph-Salisbury is a Presidential Fellow at the University of Manchester. His primary research interests are in Race, Ethnicity and Anti-racism. His forthcoming monograph is entitled *Black Mixed-Race Men, Transatlanticity, Hybridity and 'Post-Racial' Resilience*, and he is the co-editor of a forthcoming edited collection, *The Fire Now: Anti-Racist Scholarship in Times of Explicit Racial Violence*.

Yaojun Li is Professor of Sociology at School of Social Sciences, University of Manchester, and a Fellow of the Royal Society of Arts (FRSA). His research interests are in social mobility, social capital, socio-economic integration of minority ethnic groups and cross-country comparisons. He has published over 90 papers, book chapters and research reports, and conducted over 20 projects funded by academic and government agencies in Britain and other countries. His edited book *The Handbook of Research Methods and Applications on Social Capital* was published in August 2015 and his co-authored book with Professor Anthony Heath on *Key Concepts in the Social Sciences: Social Mobility* will be published in 2018. He also co-authored some chapters in Anthony Heath's *Social Progress in Britain* (Oxford University Press, 2018) and his new book (co-edited with Yanjie Bian) on *Social Inequalities in China* will be published by World Scientific and Imperial College Press.

Gary Loke is Head of Policy at Equality Challenge Unit, a central source of research, advice and leadership on equality in UK higher education, and colleges in Scotland. Gary has worked for a range of equality organisations on issues including age discrimination in social care and minority ethnic people's access to information and public services in a rural context.

Uvanney Maylor is Professor of Education and was Director of the Institute for Research in Education at the University of Bedfordshire (2013–2017). She is a former director of Multiverse and was a member of the Higher Education Funding Council for England Research Excellence Framework (2014) Education sub-panel. Her research interests are in the areas of race, ethnicity, diversity, culture and equity in education.

Heidi Safia Mirza is Visiting Professor of Race, Faith and Culture at Goldsmith's College, University of London and Emeritus Professor in Equalities Studies, UCL Institute of Education. She is known for her pioneering intersectional research on race, gender and identity in education and has an international reputation for championing equality and social justice for Black, Asian and Muslim women and young people through educational reform. Coming from Trinidad and schooled in Britain, she is one of the few women of colour professors in UK. She is author of several best-selling books including, *Young Female and Black*, which was voted in the BERA top 40 most influential educational studies in Britain. Her other publications include *Black British Feminism; Race Gender and Educational Desire: Why black women succeed and fail; Black and postcolonial Feminisms in New Times*, and most recently, *Respecting Difference: Race, faith, and culture for teacher educators*.

Michael Adrian Peters is Professor of Education at the University of Waikato, New Zealand and Emeritus Professor in Educational Policy, Organization, and Leadership at the University of Illinois at Urbana–Champaign. He is the executive editor of the journal, *Educational Philosophy and Theory*, and the founding editor of four international e-journals, *Policy Futures in Education*, *E-Learning and Digital Media*, *Knowledge Cultures* and *The Video Journal of Education & Pedagogy*. His interests are in education, philosophy and social theory, and he has written over eighty books and 500 papers. He is a lifelong Fellow of the New Zealand Academy of Humanities, an Honorary Member of the Royal Society of NZ, and a life member of the Society for Research in Higher Education (UK), and the Philosophy of Education Society of Australasia. He was awarded honorary doctorates by State University of New York (SUNY) in 2012 and University of Aalborg in 2015.

Andrew Pilkington is Professor of Sociology at the University of Northampton. He is currently Associate Director of the Centre for Children and Youth and Director of the Equality and Diversity Research Group. His research has especially focused on issues relating to race and ethnicity, and he has published widely in this area, including *Racial Disadvantage and Ethnic Diversity in Britain* (Palgrave, 2003) and, with Shirin Housee and Kevin Hylton, an edited collection, *Race(ing) Forward: Transitions in Theorising Race in Education* (HEA, 2009). His most recent book is *Institutional Racism in the Academy: A Case Study* (Trentham, 2011).

Diane Reay grew up in a working class, coal mining community before becoming an inner city, primary school teacher for 20 years. She is now a Visiting Professor at the LSE and Emeritus Professor of Sociology of Education at the University of Cambridge. Her main research interests are social justice issues in education, Pierre Bourdieu's social theory, and cultural analyses of social class, race and gender. Her most recent book is *Miseducation: Inequality, Education and the Working Classes* Policy Press, 2017.

John T. E. Richardson was Professor in Student Learning and Assessment in the Institute of Educational Technology at the Open University until his retirement in July 2017. His main research interests were concerned with the relationship between students' perceptions of their courses of study in higher education and the approaches to studying that they adopt on those courses. He also carried out institutional research on the evaluation of courses. He completed a literature review on the role of ethnicity and gender as predictors of degree attainment as part of the HEA/ECU Ethnicity, Gender and Degree Attainment Project and was a member of the team that produced a report for the Funding Council on league tables and their impact on higher education institutions. He is now Emeritus Professor in student learning at the Open University.

Nicola Rollock is a Reader in Equity and Education at Goldsmiths, University of London, UK and Patron of the Equality Challenge Unit's Race Equality Charter. She is interested in improving the ways in which we commonly think about racism and in identifying solutions to persistent race inequalities within the education system and the workplace.

She is lead author of the award-winning book *The Colour of Class: The Educational Strategies of the Black Middle Classes* which documents the experiences of Black British middle-class families as they work to navigate their children successfully through the education system.

Tania Saeed is Assistant Professor at the Lahore University of Management Sciences (LUMS), Pakistan. She is the author of *Islamophobia and Securitization. Religion, Ethnicity and the Female Voice* (Palgrave Macmillan). She read for a D.Phil. in Education at the University of Oxford, and an M.Sc. in Gender, Development and Globalisation at the London School of Economics and Political Science.

Stuart Whigham is a Lecturer in Sport, Coaching and Physical Education in the Department of Sport, Health Sciences and Social Work at Oxford Brookes University. Before entering the field of higher education, Stuart previously taught PE and Sport in secondary, sixth form and further education settings, before commencing postgraduate studies in his specialist area of the sociology and politics of sport. He has recently completed Doctoral studies at Loughborough University under the supervision of Professor Alan Bairner, with a specific focus upon the politics of the 2014 Glasgow Commonwealth Games.

List of Figures

List of Tables

Part I
Introduction

1

Racism in Higher Education: 'What Then, Can Be Done?'

Heidi Safia Mirza

'What does it mean when the tools of a racist patriarchy are used to examine the fruits of that same patriarchy? It means that only the most narrow perimeters of change are possible and allowable'... 'For the master's tools will never dismantle the master's house. They may allow us temporarily to beat him at his own games, but they will never enable us to bring about genuine change.' (Audrey Lorde 2007: 110–112: Comments at Second Sex Conference, New York, September 29, 1979)

This book grew out of the seminar series *Aiming Higher: Race Inequality and Diversity in the Academy*, initiated and convened by UK's foremost race-relations think-tank, the Runnymede Trust. The outcome, the *Aiming Higher* report (Alexander and Arday 2015) centred around two main and interlinked areas of concern for Black and Minority Ethnic staff and students in the British higher education

H. S. Mirza (✉)
Goldsmiths College, University of London, London, UK
e-mail: heidi.mirza@gold.ac.uk

© The Author(s) 2018
J. Arday and H. S. Mirza (eds.), *Dismantling Race in Higher Education*,
https://doi.org/10.1007/978-3-319-60261-5_1

system; namely the white privilege that lies at the heart of the elite institutional culture, and the subsequent unequal opportunities and outcomes for BME[1] academics and students who 'strive to survive' within that culture.

The findings of the Runnymede report were indeed alarming. The evidence they unearthed of complex entrenched institutionalised gendered and classed racial discrimination in British universities speaks for itself. The Aiming Higher research team found students of colour are less likely to be admitted to elite 'Russell group' universities, even when they have 'like for like' entry grades. BME students are to be found mainly in the 'new' university sector with its lesser market value, and are less likely than their White counterparts to be awarded a good honours degree or find good jobs commensurate with their qualifications when they graduate. Those who manage to navigate the perilous journey into a career in the Academy disproportionately find themselves on insecure fixed term contracts and lower pay. The most shocking evidence of this 'crisis of race' in British higher education, is the dearth of senior Black and Minority Ethnic academics. In comparison to 3895 white female and 12,455 white male professors in the UK, there only 345 British women of colour professors of which 30 are Black British, 10 British Pakistani and 5 British Bangladeshi, with British Indian and British Chinese women topping the race to the bottom at 80 and 75 respectively (Alexander 2017; ECU 2016; Gabriel and Tate 2017). Emejulu (2017b) poignantly sums up the state of play in the British Academy when she says, 'To speak of universities is to recognise them as spaces of exclusion and discrimination which hide their epistemic violence behind a rhetoric of meritocracy, collegiality and the 'free exchange of ideas''.

---

[1]The acronym BME or BAME (*Black and Minority Ethnic* and *Black Asian and Minority Ethnic*) is a collective term used in official British government sources to encompass the highly differentiated racialised post-colonial but global majority 'peoples of colour' who now live and work in Great Britain (Bhavnani et al. 2005). It denotes the social construction of difference through visible 'race' (Black) and ethnic (cultural) markers. Many of the chapters in the book adopt the official convention of 'BME' while acknowledging it is a crude reduction of complex ethnic, cultural and religious differences (Alexander 2017).

David Lammy, the former Labour Minister of Higher Education commented in the Forward to the *Aiming Higher* report, '*So despite the lofty ideals of universities, they do no better, and are in fact doing worse than many other institutions in British society when it comes to race equality*' (Alexander and Arday 2015: 3). Lammy then throws down the gauntlet to the Academy, declaring, '*What then, can be done?*' As politically committed academics of colour, we could not let Lammy's challenge lie, and pick up his gauntlet by bringing together 22 of the best and brightest, new and established scholars of race and higher education to tackle this question in this unique Volume. This book thus takes up the task the Runnymede began, and Audrey Lorde in her eminent and forceful wisdom in her opening quote counsels us to do—that is to 'dismantle the masters house' of higher education. It is a forensic task, that comes at a pivotal time marking just over 50 years since the 1965 Race-Relations Act addressed the endemic racism that plagued post-war Britain (Khan 2015a). In terms of higher education reform, it also signals 50 years since the Robbins Report called for the national expansion of the university system which opened the door to a post-colonial generation of Black and Asian British students from the former colonies (Alexander and Arday 2015). Drawing on the contributing authors' meticulous evidence of facts and figures on one hand, and their rich archives of feelings and frustrations on the other, the book clearly demonstrates that indeed something has to give if, as Martin Luther King prophesied 50 years ago, and Sam Cooke immortalised in his civil rights song, 'A Change is Gonna Come'.

If British higher education is to move beyond its twentieth century bunker of anachronistic elitism and social hierarchies of privilege and modernise as 'fit for purpose', it must embrace a new era of democratisation and diversity that will ultimately define its success in the new global reach of the twenty first century (Morley 2012). The over-riding message of this Collection is clear—despite the massification and marketisation of higher education, in which universities are reconstituted as international 'big businesses' (Collini 2017), the 'masters tools' of race equality and diversity polices have not 'dismantled the masters' house' (Warikoo 2016). Instead, we find the latest tranche of 'fat cat'[2] leadership in the Academy have erected new 'walls of containment' for Black, Asian and White working classes in their expensive new architectural extensions. But like all 'walls of exclusion' forged in fear, envy and greed—the walls of Apartheid, the Berlin Wall, the walls in Gaza and Trump's Mexican walls—they outlive their time and eventually, under mass protest, crumble.

The incontrovertible evidence amassed in this book heralds an eve of change in the search for social justice and racial equality in higher education. By peeling back the mechanisms of institutional racism; exposing the spaces of white privilege; documenting the grassroots movement for decolonisation: and illuminating the bureaucratic conceit of equality and diversity policies—we suggest, in the pages that follow, that the 'game is up' and there is nowhere for those in power to hide.

Let the Facts Speak: Institutional Racism in Higher Education

Institutional racism, a concept coined in America in 1967 in the Black Power era by Kwame Ture (né Stokely Carmichael) and Charles V. Hamilton is, like the Race Equality Legislation in Britain, now marking its 50th anniversary. However, it was not until the racist murder of the Black teenager Stephen Lawrence[3] in 1993 that the concept of Institutional racism entered the lexicon of higher education in Britain. Stephen's brutal murder marked a watershed in the recognition that

---

[2]There have been several scandals followed by a call for a Government review of the inflated pay of university Vice-Chancellor's in which the highest paid earns £450,000, three times the prime minister's salary. http://www.dailymail.co.uk/news/article-5224813/Vice-chancellors-pay-Britains-worst-universities.html (accessed 15 Jan 2018).

[3]The Racially motivated murder of the black teenager Stephen Lawrence in London in 1993 and the subsequent racist mishandling of the case by the police led to the Stephen Lawrence Inquiry in 1999. https://www.theguardian.com/uk/2012/jan/03/stephen-lawrence-timeline (accessed 15 Jan 2018).

public sector organisations, including higher education, operate institutional forms of racism that are, *"less overt, far more subtle, less identifiable in terms of specific individuals committing the acts ... (and) originate in the operation of established and respected forces in society"* (Carmichael and Hamilton 1967: 4). The raft of recommendations that followed the Macpherson Report into Stephen's murder led to the 2000 Race Relations Amendment Act (RRAA) and later the 2010 Race Equality Act, which marked a hopeful start to a new millennium (Khan 2015a). In a breath of fresh air, higher education had to take on board the definition of institutional racism in the Macpherson Report, defined as, *"The collective failure of an organisation to provide an appropriate and professional service to people because of their colour, culture, or ethnic origin. It can be seen or detected in processes, attitudes and behaviour which amount to discrimination through unwitting prejudice, ignorance, thoughtlessness and racist stereotyping which disadvantage minority ethnic people."* (Macpherson 1999: para 6.34). Tasked by the law, universities were now accountable and open to external scrutiny and had no choice but to reluctantly invoke the principles equality of opportunity and abide by the 'Positive Duty' to promote and value difference and diversity in their hallowed halls. However, as the seminal book, *Institutional Racism in Higher education* (Law et al. 2004: 3) shows so well, British universities still managed to remain 'hideously white'.

It is this watershed moment, and the subsequent fate of institutional race equality within the sector during the following 20 years, that Andrew Pilkington skilfully unravels in his opening chapter, 'The Declining Salience of Race Equality in Higher Education' (see Chapter 2). He asks, 'Why, despite such progressive Race Equality Legislation, have we witnessed the rise, rather than the fall of disadvantages for BME students and staff?' He suggests that the underlying principles of equality enshrined in anti-discrimination Law elicits a liberal rather than radical approach to equalities, ensuring fair procedures for all, rather than fair outcomes and equitable redistribution for those who are the most discriminated against. By adopting 'colour-blind' and 'complacent' bureaucratic approaches, universities can claim to be doing something, while really doing nothing at all to change the status-quo. With endemic cultures of cynicism about 'political correctness' towards race equality, Pilkington concludes the situation facing us in universities is, 'impossible to comprehend without recognising how deeply rooted Whiteness is throughout the system'.

How the upper middle and upper classes reproduce and jealously guard their exclusive institutional spaces of elite white privilege, is the issue that concerns Diane Reay in her theoretically rich chapter, 'Race and Elite Universities in the UK' (see Chapter 3). While the 'success story' of expansion in higher education has led to a more diverse student body, it ironically has not produced a more inclusive higher education sector. Instead we find in the 'open' market place universities have become more polarised and segregated along hierarchical race and class lines. Thus, Oxford and Cambridge and the hub of 'old traditional' Russell group universities have become 'finishing schools' for the global wealthy elite, while Black and White working classes, are bound into a system of medieval like indebtedness in the lower status 'new' universities. How does this inequitable two-tier class system thrive in a seemingly open liberal democratic society? Herein lies Reay's core argument, it is the myth of meritocracy that keeps the neoliberal dream alive—that is, the belief if you work hard 'all can rise to the top'. It is a cruel dream with many working-class causalities and the few high achieving white working class and BME students that gain admission to elite universities suffer the psychological trauma of marginalisation, as well as more brutal and overt forms of racism.

It is the politics and processes behind the BME and working-class struggle to be admitted into these elite spaces of higher learning that Vikki Boliver deconstructs with clear sighted forensic aptitude in her chapter, 'Ethnic Inequalities in Admission to Highly Selective Universities' (see Chapter 4). Two decades of high rates of BME student participation has not been met with higher rates of entry into elite Russell group universities. Boliver goes straight to the horse's mouth for her data—the Universities Colleges and Admissions Service, and asks the 'million-dollar' equity question, 'why are British ethnic minority applicants to highly selective universities less likely to be offered places than white British applicants with the same grades? The rates of offer for White students were 7–12 percentage points higher than equivalently qualified Black Caribbean, Pakistani and Bangladeshi applicants, and 3–4 percentage points higher for Chinese, Indian and 'mixed' ethnic groups. Boliver deducts a possible cause for this glaring disparity, namely the racist conscious and unconscious ethnic bias of the admission processes to highly selective universities. Boliver strongly argues for determined action on the part of university senior leadership to lever tools at their disposal if institutional racism is to be challenged at its root.

The lower attainment of BME students in relation to White students is a long-standing problem and an indicator that something is, 'rotten in the state of Denmark'.[4] John Richardson's detailed and considered chapter, 'Understanding the Under-Attainment of Ethnic Minority Students' (see Chapter 5) aims to shed light on what is 'known and not known' about this ubiquitous and persistent phenomenon. Richardson takes the latest data that is available and deconstructs a national picture of BME degree attainment. Richardson is unequivocal that the aspirations of ethnic minority students do not explain the UK situation and deduces if 'ethnicity per se' is not a factor in explaining the attainment gap, and entry qualifications are controlled for, then the factors that are responsible for the ethnic differences in attainment must, to some degree, be institutional. He tentatively suggests that they could result, at least in part, from the teaching and assessment practices that are adopted in different institutions and academic subjects. Richardson ultimately concludes the phenomena of lower attainment still remains an 'unknown'. With very little official academic appetite to find out why, vulnerable BME students are left to flounder, while powerful institutions charged with their educational well-being remain with their heads well and truly buried in the 'equality sand'.

The issues for of social mobility for BME students do not stop with disadvantages in degree attainment. In a robust and careful analysis of ethnic differences in degree-level education and access to the professional-managerial salariat, Yaojun Li in his chapter, 'Unequal Returns' (see Chapter 6) asks what are the employment outcomes for BME graduates with degrees? First, aspirations are clearly not a problem as ethnic

---

[4]Quote from the play Hamlet. See, Shakespeare, W. (1993) *The Complete Works of William Shakespeare*. Available at http://shakespeare.mit.edu/index.html (accessed 15 Jan 2018).

minorities were more likely than the majority white group to have degree-level education. Li's meticulous analysis of the best available British national survey data shows a complex pattern of both polarisation and stratification in education for minority groups. He finds parental class and education plays a very important role hence Caribbean, Bangladeshi and Pakistani groups were overrepresented in the lowest levels of education, while Chinese, Indians and Black Africans outperform the white UK majority by large margins. Yet, and this is the shocking finding, despite all their educational achievements, second generation British born ethnic minority women, but more so men face a considerable 'ethnic penalty' in terms of pay and accessing professional-managerial positions compared to their white peers. For them higher education did not level the playing field of equality in employment, and as Li concludes, 'the ethnic penalty is a litmus test of social equality in British society'.

Just as BME students do not enjoy parity with their white counterparts in the professional world of work, BME academic staff also face quantifiable barriers to their career progression in UK higher education institutions. In their illuminating chapter, 'Should I Stay or Should I Go' (see Chapter 7), Kalwant Bhopal, Hazel Brown and June Jackson reveal new survey evidence showing that as many as 83.6% of Black, Asian and mixed race academics consider voting with their feet to leave Britain to seek work in more equitable 'greener pastures' overseas. In examining the push and pull factors that determine their desire to move, Bhopal et al. found BME academics are more likely to experience subtle, covert forms of racism, are less likely to be pushed forward for promotion, and less likely to be in senior decision-making roles, compared to their White colleagues. Interviewees spoke about how white senior academics often excluded them from accessing the necessary 'prestige' social and cultural capital needed to progress in the academy. The informal nature of this type of behaviour had an exclusionary impact on the experiences of BME academics whose legitimacy to occupy senior roles was frequently challenged in cruel and overtly racist ways such as taunting and belittling them. Bhopal and her colleagues suggest senior leaders are culpable by allowing, 'a culture where race equality is not being prioritised within the sector'.

Outsiders Within the Academy: Surviving the 'Sheer Weight of Whiteness'

The Black feminist theorist, Patricia Hill Collins (1998) developed the powerful concept, '*outsider-within*' to describe the liminal border space of marginalisation she experienced as a woman of colour working inside white academy. She writes, "*For my own survival I chose the term outsider-within to describe the location of people who no longer belong to any one group ... individuals like me who appear to belong, because we possess both the credentials for admittance and the rights of formal membership*" (Collins 1998: 5). Being a highly visible 'raced' professional in public spaces that were previously closed and homogenous with respect to race and gender, has led to reconfigured patterns of institutionalised racism for Black and Minority Ethnic 'outsiders' who now, by law have been allowed into these exclusive 'spaces of whiteness'. In these desegregated work environments, a climate of unease evolves. Microaggressions and surveillance strategies become increasingly important to ensure Black and Minority Ethnic staff remain manageable, safe, unraced and assimilated (Gabriel and Tate 2017). In the following chapters the contributing authors interrogate the ways in which gender, race and class are lived out in the boardrooms, corridors and classrooms of our universities. Our aim in this section is to understand the multiple and complex ways in which structures of power reproduce intersectional social divisions in the everyday lives of Black and Minority Ethnic people who inhabit these still unreconstructed 'spaces of whiteness'.

In their chapter, 'Are You Supposed to Be in Here?' (see Chapter 8) Remi Joseph-Salisbury and Azeezat Johnson draw on autoethnographic accounts of teaching and studying 'race' in racist universities. They ask, 'What does it mean for academics of colour who are studying race(ism) to be subjected to the same racist oppressions within the academe?' In the rarefied space of the academe 'everyday' race inequalities are seen as existing outside of the institution rather than produced through the academe. By centring their own experiences, Joseph-Salisbury and Johnson point to the pervasiveness of white supremacy within these legitimised spaces of knowledge production, deconstructing how racist and sexist microaggressions are a form of systemic, everyday racism. Joseph-Salisbury as a Black mixed-race man finds he is more intelligible as the Black male trespasser than as an academic. Azeezat Johnson is seen as a 'native informant' when her Black and Muslim female body is fetishised by a majority white audience. Joseph-Salisbury and Johnson generously share their 'epistemes of Blackness' for surviving in HE, which given the insurmountable task, one option is to leave the academy!

Using the Critical Race Theory (CRT) tool of counter narrative and semi-biography, Jason Arday in his chapter, 'Being Black, Male and Academic' (see Chapter 9), allows us the privilege of entering his world as a Black, male early career academic. In his deeply personal and poignant account of exclusion and marginalisation, he shares his struggle to survive and carve out a career in academia. His 'hidden' inner battle to overcome his hurdles as an autistic learner is very different from his outward facing presence as a 'visible' Black male, which unsettles the normativity of Whiteness within academia. He constantly questions if he has the credentials to be a 'real' academic when he is routinely turned down at interviews despite his professional and academic experience and the equal opportunities mantra, 'We value a diverse work force'. He notices how the all-white interview panels flinch awkwardly when he comes into the room, and is inevitability turned down, as his 'face does not fit'. Students think he is a rapper, and colleagues refer to him as a 'dark horse' and imagine his popularity as lecturer is because 'Black is the new cool'. Sharing his story is not only cathartic for Arday, but a gift for us. In a dream, he tells his 18-year-old self, who could not read or write, no matter the mountains he has to climb in this white world, he has already reached his Everest.

While BME academic staff are captured in the institutional cultures of whiteness in the academy, so too are the students. Heidi Mirza in her chapter, 'Black Bodies 'Out of Place' in Academic Spaces' (see Chapter 10) turns her attention to the institutional 'flashpoints' where the intersectionality of race, gender, faith and culture plays out at critical moments for students of colour. Though it is claimed we live in 'colour-blind' post-race times, Mirza finds that rather than racism fading away, new patterns of insidious racism are evolving which can be mapped in the micro-institutional practices of recruitment, retention and progression that mark the life cycle of a student's journey. Just getting in the university door was a trial for one African Caribbean young man. Other BME students are cut adrift in hostile 'anti-equality' learning environments, while Muslim students encounter overt anti-Islamic discrimination. Mirza found that while the white tutors wanted an open dialogue about tackling their racism, an intellectual and institutional 'safe space' to develop such critical consciousness was not yet on the horizon.

How do two white male lecturers create such an institutional 'safe space' is the subject of Michael Hobson's and Stuart Whigham's challenging chapter. 'Am I Too White to Talk About Being Black?' (see Chapter 11). It is not often that we get to hear white male academics critically reflect on their privilege and the frailties of their anti-racist teaching practice and pedagogy. Hobson and Whigham reflect upon their impossibility to empathise with the racialised experiences of BME students, and the potential risk that their attempt to do so will lead to a tokenistic discussion of race, which reinforces the students' inequality and their white privilege. The autoethnographic accounts of their engagement with issues of race and racism in the classroom, such as how to react when students use the 'n' word, or using pedagogic devices such as ball games that mimic hierarchies of race and class, makes for uncomfortable reading. However, as they themselves admit, if white male lecturers are to move out of the comfort zone of inviting people of colour to deliver the one 'special lecture on race' per term, then it is critical for them to move beyond introspection and 'navel gazing' about their white 'vulnerability' when tasked to deliver important curriculum content on racism in sport.

Whiteness is clearly classed, gendered, and raced, and the true 'vulnerability' of certain disadvantaged and stigmatised 'white' groups in higher education is the focus of Kate D'Arcy and Lisa Galloway in their chapter, 'Access and Inclusion for Gypsy and Traveller Students' (see Chapter 12). The complexity of the educational issues gypsy and traveller communities face are carefully unpacked in this rare but important chapter. Gypsy and traveller children and young people who struggle to achieve educationally within the state system, find themselves caught between overt prejudice and low expectations of schools and authorities on the one hand, and the rightful suspicion and lack of trust of such institutions within their communities on the other. This pattern extends into further and higher education for the few who do enter its ranks and these students evolve specific coping strategies such as '*fight, flight and playing White*' in order to deal with the cultural dissonance and social exclusion they experience. As D'Arcy and Galloway show successful policies of inclusion rest on building trust and respect, as well as emotional and financial support, but most of all it depends on the political will to do so.

The fate of racially stigmatised groups in higher education is deeply concerning. Muslim students, now labelled as the new 'folk devils', are freely and openly subjected to suspicion and official surveillance in higher educational institutions. The ways in which pervasive racist Islamophobic discourses have become legitimated and institutionalised within the academy is deftly deconstructed by Tania Saeed in her chapter, 'Islamophobia in Higher Education' (see Chapter 13). Universities are now tasked under the law to 'prevent' the radicalisation of 'vulnerable' young Muslims, and are bound by a statutory responsibility to inform on would-be terrorists. However, the welfare services in universities set up to support and monitor young Muslim men and women 'vulnerable' to Islamophobia are failing to provide an adequate service. Saeed's research asks, 'how can universities create an atmosphere of *no tolerance* against Islamophobia that the students trust?' One solution is to build the capacity of existing welfare officers to reach out and communicate with Muslims including protecting Hindus and Sikhs who are also attacked for being Muslim in the hysterical climate of state sanctioned Islamophobia.

Seize the Day! The Irresistible Rise of Decolonising Movements

Decolonising higher education, as Bhambra (2007: 872) observes, is a 'postcolonial thought-revolution' that unsettles and reconstitutes standard processes of knowledge production'. From the dominant western narratives of European modernity at the heart of the academy's 'hidden curriculum', to the material manifestation of imperial and colonial legacies embodied in the statues and buildings that celebrate this racist violent past, we find a new generation of scholars calling for decolonial dialogues 'that offer the possibility of a new geopolitics of knowledge' (Bhambra 2014: 120; Khan 2015b). Histories of decolonising movements which aim to decentre the dominance of the Western canon of European thought are rooted in a long history for racial justice that reaches back to the early twentieth century when Black and Asian anti-colonial and liberation scholars in India and Africa began their intellectual struggle for freedom and independence from British imperial rule. Scholars such as John La Rose, Franz Fanon, and Una Marson championed Marcus Garvey's call to 'free the mind from mental slavery', as immortalised in the well-beloved lyrics of the late great Bob Marley. What is striking now, in the technological age of social media, is the virulent and hostile exchanges that characterises the White establishment's backlash against students of colour who challenge the dominant narrative of the centrality of European modernity (Gopal 2017). The battle ground for a more open political and culturally representative curriculum and safe spaces to work this out are ridiculed as 'politically correct', a fundamental threat to liberal democracy, and an affront to the sanctity of (white) 'freedom and speech' (Ahmed 2015). What is clear from the debates recorded in the chapters here, is that the decolonising movement represents a 'tipping point', marking a fundamental shift in global power relations, in which the old colonial regimes of the fading metropole—characterised by class elitism and white supremacy, are being challenged by the 'irresistible' demands of a new tech savvy multicultural generation of international students (Caluya et al. 2011). With their thirst for new ways of thinking to 'feed and free' their minds they will vote for the best university to serve their needs …with their feet!

Michael Peters, in his chapter, 'Why Is My Curriculum White?' (see Chapter 14). Makes the point that the campaign to counter the narrow-mindedness of university courses is gathering pace because students demand disciplines such as Philosophy should investigate *all* human existence. Indeed, the University College London (UCL) student campaign, *Why is My Curriculum White?* Does not simply dismiss white, western, or male thinking simply on the premises that it is white, western, or male, but suggests it should embrace modern inclusive philosophical concepts of personhood, human rights, justice and modernity which are deeply shaped by 'race'. This inclusive and intellectually curious approach Peters advocates, has its roots in the long arc of anti-colonial and decolonial history. In a scholarly analysis originating with the Negritude movement in the 1930s, he incisively charts the impact of Black radical thought from the Civil Rights and Black Studies movement in the 1960s, to the more recent academic movements of critical race theory and anti-racism in 1980s and 1990s. Ultimately, Peters asks if the tradition of 'white male and pale Philosophy' to which he belongs has the capacity to acknowledge the racism that informs the root of the discipline. As a teacher and activist, his answer is one of enduring hope that it can.

The story of hope and belief in a better world underscores Kehinde Andrews' passionate contribution in this chapter, 'The Black Studies Movement in Britain' (see Chapter 15). The exclusion of whole swathes of legitimate 'Black knowledge' from the curriculum constitutes a crisis in British higher education. In his support for the radical statement, 'the university is not racist—the university *is* racism', Andrews alludes to the fact that the very structures and systems within the university are designed to reproduce the white privileged elite. Given its history, it is a myth to ever presume the university could ever be progressive, and we should expect nothing other than racism from the academy. As he states, 'If university is the disease, then it cannot be the cure'. Drawing on Malcom X and the Black Studies movement in the USA, Andrews vision is for the liberation of people of African descent through revolutionary education, in which history, literature, and mathematics are taught as instruments for change. The strength and legitimacy of Black Studies is that it is embedded in grassroots local communities from which Black intellectuals organically emerge. Racial justice and true democratisation cannot be top down, it must be '*by* the people *for* the people'.

In his evocative and moving chapter, 'Free, Decolonised Education' (see Chapter 16), Adam Elliot-Cooper weaves a powerful personal tale of his journey to South Africa in the wake of the 2015 *Rhodes Must Fall* students uprising. From the grand white-washed buildings now covered in Black power graffiti, he reflects on the student campaign that successfully brought down the statue of the vile racist British colonialist Cecil Rhodes. The statue was symbolic of the imperial logic of white privilege that still dominates the South African higher education system 25 years after the collapse of the reign of terror that was Apartheid. What Elliot-Cooper observes is the spontaneous power of such movements to spread like a flame to the metropole of Oxford and London where students also rose up in the university colleges of SOAS and UCL (Emejulu 2017a). In conclusion Elliot-Cooper asks what can those of us in the old centre of Empire do to ensure that our academic work, forged in imperial disciplines such as Geography, do to dismantle colonialism and its legacies. He gives us much food for thought.

Anuradha Henriques and Lina Abushouk share a fascinating account their engagement in the decolonial student movement in their chapter, 'Decolonising Oxford' (see Chapter 17). As they point out the *#ITooAmOxford* campaign, the magazine, *Skin Deep* and the *#RhodesMustFall Oxford* (*RMFO*) movement, like the student activism of their eminent Oxford predecessor, the late great Black British social theorist Stuart Hall, are all political interventions that emerged at a particular historical conjuncture. It is the organic coming together of politics, history and technology, ignited by the spark of decolonial student activism in America and South Africa, that created the moment for their activism to emerge. Henriques and Abushouk call for students to overcome apathy and docility in the neoliberal university, and link together in global solidarity to decolonise the academy from within, is a powerful call to arms.

Brick Walls and Tick-Boxes: The 'White-Washing' of Equality and Diversity Policies

In her opening, searing and eloquent statement that defines this book, Audrey Lorde invites us to consider the racialised consequences of the bureaucratic 'diversity industry' that has burgeoned in the academy despite persistent racial inequality. In this final section the authors collectively unmask the ways in which the huge swathes of equality policies and diversity practices effectively function as the 'master's tools'. Equality and diversity documents that circulate from the boardroom to the classroom constitute 'non-performative' institutional 'speech acts' in which simply having a good race equality policy gets translated into *being good at race equality* (Ahmed 2012). Thus we find in the 'master's house' saying you are *for* equality, becomes as good as *doing* equality, which explains why, when it comes to policy solutions, '*the more things change the more they stay the same.*'

In her chapter, 'The Heart of Whiteness' (see Chapter 18), Nicola Rollock empathically uses CRT to illuminate exactly how these bureaucratic racist technologies of concealment operate. Drawing on her personal account as a woman of colour she finds she is seldom the author of her own destiny on the academic stage. That power remains the privileged domain of White male and female academics who police and control academic spaces. Much of their power lies in the subtlety of everyday racial microaggressions, such as when she was cynically told by a senior white female colleague, 'it would be so different if you were in charge', which put her in her place and serves to remind her that she is less than white. In assessing applications for the rigorous Race Equality Charter, of which she is a Patron, Rollock observes the few successful institutions are the ones where whites are cognisant of their actions and racial justice is named, embedded and enacted within the normality of institutional life.

In her chapter, 'Rocking the Boat' (see Chapter 19), Sara Ahmed skilfully and poetically explains why women of colour tend to be seen as diversity workers or end up becoming diversity workers in universities. Those who do not quite inhabit the norms of an institution are often given the task of transforming these norms, and find themselves relegated to diversity committees or equality task forces to do so. This knowing act of strategic 'tick box inclusion' creates the appearance of an institution being a place of 'happy diversity'. However, for women of colour being a 'happy symbol of diversity' is hard work, and they find themselves caught between 'not rocking the boat' or banging their head against institutional 'brick walls' if they the challenge the entrenched institutional systems of racist and sexist collusion. To complain, show anger, or dissent is a dangerous business, and many have to leave their universities to survive, as indeed Ahmed had to do. Resignation under these conditions is a powerful act of resistance, dignity and voice.

With the gaze firmly on the bodies of Black and brown people in the 'equality game', you may well ask, what does senior white leadership have to do with it? Well everything as Uvanney Maylor sensitively explores in her chapter, 'Educational Leadership for Social Justice' (see Chapter 20). In recounting the shocking lack of respect displayed towards her by a White male governor who blurts out, 'you don't look like a Professor', she is prompted to ask if he or the senior governance team have ever received any race equality training? If this is *still* the face of elite white patriarchal leadership in higher education today, the question is how can we ever achieve a model of social justice in higher education that speaks to issues of fairness and representation? For Maylor true social justice means valuing and promoting the leadership capabilities of Black staff such that they become 'part of the fabric' of what higher education institutions can and should be.

However, as Penny Jane Burke, explains, higher education as a vehicle for social justice will remain an elusive vision if the fundamental excluding processes of racist misrecognition and redistribution are not tackled. In her theoretically rich chapter, 'Trans/forming Pedagogical Spaces' (see Chapter 21), Burke explains, misrecognition is a form of symbolic violence in which only certain persons are seen as 'worthy' and authentic university participants. Although there are important differences between groups targeted by higher education policies to Widen Participation, such as 'Black and Minority Ethnic', 'Low Socio-economic Groups', 'Mature', 'Part-time', and 'Students with Disabilities, these homogenising policy categorisations often perpetuate a pathologising neo-colonial gaze. Thus, as Burke concludes policy and practice to tackle institutional racism must be fine-tuned to the intersectional formations of difference within and across different communities if universities are to provide genuine opportunities for social mobility through policies of Widening Participation.

It is fitting that the last word in this collection should be given to one of our leading policy makers in the field of Race Equality in higher education. Gary Loke, in his summation of the collection, 'So What Next? A Policy Response' (see Chapter 22), observes three outstanding things that define this moment in race equality in higher education. First, is the complexity of definitions and inequalities—from what we mean by 'White' in the context of class differences, to what constitutes the category BME and the important ethnic and class and gender differences within these groups. This complexity, he suggests, calls for a more nuanced approach to equality. Secondly, Loke observes institutional racism is still endemic. This is evidenced among other things by the lack of progression for Black academics and the exclusion of students of colour from elite universities. Third, policy initiatives such as the Race Equality Charter, which he champions, provides a hopeful horizon to hold universities to task. However, given the Government's retraction of the monitoring and accountability powers enshrined in the Equality Act, there still appears to be few carrots and no sticks left to beat the HE sector with!

Conclusion: 'What Then, Can Be Done?'

In reviewing the incontrovertible evidence amassed in this book on the shocking state of racial inequality in our British universities, we return to Lammy's lament, 'What then, can be done?'

The launch of this Collection represents an important moment of critical intervention into the wider debates concerning the future of the Higher Education sector in Britain. 50 years on from the progressive twentieth century reforms to expand higher education, the birth of the concept institutional racism, and the landmark civil rights and Race Equality legislation in Britain and America, we find ourselves at a moment of consolidation and reflection.

The chapters in the book document the scale of 'What's to be done'. We see how the entrenched mechanisms of institutional racism, from the overt admission processes, to covert everyday microaggressions operate to keep the academy an enclave of white privilege. We dismantle the ruse of equality and diversity policies which have become no more than a sham, a slick bureaucratic performance which contains the problem, but leaves the rot. We hear the voices of students and scholars who speak back to these institutions of higher learning with their revolutionary calls to decolonise the still impenetrable hub of imperial white knowledge production—and like them, we ask not 'What's to be done'—but 'How can we do it?'

In looking towards the future, we would argue a key starting point for those who are committed to social justice and racial equality in the academy is to not ask, 'What then, can be done?', but rather '*What's the nature of changing terrain on which we struggle?*'. Over the past 15 years we have witnessed a revolution in the marketisation of the knowledge economy, culminating in the 2017 Higher Education and Research Act. No longer are Universities semi-autonomous institutions of scholarly pursuit. They now are expected to behave like business enterprises, operating in a highly regulated but competitive commercial marketplace (Collini 2017; Emejulu 2017b). This complete neoliberal transformation of the Academy has huge implications for Black and Minority Ethnic students, staff and service workers, given the already exclusionary racist institutional practices that remain at the sectors core. Vulnerable BME students indebted by the burden of high fees and exposed to the open market of 'choice' are now expected to put their faith and futures in the dubious mechanisms of 'student satisfaction' that drives the Teaching Excellence Framework (TEF) and the controversial quango, the 'Office for Students' who will regulate it. In this 'brave new world' of profit and privilege, Black and Minority Ethnic early career academics are faced with the precarity of teaching-only or short-term contracts and find themselves increasingly casualised, deskilled and disposable in the competitive world of 'League tables' and the brutal funding metrics of the Research Excellence Framework (REF). In this new terrain of struggle 'dismantling the masters house', as it is being systematically rebuilt will shape our challenge ahead. Armed with the contents of this book we at least have a head start!

References

Ahmed, S. (2012). *On Being Included: Racism and Diversity in Institutional Life*. Durham: Duke University Press.

Ahmed, S. (2015, June 25). Against Students. https://feministkilljoys.com/2015/06/25/against-students/.

Alexander, C. (2017). Breaking Black: The Death of Ethnic and Racial Studies in Britain. *Ethnic and Racial Studies*. https://doi.org/10.1080/01419870.2018.1409902.

Alexander, C., & Arday, J. (Eds.) (2015). *Aiming Higher: Race, Inequality and Diversity in the Academy*. London: Runnymede Trust. https://www.runnymedetrust.org/uploads/Aiming%20Higher.pdf.

Bhambra, G. K. (2007). Sociology and Postcolonialism: Another 'Missing' Revolution? *Sociology, 41*(5), 871–884. https://doi.org/10.1177/0038038507080442.

Bhambra, G. K. (2014). Postcolonial and Decolonial Dialogues. *Postcolonial Studies, 17*(2), 115–121. https://doi.org/10.1080/13688790.2014.966414.

Bhavnani, R., Mirza, H., & Meetoo, V. (2005). *Tackling the Roots of Racism: Lessons for Success*. Bristol: Policy Press.

Caluya, G., Probyn, E., & Shvetal, V. (2011). 'Affective Eduscapes': The Case of Indian Students Within Australian International Higher Education. *Cambridge Journal of Education, 41*(1), 85–99.

Carmichael, S., & Hamilton, C. V. (1967). *Black Power: The Politics of Liberation in America* (1st ed.). New York: Vintage Books.

Collini, S. (2017). *Speaking of Universities*. London: Verso.

Collins, P. H. (1998). *Fighting Words: Black Women and the Search for Justice*. Minneapolis: University of Minnesota Press.

Emejulu, A. (2017a, January 12). Another University Is Possible. https://www.versobooks.com/blogs/3044-another-university-is-possible. Accessed 15 Jan 2018.

Emejulu, A. (2017b, March 29). *The University Is Not Innocent: Speaking of Universities*. London: Verso. https://www.versobooks.com/blogs/3148-the-university-is-not-innocent-speaking-of-universities. Accessed 15 Jan 2018.

Equality Challenge Unit (ECU). (2016). *Equality in Higher Education: Statistical Report 2016*. http://www.ecu.ac.uk/publications/equality-in-higher-education-statistical-report-2016. Accessed 15 Jan 2018.

Gabriel, D., & Tate, S. A. (Eds.). (2017). *Inside the Ivory Tower: Narratives of Women of Colour Surviving and Thriving in Academia*. London: Trentham UCL Press.

Gopal, P. (2017, October 27). Yes, We Must Decolonise: Our Teaching Has to Go Beyond Elite White Men. *The Guardian*. https://www.theguardian.com/commentisfree/2017/oct/27/decolonise-elite-white-men-decolonising-cambridge-university-english-curriculum-literature. Accessed 15 Jan 2018.

Khan, O. (Ed.). (2015a). *How Far Have We Come? Lessons from the 1965 Race Relations Act*. London: Runnymede Trust. https://www.runnymedetrust.org/uploads/publications/pdfs/Race%20Relations%20Act%20Perspectives%20report.pdf. Accessed 15 Jan 2018.

Khan, O. (2015b). #RhodesMustFall: A Movement for Historical and Contemporary Recognition of Racial Injustice. https://www.runnymedetrust.org/blog/rhodesmustfall-a-movement-for-historical-and-contemporary-recognition-of-racial-injustice-part-1. Accessed 15 Jan 2018.

Law, I., Phillips, D., & Turney, L. (Eds.). (2004). *Institutional Racism in Higher Education*. Stoke on Trent: Trentham Books.

Lorde, A. (2007). *Sister Outsider: Essays and Speeches* (2nd ed.). New York: Crossing Press.

Macpherson, W. (1999). *The Stephen Lawrence Inquiry: Report of an Inquiry by Sir William Macpherson*. London: HMSO.

Morley, L. (2012). Researching Absences and Silences in Higher Education: Data for Democratisation. *Higher Education Research & Development, 31*(3), 353–368. https://doi.org/10.1080/07294360.2011.634385.

Warikoo, N. (2016). *The Diversity Bargain: And Other Dilemmas of Race, Admissions and Meritocracy at Elite Universities*. Chicago, IL: University of Chicago Press.

Part II
Let the Facts Speak: Institutional Racism in Higher Education

2

The Rise and Fall in the Salience of Race Equality in Higher Education

Andrew Pilkington

Introduction

What initially prompted me to address the issue of race and higher education was the murder of a young Black man, Stephen Lawrence in 1993 because of the colour of his skin. The subsequent flawed police investigation eventually led to an official inquiry chaired by Sir William Macpherson. The report published in 1999 was extraordinarily damning: 'The [police] investigation was marred by a combination of professional incompetence, institutional racism and a failure of leadership by senior officers' (Macpherson 1999: para 46.1). And the political response, as exemplified by the Home Secretary's response to the report, was equally forthright: 'In my view, any long-established, white-dominated organisation is liable to have procedures, practices and a culture that tend to exclude or to disadvantage non-white people' (Hansard 1999: col 391).

A. Pilkington (✉)
University of Northampton, Northampton, UK
e-mail: Andrew.pilkington@northampton.ac.uk

© The Author(s) 2018
J. Arday and H. S. Mirza (eds.), *Dismantling Race in Higher Education*,
https://doi.org/10.1007/978-3-319-60261-5_2

27

The acceptance by a senior judge and leading Minister of the charge of institutional racism was unprecedented and inaugurated what I have labelled 'a radical hour' when the state seemed to be serious about promoting race equality (Pilkington 2014).

Prior to the Stephen Lawrence Inquiry, very little attention was paid to race and ethnicity in relation to higher education in the UK (Neal 1998; Law et al. 2004; Pilkington 2011). As one writer puts it, 'The university sector... remained relatively insulated from other policy developments in councils, schools, the health service and the police with regards to challenging racism and promoting ethnic and cultural diversity' (Law 2003: 519). Such detachment was also evident in research where 'in contrast to the large amount of work on race and schooling in Britain, relatively little [had] been written on "race" and higher education' (Jacobs and Hai 2002: 171). The advent of the Labour government in 1997 and the subsequent publication of the Macpherson report provided a jolt to the sector. Renewed impetus was given to equality initiatives and the limitations of equal opportunity policies in generating cultural change and combating racial disadvantage were more widely recognised.

This chapter surveys the two decades since 1997 to examine how the higher education sector in general and one university in particular has addressed race and ethnicity. It will draw upon a growing research literature to evaluate the major policy initiatives. I shall argue that the salience of race equality which rose dramatically in the aftermath of the publication of the Macpherson report, and the government's response to it, has not been sustained. While new policy initiatives periodically emerge, what is remarkable in my view is the failure of the higher education sector in the last twenty years to transform the experience of Black and Minority Ethnic (BME) staff and students. Racial disadvantage remains stubbornly persistent, as we shall see.

The Increasing Salience of Race Equality

For a brief period in the first few years of the new millennium, the state exerted considerable pressure on universities to address race equality. Two issues in particular were highlighted in major research publications.

The first related to staffing. A report published a few months after the Macpherson report in June 1999, pointed to disadvantages experienced by academic staff from minority ethnic groups (Carter et al. 1999). The disadvantages related to recruitment, employment status and career progression, with some BME staff reporting experiences of racial discrimination and harassment. A few years later, another major study pointed to disadvantages experienced by BME students. The latter were less likely to be found in old universities, more likely to drop out, less likely to be awarded good honours degrees and more likely to do less well in the labour market (Connor et al. 2004).

Acknowledging these to be the central issues in higher education pertaining to race, the state cajoled universities to address race equality through two strategies for higher education, notably those concerned with widening participation and human resources. The first sought to promote equality and diversity in the student body, while the second was concerned with promoting equal opportunities in staffing. While the specific mechanisms employed to promote widening participation and equal opportunities have changed over time, the annual funding letters from the government to the Higher Education Funding Council for England (HEFCE) reveal that these remain government 'priorities' (HEFCE 2016a). In addition to these colour blind strategies, the state also for a period required universities along with other public organisations to develop race equality policies and action plans following new race relations legislation in 2000.

How successful were these colour blind strategies in promoting race equality? However effective these strategies may have been in relation to other equality strands, they do not seem to have made significant inroads in combating race inequality.

The primary concern of widening participation strategies is social class. The result is that the needs of BME students have been of marginal concern to policy makers (Aimhigher 2006). The focus of policy on admissions to the sector as a whole glossed over the differentiated nature of the higher education sector and overlooked the different rates of return from gaining access to higher education (Reay et al. 2005). In particular it failed to address the fact that BME students, though well represented in the sector as a whole, are underrepresented in the more prestigious institutions and continue to be less likely than White students to gain good honours degrees. A study exploring in depth widening participation initiatives indicates 'that the sector generally prioritises pre-entry and access initiatives at the expense of interventions once students have entered HE' (Thomas et al. 2005: 193). This finding is significant and has adverse consequences for minority ethnic groups who are more likely to gain access to the sector but disproportionately face problems in succeeding.

Turning to strategies promoting equal opportunities, a series of audits reveal significant lacunae. One reveals that many key staff do not believe in the importance of EO (HEFCE 2005a), while other research indicates that many staff are in fact highly sceptical of the efficacy of equal opportunities policies (Deem et al. 2005). Furthermore, analysis of university equal opportunities strategies identifies significant deficiencies in monitoring (HEFCE 2002/14: para 143 in HEFCE 2007) and in target setting (HEFCE 2003/37: para 27 in HEFCE 2007). Since it has been widely recognised for a long time that an organisation intent on preventing or detecting racial discrimination needs to undertake both 'ethnic monitoring and the setting of targets' (Sanders 1998: 38), the evidence pointing to failures in data gathering and target setting suggest that many HEIs have not taken equal opportunities policies seriously, at least when it comes to race. This suggestion is confirmed by official evaluations of human resources strategies which indicate that the implementation of equal opportunities strategies continued to exhibit a greater concern with gender than race issues (HEFCE 2005b). Previous research had indicated that equal opportunities policies in higher education tend to focus on gender rather than race (Neal 1998; Law et al. 2004). The evidence above that the implementation of equal opportunities strategies entailed a greater concern with gender than race issues suggests that this prioritisation persists.

Let us turn to an approach that is explicitly concerned with race. The government's major response to the Macpherson report was a legislative initiative, the Race Relations (Amendment) Act (RRAA), 2000. The Act extended the scope of the 1976 Race Relations Act by covering public bodies which had been previously exempt and making it unlawful for public authorities to discriminate in carrying out any of their functions. While this Act, like previous race relations legislation, prohibited unlawful discrimination, a new approach was also evident. For the first time, a general statutory duty was placed on all public authorities, and specific duties on some authorities, to eliminate racial discrimination (including indirect discrimination), promote good race relations and facilitate equality of opportunity. The Act gave the Commission for Racial Equality (CRE) the power to develop a statutory code of practice and provide guidance to public authorities on how to meet the general duty and any specific duties introduced by the Home Secretary. By enjoining public bodies in this way to develop policies and plans which promote racial equality, the RRAA adopted a very different approach to that embodied in previous race relations legislation: public authorities were now being required to take a pro-active stance to racial equality and thus take the lead in eliminating racial discrimination, promoting good race relations and facilitating equal opportunities.

While the colour blind strategies were not very successful in promoting race equality, the race relations legislation introduced in 2000 proved more effective, at least for a time. Under RRAA, universities were obliged to develop race equality policies and action plans by May 2002. These policies and action plans needed to meet both the general and specific duties laid down by the legislation. The specific duties for HEIs were:

- Prepare and maintain a written race equality policy and implementation plan;
- Within the policy and plan assess the impact of institutional policies on staff and students from different racial groups;
- Within the policy and plan monitor the applications, admissions and progression of students;
- Within the policy and plan monitor the recruitment and development of staff;
- Within the policy and plan set out arrangements for publishing the race equality policy and the results of monitoring impact assessments and reviews.

What is interesting about these specific duties is what they prioritise. They do not, unlike the *Anti-Racist Toolkit* produced by Leeds University (Turney et al. 2002), focus on teaching and research, but on widening participation and equal opportunities (Sharma 2004). The colour blind widening participation and equal opportunity policies may have, as we have seen, bypassed minorities, but targeted policies it was hoped would make a difference.

University race equality policies and action plans were subsequently audited in 2003 and 2004. While the initial audit found more than a third of higher education institutions (HEIs) had not satisfactorily met their statutory obligations (John 2003), subsequent audits were more upbeat and pointed to the considerable progress travelled by the majority of HEIs (OPM 2004a, b). Given that a report published a mere 5 years earlier indicated that only a few HEIs had a race equality policy at all, such an upbeat position is understandable. However, it should be noted that these audits were desk based and that the reality on the ground might be very different.

So what can we provisionally conclude? Colour blind government strategies to widen participation and promote equal opportunities seem to have had minimal impact in combating race inequality in the period that we have examined. By contrast, the more targeted RRAA seems to have had more impact, at least in the sense of generating race equality policies and plans.

We need to be circumspect, however. Even when legislation had insisted on the production of race equality policies and action plans and guidance had been provided to aid the production process, the requisite policies and action plans were often initially lacking, and significant pressure had to be exerted to ensure minimal compliance (John 2003). What is more, when (some of) those institutions that had produced exemplary policies were followed up eighteen months to two years later, those Institutions had generally done very little to translate their first class policy into meaningful action (John 2005: 593–594). The reviews that we have drawn upon here have perforce been focused on documents but there is a danger of being too reliant on documents. This is that we confuse what is written in strategic and policy documents with what actually happens in institutions. Since strategic and policy documents often serve as the public face of the university, an inordinate amount of time can go into getting them just right. This can mean that writing documents and having good policies becomes a substitute for action: as an interviewee in one study (Ahmed 2012) puts it, "you end up doing the document rather than doing the doing" (Ahmed 2007).

Conscious of the dangers of reliance on official documents, I conducted an ethnographic investigation of one university in the decade following the publication of the Macpherson report (Pilkington 2011). A colleague has subsequently extended the investigation to 2013 (Crofts 2013). The university is a new university in Central England and will be identified as Midshire University.

What is immediately apparent is that at different times more or less attention has been placed on race equality. At certain points, the university has made a serious effort to address the issue of race equality. At other times, the issue has not been on the institution's radar. The development of equal opportunity policies from 1989 onwards eventually led to the development of action plans for different strands of equality. A race equality plan was devised between 1992 and 1994. This was updated and launched in 1996 and can be considered to be a relatively advanced policy at this time. Within an extraordinarily short time, however, the policy had been forgotten. Indeed the subsequent requirement under the RRAA to develop by May 2002 a race equality policy and action plan was not appropriately met. The university was subsequently required to resubmit its policy and action plan to HEFCE within a limited time period. This provided an opportunity for race equality champions within the university to develop a robust policy and action plan and persuade senior management to put in place appropriate resources to support the policy and plan. It is noteworthy that what prompted the recovery was not the race relations legislation per se but the independent review which indicated the university was non-compliant.

Race equality subsequently had a higher priority within the university. New governance arrangements and the arrival of two equality and diversity officers in 2004 subsequently gave equality and diversity generally and race in particular a higher profile. And there is no doubt that for some years significant progress was made. The conditions facilitating this included (for a period) external pressure on the university, support from some key senior staff and the presence of highly effective equality and diversity officers.

The Declining Salience of Race Equality

The middle of the first decade of the new millennium represented the university's high point in terms of addressing race equality. Since then external pressure from the government has ineluctably declined (Feldman 2012). Although lip service continues to be paid in government pronouncements and some strategies to race equality and ethnic diversity, other government agendas prompted by concerns over increasing net migration, disorder and terrorism subsequently marginalised one concerned with race equality. This is evident in relation to the way new legislation introduced by the Labour government in 2010 has been subsequently implemented.

The Equality Act 2010 extended the general duties (now labelled the public sector equality duty), initially identified in the race relations legislation, to different strands of equality, with the Equality and Human Rights Commission (EHRC), a body that had been set up earlier to replace a series of bodies focused on distinct strands of equality, being charged with having an enforcement role. Over time, however, and especially since the Coalition government (2010) and subsequent Conservative government (2015) took power, the requirements embodied in the legislation have been eroded. Thus the specific duties, enshrined in statutory codes of practice, including the requirement to have in place an equality action plan and conduct equality impact assessments have been replaced by the need, on which there is merely guidance, to publish limited data and set one or more objectives. And at the same time, the red tape challenge and the significant cut in funding for the EHRC signal that racial equality is sliding down the government's agenda.

The Periodic Emergence in Policy Discourse of Race Equality

Inevitably I have been constructing a narrative in this chapter and it is a narrative that seeks to present a coherent story. Race equality and ethnic diversity have been deprioritised as other governmental agendas rise to prominence. In the process the external pressure on the university sector has waned with the result that there is a very real danger that the gains that have been made will not be maintained let alone built upon. It is important, however, not to overstate my case or assume complete consistency in the government's approach. What should be noted in this context is the continuing concern of some parts of the machinery of government with racial equality throughout the period I have been discussing.

A seeming case in point is the *Ethnicity and Degree Attainment Project*. This arose out of the findings of a research study published in January, 2007 which demonstrated that, even after controlling for a plethora of contributory factors, minority ethnic status generally had an adverse effect on degree attainment (Broecke and Nicholls 2007). The findings prompted the Department for Innovation, Universities and Skills (DIUS) and the English and Welsh funding councils to commission the Higher Education Academy and Equality Challenge Unit to undertake a project to explore possible causes and practical responses. The project culminated in a report that was launched at a conference in January, 2008. On possible causes, the report concluded: 'The causes of degree attainment variation...were found to be unlikely to be reducible to single, knowable factors' and on practical responses, the report made two key recommendations: 'There is a need to ensure that the valuable information gained from data sources...are used as a means of reflective institutional analysis and action planning' and 'HEIs need to implement systems that can evaluate, review and design teaching, learning and assessment activities in light of data on degree attainment variation' (Higher Education Academy 2008: 3–4). What was disturbing as an attendee at the conference was the sense of déjà vu. The audience comprised of academics rather than administrators, but the key recommendations and much of the discussion were not dissimilar to those at conferences six years earlier designed to prepare universities to meet their duties under the RRAA. While the report itself does acknowledge that 'higher education institutions are legally required to gather data... and then take action against any adverse findings' (Higher Education Academy 2008: 13), the recommendations were presented to the conference as though they were new. It is both remarkable and revealing how quickly previous initiatives had been forgotten. It is remarkable because of the short time that had elapsed since universities were required to demonstrate how they were meeting the specific duty 'to monitor the applications, admissions and progression of students by racial group'. It is revealing because it raises serious doubts about whether the sector is any longer under pressure to take race seriously and, in the seeming absence of such pressure, whether it is likely to take any sustained action to promote race equality and ethnic diversity. In this context it is revealing to note that less than half the access agreements, which universities are obliged to produce for formal approval by the Office for Fair Access, 'address the persistent gap in attainment rates for students from different ethnic minority groups' and this despite the fact that this issue is supposedly central to 'the national strategy for access and student success' (OFFA 2016: 3). It is difficult not to conclude that this episode exemplifies lip service being paid to racial equality and ethnic diversity.

This judgement is confirmed in my view by successive funding letters from the government to HEFCE (2016a) which consistently identify widening participation as a priority but at the same time periodically acknowledge the continuing failure of elite universities to increase significantly their enrolment of students from disadvantaged backgrounds. The government's most recent proposal to improve opportunities for students from disadvantaged groups (which it is recognised incorporate many BME groups) is contained in the HE White paper (DfBIS 2016). The emphasis yet again is on the obligation for HEIs to publish data! As the ECU (2016) optimistically puts it, 'HEIs will be required to publish data on application, offer and progression by ethnicity, gender and socioeconomic background. Provision of this information, along with overall participation rates, continuation rates, degree attainment and outcome and employment outcomes will help the sector to understand the barriers that exist—and put in place measures to overcome disadvantage'. While it would be an exaggeration to say that equality and diversity, and concomitantly race equality and ethnic diversity, have completely disappeared as policy objectives, the contrast between the policy initiatives at the beginning of the century which demanded the production of action plans and this latest initiative which merely 'nudge[s] universities into making the right choices and reaching out in the right ways' as part of 'our ambitious (sic) "2020 agenda" for BME communities' (Cameron 2016: 2–3) could not be more palpable.

The consequence of the declining salience of race equality in government pronouncements and the decreasing pressure on universities to promote race equality has been felt graphically at Midshire University. At the university, this initially entailed increasing resistance to an equality and diversity agenda, but eventually led to the disappearance of any dedicated committees or equality and diversity officers (Crofts 2013). This development was justified in terms of mainstreaming but has in fact entailed a reversal of the progress made in the preceding years to meet the general and specific duties of the race relations legislation.

What is remarkable is that at the same time, evidence of racial disadvantage remains stubbornly persistent. In my study, I found the following: persistent ethnic differentials in the student experience that adversely impact on BME students and point to possible indirect discrimination; ethnic differentials in staff recruitment that adversely impact on Black and Asian applicants and point to possible indirect discrimination; (some) minority ethnic staff subject to racism and (some) White staff cynical about political correctness; an overwhelmingly White senior staff team, with no evident efforts to transform this situation; low priority given to the implementation of a race equality action plan; few staff skilled in intercultural issues; many staff not trained in equality and diversity; and few efforts made to consult Black and Asian communities.

We cannot of course generalise from this case study to the sector as a whole. Nonetheless, what we have found at Midshire University resonates with findings elsewhere (Turney et al. 2002; Bhattacharya 2002; Major 2002; Bhopal 2016) and points to what one author has called 'the sheer weight of Whiteness' (Back 2004: 1). It is impossible to comprehend the persistence of racial disadvantage and the failure to combat this without recognising 'how deeply rooted Whiteness is throughout the … system' (Gillborn 2008: 9). While minority ethnic staff are typically conscious of this, often for White staff (including White researchers) '… the Whiteness of the institution goes unnoticed and is rationalised into a day-to-day perception of normality' (Law et al. 2004: 97). It is crucial therefore that we are reflexive and do not let 'the "whiteness" of the academy ….go unnoticed and uncommented' (Clegg et al. 2003: 164; Frankenberg 2004).

Continuing Racial Disadvantage in the HE Sector: BME Staff and Students

Research continues to demonstrate that individuals from minority ethnic communities disproportionately experience adverse outcomes (Grove 2015). While there is some variability by ethnic group since BMEs are by no means a homogeneous category, BME staff and students experience considerable disadvantage. BME academic staff are more likely to be on fixed term contracts, continue to experience significant disadvantage in career progression, especially in gaining access to the senior ranks of university management, and there remains an ethnic pay gap virtually 2 decades after the publication of the Macpherson report (Leathwood et al. 2009; ECU 2011; Ratcliffe and Shaw 2014). Indeed a recent report based on interviews with BME staff is sceptical that much has changed in the last 20 years: the vast majority continue to experience subtle racism and feel outsiders in the White space of the Academy (Bhopal 2016). Meanwhile BME students continue to be less likely to be enrolled at elite universities (UCAS 2016) and awarded good honours degrees even when prior attainment and socio-economic status have been taken into account (Broeke and Nicholls 2007; HEA 2008), and to experience lower retention rates and progression rates from undergraduate study to both employment and postgraduate study (OFFA 2016; HEFCE 2016b). In this context it is not altogether surprising that they express significantly less satisfaction with their university experience (Havergal 2016). And yet, despite this evidence of the remarkable persistence in racial disadvantage, universities are extraordinarily complacent.

Legislation and Equality

This complacency partly stems from the dominance in the academy and much of society of a liberal perspective on equality. We can distinguish two broad perspectives on equality—liberal and radical. The first is concerned to promote fair or like treatment and to this end seeks to devise '*fair procedures*' so that everybody, regardless of race, receives the same treatment and 'justice is seen to be done' (Noon and Blyton 1997: 177). The emphasis in this approach is upon sanctions against any form of racially discriminatory behaviour. The second 'represents a more radical approach since it suggests that policy makers should be concerned with the *outcome*, rather than the *process*, and should therefore be seeking to ensure a *fair distribution of rewards*' (Noon and Blyton 1997: 182). To treat everybody the same is, in this view, to ignore pertinent differences between people and does little to eradicate disadvantage which stems from discrimination in the past and current institutional practices which result in indirect discrimination. To ensure fair outcomes—such as an ethnically balanced workforce—what are needed are not merely sanctions against racial discrimination but measures which entail positive discrimination i.e. preferential treatment of disadvantaged groups.

The liberal perspective has primarily informed legislation and policies in the UK. Take the 1976 Race Relations Act. The emphasis was on like treatment, with the law enabling sanctions to be deployed against those found to be guilty of racial discrimination. Positive discrimination was not permitted and the 'overall thrust was individualist' with the legal process demanding proof that 'individual members of racial groups [had] suffered discrimination' before racial discrimination could be established and sanctions deployed (Pilkington 2011: 66). Nonetheless, the Act did move beyond like treatment in two respects. Firstly, the recognition that discrimination took indirect forms entailed an acknowledgement that practices, which treated people in the same way, could disproportionately and adversely effect some groups more than others. Secondly, organisations were encouraged under the Act to counter the effects of past discrimination and redress the under representation of minority groups by developing positive action programmes. The rationale for such programmes, which included targeted advertising campaigns and training courses, was 'to encourage the previously disadvantaged to the starting gate for jobs, promotion and other opportunities' (Blakemore and Drake 1996: 12). Once at the starting gate, however, and in contrast to the situation which prevailed in the United States from the mid 1960s to (at least) the late 1980s and has developed in Northern Ireland since 1989 (Noon and Blyton 1997), no preferential treatment was permitted and legally enforceable quotas for disadvantaged groups were expressly disallowed.

The government's major response to the Macpherson report was, as we have argued above, a legislative initiative, the RRAA, 2000. While this Act, like previous race relations legislation, was partly informed by the liberal perspective and thus prohibited unlawful discrimination, the Act was also informed by the radical perspective and adopted an approach that required public bodies to take the lead in eliminating racial discrimination, promoting good race relations and facilitating equal opportunities. To this end universities were required to produce race equality action plans in order to facilitate fair *outcomes*. Unfortunately, many of the key players in the university sector adopt a liberal perspective on equality and believe fair procedures are what is important (Deem et al. 2005; Crofts 2013). They see themselves as liberal and believe existing policies ensure fairness and in the process ignore adverse outcomes and do not see combating racial/ethnic inequalities as a priority. This points in my view to the sheer weight of whiteness (if not institutional racism) which will remain intact unless significant pressure is placed on universities to change.

What Is to Be Done?

Universities will not be able to promote race equality and combat the adverse outcomes faced by BME staff and students unless they see it as their responsibility to take ameliorative action. No truck should be given to a deficit model which explains away the racial disadvantage faced by BME staff and students evidenced above. While there may be no easy answers, the key starting point is for universities to ask what they can do to ensure more *equitable outcomes*. Do we have forums which enable us effectively to consult with BME staff and students? What measures need to be taken to ensure diversity in leadership? Are there unconscious biases in selection and promotion boards at play which need to be dismantled? And so on.

We can distinguish two ideal typical approaches.

The first is sceptical as to whether universities will as a matter of course promote race equality and ethnic diversity. External pressure in this view is vital to facilitate change. To this end, the first approach believes that legislation and the enforcement of that legislation are crucial; sees a need for there to be a focus on race equality rather than equality in general; adopts a radical perspective on equality; identifies the need for action plans with clear targets which are regularly audited; requires publication of time series and comparative data to ensure transparency; and identifies the need for periodic inspection by an independent body.

The second approach is very different in visualising universities as having an inherent interest in promoting race equality and ethnic diversity in a highly competitive global marketplace where universities compete for students and require a diverse workforce. Legislation compelling universities to act in particular ways, according to this approach, is less effective than nudges and persuasion to remind them to utilise appropriate data to identify and dismantle barriers to equal opportunities for individuals from disadvantaged groups. Rather than imposing mandatory requirements, it is deemed preferable for universities to set their own objectives in the light of their own particular circumstances, Independent bodies ideally will identify good practice and disseminate it widely to the sector and even give awards to those universities who manifest good practice. In the process, universities will not merely comply with external demands but steadily transform themselves.

While neither of these two approaches can be found in their pure form in the real world, there is little doubt that the period we have examined has witnessed the transition from an approach close to the first ideal type to an approach close to the second. Both approaches have some merits. It is probably evident that I have greater sympathy for the first approach and thus welcome EHRC's recent call for a comprehensive race equality strategy (EHRC 2016). Adoption of this approach following publication of the Macpherson report did entail some progressive change in the sector and its abandonment prevented this being sustained both at the sectoral level and at Midshire University. It would be utopian to anticipate the return of this approach in the near future. And the second approach can entail progressive change in some universities, as evidenced by those who have met the requirements for a bronze award of the race equality charter.

References

Ahmed, S. (2007). "You End Up Doing the Document Rather Than Doing the Doing": Diversity, Race Equality and the Politics of Documentation. *Ethnic and Racial Studies, 30*(2), 235–256.

Ahmed, S. (2012). *On Being Included: Racism and Diversity in Institutional Life*. London: Duke University Press.

Aimhigher. (2006). *A Review of Black and Minority Ethnic Participation in Higher Education*. http://www.aimhigher.ac.uk/sites/practitioner/resources/Conf%20Summary%20report%. Last Accessed 20 Nov 2011.

Back, L. (2004). Ivory Towers? The Academy and Racism. In I. Law, D. Phillips, & L. Turney (Eds.), *Institutional Racism in Higher Education*. Stoke on Trent: Trentham Books.

Bhattacharya, G. (2002, January 15). The Unwritten Rules of the Game: Imagine Working in a Place Where the Rules Aren't the Same for Everyone. *The Guardian*. http://www.guardian.co.uk/education/2002/jan/15/raceineducation.race1. Last Accessed 24 Mar 2013.

Bhopal, K. (2016). *The Experiences of Black and Minority Ethnic Academics: A Comparative Study of the Unequal Academy*. London: Routledge.

Blakemore, K., & Drake, R. (1996). *Understanding Equal Opportunity Policies*. London: Prentice Hall.

Broecke, S., & Nicholls, T. (2007). *Ethnicity and Degree Attainment* (Research Report RW92). London: Department for Education and Skills.

Cameron, D. (2016). *Watch Out Universities; I'm Bringing the Fight for Equality to You*. https://www.gov.uk/government/speeches/watch-out-universities-im-bringing-the-fight-for-equality-in-britain-to-you-article-by-david-cameron. Last Accessed 29 June 2016.

Carter, J., Fenton, J., & Modood, T. (1999). *Ethnicity and Employment in Higher Education*. London: Policy Studies Institute.

Clegg, S., Parr, S., & Wan, S. (2003). Racialising Discourses in Higher Education. *Teaching in Higher Education, 8*(2), 155–168.

Connor, H., Tyers, C., & Modood, T. (2004). *Why the Difference? A Close Look at Higher Education Minority Ethnic Students and Graduates* (Research Report RR448). London: Department for Education and Skills.

Crofts, M. (2013). *The Impact of the Public Sector Equality Duties on Higher Education: A Case Study*. Northampton: University of Northampton.

Deem, R., Morley, L., & Tlili, A. (2005). *Negotiating Equity in Higher Education Institutions.* http://www.hefce.ac.uk/pubs/redreports/2005/rd10_05/rd10_05doc. Last Accessed 30 May 2010.

Department for Business, Innovation and Skills. (2016). *Higher Education: Success as a Knowledge Economy—White Paper.* https://www.gov.uk/government/publications/higher-education-success-as-a-knowledge-economy-white-paper. Last Accessed 28 June 2016.

ECU (Equality Challenge Unit). (2011). *Experience of Black and Minority Ethnic Staff in Higher Education in England.* London: ECU.

ECU. (2016). *ECU Responds to White Paper.* http://www.ecu.ac.uk/news/ecu-responds-to-he-white-paper/. Last Accessed 28 June 16.

Equality and Human Rights Commission. (2016). *Healing a Divided Britain: The Need for a Comprehensive Race Equality Strategy.* https://www.equalityhumanrights.com/en/publication-download/healing-divided-britain-need-comprehensive-race-equality-strategy. Last Accessed 16 Sept 2016.

Feldman, S. (2012, November 29). Opportunity Blocks. *Times Higher Education.*

Frankenberg, R. (2004). On Unsteady Ground: Crafting and Engaging in the Critical Study of Whiteness. In M. Bulmer & J. Solomos (Eds.), *Researching Race and Racism* (pp. 104–118). London: Routledge.

Gillborn, D. (2008). *Racism and Education.* London: Routledge.

Grove, J. (2015, November 5). Black and Ethnic Minorities Still Have Mountains to Climb in Higher Education. *Times Higher Education.*

Hansard. (1999, February 24). *Stephen Lawrence Inquiry.* http://www.publications.parliament.uk/pa/cm199899/cmhansard/vo990224/debtext/90224-21.htm. Last Accessed 23 Aug 2012.

Havergal, C. (2016, June 9). BME Students Are Not Satisfied. *Times Higher Education.*

Higher Education Academy. (2008). *Ethnicity, Gender and Degree Attainment Project: Final Report.* London: ECU.

HEFCE (Higher Education Funding Council for England). (2005a). *Equal Opportunities and Diversity for Staff in Higher Education.* http://www.hefce.ac.uk/pubs/hefce/2005/05_19/05.19.pdf. Last Accessed 29 May 2012.

HEFCE. (2005b). *HEFCE Race Equality Scheme.* http://www.hefce.ac.uk/pubs/hefce/2005/05_04/. Last Accessed 26 June 2016.

HEFCE. (2007). *Rewarding and Developing Staff in Higher Education.* http://www.hefce.ac.uk/lgm/hr/reward/. Last Accessed 21 Aug 2012.

HEFCE. (2016a). *Grant Letter from the Secretary of State to HEFCE.* http://www.hefce.ac.uk/funding/govletter/. Last Accessed 27 June 2016.

HEFCE. (2016b). *Differences in Employment Outcomes: Comparison of 2008–09 and 2010–11 First Degree Graduates.* http://www.hefce.ac.uk/pubs/year/2016/201618. Last Accessed 15 Sept 2016.

Jacobs, S., & Hai, J. (2002). Issues and Dilemmas: "Race" in Higher Education Teaching Practices. In F. Anthias & C. Lloyd (Eds.), *Rethinking Anti-racisms.* London: Routledge.

John, G. (2003). *Review of Race Equality Policies and Action Plans in HEFCE-Funded Higher Education Institutions.* http://www.hefce.ac.uk/lgm/divers/ecu. Last Accessed 30 Oct 2012.

John, G. (2005). *Taking a Stand.* Manchester: Gus John Partnership.

Law, I. (2003). University Teaching in Ethnicity and Racism Studies: Context, Content and Commitment. *Ethnic and Racial Studies, 26*(3), 517–522.

Law, I., Phillips, D., & Turney, L. (Eds.). (2004). *Institutional Racism in Higher Education.* Stoke on Trent: Trentham Books.

Leathwood, C., Maylor, U., & Moreau, M. P. (2009). *The Experience of Staff Working in Higher Education.* London: Equality Challenge Unit.

MacPherson, W. (1999). *The Stephen Lawrence Inquiry: Report of an Inquiry by Sir William Macpherson of Cluny.* London: HMSO.

Major, L. (2002, January 15). Incredible Islands. *The Guardian.* http://www.guardian.co.uk/education/2002/jan/15/raceineducation.race1. Last Accessed 27 June 2016.

Neal, S. (1998). *The Making of Equal Opportunity Policies in Universities.* Buckingham: SRHE/Open University Press.

Noon, M., & Blyton, P. (1997). *The Realities of Work.* London: Macmillan.

OFFA (Office for Fair Access). (2016). *Topic Briefing: BME Students.* https://www.offa.org.uk/universities-and-colleges/guidance-and-useful-information/topic-briefings/offa-topic-briefing-bme-students/. Last Accessed 28 June 2016.

OPM (Office of Public Management). (2004a). *Assessment of Race Equality Policies and Plans in HEFCE-Funded HEIs.* http://www.hefce.ac.uk/Pubs/rdreports/2004/rd09_04/. Last Accessed 1 Dec 2011.

OPM (Office of Public Management). (2004b). *Review of Progress in Race Equality.* http://www.hefce.ac.uk/Pubs/rdreports/2004/rd09_04/. Last Accessed 1 Dec 2011.

Pilkington, A. (2008). From Institutional Racism to Community Cohesion: The Changing Nature of Racial Discourse, *Sociological Research Online, 13*(3). http://www.socresonline.org.uk/13/3/6.html. Last Accessed 27 June 2016.

Pilkington, A. (2011). *Institutional Racism in the Academy: A UK Case Study.* Stoke on Trent: Trentham Books.

Pilkington, A. (2014). The Sheer Weight of Whiteness in The Academy: A UK Case Study. In R. Race & V. Lander (Eds.), *Advancing Race and Ethnicity in Education.* Basingstoke: Palgrave.

Ratcliffe, R., & Shaw, C. (2014). *White Males Monopolise Best Paid Jobs in UK Universities, Report Shows.* https://www.theguardian.com/higher-education-network/2014/nov/18/-sp-white-males-monopolise-highest-paid-jobs-uk-universities. Last Accessed 27 June 2016.

Reay, D., David, M., & Ball, S. (2005). *Degrees of Choice.* Stoke on Trent: Trentham Books.

Sanders, P. (1998). Tackling Racial Discrimination. In T. Blackstone, B. Parekh, & P. Sanders (Eds.), *Race Relations in Britain* (pp. 36–52). London: Routledge.

Sharma, S. (2004). Transforming the Curriculum. In I. Law, D. Phillips, & L. Turney (Eds.), *Institutional Racism in Higher Education* (pp. 105–118). Stoke on Trent: Trentham Books.

Thomas, L., May, H., Houston, M., Knox, J., Lee, M., Osborne, M. et al. (2005). *From the Margins to the Mainstream.* London: Universities UK.

Turney, L., Law, I., & Phillips, D. (2002). *Institutional Racism in Higher Education Toolkit Project: Building the Anti-racist HEI.* http://www.leeds.ac.uk/cers/toolkit/toolkit.htm. Last Accessed 16 Aug 2005.

UCAS. (2016). *UCAS Publishes First Equality Reports for Individual Universities.* https://www.ucas.com/corporate/news-and-key-documents/news/ucas-publishes-first-equality-reports-individual-universities. Last Accessed 29 June 2016.

3

Race and Elite Universities in the UK

Introduction: Elite Universities and Their Centrality in the Reproduction of Educational Inequalities

Although the central focus of this chapter is the issue of race and how it is dealt with by Britain's elite universities, in order to fully understand the way race works in our elite institutions, at the outset a broader lens is needed, one that initially steps back and examines not only the mission and purpose of these few select universities but also how they justify and explain their selectivity and elitism to themselves and others. This requires an interrogation of the meritocratic ideal that Oxbridge and other elite universities hold dear. It also requires an analysis of the powerful ways in which educational systems, including their universities, work to reproduce the existing order rather than transform it, and to this end, I have drawn on the work of Pierre Bourdieu.

D. Reay (✉)
Sociology of Education, University of Cambridge, Cambridge, UK
e-mail: dr311@cam.ac.uk

© The Author(s) 2018
J. Arday and H. S. Mirza (eds.), *Dismantling Race in Higher Education*,
https://doi.org/10.1007/978-3-319-60261-5_3

When Michael Young coined the term meritocracy in his 1958 satire 'The Rise of the Meritocracy', he introduced into popular understanding an ideal long cherished in British society: 'may the best person win'. The meritocratic paradigm, if not the term itself, has been a cornerstone of liberal and social democratic thought for the last two centuries (Miller 1999). And despite Young's pessimistic account of the dangers of meritocracy it has become widely accepted as an ideal in liberal democratic societies. A meritocratic system is a competition in which there are clear winners and losers, but in which the resulting inequalities are justified on the basis that participants have an equal opportunity to prove themselves (Miller 1999). The fantasy made clear in 'The Rise of Meritocracy' is that education is supposed to be meritocratic. But in the twenty-first century the reality is that it has become a powerful mechanism of legitimation of social closure and exclusion (Dorling 2015). We have an educational system where the norm is to misrecognise and reward the benefits of a privileged class background as deriving from individual effort and ability (Brown 1990). A crucial part of this operation of reproducing the British elite, and nurturing and expanding its academic, cultural and social capital, is carried out by Oxbridge and a small number of other elite universities (Savage 2015).

In understanding the educational processes that work to exclude and eliminate all but a small elite, the work of Pierre Bourdieu is particularly helpful. His books, Reproduction in Education, Society and Culture (1977), The Inheritors (1979), and State Nobility (1996) all explain in meticulous detail how the educational system works to consecrate a white upper-class elite, and the key role of the most selective universities in this process. As in 1960s and 1970s France, of which Bourdieu was writing, we find in contemporary Britain the majority of students also remain excluded from the most prestigious institutions. Rather than acting primarily as an avenue for social mobility, the educational system encourages social reproduction by indirectly rewarding the cultural experiences, dispositions, and talents of the elite classes (Reay 2017). In State Nobility the grandes écoles, France's equivalent of Oxbridge, required a clear demonstration of achievement at admission, and thus nominally "represented the institutional embodiment of French meritocracy" (Swartz 1997: 193).

In his study of the preparatory academies that often lead to enrollment at the grand écoles, Bourdieu (1996: 73–127) considered several forms of symbolic capital that accumulated within elite postsecondary institutions. Due to the competitive admissions process and harrowing academic requirements, students at the preparatory academies constituted a highly selected and homogenous group that shared similar experiences of educational success (Bourdieu 1996: 76–83). Despite making claim to a meritocratic ideal, the preparatory schools and grand écoles conferred a wide range of institutionalised cultural and social capital. As Bourdieu wrote:

> When the process of social rupture and segregation that takes a set of carefully selected chosen people and forms them into a separate group is known and recognized as a legitimate form of election, it gives rise in and of itself to symbolic capital that increases the degree of restriction and exclusivity of the group so established … Each of the young people brought together becomes rich by proxy in all the current symbolic capital… as well as all the potential symbolic capital (exceptional jobs, famous works, etc.) brought in by each of his classmates as well as the entire society of alumni. (Bourdieu 1996: 79)

This is what our elite universities in Britain are also doing, not only recognising and rewarding the embodied cultural capital common to the elite classes, but also generating institutionalised cultural capital by bestowing highly valued academic credentials. The notion of an Oxbridge graduate's intellectual qualities and qualifications for leadership in society extend well beyond the university to wider society, and hence graduation symbolically endows students with membership in that high-status group. As Bourdieu goes on to argue such credentials confer a range of positive designations—similar to the bestowal of titles of nobility (Bourdieu 1996: 102–123)—and link to the symbolic resources of other classmates and alumni, a form of institutionalised social capital. In short, a prestigious alma mater entitles even the least successful graduate to share in the "exceptional properties accumulated by all of its members, and particularly by the most prestigious among them" (Bourdieu 1996: 114).

Bourdieu is also very clear about how far from meritocratic these processes are:

> Given that this enterprise of hothouse cultivation is carried out on ado-
> lescents who have been selected and who have selected themselves
> according to their attitude toward the school … and who, shut up for
> three or four years in a protected universe with no material cares, know
> very little about the world other than what they have learned from
> books, it is bound to produce forced and somewhat immature minds
> that ….understand everything luminously and yet understand absolutely
> nothing. (1996: 91)

Much like the Grand Ecoles in France, Oxbridge, together with a handful of elite London institutions, operates like a closed shop for the English elite. Paul Wakeling and Mike Savage's (2015) recent work shows powerful reproductive effects of the elite universities, in particular Oxford, LSE and Cambridge (in that order) on entry to the Elite. Wakeling and Savage define this elite class as characterised by high levels of highbrow cultural capital, strong social capital as well as very high levels of household income, savings and house prices. They found no more signs of meritocracy in twenty-first century British universities than Bourdieu did in twentieth century France.

Bourdieu argues in State Nobility that:

> The strategies that an institution may implement to ensure or improve its
> position depend on the overall amount of its specific (inseparably social
> and academic) capital as well as the structure of this capital, that is, on
> the relative weight of both its academic capital (measured in terms of the
> specific value of the competences guaranteed) and its strictly social capital
> (linked to the current or potential social value of its student body present
> and past – its alumni). (Bourdieu 1996: 198)

This conferral of social capital operates in Oxbridge in a number of ways but particularly through showing a preference for "legacy" appli-cants, or students with a parent or close family member who graduated from the university. I am calling students with parents and/or family members who have themselves been to elite universities 'legacies'. A study in the US (Hurwitz 2011) showed that legacies are predominately white and affluent. Legacies also showed a distinct configuration of high levels of economic, cultural, and social capital, but lower levels of pre-university achievement relative to other students with middle class parents. The American study revealed a clear admissions bias that favoured applicants with family ties to the university. Admissions preferences for legacy applicants is an example of institutionalised social capital at elite universities, while the extent of legacy students in elite universities demonstrates high levels of reproduction. We do not have comparable data in the UK although we might ask whether such bias is replicated across Oxbridge and other elite institutions such as LSE. The evidence from my study with Stephen Ball and Miriam David (Reay et al. 2005) supports the view that legacy students are common in Oxbridge:

> Deciding where to go was probably a very unscientific process actually. My father went to Trinity College Cambridge to do law. And he was always very keen to show her Cambridge and his old college, which he did, when she was probably around thirteen. And she fell in love with it. And decided that's where she wanted to go. (mother of privately educated student in Reay et al. 2005)

> Well just since I've been born, I suppose it's just been assumed I am going to university because both my parents went to university, all their brothers and sisters went to university and my sister went to university so I don't think I've even stopped to think about it … I've just grown up with the idea that's what people do. I have always assumed I am going to university. (Nick, private school student)

Nick went on to point out that all these members of his family had been to either Oxford or Cambridge. The words in both quotes evoke images of elite conveyor belts rather than considered rational choice—it is just what 'people like us do'. This is a non-decision, almost too obvious to articulate. Rather choice was automatic, taken-for-granted and always assumed—these are examples of seamless reproduction at play but the players are all white and upper class.

Yet, meritocratic beliefs permeate the student body at Oxbridge, it is the dominant doxa. 'Doxa' is Bourdieu's (1990) term used to refer to a set of core values and discourses that has come to be taken as inherently true and necessary. Unsurprisingly in a recent research study of white upper and middle class students at Oxford, they nearly all felt they were there purely because of their effort and ability, that it had nothing to do with parental resources and privileged schooling. (Warikoo and Fuhr 2014).

It is obvious that a deeply reproductive tendency lies at the heart of Oxbridge. The most recent statistics show that the percentage of disadvantaged students gaining admission has fallen over the last five years (Havergal 2016). Unsurprisingly, elite universities are under increasing pressure to widen their access to a greater diversity of students (Parry 2016). Clearly this focus on widening access and participation centrally implicates social class, but how is race positioned within the competing tensions between ensuring meritocracy, sustaining elite status and widening access? In the next section I will look at the troubling issue of widening access to BME students at Elite universities in the UK.

Widening Participation and Access to BME Students in UK Elite Universities

While the increase in the participation of BME students in UK higher education over the last twenty years is an undoubted success story, strong concerns remain around which universities have widened their doors to BME students. Twenty-five per cent of BME students study at just 30 modern (post-1992) universities (Tatlow 2015). There are more students of Black Caribbean origin at London Metropolitan University than at all the Russell Group universities put together (Curtis 2006). In particular, the statistics continue to show a stark ethnic deficit in access to Oxbridge. Official data shows that over twenty Oxbridge colleges made no offer to Black students in 2009, and that one Oxford college had not admitted a Black student in five years. David Lammy (2010) found that in 2009, 292 Black students achieved three A grades at A Level and that 475 Black students applied to Oxbridge. However, only a handful were admitted, including just one British Black Caribbean student to Oxford. As a result, British-born Black Caribbean students had a 2.9% success rate for admission, in contrast to the 27.6% success rate for white applicants. In response David Cameron, the Prime Minister at the time, insisted 'we have got to do a lot better' but the following year the number of Black students admitted to Oxbridge actually fell by almost a third to just 36. As the following statistics demonstrates, there has been little improvement since then. In 2013 the success rate of White students applying to Oxford was 25.4% (Oxford University 2014). The success rate of Bangladeshi students was 6.7%, that of Pakistani students 6.5%, while Black Caribbean students had a 14.3% success rate and Black African students a 13% success rate. Cambridge University was doing only slightly better (Cambridge University 2014). While Black Caribbean applicants had a 24.3% chance of success compared to White applicants' 29% success rate, Black African students had a 9.2% chance of success, and Bangladeshi and Pakistani students 13.8 and 13.6% respectively.

The disparities in rates of admission remain substantial for White and BME applicants, even after entry qualifications have been taken into account (Boliver 2013). As Vikki Boliver (2016) states, even very highly qualified ethnic minority applicants are substantially less likely than their white counterparts to be offered places on some of the most competitive courses at Oxbridge. We can see from the latest admissions statistics available from Cambridge University (see Table 3.1), that although the success rates of some BME groups have improved, that of other groups like Black Caribbean have significantly worsened while the Pakistani success rate has also fallen slightly (Cambridge University 2015).

In 2014 only two Black Caribbean students started a degree at Cambridge. If all Black undergraduates are included the number rises to 35. Oxford was doing even worse, averaging 26 Black students a year between 2012 and 2014 (Halls 2016). In 2016, David Cameron, the Prime Minister at the time, in a call for greater transparency in university admissions, lambasted the elite universities for failing to make any progress in relation to BME admissions:

Table 3.1 Home Applicants, offers and acceptances to Cambridge by ethnic origin and gender 2014

Ethnicity	Applicants				Offers				Acceptances and success rates				
	Male	Female	Total	%	Male	Female	Total	%	Male	Female	Total	%	Success rate (%)
Black Caribbean	14	13	27	0.3	3	3	6	0.2	1	1	2	0.1	7.4
Black African	86	99	185	1.9	22	17	39	1.3	19	14	33	1.3	17.8
Black Other	3	7	10	0.1	1	0	1	0.0	0	0	0	0.0	0.0
Indian	306	162	468	4.9	103	61	164	5.4	94	53	147	5.8	31.4
Pakistani	78	65	143	1.5	10	14	24	0.8	7	12	19	0.7	13.3
Bangladeshi	35	20	55	0.6	10	3	13	0.4	10	3	13	0.5	23.6
Chinese	121	107	228	2.4	34	35	69	2.3	26	29	55	2.2	24.1
Asian Other	93	49	142	1.5	24	16	40	1.3	21	16	37	1.5	26.1
Mixed White and Black Caribbean	33	35	68	0.7	12	6	18	0.6	10	4	14	0.5	20.6
Mixed White and Black African	12	15	27	0.3	2	3	5	0.2	1	3	4	0.2	14.8
Mixed White and Asian	169	139	308	3.2	64	41	105	3.5	56	35	91	3.6	29.5
Mixed Other	68	67	135	1.4	18	28	46	1.5	14	25	39	1.5	28.9
Other	64	38	102	1.1	19	9	28	0.9	16	8	24	0.9	23.5
Unknown	241	160	401	4.2	43	26	69	2.3	16	8	24	0.9	6.0
White	4023	3294	7317	76.1	1238	1176	2414	79.4	1045	1004	2049	80.3	28.0
Totals	5346	4270	9616	100.0	1603	1438	3041	100.0	1336	1215	2551	100.0	26.5

From Cambridge University Undergraduate Admissions Statistics: 2014 cycle

It is striking that in 2014, our top university, Oxford, accepted just 27 black men and women out of an intake of more than 2,500. I know the reasons are complex, including poor schooling, but I worry that the university I was so proud to attend is not doing enough to attract talent from across our country. (Cameron 2016)

More recent statistics (Adams and Bengtsson 2017) reveal even more shocking racial disparities in Oxbridge admissions. The data showed that just 1.5% of all offers from the two universities to UK A-level students went to Black British candidates. Nearly one in three Oxford colleges failed to admit a single Black British A-level student in 2015, while one Oxford College has only offered one place to a Black British A-level student in six years. As David Lammy (2017) concluded 'Seven years have changed nothing at Oxbridge. In fact, diversity is even worse'. The evidence on BME admissions to Oxbridge clearly raises serious causes for concern across the political spectrum, but what happens when BME students are offered and accept a place? As is evident in the following section, widening access and participation is only part of the problem of tackling racial inequalities and exclusions in relation to elite universities.

Being a BME Student at an Elite UK University

It was a complete shock, it was different from anywhere else I have ever been, it was too traditional, too old fashioned, from another time altogether. I didn't like it at all. It was like going through a medieval castle when you were going down the corridors. It was like a proper castle, and I was thinking—where's the moat, where's the armour? Save me from this. You know, you expect little pictures with eyes moving around, watching you all the time. And I just didn't like the atmosphere, not one bit. (Ong cited in Reay et al. 2005)

In this quote Ong, a Chinese working class student, tries to explain why he turned down an offer from Cambridge; a place he says all his friends thought he was mad to refuse.

Then there was Candice, a Black working-class student, who raises a collective dilemma facing Black students when she discusses her desire to go to 'a good university':

> It's been really scary thinking that you could have made the wrong deci-
> sion, very anxiety inducing… . I think it's more difficult if no one in
> your family's been there. I think in a funny sort of way it's more difficult
> if you're Black too…. Because you want to go to a good university but
> you don't want to stick out like a sore thumb. It's sad isn't it? I've sort of
> avoided all the universities with lots of Black students because they're all
> the universities which aren't seen as so good. If you're Black and not very
> middle class and want to do well then you end up choosing places where
> people like you don't go and I think that's difficult. (Candice: Cited in
> Reay et al. 2005)

What is apparent in both Ong's and Candice's narratives is how different, even alien, elite universities appear to BME students. Both quotes
reveal a class and ethnic distance, in relation to the elite universities
(Reay et al. 2005). We found, in the research study these quotes are part
of, that most BME students were hesitant about entering institutions
with small numbers students or staff from their own ethnic background,
and desired to go to institutions with an ethnic mix (Ball et al. 2002).
The higher education choice process, as Candice's words reveal, often
involved treading a fine line between the desire to 'fit in' and being stereotyped in predominantly white settings. A number of BME students
went as far as to talk about specific universities (predominantly in the
elite category) that had racist reputations. So Temi, a Black middle class
student, told me "They say it is very white there and a bit racist, so not
really a good one, don't go there". Because historically Whiteness has
rarely been problematised within social theory (although see Gillborn
2008) elite universities have seldom been conceptualised as racialised environments. Their overriding Whiteness is read as normative, it
is part of the taken-for-granted assumptions of what elite universities
are, and who they are for. Yet, as Nicola Rollock (2014: 449) argues,
by constructing a racial fantasy in which Whiteness is invisible and
therefore does not count White people are able to collude in practices

which 'other' and racially subjugate people of colour and reject their (racialised) experiences as valid. As Temi's words indicate, what constitutes a good university cannot be separated out from issues of race. In a later study of students I conducted at Cambridge, all nine working class students described the university as 'a white, middle class bubble'. And we found many of the same feelings and attitudes that led a majority of high achieving, BME working class students, like Ong, to decide Oxbridge was not for them (Reay et al. 2009).

So university choice is difficult, painful even, for many BME students, but even for those students who decide on elite institutions and gain a place, difficulties continue. Research on the experiences of ethnic minority students at UK universities finds racism to be commonplace (National Union of Students 2011). The paucity of BME students in elite HE means that the very few Black students who do make it to the elite universities have to confront social, psychological as well as academic challenges. Black students at both Oxford and Cambridge have set up websites to chronicle their experiences of being in an overwhelmingly white institution and the prejudice and bigotry they have to face (http://wetooarecambridge.tumblr.com/). Attitudes and opinions Black students have to deal with range from the deeply shocking to the profoundly ignorant. Black students report being racially abused, mistaken for tourists, having their hair inappropriately touched, and being told they speak good English for a Black person (Wilkinson 2014). Their words vividly bring to life the psycho-social challenges of being an outsider on the inside. And when we move from qualitative accounts to quantitative surveys of the Black student experience there is further evidence of how an alien, intimidating, academic culture impacts on BME student attainment (Table 3.2).

The Cambridge research this table comes from focused on the British Caribbean, Pakistani and Bangladeshi groups as causing the most concern (Scales and Whitehead 2006). It found, in relation to these three groups, that 50% of those who said they had strong fears about not fitting in got a 1st or 2:1 compared with 80% of those who had no such fears. A further finding was that 47% of those who said there were 'lots of things they can't afford' in day-to-day life gained a 1st or 2:1 compared to 77% of those who said they 'have enough money to do

Table 3.2 University of Cambridge examination results for years 2001, 2002, 2003 combined by ethnic group

Ethnicity	1st/2:1 number	1st/2:1 (%)	2:2/3rd number	2:2/3rd (%)
White	14,557	77.25	4283	22.75
Chinese	781	76	246	24
Indian	598	70.5	250	29.5
Pakistani	99	62	61	38
Bangladeshi	43	59	30	41
Black British-Caribbean	44	59.5	30	40.5
Black British-African	107	72.3	41	27.7

everything they want'. Poverty had a major impact. Those who received money from their parents are much more likely to gain good examination results. 75% got a 1st or 2:1 compared with only 45% of those who said they received no money from their parents. Relatedly, vacation working showed a strong significant relationship with examination performance. Only 47% of those who undertook paid vacation work to fund their education achieved good examinations grades compared to 78% of those who did not. As Metcalf points out:

> The current HE financial system has lead to an increasingly polarised university system, those that facilitate term-time working and those that do not, with the more prestigious universities tending to be in the latter category. This distorts the university choice of those who need to work during term-time, inhibiting their access to prestigious universities. (Metcalf 2003: 315)

Vacation employment might reduce the financial problems of students from poor families. However, the Cambridge research reported that those students who did paid work in vacations were much less likely to get a good degree, and that:

> Some students were in situations of severe financial hardship. Amongst these students are a number from single-parent families and larger families whose parents are less likely to be able to offer them financial help and support. (Scales and Whitehead 2006)

Here we see class compounding race to reproduce very unmeritocratic cultures and outcomes. But the inequalities faced by the low income BME students that Scales and Whitehead uncovered are set to increase even further from 2017 onwards, as the Conservative government has decided to axe student maintenance grants for UK's poorest students, a group who are disproportionately from BME backgrounds (Institute of Race Relations 2016).

A more recent study that examined the experiences of seventeen Black male students at ten Russell Group universities (Dumangane 2015) included 4 students who were studying at Oxbridge. The other universities attended were the University of Birmingham, University of Bristol, Cardiff University, Durham University, Exeter University, LSE, Manchester University, and UCL. The Oxbridge students, in particular, expressed surprise, disappointment, and a sense of puzzlement about their white peers' attitudes and perceptions. Ted, a middle class British Caribbean Oxbridge graduate, recounted an incident when one of his white Oxbridge friends made a comment about 'a Black guy driving a BMW'. The friend queried where he got the car from, asserting 'he must have got it by dodgy means'. Such stereotypes abounded in the perceptions of white students the Black students encountered in Oxbridge. John, a British African, middle class student, told of the group of white girls he and his two Black friends met at university who held the view that "all a Black man could afford to do was take a girl to KFC or one of those stereotypical chicken places". Dwayne, a working class, British Caribbean Oxbridge graduate, said with a degree of incredulity:

> One of my friends, this was like whilst we were becoming friends: he said that the first time he met me he thought I was going to stab him.

John, Dwayne, and Ted went on to attribute their friends' comments to ignorance rather than racism, opting to moderate their blackness (Wilkins 2012), rather than challenge discriminatory comments. However, Dumangane (2015) found that Black Oxbridge students did not only have to deal with misconceptions and prejudice from fellow students, they often had uncomfortable and distanced relationships with academic staff. Ted explained how his relationship with his tutor differed qualitatively from the relationship his friend had with the same tutor:

> She would always tell me about how [the tutor] would tell her all this stuff about his life, and how they would talk a lot about stuff beyond the subject itself. Beyond the subject matter of English. And I never had that relationship with him. He never opened up in that way to me. Or spoke to me about much apart from the degree. (Ted: Cited in Dumangane 2015)

What we glimpse very powerfully through Dumangane's (2015) analysis is the degree of compromise and concession made by the Black students as they struggle to survive what often feels like an alien and unyielding environment. Discrimination continues to be an everyday reality, allowing racism, as it seeps into mundane everyday interactions, to be seen as normative and ordinary. They are dealing with countless little discrepancies between habitus and the unfamiliar field of elite white HE that contribute to a sense of being an outsider despite their efforts to fit in.

Conclusion

As I write in my recent book *Miseducation* (Reay 2017):

> The troubling paradox of widening access and democratisation of higher education is that, despite its democratic intentions, widening access has brought an intensification of class and racial inequalities between different levels of higher education. Growing diversity within the field of HE, rather than producing a more inclusive higher education, has resulted in a segregated and increasingly polarised system. (121)

Despite the pervasive focus within the HE field on elite means best and modern means worst, there is a need for a more philosophic discussion about what 'the best' constitutes in the HE context. The overwhelming dominance of whiteness in our elite universities is rarely problematised. Yet, the paucity of BME students in the elite university sector, and the

difficulties they experience if they do gain admission, demands a recon-
ceptualisation of elite higher education as a space of white hegemony,
and a recognition that changes need to be made. Currently, Oxbridge
admits 0.4% of each age cohort based on academic performance (Clark
2015). This may appear to be meritocratic but it is also highly elitist.
The beneficiaries are the white English upper classes. As a consequence,
Oxbridge remains the equivalent of 'a finishing school' for the private
school system, polishing, refining and accentuating the elitism and sense
of superiority acquired in earlier schooling. In this process Black students across social class are often marginal and marginalised, small in
numbers and peripheral to the main work of the elite universities which
is, as it always was, educational reproduction.

But this does not have to be the case. As Nahai (2013) demonstrates,
The University of California, Berkeley has managed to achieve one of
the most racially, ethnically and socioeconomically diverse student populations of any top US research university, without any fall in its academic results. It has achieved this by accepting a mandate "to seek an
undergraduate student body that reflects the ethnic, racial and social
class composition of the Californian state's high school graduating class"
(Douglass and Thomson 2012: 74). There is also a stated commitment
to reduce the number of legacy students, who are predominantly white.
Although this 'parity model' is almost impossible to achieve, it drives
university admissions policy. Over 60% of Berkeley's intake have at least
one parent who is foreign born (Douglass and Thomson 2010), and
it draws growing numbers of its lower-income students from increasingly diverse Asian and Asian-Pacific ethnic groups (Douglass and
Thomson 2012). Berkeley has succeeded where Oxbridge has failed. It
has achieved a social and ethnic diversity that our elite universities are
nowhere near achieving. So one way forward would be to institute policies that move towards a diverse intake that better reflects the UK population. As Douglass and Thomson (2012: 85) conclude, based on data
that shows Berkeley's low income and BME students do just as well, if
not better, than their wealthy white counterparts, it may well be that
if Oxford and Cambridge were to become more representative of UK
society in general, they would not suffer increased attrition rates or a
lowering of academic quality.

Greg Clark (2015) suggests another possible alternative that ameliorates rather than challenges meritocracy. He proposes the identification of a much larger share of students equally able to benefit from an Oxbridge education. The suggestion he makes of including all those with 3 A grades at A-level, would widen the pool from which the Oxbridge elite are drawn to 3% of each age cohort. He then argues that admissions to Oxbridge could be based on randomly selecting from this pool. This system, similar to the one used in Dutch medical schools, would result in proportionately more students without privileged family backgrounds being admitted. Oxbridge would be less elite, and more diverse both racially and in terms of social class.

A more radical approach would be to pay serious attention to the concept of the comprehensive or common university. In the mid-twentieth century R. H. Tawney put the case for a common school asserting that 'the English educational system will never be one worthy of a civilised society until the children of all classes in the nation attend the same schools' (Tawney 1964: 144). But in a twenty-first century where the elite universities, and in particular Oxbridge, increasingly represent a racial as well as a class ceiling, privileging and protecting the social and economic hegemony of a tiny white elite, it is time to pay serious consideration to the concept of 'the common university' or what Selina Todd (2015) terms 'the comprehensive university'. Todd argues that a comprehensive university system would mean redistributing funds to ensure equality, and abolishing selection criteria, but is vital if we want to raise opportunities within higher education for women, for Black and Minority Ethnic people, and for the disadvantaged.

What is clear is that clinging to the meritocratic principle as a way of achieving fairness in relation to university admission and participation will not work. For over thirty years sociologists of education have been pointing out that educational choice is based on the resources and social power and networks of the parents rather than the ability and effort of the child (Brown 1990; Gewirtz 2001; Reay 2015). Meritocracy has become the educational equivalent of the emperor with no clothes, all ideological bluff with no substance. We do not have a meritocracy, or anything approaching a meritocracy. Yet, the elite universities continue to justify their elitism on the premise that they operate in a meritocratic society. It is increasingly apparent that a socially just approach that gives

BME students, across ethnic diversity and class differences, a fair chance of admittance, and equal opportunities to high achievement and social acceptance once they are studying at elite institutions, requires just and impartial solutions rather than yet more bland rhetoric about meritocracy.

References

Adams, R., & Bengtsson, H. (2017, October 17). Oxford Accused of 'Social Apartheid' as Colleges Admit No Black Students. *The Guardian*, p. 23.

Ball, S. J., Davies, J., David, M., & Reay, D. (2002). 'Classification' and 'Judgement': Social Class and the Cognitive Structures of Choice of Higher Education. *British Journal of Sociology of Education, 23*(1), 51–72.

Boliver, V. (2013). How Fair Is Access to More Prestigious UK Universities? *British Journal of Sociology, 64*(2), 344–364.

Boliver, V. (2016). Exploring Ethnic Inequalities in Admission to Russell Group Universities. *Sociology, 50*(2), 247–266.

Bourdieu, P. (1990). *In other words*. Cambridge: Policy Press.

Bourdieu, P. (1996). *The State Nobility: Elite Schools in the Field of Power.* Cambridge: Polity Press.

Bourdieu, P., & Passeron, J.-C. (1977). *Reproduction in Education, Society and Culture.* London: Sage.

Bourdieu, P., & Passeron, J.-C. (1979). *The Inheritors, French Students and Their Relation to Culture.* Chicago: University of Chicago Press.

Brown, P. (1990). The 'Third Wave': Education and the Ideology of Parentocracy. *British Journal of Sociology of Education, 11*(1), 65–85.

Cambridge University. (2014). *Undergraduate Admissions Statistics—2013 Cycle.* Cambridge: Cambridge Admissions Office.

Cambridge University. (2015). *Undergraduate Admissions Statistics—2014 Cycle.* Cambridge: Cambridge Admissions Office.

Cameron, D. (2016, January 31). Watch Out, Universities; I'm Bringing the Fight for Equality in Britain to You. *The Sunday Times*, p. 25.

Clark, G. (2015, February 4). Social Mobility Barely Exists but Let's Not Give Up on Equality. *The Guardian*.

Curtis, Polly. (2006, January 3). Segregation, 2006 Style. *The Guardian*. http://education.guardian.co.uk/racism/story/0,,1676678,00.html.

Dorling, D. (2015). *Injustice: Why Social Inequality Still Persists.* Bristol: Policy Press.

Douglass, J. A., & Thomson, G. (2010). The Immigrant's University: A Study of Academic Performance and the Experiences of Recent Immigrant Groups at the University of California. *Higher Education Policy, 23,* 451–474.

Douglass, J. A., & Thomson, G. (2012). Poor and Rich: Student Economic Stratification and Academic Performance in a Public Research University System. *Higher Education Quarterly, 66*(1), 65–89.

Dumangane, C. (2015). *Exploring the Narratives of the Few: British African Caribbean Male Graduates of Elite Universities in England and Wales* (Ph.D. thesis). University of Cardiff.

Gewirtz, S. (2001). Cloning the Blairs: New labour's Programme for the Re-socialisation of Working-Class Parents. *Journal of Education Policy, 16*(4), 365–378.

Gillborn, D. (2008). *Racism and Education: Coincidence or Conspiracy?* London: Routledge.

Halls, A. (2016, January 24). If You're White and Wealthy, Your Dreaming Spires Await. *The Sunday Times.*

Havergal, C. (2016, February 18). Elite Universities 'Going Backwards' on Widening Access. *Times Higher Education.* https://www.timeshighered-ucation.com/news/elite-universities-going-backwards-widening-access. Accessed 16 Feb 2016.

Hurwitz, M. (2011). The Impact of Legacy Status on Undergraduate Admissions at Elite Colleges and Universities. *Economics of Education Review, 30*(3), 480–492.

Institute of Race Relations. (2016). *Inequality, Housing and Employment Statistics.* http://www.irr.org.uk/research/statistics/poverty/.

Lammy, D. (2010, December 7). The Oxbridge Whitewash. *The Guardian,* p. 28.

Lammy, D. (2017, October 20). Seven Years Have Changed Nothing at Oxbridge. In Fact, Diversity Is Even Worse. *The Guardian,* p. 7.

Metcalf, H. (2003). Increasing Inequality in Higher Education: The Role of Term-Time Working. *Oxford Review of Education, 29*(3), 315–329.

Miller, D. (1999). *Principles of Social Justice.* Cambridge: Harvard University Press.

Nahai, R. (2013). Is Meritocracy Fair? A Qualitative Case Study of Admissions at the University of Oxford. *Oxford Review of Education, 39*(5), 681–701.

National Union of Students. (2011). *Race for Equality: A Report on the Experiences of Black Students in Further and Higher Education.* London: National Union of Students.

Oxford University. (2014). *Undergraduate Admissions Statistics: 2013 Entry*. Oxford: Oxford Admissions Office.

Parry, G. (2016). Access, Equity, and Participation of Disadvantaged Groups. In B. Jongbloed & H. Vossensteyn (Eds.), *Access and Expansion Post-Massification: Opportunities and Barriers to Further Growth in Higher Education Participation*. Abingdon: Routledge.

Reay, D. (2015). White Middle Class Families and Urban Comprehensives: The Struggle for Social Solidarity in an Era of Amoral Familism. *Families, Relationships and Society, 3*(2), 235–249.

Reay, D. (2017). *Miseducation: Inequality Education and the Working Classes*. Bristol: Policy Press.

Reay, D., Crozier, G., & Clayton, J. (2009). Strangers in Paradise: Working Class Students in Elite Universities. *Sociology, 43*(6), 1103–1121.

Reay, D., David, M. E., & Ball, S. (2005). *Degrees of Choice: Social Class, Race and Gender in Higher Education*. Stoke-on-Trent: Trentham Books.

Rollock, N. (2014). Race, Class, and 'the Harmony of Dispositions'. *Sociology, 48*(3), 445–451.

Savage, M. (2015). *Social Class in the 21st Century*. Milton Keynes: Pelican Books.

Scales, J., & Whitehead, J. (2006, March 15). The Undergraduate Experience of Cambridge Among Three Ethnic Minority Groups. *The Cambridge Reporter*.

Swartz, D. (1997). *Culture and Power: The Sociology of Pierre Bourdieu*. Chicago: University of Chicago Press.

Tatlow, P. (2015). Participation of BME Students in UK Higher Education. In C. Alexander & J. Arday (Eds.), *Aiming Higher: Race, Inequality and Diversity in the Academy*. London: Runnymede Trust.

Tawney, R. H. (1964). *Equality*. London: Unwin Books.

Todd, S. (2015, September 22). Let's turn Oxbridge into a comprehensive. *The Guardian*.

Wakeling, P., & Savage, M. (2015). Entry to Elite Positions and the Stratification of Higher Education in Britain. *The Sociological Review, 63*(2), 290–320.

Warikoo, N., & Fuhr, C. (2014). Legitimating Status: Perceptions of Meritocracy and Inequality Among Undergraduates at an Elite British University. *British Educational Research Journal, 40*(4), 699–717.

Wilkins, A. (2012). "Not Out to Start a Revolution": Race, Gender, and Emotional Restraint Among Black University Men. *Journal of Contemporary Ethnography, 41*(1), 34–65.

Wilkinson, H. (2014, March 10). I, Too, Am Cambridge: Students Speak Out Against Racial Discrimination in Cambridge. *Varsity.*

Young, M. (1958). *The Rise of the Meritocracy.* London: Pelican Books.

4

Ethnic Inequalities in Admission to Highly Selective Universities

Vikki Boliver

Introduction

Young people from British ethnic minority backgrounds have been *more likely* than their white British peers to go to university for more than two decades (Modood 1993). By 2010/2011, enrolment rates for 18–19 year olds ranged from 37.4 to 75.7% for those from Black Caribbean and Chinese backgrounds respectively, compared to 32.6% for young people from the white British group (Crawford and Greaves 2015). However, some ethnic minority groups remain significantly under-represented in the UK's most academically selective and prestigious universities. Black Caribbean, Bangladeshi and Pakistani students made up just 0.5, 0.6 and 1.8% of all entrants to the twenty universities that were members

V. Boliver (✉)
Department of Sociology, Durham University, Durham, UK
e-mail: Vikki.Boliver@durham.ac.uk

© The Author(s) 2018
J. Arday and H. S. Mirza (eds.), *Dismantling Race in Higher Education*,
https://doi.org/10.1007/978-3-319-60261-5_4

of the prestigious Russell Group[1] in 2010–2012, despite constituting 1.1, 1.2 and 2.5% of all 15–29 year olds in England and Wales (Boliver 2015a). Young people from Indian, Chinese, and 'Mixed' ethnic backgrounds, in contrast, were found to be well-represented at Russell Group universities in 2010–2012 (Boliver 2015a).

Ethnic group differences in rates of participation at highly academically selective universities are driven partly by differences in prior achievement. On average Black Caribbean, Bangladeshi and Pakistani students are outperformed at key stages 4 (GCSE) and 5 (A-level) by white British students, who are, in turn, outperformed by students of Chinese and Indian origin (Crawford and Greaves 2015). But a number of studies point to a further possible cause, namely ethnic bias in admission to highly selective universities. Research drawing on data supplied by the Universities and Colleges Admissions Service (UCAS)—the administrative body that processes almost all applications to full-time courses of higher education in the UK—has found that British ethnic minority applicants to highly selective universities in the 1990s, 2000s and early 2010s were less likely to be offered places than white British applicants with the same grades at key stage 5 (Modood and Shiner 1994; Shiner and Modood 2002; Zimdars et al. 2009; Boliver 2013, 2015a, 2016; Noden et al. 2014). One study reported that the rate at which white applicants to Russell Group universities were offered places in 2010–2012 was 7–12 percentage points higher than the rate for equivalently qualified Black Caribbean, Pakistani and Bangladeshi applicants, and 3–4 percentage points higher than the rate for equivalently qualified applicants from the Chinese, Indian and 'mixed' ethnic groups (Boliver 2015a). Disparities in offer rates have been shown to persist even after factoring in information about applicants' A-level subject choices and the popularity of their chosen degree programmes

---

[1]The Russell Group purports to represent twenty-four "leading UK universities", specifically the universities of Birmingham, Bristol, Cambridge, Cardiff, Durham, Edinburgh, Exeter, Glasgow, Imperial, King's, Leeds, Liverpool, LSE, Manchester, Newcastle, Nottingham, Oxford, Queen Mary, Queen's Belfast, Sheffield, Southampton, UCL, Warwick and York. The universities of Durham, Exeter, Queen Mary and York joined the Russell Group in 2012. For empirical evidence that the Russell Group universities (excepting Oxford and Cambridge) are in fact no more "leading" than many other 'old' (pre-1992) universities, see Boliver (2015b).

(Noden et al. 2014; Boliver 2016), and have been found to be particularly large for courses which attract large numbers of ethnic minority applicants (Boliver 2016).

Concerns that admissions to highly selective universities may be unfairly biased against ethnic minority applicants have been repeatedly dismissed by the public relations wing of the elite Russell Group of universities (Russell Group 2013, 2015), which has pointed out that the studies cited above do not take into account all information relevant to university admissions, such as the specific academic entry requirements of courses applied to and other indicators of applicant merit besides grades achieved at key stage 5. These are legitimate criticisms; but it is noteworthy that the Russell Group has been content to simply dismiss concerns about possible ethnic bias in admissions as unfounded, rather than call for a more thorough and complete analysis to be undertaken. Notwithstanding the Russell Group's seeming lack of inquisitiveness, it has not been possible in any case for academic researchers to undertake further analysis of UCAS data in order to address the shortcomings of previous research. For the last few years, UCAS has been unwilling to share with academic researchers the detailed, anonymised, individual-level data needed for such analysis, citing concerns about jeopardising applicants' trust in their service (UCAS 2015a). In lieu of sharing data with academic researchers, UCAS issued a press-release in 2013 and an Analysis Note in 2015 reporting that its own in-house analysis had found only small ethnic group differences in offer rates after taking predicted key stage 5 results and choice of degree programme into account (Grove 2013; UCAS 2015b). UCAS noted that these small differences in offer rates could to be attributable to differences in the quality of other aspects of applications besides prior attainment, such as personal statements or performance at interview.

The fact that researchers and policy makers have been unable to access detailed anonymised UCAS data for research purposes for several of years was highlighted by the Social Mobility and Child Poverty Commission as a major obstacle to identifying and removing the barriers to fair access to higher education (Machin 2015). In response, the UK government announced in its 2016 Higher Education White Paper:

> We will enhance transparency, opening up data held by the sector, informing choice and promoting social mobility. (DBIS 2016: 41)

More specifically the White Paper set out three important proposals. First, the White paper proposed to "place a duty on institutions to publish application, offer, acceptance and progression rates, broken down by gender, ethnicity and disadvantage". This has prompted the UCAS to publish for the first time in 2016 detailed statistics on the number of applications and offers processed by 132 UK universities between 2010 and 2015 (UCAS 2016a). Section two of this chapter asks what these newly-released statistics tell us about the extent and causes of ethnic group differences in offer rates at a Russell Group universities.

Second, the White Paper proposed to "require those organisations who provide shared central admissions services (such as UCAS) to share relevant data they hold with Government and researchers in order to help improve policies designed to increase social mobility" (DBIS 2016: 41). This has resulted in UCAS revising its data sharing policy, reinstating the ability of accredited researchers to securely access anonymised individual-level application and offer data for the 2016 admissions cycle onwards from 2017 (UCAS 2016b). The greater availability of data on university admissions is a welcome development for researchers and policy-makers keen to understand and address the causes of lower elite university admission rates for ethnic minority students. The close of section two of this chapter discusses what more we will be able to learn once detailed, individual-level applications and admissions data becomes available to researchers again from 2017 onwards.

Third, in response to concerns about the possible influence of unconscious bias and other inadvertently discriminatory practices on admissions decision-making (Boliver 2013, 2015a, 2016; Cameron 2015), the White Paper reported that the government had "asked UCAS to consult the higher education sector on the feasibility of introducing name-blind applications for prospective students [...to...] potentially help reduce unfairness and inequality" (DBIS 2016: 41). UCAS has since published a report on the results of this consultation on name-blind admissions (UCAS 2016c), and it has been announced that name-blind admissions will be trialled for some courses at four UK universities—Exeter, Huddersfield, Liverpool and Winchester—during the 2016/2017 admissions cycle (Havergal 2016). Section three of this chapter discusses the likely impact of unconscious bias on university admissions decisions, and challenges the idea that name-blind admissions is the best way to tackle it. The chapter closes by arguing that what is needed instead is determined action on the part of universities to foster an institutional culture in which ethnic biases in university admissions and other domains of university life are confronted and redressed.

Ethnic Group Differences in Russell Group University Offer Rates

In June 2016 UCAS published for the first time detailed statistics on applications to and admissions offers made by 132 UK universities between 2010 and 2015, broken down by broad ethnic group (UCAS 2016a). Analysis of these statistics reveals two seemingly encouraging trends. First, the absolute number of ethnic minorities receiving a place at a Russell Group university increased by more than 40% in the period between 2010 and 2015, outpacing the rate of growth in the number of White entrants to these universities during the same period.[2] Secondly, offer rates increased by 11 percentage points for Asian applicants to Russell Group universities between 2010 and 2015, and by 14 percentage points for Russell Group applicants from the Black and 'mixed' ethnic groups, indicating that when ethnic minority students apply to Russell Group universities they are more likely to get in than ever before.

However, these trends may not be as encouraging as they first appear. Much of the increase in the number of British ethnic minority entrants to Russell Group universities is due to the fact that the number of *applications* submitted to Russell Group universities by students from ethnic minority backgrounds increased by some 22% between 2010 and 2015,

---

[2]All statistics in this section based aggregate data published by in UCAS in June 2016, authors' own calculations.

whereas the number of applications from white students declined by half a percent during the same period. Moreover, much of the rise in offer rates for ethnic minority applicants to Russell Group university is due to the fact that these universities are now admitting a higher proportion of *all* applicants than in the past: 64% of all applications were met with an offer of a place in 2015, compared to just 53% in 2010, with offer rates rising for white applicants as well as for ethnic minority applicants, by some 11 percentage points. So while there are more ethnic minority students applying to and entering Russell Group universities than ever before, and while ethnic group differences in offer rates have become slightly less unequal in recent years, offer rates nevertheless remain substantially lower for ethnic minority applicants to Russell Group universities than for white applicants to these universities. In 2015, the offer rate was 67% for white applicants to Russell Group universities considered collectively, compared to 63% for applicants from 'mixed' ethnic backgrounds, 54% for Asian applicants, 49% for those from 'other' ethnic groups, and just 41% for Black applicants. The question remains, therefore, whether ethnic minority applicants are as likely to be offered places at Russell Group universities as comparably qualified white applicants.

It is clear from the UCAS statistics cited above that there is a large 'raw gap' between offer rates for white applicants to Russell Group universities and those for applicants from ethnic minority backgrounds. But it is important to also calculate the 'net gap' in offer rates; that is, the difference in offer rates after taking into account the fact that the degree programmes chosen by ethnic minority applicants tend to be more heavily oversubscribed than is the case for white applicants, and that some ethnic minority groups apply with prior attainment levels that are lower (Black, Pakistani and Bangladeshi applicants) or higher (Chinese, Indian and 'mixed' ethnicity applicants) than their white peers (Boliver 2016). Helpfully, the UCAS statistics also include what they term 'average offer rates' for the sub-set of applicants who applied to university straight from school at age 18. 'Average offer rates' describe the offer rate for all applicants, irrespective of ethnicity, whose chose the same degree programmes and applied with the same predicted key stage 5 grades as members of the ethnic group in question. Taking the difference between average offer rates and raw offer rates gives us the size of the 'net gap' between offer rates for white as compared to ethnic minority applicants; that is, the size of the gap after taking differences in course choice and predicted key stage 5 attainment into account. If there is a substantial 'net gap' in offer rates, this could be considered *prima facie* evidence of the possibility of some form of ethnic bias in admissions.

Looking across the UK university sector as a whole, the 'net gap' in offer rates appear modest. Average offer rates are 1.6 percentage points lower for Asian applicants than for white applicants, 3 percentage points lower for Black applicants, 0.6 percentage points lower for 'mixed' ethnicity applicants, and 2.3 percentage points lower for applicants from 'other' ethnic minority groups. Commenting on the size of the 'net gap' in offer rates across the UK university sector as a whole, UCAS stated that "the offer-making process operated by universities is broadly fair" (UCAS 2016a).

The Russell Group put it more strongly, claiming that "New analysis from UCAS finds no evidence of bias in the admissions system" (Russell Group 2016a). However, as Fig. 4.1 shows, the 'net gap' is rather larger for some Russell Group universities than for the sector as a whole. For Asian applicants, the 'net gap' in offer rates relative to white applicants is a substantial 5.4 percentage points at Imperial College London, 6.5 percentage points at Queens Belfast, and 9 percentage points at the University of Oxford. For Black applicants, the 'net gap' in offer rates relative to white applicants is 5 percentage points at Birmingham University and Cardiff University, 7 percentage points at Glasgow University and Kings College London, and 8.7 percentage points at Imperial College London.[3] Moreover, the vast majority of the data points in Fig. 4.1 (40 out of 48) evidence a 'net gap' (of various magnitudes) in favour of white applicants.

---

[3]Bars for 'other ethnicity' applicants are not shown in Fig. 4.1. However, a similar pattern is evidence, with a 'net gap' for 'other ethnicity' applicants relative to white applicants of 5.4 percentage points at Manchester University, 6 percentage points at Southampton University, and nearly 10 percentage points at the University of Oxford and Imperial College London. Bars for 'mixed ethnicity' applicants are also not shown in Fig. 4.1. For 'mixed ethnicity' applicants the 'net gap' is generally smaller, typically less than 2 percentage points.

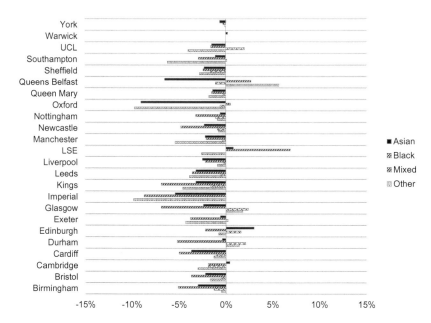

Fig. 4.1 'Net gap' in Russell Group offer rates relative to white applicants, 2015 (*Source* UCAS (2016a))

While Fig. 4.1 shows that overall net gaps in offer rates for different ethnic groups were substantial for many Russell Group universities in 2015, it is also clear that a small number of universities had overall net gaps that were effectively zero—notably Cambridge, Durham, Exeter, LSE, Nottingham, Warwick and York in relation to the net gap between Asian and white applicants; and for Oxford, Warwick and York in relation to the net gap between Black and white applicants. Figure 4.1 also shows that at one Russell Group university—the LSE—the net gap in fact favoured Black applicants over white applicants. These anomalies beg the question: has the equitableness of admission to these and other Russell Group universities improved in recent years?

Because the UCAS statistics stretch back to 2010 it is possible to compare the size of the net gaps in offer rates for 2015 to the size of the net gaps five years previously. Figure 4.2 displays the net gaps as they were in 2010. Comparing Figs. 4.2 to 4.1, it is clear that most Russell

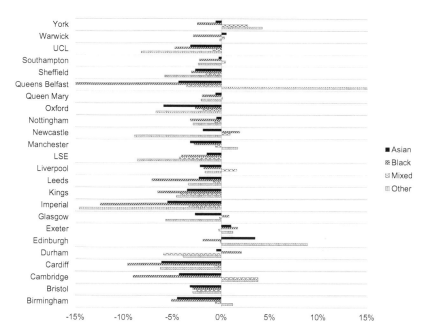

Fig. 4.2 'Net gap' in Russell Group offer rates relative to white applicants, 2010 (*Source* UCAS (2016a))

Group universities were doing rather worse by ethnic minority applicants in 2010 than they were by 2015, including several of the universities that were anomalous in 2015 for having net gaps that were negligible (e.g. York and Warwick) or which favoured ethnic minority applicants (LSE). It is not obvious what has caused net gaps in offer rates to become smaller over time. One possibility is that ethnic minority applicants to these universities are better qualified than they were in the past. Another possibility is that these universities have begun to take seriously concerns about ethnic bias in admissions and have begun to take the steps needed to address them. This second possibility is an encouraging thought, but it is clear that more needs to be done to fully equalise offer rates for comparably qualified applicants from different ethnic groups.

It is important to appreciate that the 'net gaps' in offer rates presented in Figs. 4.1 and 4.2 relate only to those who applied to university straight from school at age 18. This is important because only two-thirds of all applications to Russell Group universities in 2015 came from 18 year olds, whereas one third were submitted by those aged 19+ after taking a 'gap year' or a longer break from education before returning as a mature student. Given that the raw gap in offer rates is somewhat larger for applicants aged 19+ than it is for applicants aged 18 (UCAS 2016a), it seems likely that including applicants of all ages in the calculation of 'net gaps' would paint a rather bleaker picture.

It is also important to note that the 'net gaps' in offer rates presented in Figs. 4.1 and 4.2 are averages for each institution as a whole. As such, they tell us nothing about the equitableness or otherwise of offer rates for specific degree programmes. This matters because ethnic minority applicants are known to choose some areas of study at much higher rates than their white peers, including Medicine and Dentistry, Computer Science, Law, and Business and Administration, and previous research has shown that the net gap in offer rates is particularly large for courses which attract disproportionately high numbers of ethnic minority applicants (Boliver 2016). This suggests that there may be substantial net gaps in offer rates for particular courses even for universities for which the overall net gap in offer rates is small or non-existent.

As discussed earlier, from 2017, researchers will be permitted once more to access in anonymised form the individual-level applications and admissions data held by UCAS. Access to this data will enable researchers to examine the equitableness of offer rates for applicants of all age groups, not just 18 year olds, and to drill down to the level of specific degree programmes at each institution, in addition to examining the patterns for each institution overall. Access this this data will also enable researchers to investigate whether ethnic group differences in offer rates are related to corresponding differences in performance at GCSE, given that some universities use this as an additional selection criterion; choice of key stage 5 qualification, given that some universities prefer A-level qualifications over more vocational qualifications such as BTEC and Access to Higher Education courses; choice of subjects at A-level, given that some courses stipulate A-level subject requirements and others prefer so-called 'facilitating subjects' (Russell Group 2016b); and mismatches between applicants' predicted and achieved grades at key stage 5, given that offers of university places are typically made before applicants' achieved grades are known. All of the factors listed above may be working to the detriment of ethnic minority applicants' chances of gaining a place at a highly selective university.

Unconscious Bias, Name-Blind Admissions, and Fostering an Inclusive Institutional Culture

While ethnic group differences in offer rates from Russell Group universities have improved over time, several universities clearly continue to have substantial overall net gaps, and it seems likely that net gaps also exist for specific degree programmes within universities, possibly even for institutions with negligible net gaps overall. Until individual-level UCAS data becomes available again for more detailed analysis, the possibility of ethnic bias on the part of admissions decision-makers cannot be ruled out.

The possibility of 'unconscious bias' on the part of decision-makers has been raised by the higher education sector's equalities body the Equality Challenge Unit (ECU) (2013), and by the former Prime Minister David Cameron MP (Cameron 2015), as a likely cause of unequal offer rates for different ethnic groups. The ECU defines unconscious bias as:

> a term used to describe the associations that we hold which, despite being outside our conscious awareness, can have a significant influence on our attitudes and behaviour. Regardless of how fair minded we believe ourselves to be, most people have some degree of unconscious bias. The means that we automatically respond to others (e.g. people from different racial or ethnic groups) in positive or negative ways. These associations are difficult to override, regardless of whether we recognise them to be wrong, because they are deeply ingrained into our thinking and emotions. (ECU 2013: 1)

The ECU also uses the term 'implicit bias' to refer to the stereotypes that may continue to influence peoples' attitudes and behaviour even after they become more aware of them (i.e. as they become less 'unconscious'). As the ECU makes clear, recognising that unconscious or implicit bias may affect decision-making "must not replace an acknowledgment that explicit bias and discrimination exist and continues to be an issue in the higher education sector" (ECU 2013: 4). However, it is unconscious and implicit forms of bias that are currently in the spotlight.

There is a significant degree of scope for unconscious bias to be at play when it comes to university admissions decisions, particularly for courses which attract a high ratio of well-qualified applicants per course places available. This is because although information about applicants' ethnic origins is *not* shared with universities prior to admissions decisions being made, admissions selectors do see a range of other information that are likely to give clues as to ethnic origin (and gender and social class background). Admissions selectors see each applicant's name, which may connote membership of a particular ethnic group, particularly for Asian applicants but also potentially for applicants from the Black Caribbean and Black African groups. Admissions selectors see each applicant's home address and the school they attend, which may also be suggestive of ethnicity given the high degree of residential concentration of British ethnic minority communities (although this has been decreasing over time, see Catney 2015). Admissions selectors also see what an applicant says about themselves in their personal statements, where language use or references made to personal experiences and interests may also signal an applicant's ethnicity. For courses which require shortlisted applicants to attend a formal interview, an applicant's ethnicity (and gender and social class) are of course likely to be highly visible. These signals as to an applicant's ethnicity may lead admissions selectors to make biased decisions, perhaps based on an unconscious association of the applicant with societal stereotypes about their ethnic group, or an unconscious preference for recruiting students in their own (typically white upper-middle-class) image (ECU 2013).

There is evidence from labour market studies that applicant names do influence selection decisions. A UK study commission by the Department for Work and Pensions found that job applicants with White British sounding names were more likely to be shortlisted than applicants with names more commonly associated with British ethnic minority groups (Wood et al. 2009). These findings echo the results of many similar studies in the US (see e.g. Pager 2009). The evidence in relation to higher education admissions is more limited than that for job hiring. However, in the UK, a now-dated study of medical school admissions found that applicants from ethnic minority groups were 1.46 times less likely to be accepted even when qualifications and other factors were taken into account, and that those with non-European-sounding surnames were less likely to be offered places than other applicants with comparable qualifications (McManus et al. 1995). More recent experimental evidence from the US found that identical emails from prospective postgraduate students were more likely to receive a response from US college professors if the sender's name indicated they were white rather than African American, Hispanic, Indian or Chinese (Milkman et al. 2015).

In response to concerns about the possibility of unconscious bias in university admissions, the UK government has advocated that UCAS applications should be name-blind (Cameron 2015; DBIS 2016). But would simply removing applicants' names mitigate the possible influence of unconscious bias on university admissions decisions? Even if it would, is it enough?

UCAS was tasked with consulting the higher education sector about the proposal and reported its findings and recommendations in August 2016 (UCAS 2016c). UCAS reported that respondents to the consultation raised concerns about the efficacy of simply removing applicant names from the top of application forms given that names are likely to appear elsewhere on the form, for example in an applicant's email address or teacher's reference, and given that other information provided could still provide clues as to an applicant's ethnicity, including the applicant's home address, school attended, personal statement, qualifications taken in another language, and so on. Respondents also expressed concerns that going name-blind would prove detrimental to attempts to take positive action to support applicants from ethnic minority backgrounds and other under-represented groups, for example by making it more difficult to use contextual data in admissions or to target 'conversion' activities focused on encouraging applicants from under-represented groups to accept offers of places.

These criticisms of name-blind admissions notwithstanding, UCAS's first of seven recommendations was that name-blind admissions should be piloted locally by higher education providers, so as to "test its applicability to HE admissions, its efficacy in addressing concerns about unconscious bias, and to better understand the likely costs of a widespread implementation" (UCAS 2016c: 15). It was subsequently announced that name-blind admissions trials would be implemented for selected courses at the universities of Exeter, Huddersfield, Liverpool and Winchester during the 2016/2017 admissions cycle.[4] This may yield useful quasi-experimental data, but it is unlikely to lead to name-blind admissions being rolled out nationally because of the impracticalities mentioned above.

But more importantly, even if it was practicable to disguise applicants' ethnic backgrounds on their UCAS application forms, such a move would fail to address the underlying causes of any ethnic bias in offer making. If admissions decisions *are* influenced by conscious or unconscious bias, then the solution is not to remove information that triggers those biases, but to develop processes and foster cultures in which such biases are recognised and redressed, and not just at the point of admissions, but across all domains of university life. Name-blind admissions, even if it could be done, would not be enough.

Developing Genuinely Inclusive Practices and Cultures Within the Academy

Rather attempting to disguise the ethnicity of university applicants, whether by removing names from UCAS forms or by other means, universities need to face the problem of possible unconscious bias more frontally. This means universities looking closely and critically not only at current practices within the university, but also at the wider institutional culture.

---

[4]At Exeter, Huddersfield, Liverpool at Winchester in 2015, the overall net gap in offer rates between Black and white applicants was 3.7, 1.6, 2.7, and 2.2 percentage points respectively, while that between Asian and white applicants was 0.5, 4.5, 2.4 and 1.0 percentage points respectively.

In terms of practices, universities could provide equality and diversity and unconscious bias training to those involved in the selection of students. Many universities already train staff to understand and follow equalities legislation, and to be recognise and take steps to mitigate unconscious bias, when recruiting to academic and administrative posts within the university. This kind of training could be rolled out to those involved in the selection of students, drawing on the unconscious bias training materials produced for the higher education sector by the ECU (2013). Encouragingly, Supporting Professionalism in Admissions has produced a good practice guide focusing specifically on university admissions (SPA 2015), and has begun offering unconscious bias training courses to universities nationally, in line with UCAS's second recommendation to the sector.

UCAS has also recommended that universities institute a system of double-checking rejected applications (UCAS recommendation 4); that they proactively monitor their own admissions data throughout the admissions cycle with a view to identifying and addressing any illegitimate gaps in offer rates by ethnic group (UCAS recommendation 3); that they engage in and with research examining whether and if so how unconscious bias influences admissions decisions (recommendation 5); and that they consider what other steps may need to be taken to address ethnic disparities in admissions chances where they occur (recommendation 7).

Unlike the proposal for name-blind UCAS forms, the above recommendations from UCAS would be steps in the right direction. But it is notable that they focus exclusively on institutional practices, with little said about wider institutional cultures. This is problematic given that ethnic inequalities in higher education are not confined to admissions, but are evident in all domains of university life. Research shows that ethnic minority students and staff commonly experience institutional and personal racism within the academy, both subtle and overt (NUS 2011; Pilkington 2011). Moreover, ethnic minority students graduate with significantly lower marks on average than white students who entered university with the same A-level grades, with rates of achieving a first or upper second class degree around fifteen percentage points lower for students from ethnic minority backgrounds as compared to comparably qualified white students (HEFCE 2015). It is also clear that ethnic minorities are significantly under-represented among academics working in UK universities and face institutional bias when applying for academic jobs and for internal promotion (Arday 2015; Bhopal and Jackson 2013). All of this indicates that ethnic bias within UK universities, unconscious or otherwise, is not confined to admissions decision-making but is widespread. This in turn indicates that the solution requires change not only to institutional processes, but to wider institutional cultures too.

If unconscious ethnic bias exists in the academy (and all the more so if conscious ethnic bias exists), there is an urgent need for universities to work harder to actively foster an institutional culture which is genuinely inclusive and which genuine values diversity. Researchers have documented the failure of equality and diversity policies which focus on institutional practices but do not address institutional cultures; the mere existence of equality and diversity policy documents has been noted to foster the illusion that problems have been dealt with, and to result in continuing bias and discrimination being ignored or downplayed (Pilkington 2011; Ahmed 2015). More is needed besides good intentions on paper even where these result in piecemeal changes to practice.

A valuable model of how universities can begin to develop genuinely inclusive institutional cultures is provided by the ECU through its development of a Race Equality Charter since 2012. Application to ECU for Charter membership requires unequivocal recognition of the fact that ethnic inequalities in higher education exist and that long-term institutional cultural change is needed to remedy them, together with a commitment from the Vice-Chancellor and senior management team to take action.[5] Participating universities can then work towards a Race Equality Chartermark which is awarded to institutions that are able to demonstrate how their commitment to these principles translate *effectively* into practice. So far, only 25 of the UK's 130+ higher education institutions have signed up to the Charter, and just 8 have met the standard required to receive a first-level (bronze) Charter Mark award. Widespread take-up of Race Equality Charter membership in the future offers one of the best hopes of successfully tackling ethnic bias within higher education in admissions and beyond.

---

[5]http://www.ecu.ac.uk/equality-charters/race-equality-charter/about-race-equality-charter/.

References

Ahmed, S. (2015). Doing Diversity Work in Higher Education. In C. Alexander & J. Arday (Eds.), *Aiming Higher: Race, Inequality and Diversity in the Academy. Runnymede Perspectives* (pp. 6–7). London: Runnymede.

Arday, J. (2015). Creating Space and Providing Opportunities for BME Academics in Higher Education. In C. Alexander & J. Arday (Eds.), *Aiming Higher: Race, Inequality and Diversity in the Academy. Runnymede Perspectives* (pp. 15–18). London: Runnymede.

Bhopal, K., & Jackson, J. (2013). *The Experiences of Black and Minority Ethnic Academics: Multiple Identities and Career Progression.* Southampton: University of Southampton EPSRC.

Boliver, V. (2013). How Fair Is Access to More Prestigious UK Universities? *British Journal of Sociology, 64*(2), 344–364.

Boliver, V. (2015a). Why Are British Ethnic Minorities Less Likely to Be Offered Places at Highly Selective Universities? In C. Alexander & J. Arday (Eds.), *Aiming Higher: Race, Inequality and Diversity in the Academy. Runnymede Perspectives* (pp. 15–18). London: Runnymede.

Boliver, V. (2015b). Are There Distinctive Clusters of Higher and Lower Status Universities in the UK? *Oxford Review of Education, 41*(5), 608–627.

Boliver, V. (2016). Exploring Ethnic Inequalities in Admission to Russell Group Universities. *Sociology, 50*(2), 247–266.

Cameron, D. (2015). PM: Time to End Discrimination and Finish the Fight for Real Equality, Prime Minister's Office. Available at https://www.gov.uk/government/news/pm-time-to-end-discrimination-and-finish-the-fight-for-real-equality.

Catney, G. (2015). The Changing Geographies of Ethnic Diversity in England and Wales, 1991–2011. *Population, Space and Place, 22*(8), 750–765.

Crawford, C., & Greaves, E. (2015, November). *Socio-economic, Ethnic and Gender Differences in HE Participation* (BIS Research Paper No. 186). London: Department for Business, Innovation and Skills.

DBIS. (2016). *Higher Education: Success as a Knowledge Economy.* London: Department for Business, Innovation and Skills. Cm 9258.

ECU. (2013). *Unconscious Bias in Colleges and Higher Education: Handbook for Trainers.* London: Equality Challenge Unit.

Grove, J. (2013, May 2). 'Small' Russell Group Racial Bias in Admissions: Ucas. *Times Higher*. Available at http://www.timeshighereducation.co.uk/news/small-russell-group-racial-bias-in-admissions-ucas/2003594.article.

Havergal, C. (2016, September 8). Four Universities to Trial Name-Blind Applications. *Times Higher*. Available at https://www.timeshighereducation.com/news/four-universities-trial-name-blind-applications.

HEFCE. (2015). *Differences in Degree Outcomes: The Effect of Subject and Student Characteristics*. London: Higher Education Funding Council for England.

Machin, D. (2015). *Data and Public Policy: Trying to Make Social Progress Blindfolded. A Report for the Social Mobility and Child Poverty Commission*. London: HMSO.

McManus, C., Richards, P., Winder, B. C., Sproston, K. A., & Styles, V. (1995). Medical School Applicants from Ethnic Minority Groups: Identifying if and When They Are Disadvantaged. *British Medical Journal, 310*, 496.

Milkman, K. L., Akinola, M., & Chugh, D. (2015). What Happens Before? A Field Experiment Exploring How Pay and Representation Differentially Shape Bias on the Pathway into Organizations. *Journal of Applied Psychology, 100*(6), 1678–1712.

Modood, T. (1993). The Number of Ethnic Minority Students in British Higher Education: Some Grounds for Optimism. *Oxford Review of Education, 19*, 167–182.

Modood, T., & Shiner, M. (1994). *Ethnic Minorities and Higher Education: Why Are There Differential Rates of Entry?* London: Policy Studies Institute.

Noden, P., Shiner, M., & Modood, T. (2014). University Offer Rates for Candidates from Different Ethnic Categories. *Oxford Review of Education, 40*(3), 349–369.

NUS. (2011). *Race for equality: A Report on the Experiences of Black Students in Further and Higher Education*. London: National Union of Students.

Pager, D. (2009). Discrimination in a Low-Wage Labor Market: A Field Experiment. *Journal American Sociological Review, 74*(5), 777–799.

Pilkington, A. (2011). *Institutional Racism in the Academy: A UK Case Study*. Stoke-on-Trent: Trentham Books.

Russell Group. (2013). *Russell Group Comment on Access Research*. Press Release. Available at www.russellgroup.ac.uk/russell-group-latest-news/154–2013/5485-russell-group-comment-on-accessresearch/.

Russell Group. (2015). *University Access Research*. Press Release. Available at http://russellgroup.ac.uk/news/university-access-research/.

Russell Group. (2016a, June 9). *UCAS Admissions Data*. Press Release. Available at http://russellgroup.ac.uk/news/ucas-admissions-data/.

Russell Group. (2016b). *Informed Choices: A Russell Group Guide to Making Decisions about Post-16 Education*. London: Russell Group. Available at http://russellgroup.ac.uk/for-students/school-and-college-in-the-uk/subject-choices-at-school-and-college/.

Shiner, M., & Modood, T. (2002). Help or Hindrance? Higher Education and the Route to Ethnic Equality. *British Journal of Sociology of Education, 23*(2), 209–232.

SPA. (2015). *SPA Good Practice Considerations in Admissions on Unconscious and Implicit Bias in Admissions*. Cheltenham: Supporting Professionalism in Admissions.

UCAS. (2015a). *Survey of 2015 Cycle UCAS Applicants on the Use of Their Personal Data*. Cheltenham: UCAS. Available at https://www.ucas.com/sites/default/files/ucas_applicant_data_survey_key_results_0.pdf.

UCAS. (2015b). *Offer Rates to Different Ethnic Groups Close to Expected Values. Analysis note 2015/05*. Cheltenham: UCAS. Available at https://www.ucas.com/sites/default/files/gbanalysis_note_2015_05_web_0.pdf.

UCAS. (2016a). *UCAS Undergraduate Reports by Sex, Area Background, and Ethnic Group*. Cheltenham: UCAS. Available at https://www.ucas.com/corporate/news-and-key-documents/news/ucas-publishes-first-equality-reports-individual-universities.

UCAS. (2016b). *Our Personal Data Policy*. UCAS: Cheltenham. Available at https://www.ucas.com/corporate/about-us/our-personal-data-policy.

UCAS. (2016c). *Unconscious Bias Report 2016*. Cheltenham: UCAS. Available at https://www.ucas.com/file/74801/download?token=M80wi05k.

Wood, M., Hales, J., Purdon, S., Sejersen, T., & Hayllar, O. (2009). *A Test for Racial Discrimination in Recruitment Practices in British Cities*. Department for Work and Pensions Research Report No. 607. London: HMSO.

Zimdars, A., Sullivan, A., & Heath, A. (2009). Elite Higher Education Admissions in the Arts and Sciences: Is Cultural Capital the Key? *Sociology, 43*(4), 648–666.

5

Understanding the Under-Attainment of Ethnic Minority Students in UK Higher Education: The Known Knowns and the Known Unknowns

John T. E. Richardson

Introduction

This chapter is concerned with the attainment (and specifically with the under-attainment) of ethnic minority students in UK higher education. First, I will review the evidence that shows that the academic attainment of ethnic minority students who have been awarded first degrees is less than that of White students. Second, I will describe an explanation for this disparity in attainment based upon the experience of people from different ethnic minorities in the US, but I will suggest that it does not fit the UK situation. Third, I will consider whether there are differences between White students and ethnic minority students in their experience of higher education. Finally, I will indicate what further research is needed on this topic.

First, however, a few preliminary remarks. I use the term 'ethnicity' in preference to the term 'race', because the latter is associated with long

J. T. E. Richardson (✉)
Institute of Educational Technology, The Open University,
Milton Keynes, UK
e-mail: john.t.e.richardson@open.ac.uk

© The Author(s) 2018
J. Arday and H. S. Mirza (eds.), *Dismantling Race in Higher Education*,
https://doi.org/10.1007/978-3-319-60261-5_5

discredited theories concerning human behaviour, character and social organisation (Platt 2011: 71–72; Fenton 1996; Tobias 1996). The labels used to identify different ethnic groups differ from country to country and evolve over time in each country. As Fenton (1996) remarked in commenting on the classification used in a previous UK census, the categories are a mixture based partly on skin colour and partly on national, regional or continental origin. They mainly reflect the messy cultural and colonial history of the UK. Nevertheless, they are valid to the extent that people from different ethnic groups are prepared to use them to describe themselves.

Information about the ethnicity of students in UK higher education is based on their self-identification at the time of their registration: that is, they are asked to choose an ethnic group with which they most identify from a list similar to that used in the national census. Certain minority groups (such as Travellers or people with an Irish background) are included in the category 'White', but the relevant subcategories are not used consistently across the different nations that constitute the UK and are not employed in published statistics regarding students in higher education. Consequently, research using these statistics tends to suggest that the category of White students is both homogeneous and unproblematic, when neither is the case (Platt 2011: 74–75; Bird 1996: 96–97; Fenton 1996). Moreover, educational researchers tend to use the expression 'ethnic minority' (or 'minority ethnic') to refer only to non-White students. Although strictly incorrect, this practice will be followed in this chapter.

First-Degree Attainment in White and Ethnic Minority Students

In previous research into the attainment of White and ethnic minority students in the UK, the most common index of attainment is based on the classification of first degrees. These are usually designated by the title of 'Bachelor', although enhanced degrees taken by students intending to be professional scientists and engineers are commonly designated by the title of 'Master', as are degrees in the humanities and social sciences conferred by the four Ancient Scottish universities (Aberdeen, Edinburgh, Glasgow and St. Andrews). Most programmes lead to degrees that are awarded with honours; these are usually classified as first, second or third class, and the second class is usually categorised into an upper division and a lower division. A degree that is awarded with either first-class or upper second-class honours is often described as a 'good' degree.

Students from ethnic minorities in the UK are less likely to obtain good degrees than are White students. Connor et al. (1996) surveyed students who had graduated from four institutions of higher education in 1993. They found that 65% of the White students had obtained good degrees, but that only 39% of the non-White students had obtained good degrees. Subsequently, this pattern was confirmed in analyses based on UK-domiciled graduates from all UK institutions of higher education (Social Mobility Advisory Group 2016: 19; Richardson 2008, 2015; Fielding et al. 2008; Broecke and Nicholls 2007; Elias et al. 2006; Leslie 2005; Connor et al. 2004; Naylor and Smith 2004; Owen et al. 2000).

However, the overall proportion of students awarded good degrees has increased over this period, rising to 73.2% in 2015–2016 (Higher Education Statistics Agency 2017). To compare the results obtained in different years, it is necessary to convert the raw percentages to odds ratios. If the probability of the members of one group exhibiting a particular outcome is p (for example, 0.60), the odds of this are $p/(1-p)$ (that is, 0.60/0.40 or 1.50). If the probability of the members of another group exhibiting the same outcome is q (for example, 0.70), the odds of this are $q/(1-q)$ (that is, 0.70/0.30 or 2.33). The ratio between these odds is $1.50/2.33 = 0.64$. In other words, the odds of the members of the first group exhibiting the relevant outcome are 64% of the odds of the members of the second group exhibiting that outcome. Odds ratios vary from 0 (when $p=0$ or $q=1$) to infinity (when $p=1$ or $q=0$), and an odds ratio of 1 means that there is no difference in the odds of the two groups exhibiting the outcome in question (when $p=q$).

Table 5.1 shows the odds ratios comparing students from different non-White ethnic groups with White students in terms of the proportions of good degrees and first-class degrees over the last 20 years. Overall, the odds of a non-White student obtaining a good degree are about half those of a White student obtaining a good degree. The attainment gap is greater in Black students than in Asian students, and it is greater in Asian students than in students of Chinese, Mixed or Other ethnicity. This pattern has been broadly consistent from one year to another. In general, the odds ratios relating to the attainment of first-class honours are similar to the odds ratios relating to the attainment of good degrees. The latter show no systematic change over the last 20 years, but the former show an increase for seven of the nine ethnic groups in the most recent data.

Previous research showed persistent differences in attainment among ethnic minority students (Richardson 2008). For instance, the trend for Asian and Black students to be less likely to obtain good degrees than White students is greater in older students than in younger students, greater in women than in men, and greater in some subjects than in others. The attainment gap in Asian students is greatest in those who take combined degrees and least in those who take degrees in medicine and dentistry[1]; and the attainment gap in Black students is greatest in those who take combined degrees and least in those who take degrees in agriculture. The trend for Asian and Black students to be less likely to obtain good degrees than White students is greater in part-time students than in full-time students and is greater at 'new' universities (mainly former polytechnics that have become chartered institutions since 1992) than at 'Russell Group' universities (high-ranking research-intensive institutions).

---

[1]In the UK, degrees that qualify students to practise medicine, dentistry or veterinary science are not classified. However, many of these students take intercalated or intermediate degrees after their second or third year of study, and these are classified in the usual manner. Richardson and Woodley (2003) found that these students were more likely to obtain good degrees and were more likely to obtain first-class honours than were students in any other subjects. Nevertheless, on the basis of a systematic review and meta-analysis of the research literature, Woolf et al. (2011) concluded that non-White students consistently performed less well than White students at all levels of UK medical education.

Table 5.1 Odds ratios comparing academic attainment in different ethnic groups

	1997–1998	1998–1999	2001–2002	2004–2005	2011–2012	2015–2016
Good degrees						
Black Caribbean	0.35	0.34	0.36	0.36	0.33	0.35
Black African	0.25	0.27	0.30	0.31	0.30	0.30
Black Other	0.43	0.38	0.43	0.33	0.29	0.28
Indian	0.52	0.52	0.56	0.54	0.60	0.67
Pakistani	0.43	0.40	0.43	0.39	0.39	0.45
Bangladeshi	0.40	0.45	0.44	0.41	0.43	0.51
Asian Other	0.58	0.60	0.53	0.59	0.67	0.49
Chinese	0.67	0.60	0.59	0.55	0.48	0.72
Mixed	–	–	0.88	0.86	–	–
Other	0.75	0.72	0.68	0.57	0.70	0.66
Not known	0.91	0.89	–	0.54	0.44	0.29
All non-White	0.48	0.47	0.49	0.49	0.47	0.48
First-class degrees						
Black Caribbean	0.25	0.15	0.25	0.23	0.26	0.37
Black African	0.18	0.26	0.29	0.27	0.29	0.35
Black Other	0.41	0.32	0.41	0.29	0.30	0.33
Indian	0.53	0.53	0.59	0.59	0.63	0.75
Pakistani	0.39	0.47	0.39	0.39	0.45	0.52
Bangladeshi	0.36	0.52	0.32	0.36	0.47	0.53
Asian Other	0.66	0.67	0.65	0.60	0.76	0.58
Chinese	0.87	0.74	0.81	0.63	0.66	0.83
Mixed	–	–	0.87	0.82	–	–
Other	0.82	0.84	0.78	0.69	0.73	0.70
Not known	1.06	0.88	–	0.67	0.71	0.50
All non-White	0.51	0.51	0.53	0.51	0.52	0.56

Note The odds ratios compare the likelihood of obtaining good degrees and first-class degrees in different groups of non-White students using White students as a reference group. '–' means that the relevant category was not employed. The data have been obtained or calculated from the following published sources: 1997–1998 and 1998–1999, Owen et al. (2000); 2001–2002; Connor et al. (2004); 2004–2005, Richardson (2008); 2011–2012, Richardson (2015). The data for 2015–2016 have been calculated from a HESA dataset subject to the following acknowledgement.
Source HESA Student Record 2015–2016, January 2017. Copyright HESA Limited 2017. All data are reproduced by permission of HESA Limited. HESA cannot accept responsibility for any inferences or conclusions derived from the data by third parties

Researchers using econometric techniques have confirmed that White students are still more likely to obtain good degrees than students from other ethnic groups when the effects of other demographic and institutional variables have been statistically controlled (*Student Ethnicity* 2010; Broecke and Nicholls 2007; Naylor and Smith 2004). Even so, when the effects of entry qualifications have been statistically controlled, the odds ratio comparing the likelihood of Asian and White students being awarded good degrees increases from 0.50 to 0.71, while the odds ratio comparing the likelihood of Black and White students being awarded good degrees increases from 0.33 to 0.60 (Richardson 2008). Thus, about half of the disparity in attainment between White students and non-White students is attributable to differences in their entry qualifications. The under-attainment of many ethnic minorities in UK secondary education is, of course, well-documented (Casey 2016: 81–83; Equality and Human Rights Commission 2015: 23–24).

Explaining the Attainment Gap

Nearly 40 years ago, in a classic analysis of differential attainment, Ogbu (1978) pointed out that, across a variety of countries, structural inequalities tended to impair the educational aspirations and achievement of people from ethnic minorities. He subsequently elaborated this account in writing about differences across ethnic groups in high-school attainment in the US (Ogbu 1983, 1987). He distinguished between two different kinds of ethnic minority: 'immigrant minorities' who had migrated voluntarily to their host societies and 'caste-like minorities' who had been incorporated into those societies involuntarily. Ogbu suggested that poor motivation and attainment were a characteristic of students from the latter groups but not of students from the former groups. This appeared to provide a plausible explanation for the relatively good attainment of Chinese, Japanese and Filipino students in the US (whom Ogbu characterised as immigrant minorities) and the relatively poor attainment of Black and Hispanic students in the US (whom he characterised as caste-like minorities). A similar analysis was provided more recently by Chua and Rubenfeld (2014).

A second tenet in Ogbu's account was that members of caste-like (or 'involuntary') minorities exhibited 'cultural inversion': 'the tendency for members of one population, in this case involuntary minorities, to regard certain forms of behaviors, certain events, symbols and meanings as not appropriate for them because they are characteristic of members of another population (e.g., white Americans)' (Ogbu 1987: 323). In particular, Black students were led to reject the beliefs, attitudes and behaviour that would support high attainment because they were regarded as 'acting White'; consequently, these students became disengaged from their studies and were more likely to experience academic failure (Fordham and Ogbu 1986).

Others have criticised Ogbu's analysis (Comeaux and Jayakumar 2007), and it certainly does not provide an adequate fit to the situation in UK higher education. First, it should be noted that Asian and Black students are members of ethnic groups who originally migrated to the UK voluntarily. They would therefore count as immigrant minorities on Ogbu's theory, and their academic attainment would be expected to match that of White students. Nevertheless, Table 5.1 shows that both groups have been consistently less likely than White students to obtain good degrees and less likely to obtain first-class degrees.

The idea that ethnic minority students reject the beliefs, attitudes and behaviour associated with participation in higher education also does not fit the facts. Connor et al. (2004: 42–43) estimated that in 2001– 2002 the participation rate in UK higher education was 38% for White people but 56% for people from ethnic minorities. More recently, the Department for Education (2015: 10) reported that in 2012–2013 45% of White school-leavers entered higher education in the UK compared with 64% of Asian and 62% of Black school-leavers. In fact, the higher participation rate of people from ethnic minorities could be taken as a factor in the under-attainment of students from ethnic minorities if one assumes that entrants to higher education are drawn from the upper region of some distribution of ability (Leslie 2005). On this assumption, 'more will mean worse' (Amis 1960: 8) because average attainment will vary inversely with the participation rate. Even so, most researchers consider that differences in the qualifications of entrants to UK higher education between White students and ethnic minority students are more likely to be due to inequities in attainment in secondary education (Richardson 2008).

Experiences of White and Ethnic Minority Students

As noted earlier, White students are still more likely to obtain good degrees than students from other ethnic groups when differences in their entry qualifications have been taken into account. Some have suggested that poor attainment in ethnic minority students is due to the nature of their interactions with their teachers and other students (Comeaux and Jayakumar 2007). More specifically, it has been argued that students from ethnic minorities encounter discriminatory teaching and assessment practices or more subtle exclusionary attitudes and behaviour on the part of their teachers and classmates (Osler 1999). A survey by Connor et al. (2004) found no clear evidence that any group of ethnic minority students felt disadvantaged in comparison with White students, but several small-scale qualitative studies reviewed by Singh (2011: 29–30) suggested that the experience of ethnic minority students was unsatisfactory in certain respects.

In the National Student Survey, which is administered annually to final-year students in most UK institutions of higher education, White students do tend to give more favourable ratings of their programmes than Asian or Black students. However, the effects are small and only achieve statistical significance because of the very large sample size (around 150,000 students in each of the first three years of the Survey's administration). The effects are also inconsistent from year to year (Fielding et al. 2008; Surridge 2008). Richardson (2015) concluded that any differences in the experience of higher education in White and ethnic minority students were not sufficient to explain the dramatic differences in their attainment.

Mountford-Zimdars et al. (2015) considered the possible factors responsible for variations in student attainment in higher education. They identified four kinds of factor: curricula and learning;

relationships between staff and students; social, cultural and economic capital; and psychosocial and identity factors. They concluded:

> The most effective interventions reduce gaps in outcomes by making improvements to the students' learning, boosting their engagement in HE [higher education], enhancing their wider student experience, and raising their confidence and resilience levels. Damaging psychological effects can arise from stereotyping, particularly the negative effects on students' self-confidence if HE staff or peers project bias, either consciously or unconsciously. Universal interventions avoid stereotyping, but targeted interventions remain necessary and useful in cases where the needs of specific student groups require systematic attention. (iii)

The researchers' framework proved to be useful in a subsequent investigation into differential attainment among medical students and trainee doctors (Woolf et al. 2016). Unfortunately, the analysis presented by Mountford-Zimdars et al. is limited because it conflated variations in attainment related to socio-economic background, disability and ethnicity. The researchers also treated students from lower socio-economic backgrounds, disabled students and ethnic minority students as homogeneous populations. Most important, both their investigation and that of Woolf et al. (2016) reported the perceptions of key stakeholders (professional groups, learned societies, funding agencies and student organisations in the former case; students, teachers and trainers in the latter case) and did not provide any objective evidence regarding the causes of differential attainment.

Differential Attainment at the Module Level

National statistics on the classes of first degrees awarded by UK higher education institutions are collected by the Higher Education Statistics Agency (HESA). However, HESA does not collect data on the attainment of postgraduate students, and hence little is known about the attainment of postgraduate students from ethnic minorities. However, Woolf et al. (2011) found that the attainment gap between White and ethnic minority medical students was similar on postgraduate and undergraduate programmes. This suggests that there may well be significant under-attainment on the part of ethnic minority students on postgraduate programmes in other subjects, too.

On undergraduate programmes, a student's class of degree is usually determined by the marks or grades achieved on individual course units or modules. Factors responsible for variations in the proportion of good degrees are thus likely to have affected attainment at the module level. Evidence on the role of ethnicity in student attainment has been obtained in the case of students who were taking courses with the Open University, which was created in 1969 to provide degree programmes by distance education across the UK. The University accepts all applicants over the normal minimum age of 16 onto most of its undergraduate modules without imposing any formal entry requirements. It also has a long-standing commitment to equal opportunities in both education and employment.

Despite this, the attainment gap in ethnic minority students who graduate from the Open University is similar to the attainment gap in ethnic minority students who have studied part-time at other UK institutions of higher education (Richardson 2009). At the module level, most groups of ethnic minority students are less likely than White students to complete their courses; most groups of ethnic minority students are less likely than White students to pass the courses that they have completed; and most groups of ethnic minority students are less likely than White students to obtain grades that would merit the award of a good degree (Richardson 2012a, b). In short, ethnic minority students are less likely than White students to be awarded good degrees simply because they are less likely to achieve the grades that would merit the award of a good degree.

Might the attainment gap in ethnic minority students be due to the nature of the feedback that they receive for their assignments? Richardson et al. (2015) examined four assignments that had been submitted by each of 470 ethnic minority students and 470 matched White students for an introductory arts module (making 3760 assignments in total). Consistent with previous research, the Asian and Black students had received lower marks for their assignments than did White students. The students' tutors had provided feedback on the assignments by adding their marginal comments to the electronic versions of the documents. A computer system was used to categorise this feedback based on a scheme originally devised by Bales (1950). There were only small differences between the ethnic minority students and the White students in terms of the kinds of feedback that they received, and these disappeared when the marks that they had received for their assignments were had been taken into account. These results indicate that students from all ethnic groups receive feedback that is commensurate with their marks. It follows that the origins of the attainment gap in ethnic minority students need to be sought elsewhere.

Conclusions

In UK higher education, differences in academic attainment between White students and ethnic minority students are ubiquitous and have persisted for many years. The UK is not unique in this regard. In the US, for instance, Black, Hispanic, and Native American students are less likely to complete programmes of study in higher education (Swail 2003), and they tend to obtain lower grade-point averages than White students (Horn et al. 2002: 68). In the Netherlands, ethnic minority students (mainly those with parents from the Antilles, Morocco, Surinam, or Turkey) tend to show poorer retention and take longer to graduate (Severiens et al. 2006; Hofman and Van Den Berg 2003). They also tend to obtain fewer credits and lower grades than students from the White ethnic majority (Severiens and Wolff 2008).

In the UK, at least, these differences in attainment are only partly explained by ethnic differences in students' entry qualifications. The factors that are responsible for the ethnic differences in attainment that remain when differences in entry qualifications have been taken into account have yet to be identified. The magnitude of ethnic differences in academic attainment varies from one institution to another and from one subject area to another (Richardson 2015). This suggests that they result, at least in part, from the teaching and assessment practices that are adopted in different institutions and in different academic subjects.

However, precisely which aspects of teaching and assessment practices might be responsible for variations in the attainment gap has yet to be determined.

Other research carried out at the Open University indicates that quantitative variations in the attainment of students from different ethnic groups are not reflected in concomitant qualitative variations in their experiences of studying. In particular, there seems to be little difference among students from different ethnic groups in their perceptions of the academic quality of their courses, in their ratings of their overall satisfaction with their courses, in their ratings of their own personal development as a result of taking those courses, or in their academic engagement with their courses (Richardson 2009, 2011).

Perhaps the most important point to make is that the attainment gap in ethnic minority students is a finding that is correlational rather than causal in nature (Richardson 2012a). Ethnicity per se is almost certainly not the effective variable influencing students' academic attainment. Rather, it is a proxy for other factors that are confounded with students' ethnicity. The key task for future research is to identify those factors.

Acknowledgements This chapter includes material from the articles cited as Richardson (2012a), Richardson (2015) and Richardson et al. (2015).

References

Amis, K. (1960). Lone Voices: Views of the Fifties. *Encounter, 15*(1), 6–11.

Bales, R. F. (1950). *Interaction Process Analysis: A Method for the Study of Small Groups.* Cambridge, MA: Addison-Wesley.

Bird, J. (1996). *Black Students and Higher Education: Rhetorics and Realities.* Buckingham: Society for Research into Higher Education and Open University Press.

Broecke, S., & Nicholls, T. (2007). *Ethnicity and Degree Attainment* (Research Report RW92). London: Department for Education and Skills. https://www.education.gov.uk/publications.eOrderingDownload/RW92.pdf.

Casey, L. (2016). *The Casey Review: A Review into Opportunity and Integration.* London: Department for Communities and Local Government. https://

www.gov.uk/government/uploads/system/uploads/attachment_data/file/575973/The_Casey_Review_Report.pdf.

Chua, A., & Rubenfeld, J. (2014). *The Triple Package: How Three Unlikely Traits Explain the Rise and Fall of Cultural Groups in America.* New York: Penguin.

Comeaux, E., & Jayakumar, U. M. (2007). Education in the United States: Is It a Black Problem? *Urban Review, 39*(1), 93–104.

Connor, H., La Valle, I., Tackey, N., & Perryman, S. (1996). *Ethnic Minority Graduates: Differences by Degrees* (Report No. 309). Brighton: University of Sussex, Institute for Employment Studies. http://www.employment-studies.co.uk/pubs/summary.php?id=309.

Connor, H., Tyers, C., Modood, T., & Hillage, J. (2004). *Why the Difference? A Closer Look at Higher Education Minority Ethnic Students and Graduates* (Research Report No. 552). London: Department for Education and Skills. https://www.education.gov.uk/publications/standard/publicationDetail/Page1/R552.

Department for Education. (2015). *Destinations of Key Stage 4 and Key Stage 5 Students, 2012/2013* (Statistical Release). London: Department for Education.

Elias, P., Jones, P., & McWhinnie, S. (2006). *Representation of Ethnic Groups in Chemistry and Physics.* London: Royal Society of Chemistry and Institute of Physics. http://www.rsc.org/images/Ethnic%Web_tcm18-53629.pdf.

Equality and Human Rights Commission. (2015). *Is Britain Fairer? The State of Equality and Human Rights 2015.* London: Equality and Human Rights Commission. https://www.equalityhumanrights.com/en/britain-fairer/britain-fairer-report.

Fenton, S. (1996). Counting Ethnicity: Social Groups and Official Categories. In R. Levitas & W. Guy (Eds.), *Interpreting Official Statistics* (pp. 143–165). London: Routledge.

Fielding, A. C., Charlton, C., Kounali, D., & Leckie, G. (2008). *Degree Attainment, Ethnicity and Gender: Interactions and the Modification of Effects—A Quantitative Analysis.* York: Higher Education Academy. http://www.heacademy.ac.uk/assets/documents/research/EDA_Quantitative_Report_March08.pdf.

Fordham, S., & Ogbu, J. U. (1986). Black Students' School Success: Coping with the "Burden" of "Acting White." *Urban Review, 18*(3), 176–206.

Higher Education Statistics Agency. (2017). *Higher Education Student Enrolments and Qualifications Obtained at Higher Education Providers in the United Kingdom 2015/2016* (Statistical First Release 242). Cheltenham: Higher Education Statistics Agency. https://www.hesa.ac.uk/news/12-01-2017/sfr242-student-enrolments-and-qualifications.

Hofman, A., & Van Den Berg, M. (2003). Ethnic-Specific Achievement in Dutch Higher Education. *Higher Education in Europe, 28*(3), 371–389.

Horn, L., Peter, K., & Rooney, K. (2002). *Profile of Undergraduates in U.S. Postsecondary Institutions* (Report No. 2002-168). Washington, DC: US Department of Education, National Center for Education Statistics. http://nces.ed.gov/pubs2002/2002168.pdf.

Leslie, D. (2005). Why People from the UK's Minority Ethnic Communities Achieve Weaker Degree Results Than Whites. *Applied Economics, 37*(6), 619–632.

Mountford-Zimdars, A., Sabri, D., Moore, J., Sanders, J., Jones, S., & Higham, L. (2015). *Causes of Differences in Student Outcomes*. Bristol: Higher Education Funding Council for England. http://www.hefce.ac.uk/media/HEFCE,2014/Content/Pubs/Independentresearch/2015/Causes,of,differences,in,student,outcomes/HEFCE2015_diffout.pdf.

Naylor, R. A., & Smith, J. (2004). Determinants of Educational Success in Higher Education. In G. Johnes & J. Johnes (Eds.), *International Handbook on the Economics of Education* (pp. 415–461). Cheltenham: Edward Elgar.

Ogbu, J. U. (1978). *Minority Education and Caste: The American System in Cross-Cultural Perspective*. New York: Academic Press.

Ogbu, J. U. (1983). Minority Status and Schooling in Plural Societies. *Contemporary Education Review, 27*(2), 168–190.

Ogbu, J. U. (1987). Variability in Minority School Performance: A Problem in Search of an Explanation. *Anthropology and Education Quarterly, 18*(4), 312–334.

Osler, A. (1999). The Educational Experiences and Career Aspirations of Black and Ethnic Minority Undergraduates. *Race, Ethnicity and Education, 2*(1), 39–58.

Owen, D., Green, A., Pitcher, J., & Maguire, M. (2000). *Minority Ethnic Participation and Achievements in Education, Training and the Labour Market* (Research Report No. 225). London: Department for Education and Skills. https://www.education.gov.uk/publications/eOrderingDownload/RR225.pdf.

Platt, L. (2011). *Understanding Inequalities*. Cambridge: Polity Press.

Richardson, J. T. E. (2008). The Attainment of Ethnic Minority Students in UK Higher Education. *Studies in Higher Education, 33*(1), 33–48.

Richardson, J. T. E. (2009). The Role of Ethnicity in the Attainment and Experiences of Graduates in Distance Education. *Higher Education, 58*(3), 321–338.

Richardson, J. T. E. (2011). The Academic Engagement of White and Ethnic Minority Students in Distance Education. *Educational Psychology, 31*(2), 123–139.

Richardson, J. T. E. (2012a). The Attainment of White and Ethnic Minority Students in Distance Education. *Assessment and Evaluation in Higher Education, 37*(4), 393–408.

Richardson, J. T. E. (2012b). Face-to-Face Versus Online Tuition: Preference, Performance and Pass Rates in White and Ethnic Minority Students. *British Journal of Educational Technology, 43*(1), 17–27.

Richardson, J. T. E. (2015). The Under-Attainment of Ethnic Minority Students in UK Higher Education: What We Know and What We Don't Know. *Journal of Further and Higher Education, 39*(2), 278–291.

Richardson, J. T. E., & Woodley, A. (2003). Another Look at the Role of Age, Gender and Subject as Predictors of Academic Attainment in Higher Education. *Studies in Higher Education, 28*(4), 475–493.

Richardson, J. T. E., Alden Rivers, B., & Whitelock, D. (2015). The Role of Feedback in the Under-Attainment of Ethnic Minority Students: Evidence from Distance Education. *Assessment and Evaluation in Higher Education, 40*(4), 557–573.

Severiens, S., & Wolff, R. (2008). A Comparison of Ethnic Minority and Majority Students: Social and Academic Integration, and Quality of Learning. *Studies in Higher Education, 33*(3), 253–266.

Severiens, S., ten Dam, G., & Blom, S. (2006). Comparison of Dutch Ethnic Minority and Majority Engineering Students: Social and Academic Integration. *International Journal of Inclusive Education, 10*(1), 75–89.

Singh, G. (2011). *Black and Minority Ethnic (BME) Students' Participation in Higher Education: Improving Retention and Success—A Synthesis of Research Evidence.* York: Higher Education Academy. http://www.heacademy.ac.uk/assets/documents/inclusion/ethnicity/BME_synthesis_FINAL.pdf.

Social Mobility Advisory Group. (2016). *Working in Partnership: Enabling Social Mobility in Higher Education.* London: Universities UK. http://www.universitiesuk.ac.uk/policy-and-analysis/reports/Documents/2016/working-in-partnership-final.pdf.

Student Ethnicity. (2010). *Profile and Progression of Entrants to Full-Time, First Degree Study* (Issues Paper 2010/2013). Bristol: Higher Education

Funding Council for England. http://www.hefce.ac.uk/media/hefce1/pubs/
hefce/2010/1013/10_13.

Surridge, P. (2008). *The National Student Survey 2005–2007: Findings and Trends*. Bristol: Higher Education Funding Council for England. http://www.hefce.ac.uk/media.hefce/content/pubs/indirreports/2008/rd1208/rd12_08.pdf.

Swail, W. S. with Redd, K. E., & Perna, L. W. (2003). Retaining Minority Students in Higher Education. *AHE-ERIC Higher Education Report, 30*(2), 1–187.

Tobias, P. V. (1996). Race. In A. Kuper & J. Kuper (Eds.), *The Social Science Encyclopedia* (2nd ed., pp. 260–263). London: Routledge.

Woolf, K., Potts, H. W. W., & McManus, I. C. (2011). Ethnicity and Academic Performance in UK Trained Doctors and Medical Students: Systematic Review and Meta-Analysis. *British Medical Journal, 342*(901).

Woolf, K., Rich, A., Winey, R., Needleman, S., & Griffin, A. (2016). Perceived Causes of Differential Attainment in UK Postgraduate Medical Training: A National Qualitative Study. *BMJ Open, 6*(11), 1–9.

6

Unequal Returns: Higher Education and Access to the Salariat by Ethnic Groups in the UK

Yaojun Li

Introduction

This chapter seeks to provide a more comprehensive analysis than hitherto available of the ethnic differences in higher education and access to professional-managerial (salariat) positions in contemporary UK society by linking ethnicity with generational status, family class and gender. For this purpose, I draw on the most authoritative data from the Labour Force Survey (2014–2015). The large sample size of the dataset makes it possible to differentiate ethnic groups and generational statuses in a more refined way than usually found in ethnic research, and the availability of information on parental class, together with ethnicity, generation, gender and other characteristics, offers a unique opportunity to simultaneously analyse the social foundations of ethnic differences in higher education and access to the salariat in a thorough and systematic manner.

Y. Li (✉)
Manchester University, Manchester, UK
e-mail: Yaojun.Li@manchester.ac.uk

© The Author(s) 2018
J. Arday and H. S. Mirza (eds.), *Dismantling Race in Higher Education*,
https://doi.org/10.1007/978-3-319-60261-5_6

The importance of higher education for career advancement is undisputed. Trying to obtain high levels of education by immigrants of ethnic minority heritages and their children in the 'receiving' society is a strategic investment in human capital to avoid discrimination and to ensure success in the labour market (Becker 1962). Social scientists have conducted a great deal of research on the sources and the consequences of ethnic differences in educational and occupational attainment, but such research has usually been conducted in separate manners. This chapter studies the linkage of higher education and access to the salariat whilst controlling for ethno-generational status, parental class and gender differences. It is this linkage which will make the present research a unique contribution to ethnic studies in the UK context.

It has often been observed that large-scale immigration since the Second World War has changed the socio-demographic landscapes of many developed societies. In the UK, for instance, the proportion of ethnic minorities in the population has increased nearly five-fold from less than 3% in the early 1950s to 15% in 2011 (Cheung and Heath 2007; ONS 2011). A substantial and increasing proportion of members of ethnic minority heritages belong to the second or higher generations. The continuing influx of migrants who came as adults or children, and the increasing numbers of ethnic minority heritages who were born in the country have created an on-going and imperative need to study the status, progress and obstacles of their integration into the socio-economic fabric of contemporary UK society in terms of acquiring human capital and gaining access to labour market position as commensurate with the human capital and as representing equal returns to the majority group.

Given the importance of social equality and ethnic integration, many studies have been carried out on educational and labour market attainment of the ethnic minorities in the UK. Yet due to the lack of key variables on some crucial domains such as parental class or generational status, few studies have managed to examine the link between higher education and access to the salariat whilst taking into account crucial influences exerted by parental class positions or generational changes. For instance, Lessard-Phillips and Li (2017) examined ethnic educational attainment at degree levels for multiple generations but did not link it to occupational attainment. A large number of studies looked at the ethnic situation in the labour market and found marked ethnic disadvantages but were unable to examine parental class influences. People of ethnic minority origins, even the second generation, were found to have fewer chances in training (Bhattacharyya et al. 2003), and to face 'hyper-cyclical unemployment', namely, to experience much higher levels of unemployment during economic downturns when they were three or four times as likely to be unemployed as their white peers (Li and Heath 2008; Heath and Li 2008; Li 2010); they were also less likely to find themselves in professional-managerial positions (Li and Heath 2010), and tended to receive significantly lower pay than did their white peers (Li 2012; Breach and Li 2017). Similar findings are reported in Iganski and Payne (1999), Dustmann and Fabbri (2005), Berthoud and Blekesaune (2006). Employer bias and discrimination against members of ethnic minority origins is shown to underlie much of the ethnic disadvantage (Wood et al. 2009). Disadvantages in employment, occupation and earnings as faced by members of ethnic minority heritages who possess similar educational qualifications and who share similar personal characteristics to those of the majority group are termed 'ethnic penalties' by Heath and McMahon (1997: 91).

Ethnic penalties exhibit themselves most notably in unemployment but for those fortunate enough to be in employment, the disadvantages in career advancement are shown to be mitigated (Cheung and Heath 2007). Previous studies of ethnic minority disadvantage in the labour market tend to use the micro data from the Censuses of the Population or the Labour Force Survey. These data sources contain large sample sizes as needed for ethnic research but they do not have information on parental class. When more refined analysis is conducted, such as examining the ethnic situation by generational status, the sample sizes for the ethno-generational groupings become quite small, making it necessary to limit the analysis to only a few (usually three or four) groups per generation (Cheung and Heath 2007: 532–533). When information on family class is available, researchers turned to study ethnic social mobility. For instance, Heath and McMahon (2005) compared the mobility profiles between minority and majority groups. They found that Black Caribbean, Indian and Pakistani/Bangladeshi men were well behind white men in gaining access to the most advantaged occupational positions. Yet the small samples used in the study meant that they had to confine the analysis to only a few groups. Li and Devine (2011, 2014) were unable to differentiate generational changes due to data limitations. Similarly, Platt (2005) confined her mobility analysis to Indians and Black Caribbeans. More recently, Li and Heath (2016) used datasets that contain large samples, parental class and generational status. They analysed parental effects on both unemployment risks and access to the salariat, and found that parental class played a highly important role in both respects. Similar to Cheung and Heath (2007), they found that first-generation Black Caribbean and Pakistani men were disadvantaged, being 10 and 15 percentage points behind white men in the salariat, but the second generation were generally doing well. Yet, they did not focus on higher education.

The foregoing discussion of the recent research on ethnic differences in Britain suggests two main features. Firstly, wherever data sources permit, researchers would take the advantage and include parental class, ethnicity and generational status as ascriptive factors (or as interrelated domains of social origin) which have been shown to have a powerful impact on education and, through this, on occupational attainment. The interrelationship between the expanded domains of origin, education and destination would, as shown in Fig. 6.1, constitute a reformulated OED specifically designed for research on ethnic integration, just as the classic model is for the general population (Goldthorpe 1996). The limited use of this framework is mainly due to data constraints. Secondly, a finer-grained distinction is needed on the concept of 'ethnic penalty'. Disadvantages in unemployment and low class positions as faced by the first generations certainly reflect but cannot be entirely attributed to racial discrimination, as other factors such as religion, poor human capital (overseas qualifications, poor English, unfamiliarity with the local labour market) and lack of social capital may all play a role (Heath and Martin 2012). First-generation disadvantages are thus at least partially attributable to 'migrant penalty' associated with the disruptive processes of migration. Yet, labour market disadvantages faced by the second generation who have British education

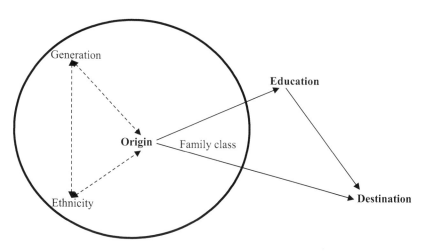

Fig. 6.1 A framework of analysis—ethno-generational status, class origin, and educational and occupational attainment (*Note* Double-headed arrows on dotted lines indicate associations and single-headed arrows on solid lines indicate causation. Ethnicity, generational status and family class are indicators of origin)

and who face no language difficulties cannot be due to the disruptive processes of migration, and can be properly termed as 'ethnic penalty'. This is especially true amongst those who possess higher levels of education obtained in UK universities. The degree to which ethnic penalty persists is a litmus test of social equality of British society. The differentiation between migrant and ethnic penalties thus calls for analyses of ethnic differences by generation, between those who came as adults or who were born in the country. In between are those who came as children or young adults, such as those arriving between ages 6 and 16 who received partial education in Britain, a group of people called the 1.5th generation in the literature (Rumbaut 2004; Lessard-Phillips and Li 2017). If ethnic penalty declines, it would be more noticeable in the attenuation of penalties in obtaining higher education and in gaining access to more advantaged occupational positions from the 1.5th to the 2nd generation.

With these considerations in mind, this chapter seeks to address the following questions:

1. How much difference is there both between the minority and the majority and among the minority groups in terms of degree-level education?
2. Do ethnic minorities find the same returns to higher education as enjoyed by the majority in terms of gaining access to the professional-managerial salariat?
3. Is there evidence of progress for the ethnic minorities over generations in both higher education and salariat access?
4. What roles do parental class and gender play in attainment of higher education and privileged occupation over and above ethnogenerational status?

Data and Methods

In order to address the research questions as outlined above, I will use the combined data from the third quarters of the labour force survey (LFS) of 2014 and 2015. The LFS is a longstanding government survey conducted since 1981 and has been much used by academic and government researchers. The reason for using this data source for the present study is that it has a large sample size and contains, for the first time in its history, information for parental class. As one of the most authoritative social surveys in the country, it also contains rich information on ethnicity, generation, educational qualification, employment status and occupational position, as well as many other demographic attributes, which makes it ideal for the present purposes. The response rates of the LFS are high, and the data files including technical reports are available at http://ukdataservice.ac.uk/get-data/key-data.aspx#/tab-uk-surveys.

The coding of the key variables (ethnicity, generational status, education, own and parental class) is adopted from standard practice (Cheung and Heath 2007; Li and Heath 2016; Lessard-Phillips and Li 2017). The analysis is confined to the working-age population, namely, age 16–65 for men and 16–63 for women excluding full-time students. Limiting the analysis to valid cases on education, ethnicity, generation, and parental class results in an analytical sample of 82,026, which is the best dataset currently available with all the crucial variables contained in one single source permitting detailed and simultaneous analysis of the ethnic stratification in higher education and access to the salariat in the UK. As ethnic minorities are generally younger than the majority group (by five years of age in the sample used), I use age-adjusted weighted analysis in this chapter following the procedure designed by Li and Heath (2016, note 12).

Results

I will start the analysis with higher education (first and higher degrees) and then move to access to the professional-managerial salariat. In each respect, I will begin with descriptive analysis before moving to statistical modelling.

The data in Table 6.1 show the educational distributions by ethno-generational status, family class and gender. Before going into detailed discussion, I wish to point out that although the focus in this chapter is on higher education, it is important to have a detailed view of the educational distribution rather than just looking at higher education which would mask considerable ethnic disadvantages. Thus six educational categories are differentiated, from higher degree to the lowest level (primary education or no formal schooling). This more differentiated view provides a fairly comprehensive educational profile in the UK. Differentiating the higher from the first degree as shown in the table has the advantage of allowing us to see the marked ethnic differences. For instance, 9% of the majority group (white UK) have higher degrees, as compared with 8 and 5% for Black Caribbeans and Bangladeshis respectively. Yet most other ethnic minority groups are more likely than the white UK respondents to have higher degrees, with white Irish and Indians being twice, and Chinese three times, as likely (17, 18 and 29% respectively).

If we group higher and first degrees together as 'higher degree', as will be the practice for the later analyses in this chapter, it can be seen that 28% of the white UK have higher education, and 16% have the lowest level (primary education or no formal schooling). Ethnic minorities are, as a whole, much more likely than the white UK to have higher

Table 6.1 Educational distribution by ethnicity, generation, family class and sex (% by row)

	Higher degree	First degree	Sub-degree	Higher secondary	Lower secondary	Primary/none	N
Ethnicity							
White UK	9	19	10	13	33	16	70,768
Ethnic minority	14	28	8	10	14	25	11,258
White Irish	17	24	12	12	16	20	472
White Other	14	27	9	10	10	30	4145
Mixed	12	28	7	13	23	17	891
Black Caribbean	8	18	10	14	30	20	732
Black African	15	28	12	9	15	22	1016
Indian	18	38	6	7	12	19	1962
Pakistani	11	21	5	11	18	33	1242
Bangladeshi	5	24	5	12	18	34	438
Chinese	29	32	5	5	9	20	360
Generation							
1st Gen	15	27	9	8	10	31	8283
1.5th Gen	10	23	8	13	23	23	1211
2nd Gen	9	19	10	13	33	15	72,532
Parental class							
Higher salariat	18	33	10	12	20	6	8943
Lower salariat	18	32	11	12	20	6	14,674
Clerical	10	22	11	13	29	15	10,550
Own-account	8	17	10	13	35	18	9562
Foremen and tech	7	17	12	13	35	16	8156
Semi routine	5	13	10	12	37	23	12,414
Routine	5	10	8	11	37	29	12,999
Not employed	4	11	7	12	33	33	4728
Sex							
Male	10	20	9	11	32	18	39,743
Female	10	20	11	13	29	16	42,283
All	10	20	10	12	31	17	82,026

Note Weighted analyses and unweighted Ns (the same below for all analyses in this chapter)
Source The Labour Force Survey (2014, 2015 quarter 3 combined, the same below for all analyses in this chapter)

education but, at the same time, they are also more likely to have the lowest education: 42 and 25% as shown in the second row of the table.

Looking more closely at the data, we find clear evidence of both ethnic polarisation and ethnic stratification in education. With regard to the former, most ethnic groups are more likely to have higher education but all groups are more concentrated in the lowest level, with white Other, Pakistani and Bangladeshi groups being twice as likely. With regard to the latter, only Black Caribbeans (at 26%) are slightly behind the white UK in higher education. Chinese and Indians are, at 61 and 56%, well above the white UK; and even white Irish, white Other, Mixed and Black African groups are around 1.5 times as likely as the white UK to have higher education, at around 40–43% versus the 28% for the white UK. Given the evidence on both the polarisation and the stratification in educational distributions, any simple notions of ethnic disadvantage or advantage in education are likely to be incomplete.

Apart from ethnic differences, there are also notable generational changes. Over 42% of the first-generation and one third of the 1.5th generation 33% have higher education, both higher than the 28% by the majority group. Among the second generation, all ethnic minority groups are more likely to have higher education than the majority group, with 58% Black Africans and Indians, and 70% Chinese being in this category.

As would be expected from the large body of literature on the sociology of education (Breen et al. 2009; Devine and Li 2013), there are striking parental class effects on educational attainment, with 52% of the respondents from higher-grade professional-managerial salariat families having higher education, which stands in sharp contrast to the 15% from routine manual or non-employed families (the latter category referring to families where neither parent was in gainful employment when the respondent was in the adolescent years, at around age 14). The mirror image of this is the evidence on the lowest level of education, with only 6% of the respondents from higher salariat families versus 33% of those from non-employed families being thus found. Gender differences are small, with women being slightly less likely than men to have the lowest level of education, at 16 and 18% respectively.

The complex interplay of ethnicity, generation, parental class and gender in their effects on education requires more refined analysis to obtain net effects. Given this, I turn to multivariate analysis with logit regression focusing on higher education (first and higher degrees combined). For ease of exposition, the coefficients from the logit models are turned into percentages using average marginal effects (AMEs) models. The data (Table 6.2) thus represent percentage-point differences for each category relative to the reference group. Three models are conducted: model 1 on ethno-generational status, model 2 adding parental class, and model further including age, age squared and gender. Note that the effects of age squared are absorbed in the age effects in the AME calculation.

Table 6.2 Average marginal effects (AME) on degree-level education

	Model 1	Model 2	Model 3
Ethnicity			
White Irish	0.127***	0.136***	0.135***
White Other	0.112***	0.135***	0.117***
Mixed	0.108***	0.104***	0.094***
Black Caribbean	−0.020	0.022	0.015
Black African	0.137***	0.144***	0.122***
Indian	0.282***	0.284***	0.267***
Pakistani	0.039**	0.103***	0.084***
Bangladeshi	0.019	0.085***	0.065**
Chinese	0.327***	0.316***	0.293***
Generation			
1st Gen	0.023**	−0.008	−0.018*
1.5th Gen	−0.048***	−0.053***	−0.036**
Parental class			
Higher salariat		0.365***	0.355***
Lower salariat		0.353***	0.342***
Clerical		0.168***	0.168***
Own-account		0.093***	0.089***
Foremen & tech		0.100***	0.100***
Semi routine		0.035***	0.037***
Not employed		−0.002	−0.005
Age			−0.001***
Female			0.009**
(N)	82,026	82,026	82,026

Note Reference groups are white UK, 2nd generation, parents in routine manual positions and male
*p < 0.05; **p < 0.01; ***p < 0.001

The data in model 1 of Table 6.2 suggest that, net of generational status, all ethnic minority groups, with the sole exceptions of Black Caribbeans and Bangladeshis, are more likely to have higher education than the majority, with the Chinese, Indians and Black Africans being 33, 28, and 14 percentage points higher, white Irish, white Other and Mixed leading by 11–13 points, and Pakistanis by 4 points. Controlling for ethnicity, the 1st are slightly more likely than the majority group to have higher education, by 2 percentage points, but the 1.5th generation are less so, being around 5 points behind.

The parental class effects, net of ethnicity and generation, are strong and have clear gradients, as shown in model 2 of Table 6.2. People from higher salariat families have a lead of 36.5 percentage points over those from routine manual families in having higher education. As Pakistani/Bangladeshi groups tend to come from more disadvantaged family positions, controlling for parental class shows that the two groups would be even more likely than the white UK to have higher education if they had similar parental class positions: an increase of approximately 6 percentage points in both cases.

Model 3 further controls for personal characteristics of age, age squared and gender. Even with all these factors taken into account, women are still found to have a higher educational profile than men, by around 1 percentage point in having first or higher degrees. Older people are less likely than younger ones to have higher education, which is understandable given the rapid expansion of higher education in the last few decades in the UK and in some other parts in the world. With the other covariates in the model taken into account, the ethnic effects in model 3 declined somewhat as compared with model 2, by 1 or 2 percentage points for most ethnic groups. Yet the overwhelming evidence still points to an ethnic premia: apart from Black Caribbeans, all other groups are more likely to have higher education than the majority. It is also the case that, other things being equal, the 1st and the 1.5th generation are less likely to have higher education.

Although all three models in Table 6.2 control for ethnicity and generation, they do not show separate ethnic differences by generation. To see such effects, I present, in Fig. 6.2, predicted probabilities of higher education on the basis of model 3 of Table 6.2.

The data in Fig. 6.2 show that, among all three generational groups, the Black Caribbeans have no statistically significantly differences with the majority group in having higher education, nor do the 1st and the 1.5th generation Bangladeshis. Apart from these, all other ethno-generational groupings are significantly above the majority in having higher education. A closer scrutiny also reveals a three-tiered structure, with Chinese and Indians taking the lead, followed by white Irish, white Other, Mixed, and Black African groups, with white UK and Black Caribbean groups being the least likely to have higher education. Generational progress is also visible for Pakistani and Bangladeshi groups, other things being equal. The findings with regard to the 2nd generation are similar to those by Cutz (2014: 180) although she was only able to analyse the situation for the four Asian groups.

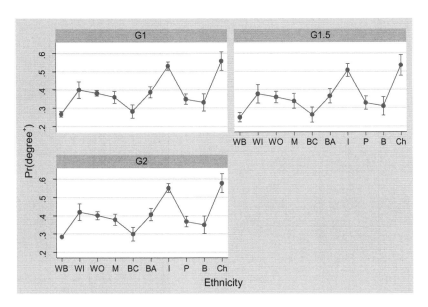

Fig. 6.2 Predictive margins with 95% confidence intervals on having degree-level education by ethnicity and generation (*Note* The predicted probabilities are based on Model 3 of Table 6.2. G1: 1st generation, G1.5: 1.5th generation, G2: 2nd generation. WB: white UK, WI: white Irish, WO: white Other, M: Mixed, BC: Black Caribbean, BA: Black African, I: Indian, P: Pakistani, B: Bangladeshi, Ch: Chinese)

Having discussed ethnic differences in higher education, I will now turn to ethnic differences in the labour market position. Previous research in this regard tends to focus on the economically active, in terms of unemployment rates (NEP 2007; Li and Heath 2008), occupational positions (Platt 2005; Li and Heath 2010), or access to the professional-managerial salariat among the active (Cheung and Heath 2007; Li and Heath 2016). Whilst such a focus is justifiable for the general population given the variegated reasons for inactivity, it is less desirable for the working-age and non-student population as used in the present study. It is reasonable to suggest that a sizeable portion of the economically inactive among this population, particularly those from ethnic minority backgrounds who tend to live in deprived areas with limited employment opportunities and elevated employer discrimination, may have involuntarily opted out of the labour market (Demireva and Heath 2017). Their cumulative experiences of job-seeking frustrations might have suggested to them that 'there is no job for me'. Such people are called 'disillusioned seekers' or 'discouraged workers' in the literature (Gallie 1988). It may also be pertinent to say that there is no clear-cut distinction between job-seeking and home-making activities, particularly for female members from some ethnic minority communities who may decide to stay at home or look for a job intermittently, pending on the prevailing family circumstances including caring responsibilities (Dale et al. 2002). Seen from this perspective, worklessness (unemployment and inactivity) may be taken as a particular, and more useful, form of disadvantage for the working-age population, with special regard to women in some ethnic minority groups. There may, to be sure, be genuine reasons for some people to stay out of the labour market, such as those with limiting long-term illness or heavy household responsibilities. Given these considerations, the following analysis will firstly show a full picture of labour market position combining occupational and employment statuses and then focus on access to the professional-managerial salariat among the employed in the multivariate modelling.

Table 6.3 shows the gross ethnic differences in the labour market, with two major features. Firstly, most ethnic minority groups are under-represented in the salariat, with Pakistanis and Bangladeshis falling behind the majority group by a big margin (13 and 14 percentage points), even though they were, as seen earlier, somewhat more likely to have higher education than the white UK respondents. Secondly, looking under the last column, one finds that broadly the same ethnic minority groups who are underrepresented in the salariat are over-represented in the routine manual and the workless positions, such as Pakistani, Bangladeshi and the two Black groups. The workless rates are markedly high for the Pakistanis and Bangladeshis. Further analysis shows that around 60% of the women in the two groups are economically inactive. There is also clear generational change, with the workless rates precipitating from 85% for the first generation to 34% for the second generation of the Bangladeshi women.

Having looked at the gross differences between ethnic groups in the labour market position, let us move to the relative ones, focusing on access to the salariat. As Iganski and Payne (1996: 129) note, it is essential to analyse ethnic position in the labour market by examining gender effects separately. Furthermore, time commitment must also be taken into account as salariat jobs tend to require full-time commitment. Thus, in the modelling part, in addition to the covariates used for educational modelling, time commitment, educational qualification, health and martial status, and number of dependent children in the family will be controlled for, as these can be expected to have significant impacts on salariat access.

Table 6.3 Labour market position by ethnicity (percentage by row)

	Salariat	Intermediate	Working class	Non-employed
White UK	35	25	17	23
White Irish	52	17	9	22
White Other	33	24	26	17
Mixed	36	20	15	29
Black Caribbean	30	26	21	24
Black African	31	17	24	28
Indian	40	21	16	23
Pakistani	22	24	13	40
Bangladeshi	21	27	16	36
Chinese	45	17	11	26
All	35	25	17	23

The data in Table 6.4 show the relative probability of being in the salariat, for men and women separately, and each with three models. For men, model 1 shows that Black Caribbeans, Pakistanis and Bangladeshis are significantly less likely to be in the salariat than white UK men. Parental class has, as can be expected, highly influential impacts, with men from higher salariat families being 31 percentage points more likely to be in the salariat positions themselves than their counterparts from routine manual working-class families, as shown in model 2. Interestingly, those from non-employed families are even less likely than those from routine manual families to be in the salariat, by 4.5 points, which is significant at the 0.001 level, showing a clear scarring effect. Education and other attributes of personal/family circumstances all show effects in the expected directions as seen in model 3. Importantly, with all these important factors taken into account, men in most ethnic minority groups show a lower probability of having salariat jobs than do white UK men with similar levels of education, similar personal characteristics, and similar family circumstances. Amidst the overall disadvantage, men of Black African, Pakistani, and Bangladeshi origins are particularly disadvantaged, being behind their white UK peers by around 9 percentage points.

Ethnic minority women are found to face lesser disadvantage than do their male counterparts. The most salient cases of disadvantage are those faced by Pakistani and Bangladeshi women but the reasons behind the differences seem chiefly attributable to personal and family circumstances. When family circumstances are taken into consideration, as shown in model 3, their disadvantages sharply declined.

Since this chapter is focused on higher education, an interesting question is whether ethnic minorities with first or higher degrees would have equal access to the salariat as do their white UK counterparts. For this, model 3 of Table 6.4 was re-run with the same covariates included but confined to those with higher education. The predicted margins were then obtained for each ethno-generational groupings, and for men and women separately. The data are shown in Fig. 6.3.

Even at the higher end of educational distribution, ethnic disadvantages persist, as seen for all three generational groups for men. A closer look shows that first and second generation Black Africans, Pakistanis

Table 6.4 Average marginal effects (AME) on access to the salariat

	Men			Women		
	Model 1	Model 2	Model 3	Model 1	Model 2	Model 3
Ethnicity						
White Irish	0.158***	0.171***	0.124***	0.237***	0.242***	0.143***
White Other	−0.016	0.007	−0.034*	0.067***	0.073***	−0.027*
Mixed	−0.010	−0.015	0.000	0.043	0.048*	0.011
Black Caribbean	−0.103***	−0.075**	−0.045	0.006	0.044	0.017
Black African	−0.050	−0.036	−0.090***	0.042	0.043	−0.004
Indian	0.085***	0.084***	−0.029	0.073***	0.076***	−0.039**
Pakistani	−0.086***	−0.037	−0.081***	−0.142***	−0.106***	−0.042*
Bangladeshi	−0.132***	−0.087*	−0.090**	−0.121***	−0.081*	−0.013
Chinese	0.193***	0.185***	0.063	0.117**	0.106**	−0.032
Generation						
1st Gen	−0.004	−0.031*	−0.079***	−0.087***	−0.103***	−0.089***
1.5th Gen	−0.058**	−0.062**	−0.020	−0.066**	−0.068***	−0.021
Parental class						
Higher salariat		0.311***	0.150***		0.268***	0.097***
Lower salariat		0.289***	0.134***		0.254***	0.094***
Clerical		0.151***	0.082***		0.138***	0.063***
Own-account		0.094***	0.043***		0.094***	0.043***
Foremen and tech		0.110***	0.063***		0.106***	0.047***
Semi routine		0.036***	0.026***		0.024**	0.010
Not employed		−0.045***	−0.011		−0.041***	−0.012
Degree+			0.362***			0.314***
Full-part time						
Part-time			−0.136***			−0.150***
Other			−0.386***			−0.409***
Age			−0.000			0.001***
Married			0.083***			0.035***
Having L-T illness			−0.137***			−0.101***
No. children under 16			−0.005*			−0.022***
(N)	39,591	39,591	39,591	42,144	42,144	42,144

Note Reference groups are white UK, 2nd generation, parents in routine manual positions, no-degree, full-time work, non-married, and no limiting long-term illness. The effects of age squared are absorbed in the age effects in the AME calculation
*p <0.05; **p <0.01; ***p <0.001

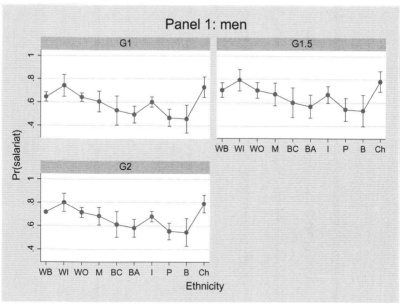

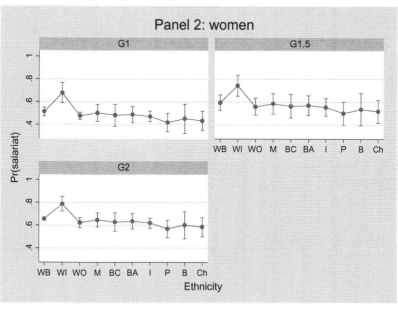

▶ **Fig. 6.3** Predictive margins with 95% confidence intervals on access to the salariat among degree-holders by ethno-generational status and sex (*Note* G1: 1st generation, G1.5: 1.5th generation, G2: 2nd generation. WB: white UK, WI: white Irish, WO: white Other, M: Mixed, BC: Black Caribbean, BA: Black African, I: Indian, P: Pakistani, B: Bangladeshi, Ch: Chinese)

and Bangladeshis, and 1.5th generation Pakistanis were significantly behind their white UK counterparts in the access rates to the salariat. Further analysis shows that, when all ethnic minorities are combined, second-generation men were around 6 percentage points less likely to have salarriat jobs, which was statistically significant at the 0.001 level. Ethnic minority women faced fewer disadvantages than their male counterparts but, apart from white Irish women, all ethnic groups in all three generations were less likely to find themselves in the salariat positions than their white UK counterparts.

Discussion and Conclusion

This chapter provided an analysis of the ethnic differences in education and labour market, focusing on higher education and access to the profession-al-managerial salariat. Generational, gender and family class differences were also examined. The main findings can be summarised as follows:

• At the overall level, ethnic minorities were well educated but at the same time they were also highly polarised: they were more likely to have degrees, but were overrepresented in the lowest level of education. There were greater differences among the ethnic minority groups in higher education than between the minority and the majority groups, with Chinese, Indians and Black Africans being well above the majority in having degree-level education. And this picture was generally the same for all three generational groupings delineated in this chapter. Family class played a crucial role but gender differences were rather small.
• The ethnic educational premia were not translated into commensurate labour market position. Many groups, particularly Pakistanis, Bangladeshis and Black Africans, were notably behind the majority in

getting salariat jobs and were overrepresented in the workless positions. The ethnic penalties were more severe for men than for women. Family class effects were still marked even when education and a whole range of personal and household circumstances were taken into account. There was some evidence of generational improvement in access to the salariat for both men and women ethnic minorities.

- Even among those with higher education, ethnic minorities, particularly men, faced marked disadvantages. Second-generation Pakistani and Bangladeshi men with degrees were around 20 percentage points behind their majority counterparts in having salariat jobs.

Overall, the analysis in this chapter shows an encouraging story for higher education but a disappointing story for access to the salariat by the ethnic minorities in the UK. While the first story is most probably due to the aspiration and determination of the minorities, first and second generations alike, in performing well in gaining higher qualifications to avoid discrimination in the labour market, the second story is a more direct reflection of unfair treatment experienced by the ethnic minorities, even amongst the second-generation degree-holders. Attainment of higher education and access to privileged class positions were not in tune with each other for the ethnic minorities. A likely explanation for this is that whilst ethnic minorities believed that they could try hard to achieve educational excellence, which many of them did as clearly demonstrated by the remarkable educational success by the 2nd generation members of Chinese, Indian, and Black African origins, they would also find that, when stepping out of education and into the realm of labour market, fates were more beyond their own control. Employers' decisions, rather than their own efforts, may play a more important role in gaining paid employment and in career advancement. In this sense, the educational success by the 1.5th and the 2nd generations may be seen as a strategic effort to try to reduce possible future employer bias and discrimination. They would have fared worse with lesser success in higher education.

Finally, it is noted that the success story of higher education by ethnic minority groups as depicted in this chapter may be too rosy. It is possible that ethnic minorities are well represented in higher education at an overall level but underrepresented in elite institutions such as in Russell

Group universities in general or in Oxford/Cambridge universities in particular. Future work could try to address this question if and when appropriate data become available. In sum, ethnic minorities face greater barriers in the labour market than in the higher education sector. Unequal returns present a serious challenge to social justice and ethnic integration in Britain.

References

Becker, G. (1962). Investment in Human Capital: A Theoretical Analysis. *The Journal of Political Economy, 70*(5), 9–49.

Berthoud, R., & Blekesaune, M. (2006). *Persistent Employment Disadvantage, 1974 to 2003*. Working Chapter of Institute for Social and Economic Research, Chapter 2006–09. Colchester: University of Essex.

Bhattacharyya, G., Ison, L., & Blair, M. (2003). *Minority Ethnic Attainment and Participation in Education and Training: The Evidence*. London: Department for Education and Skills. http://webarchive.nationalarchives.gov.uk/20130401151715/http://www.education.gov.uk/publications/eOrderingDownload/RTP01-03MIG1734.pdf.

Breach, A., & Li, Y. (2017). *Gender Pay Gap by Ethnicity in Britain—Briefing*. London: Fawcett. https://www.fawcettsociety.org.uk/Handlers/Download.ashx?IDMF=f31d6adc-9e0e-4bfe-a3df-3e85605ee4a9.

Breen, R., Luijkx, R., Müller, W., & Pollak, R. (2009). Non-persistent Inequality in Educational Attainment: Evidence from Eight European Countries. *American Journal of Sociology, 114*(5), 1475–1521.

Cheung, S., & Heath, A. (2007). Nice Work If You Can Get It: Ethnic Penalties in Great Britain. In A. Heath & S. Y. Cheung (Eds.), *Unequal Chances: Ethnic Minorities in Western Labour Markets* (pp. 505–548). Oxford: Oxford University Press.

Cutz, A. (2014). University Completion Among the Children of Immigrants. In A. Heath & Y. Brinbaum (Eds.), *Unequal Attainments: Ethnic Educational Inequalities in Ten Western Countries* (pp. 167–191). Oxford: Oxford University Press.

Dale, A., Shaheen, N., Kalra, V., & Fieldhouse, E. (2002). Routes into Education and Employment for Young Pakistani and Bangladeshi Women in the UK. *Ethnic and Racial Studies, 25*, 942–968.

Demireva, N., & Heath, A. (2017). Minority Embeddedness and Economic Integration: Is Diversity or Homogeneity Associated with Better Employment Outcomes? *Social Inclusion, 5*(1), 20–31.

Devine, F., & Li, Y. (2013). The Changing Relationship Between Origins, Education and Destinations in the 1990s and 2000s. *British Journal of Sociology of Education, 34*(5–6), 766–791.

Dustmann, C., & Fabbri, F. (2005). Immigrants in the British Labour Market. *Fiscal Studies, 26*(4), 423–470.

Gallie, D. (Ed.). (1988). *Employment in Britain.* Oxford: Basil Blackwell.

Goldthorpe, J. H. (1996). Problems of "Meritocracy". In R. Erikson & J. O. Jonsson (Eds.), *Can Education Be Equalised? The Swedish Case in Comparative Perspective* (pp. 255–287). Oxford: Westview Press.

Heath, A., & McMahon, D. (1997). Education and Occupational Attainments: The Impact of Ethnic Origins. In V. Karn (Ed.), *Ethnicity in the 1991 Census: Employment, Education and Housing Among the Ethnic Minority Populations of Britain* (pp. 97–113). London: The Stationery Office.

Heath, A., & McMahon, D. (2005). Social Mobility of Ethnic Minorities. In G. Loury, T. Modood, & S. Teles (Eds.), *Ethnicity, Social Mobility and Public Policy: Comparing the US and UK* (pp. 393–413). Cambridge: Cambridge University Press.

Heath, A., & Li, Y. (2008). Period, Life-Cycle and Generational Effects on Ethnic Minority Success in the Labour Market. *Kölner Zeitschrift für Soziologie und Sozialpsychologie, 48,* 277–306.

Heath, A., & Martin, J. (2012). Can Religious Affiliation Explain 'Ethnic' Inequalities in the Labour Market? *Ethnic and Racial Studies, 36*(6), 1–23.

Iganski, P., & Payne, G. (1996). Declining Racial Disadvantage in the British Labour Market. *Ethnic and Racial Studies, 19*(1), 113–134.

Iganski, P., & Payne, G. (1999). Socio-Economic Re-structuring and Employment: The Case of Minority Ethnic Groups. *British Journal of Sociology, 50*(2), 195–216.

Lessard-Phillips, L., & Li, Y. (2017). The Social Stratification of Education in the UK: A Study of Minority Ethnic Groups' Educational Attainment Over Three Generations. *Social Inclusion, 5*(1), 45–54.

Li, Y. (2010). The Labour Market Situation of Minority Ethnic Groups in Britain and the USA. *EurAmerica: A Journal of European and American Studies, 40*(2), 259–309.

Li, Y. (2012). Ethnic Wage Gaps in Britain and the US. In P. Lambert, R. Connelly, R. Blackburn, & V. Gayle (Eds.), *Social Stratification: Trends and Processes* (pp. 167–179). Farnham: Ashgate.

Li, Y., & Devine, F. (2011). Is Social Mobility Really Declining? Intergenerational Class Mobility in Britain in the 1990s and the 2000s. *Sociological Research Online.* http://www.socresonline.org.uk/16/3/4.html.

Li, Y., & Devine, F. (2014). Social Mobility in Britain, 1991–2011. In L. Archer, A. Mann, & J. Stanley (Eds.), *Understanding Employer Engagement in Education: Theories and Evidence* (pp. 79–91). London: Routledge.

Li, Y., & Heath, A. (2008). Ethnic Minority Men in British Labour Market (1972–2005). *International Journal of Sociology and Social policy, 28*(5/6), 231–244.

Li, Y., & Heath, A. (2010). Struggling onto the Ladder, Climbing the Rungs: Employment Status and Class Position by Minority Ethnic Groups in Britain (1972–2005). In J. Stillwell, P. Norman, C. Thomas, & P. Surridge (Eds.), *Population, Employment, Health and Well-Being* (pp. 83–97). London: Springer.

Li, Y., & Heath, A. (2016). Class Matters: A Study of Minority and Majority Social Mobility in Britain, 1982–2011. *American Journal of Sociology, 122*(1), 162–200.

National Employment Panel in Association with the EMBF. (2007). *60/76: The Business Commission on Race Equality in the Workplace*, NEP.

Office for National Statistics. (2011, March). *2011 Census: Key Statistics for England and Wales.* http://www.ons.gov.uk/ons/dcp171778_290685.pdf.

Platt, L. (2005). Intergenerational Social Mobility of Minority Ethnic Groups in Britain. *Sociology, 39*(3), 455–461.

Rumbaut, R. (2004). Ages, Life Stages, and Generational Cohorts: Decomposing the Immigrant First and Second Generations in the United States. *International Migration Review, 38*(3), 1160–1205.

Wood, M., Hales, J., Purdon, S., Sejersen, T., & Hayllar, O. (2009). *A Test for Racial Discrimination in Recruitment Practice in British Cities.* DWP Research Report 607. Leeds: Corporate Document Services.

7

Should I Stay or Should I Go? BME Academics and the Decision to Leave UK Higher Education

Kalwant Bhopal, Hazel Brown and June Jackson

Introduction

This chapter examines the experiences of Black and Minority Ethnic (BME)[1] academics in the UK higher education sector. It specifically explores how factors such as gender, age and type of university affect

This chapter is dedicated to our friend and colleague June Jackson who sadly passed away in 2017, with love.

[1]We are aware of the problems surrounding the use of the term BME. We recognise the limitations of the term and the incorrect assumption that BME groups are homogenous. We use this term to refer to those who are from Black, Asian or mixed heritage backgrounds. Furthermore, this is the term that is used by the Equality Challenge Unit in their research and references to external sources.

K. Bhopal (✉)
University of Birmingham, Birmingham, UK
e-mail: K.Bhopal@bham.ac.uk

H. Brown
University of Winchester, Winchester, UK
e-mail: hazel.brown@winchester.ac.uk

© The Author(s) 2018
J. Arday and H. S. Mirza (eds.), *Dismantling Race in Higher Education*,
https://doi.org/10.1007/978-3-319-60261-5_7

decisions to leave UK higher education to work overseas. It draws on research funded by the Equality Challenge Unit which consisted of 1200 survey questionnaires and 41 in-depth interviews to examine decision making processes in making the decision to leave UK higher education (Bhopal et al. 2015). The chapter concludes by suggesting policy recommendations for change in UK higher education for the retention and inclusion of BME academic staff.

Background and Context

The focus on career progression and opportunities for BME academics is a welcome development within UK higher education. Whilst gender has clearly taken a central focus, it is only recently that race and ethnic differences in higher education have been given greater attention. For example, career opportunities for female academic staff has been an increasing area of focus in research and policy making in the UK higher education sector over the last few decades. This work has highlighted the low representation of women at senior levels in the academy and the barriers they face to progression to senior levels (UCU 2012; Morley 2014; Savigny 2014). In particular it has focused on their under-representation in Science, Technology, Engineering, Mathematics and Medicine (STEMM subjects). The Athena Swan Charter, established a decade ago by the Equality Challenge Unit, encourages universities to review their practices to ensure equality for women, and recognises employment excellence for women in higher education in STEMM subjects (ECU 2014a). Based on their good practice in the progression of women in STEMM subjects, universities are awarded a gold, silver or bronze award. This has helped support and encourage a range of actions in universities to progress greater gender equality for women, although the limitations on women academics' careers are still apparent (Morley 2013; Manfredi et al. 2014; Savigny 2014). However, there is some suggestion that such work on gender equality fails to explore the impact of ethnicity and race. Jones (2006: 148) argues that the focus on gender 'only serves to highlight the lack of progress on the race/ethnicity front'. Pilkington (2011: 129) argues that the positive action taken in relation to gender is not reflected in inclusive policy making related to race and that, 'the same cannot be said of race where the Whiteness of senior staff is taken for granted'. Furthermore, Bhopal (2014: 13) suggests that gender experiences refer to the experiences of those 'women who share the backgrounds of the traditional academic elites'. Consequently, BME women are disadvantaged because 'the experiences of Black women academics are structured by racialised practices, from which white women may derive benefit' (Jones 2001: 159).

During the past decade there has been a significant increase in the numbers of BME UK academic staff in higher education—from 6000 staff in 2003–2004 to almost 10,700 in 2013–2014 (ECU 2015). But, BME staff are far less likely to be in senior roles compared to their White colleagues; 11.2% of UK white academics were professors compared to 9.8% of UK BME staff (of which only 4.5% were Black). There are only 20 deputy or pro vice-chancellors who are BME compared to the majority, 530 who are White (ECU 2015). There is recent evidence to suggest that BME academics remain disadvantaged in higher education. They are more likely to experience subtle, covert forms of racism, less likely to be pushed forward for promotion and less likely to be in senior decision making roles compared to their White colleagues (Bhopal and Jackson 2013; ECU 2014b). Morley (2014: 116) argues that the low percentage of BME women academics is global, rather than national, as women from a variety of nationalities are under-represented in the 'prestige economy' of research, which is the 'pathway to academic seniority and an indicator for promotion'. She also found that leadership was often perceived as a 'loss' by women—loss of status and self-esteem if they were unsuccessful in their applications, and, if successful, a loss of independence, research time and a necessity to conform to masculine 'norms and values that are alien and alienating' (2014: 119).

The most important recent policy development regarding race equality is the Race Equality Charter mark which was introduced in January 2016 in which a total of 8 out of 21 institutions were awarded a bronze charter mark. The Race Equality Charter mark works in a similar way to the Athena SWAN Charter but its main focus is on race equality, particularly in relation to improving the representation, progress and success of minority ethnic staff and students in higher education.

It is underpinned by five key principles: recognising that racism is part of everyday life and racial inequalities manifest themselves in everyday situations, processes and behaviours; individuals from all ethnic backgrounds should benefit equally from the opportunities available to them; solutions to racial inequality should have a long term impact through institutional culture change; recognising that those from minority ethnic backgrounds are not a homogenous group and such complexity must be recognised when exploring race equality; and intersectional identities should be considered when discussing race equality. The Race Equality Charter mark covers academic staff; professional and support staff; student progression and attainment and diversity in the curriculum (http://www.ecu.ac.uk/equality-charters/race-equality-charter/). It is clearly too early to tell if the Race Equality Charter will make a difference to the inclusion of BME staff in UK higher education, but if tied to funding more universities will be encouraged to sign up to it.

The Study

The study was funded by the Equality Challenge Unit and the aims of the research were:

1. To understand the extent to which UK academics consider moving to work in higher education overseas and whether there are any ethnic differences related to this;
2. To explore the push and pull factors which contribute to actual or potential overseas higher education;
3. To suggest recommendations for higher education for the retention of BME academics to UK higher education.

A total of 1200 academics participated in a survey questionnaire which was distributed to all higher education institutions in the UK. The survey was distributed via the Equality Challenge Unit as well as via established diversity networks. Following the survey questionnaire, a total of 41 participants took part in in-depth interviews. This included 14 with UK experience only, 12 currently working in the UK but with previous overseas experience, and 15 currently working overseas (12 with and three without work experience in UK higher education). The survey questionnaire data was analysed using SPSS and the qualitative data was analysed using themes and codes developed from NVIVO.

Survey Findings

The survey was open to both BME and non BME academics in order to have a comparison group. Nearly 85% of respondents were white and just over 15% were BME. Non-parametric inferential statistics (chi square test of association) were used to analyse associations between the categorical data of ethnicity, gender, age, type of institution, and motivations to leave the UK to work in HE overseas.

Who Is More Likely to Want to Move Overseas?

The survey findings suggest that BME academics (83.6%) are significantly more likely than non-BME academics (71.0%) to have ever considered moving overseas to work (chi-square $= 5.138$, df1, $p = 0.023$). No one BME group (Black, Asian, mixed race and 'other') was more likely than another to be looking for overseas work (chi-square $= 0.877$, df3, $p = 0.831$). Additionally, no significant associations were found between non-BME and BME academics with what was sought overseas (chi-square $= 9.314$, df6, $p = 0.157$), nor within BME groups (chi-square $= 12.020$, df15, $p = 0.678$). For example, the data was examined to see if academics were seeking a permanent or temporary academic post, a temporary secondment, a job outside of academia, or a move overseas to look after family members or to retire. Respondents were further asked if they were currently considering a move overseas but there were no significant differences between non-BME and BME groups, with 62.6% of white academics and 65.5% of BME respondents currently considering a move (chi square $= 0.192$, df1, $p = 0.661$). An analysis between BME groups also showed no association between ethnicity and the current desire to move overseas (chi square $= 6.424$, df3, $p = 0.093$).

This would indicate that whilst more BME academics consider a move overseas more go on to reject the idea. It is possible that more BME than white academics have family links overseas and hence find the idea of making such a move more attractive.

Where Would Respondents Want to Move to?

A significant association between ethnic identity and preferred world location of choice (chi-square = 58.365, df36, $p = 0.011$) was found. Asian respondents (19% of Asian selections) were more likely to choose to move to the Far East (e.g. China, India, Japan and Singapore) than they were to select to move elsewhere in Europe (9.5% of Asian selections). The most popular destination for Black, Asian, Mixed race and White respondents was the United States of America. Those falling into the category of 'other' race (which included Arab, Jewish and Hispanic/Latin) were most likely to select to move to a destination within Europe. This tallies with the idea that we choose our location based on family heritage. It is reasonable to assume that potential migrants look only at countries where they are able to speak the language of the native residents.

The Pull of Overseas Life: Is It Stronger for Males or Females?

Amongst all participants (BME and non-BME) 68.4% of female respondents had considered leaving the UK against 76.1% of male respondents. Females were more likely to have multiple reasons for moving overseas and males were more likely than females to be looking for a new academic post overseas (chi-square = 24.036, df7, $p = 0.001$). When White academics were removed from the data set it was found that both BME academic males and females were just as likely to be seeking work overseas. The strongest pull factor for all respondents was the existence of a full-time, permanent contract. For those that had worked overseas but had now returned to the UK both white and BME academics stated academic/professional reasons and family/personal reasons for returning.

Does University Type Make a Difference?

The data was analysed by university group (pre-1992, post 1992, university college and specialist university) and no significant associations were found between BME and non-BME respondents and their desire to leave the UK. The type of university that respondents worked in made no difference in whether they would consider working overseas.

At What Stage of Our Careers Might We Be More Likely to Consider Emigration?

When the data was analysed by both age and salary (salary being indicative of grade) it was found that BME academics were no more or less likely to be considering overseas employment at any one stage of their career life. Interestingly, non-BME academics were more likely to be considering a move overseas when at Lecturer B grade (old universities) or Senior Lecturer grade (new universities). This may be reflective of academics finding promotion difficult in the UK when trying to reach senior grades such as Reader (or Principal Lecturer).

Interview Findings

BME academics who were interviewed for this study contribute in a whole range of ways to the UK higher education sector and are in positions ranging from Researcher to Professor. This includes lecturing, carrying out research, publishing and providing student pastoral care, particularly to BME students who many report seek out the BME staff for advice and guidance. Positive career experiences, such as receiving mentoring from more senior colleagues were reported. However, there are recurring negative experiences (such as being treated as an outsider and experiencing subtle covert racism) that contribute to them considering moving overseas, away from the UK higher education sector.

Push Factors

Outsiders in the Academy—Exclusion and Negative Experiences

BME academics talked about not being accepted in the White space of the academy and having the feeling of being an 'outsider'. This was related to the predominance of white, middle class norms, specifically at senior levels of the academy, in which interviewees had to negotiate norms of whiteness. Assumptions are made by staff and students which lead to a questioning of the legitimacy of the presence of BME academics in professional roles. BME academics are not expected to occupy senior positions and their presence is frequently challenged, as demonstrated below.

And in the interview they asked me: where would you like to be in five years, or ten years or something. And I said, my goal is to become a full professor and I hope I am one of the few black women who have achieved that. And they started laughing, they said, oh no, there is a lot more people to come before you. I got up and walked out. (Black Caribbean and White, female)

And I got, I can't remember the exact number. But my official name [sounds more English] and I don't give any indication that I am of Indian origin, and I always got shortlisted by other universities for Professorships, by all these universities in the UK. But immediately they see me....their faces drop because they weren't expecting to see a Black woman. I know it was more than a dozen, I went for more than a dozen. (Asian Indian, female)

I do think a number of young black academics end up as research assistants rather than as academics in full-time posts. And I can see that happening now. There was a case where one of my PhD students, who has now moved abroad, was really qualified for a position and they didn't give it to him, they gave it to someone else. But then employed him to do the research. Because he was black [they considered] he could do the research in London among the black community. They wouldn't give him the fixed term three year research officer post. And I think that is characteristic. Either they question our ability to do intellectual work, even though you have your doctorate and you have proved yourself. And then they are quite happy to employ you as a research assistant, and collect the data which is analysed by somebody else or you might do the analysis but your name would be the last person on the list of contributors. (Black Caribbean, female)

For those whose academic work focuses on race, ethnic or Black studies, this raises additional concerns.

I think particularly, you think about the dominant universities around the country, if they get an approach from somebody who says that their focus is black people it's immediately rendering itself as being peripheral or being marginal. (Black Caribbean, male)

Barriers to Career Progression—Mentoring, Networking and Social Capital

Interviewees spoke about how white senior academics often provide mentoring, coaching and nurturing support to junior white academics, for example advising them about submitting grant applications and suggesting which journals they should publish in. The informal nature of this type of behaviour had an exclusionary impact on the experiences of BME academics who did not easily fit into this culture and have access to such social capital. Many of the interviewees find themselves unable to draw on networks of support which would enable them to access the social and cultural capital needed to progress in the academy.

The white lecturers were groomed and helped, and I just did everything on my own. I didn't get any mentoring, and I think that would help. And also how to progress in the system. It's the politics as well. If I played the game and pretended that I needed help, I think it's a game. For example, I turned down an invitation from a more senior [female] colleague and after that I found my progression more difficult. I think it's about enabling and mentoring, and valuing minority ethnic [academics]. They do value you, but they value you in order to use you. They valued my publications, but they didn't want to give me the promotion. And it is a fact that as a black person, as a minority ethnic person you have got to be twice as good as your white counterparts, I mean that's a fact. There are people, I have got so many examples, who have got fewer publications than I have and then you have got to have twice as many publications as your white counterparts and that is something that shouldn't be, that's not fair really. (Asian Indian, female)

…there was a Dean's job going within our system. I applied for it. Somebody else applied for it who only had a Masters and no business experience or anything. But they got the job. After that I heard that I was the best one on presentation and everything. And I thought, there is something here which is not quite right, they are not taking the best person for the position. I am not saying I am the best person, but whatever it is, they should have taken the best person. And I was the only one who was the Professor, I had the qualifications, more international clout and experience and all the rest of it. So it was a bit bizarre. So you just thought to yourself ok, maybe I'll just do research and I'll just trundle along making bids and all the rest of it. So then I thought, well, I am actually not being stretched any more and so I should really start looking at different ideas. (Asian Indian, male)

Pull Factors

Reasons for Considering Leaving the UK Higher Education Sector

As well as the negative experiences of the higher education sector in the UK, a combination of factors attract BME academics to higher education overseas. Several interviewees had direct contact with BME colleagues who had migrated overseas, particularly to the USA and Australia. The reports they received from their colleagues overseas contrasted significantly with the negative experiences they had in the UK, and the experiences of others. The USA was a particularly strong positive example, particularly the existence of a critical mass of BME staff in several institutions.

I got so fed up with it all. In the end I had made a lot of friends, and people I knew in the States. I rang them up one day and I told them about some of the things I had been experiencing. One of my friends said, oh, why don't you come over here. And he showed me all the different websites that you go on, and the jobs. And he gave me a little bit of information about it. And I applied for about three or four jobs. (Black Caribbean and White, female)

I thought there are so many people of African descent in the US, someone must be writing about this and I was just shocked and amazed to receive the kind of reception that I received, I went to [US university] and, I kid you not, a whole new world opened up. And: I need to take a look at this study, and take a look at that study, and have you read this, and have you read that, and treating it as though what I wanted to look at was actually of consequence. So that's what made me start to look at the US differently. (Black Caribbean, female)

For several interviewees an attraction to overseas was the opportunity to work on research areas such as race, ethnicity and Black studies which were seen as 'credible' disciplines.

In terms of finding an institutional home, obviously [for my field] it is a lot easier to do so in the US than in the UK. There are no institutional homes for black studies [in the UK]. But there were a lot of opportunities [in the US]. I was hired as a lecturer in black and minority cultures at [name of US university]. (Black Caribbean and White, male)

There is a kind of space, a kind of acceptance of work around race equality, black studies, etc. And I feel almost ashamed to have to admit it, but you go over there as a black British academic, and especially early on, you are slightly overawed, you are slightly bowled over by just seeing these senior black academics and being able to sit and listen to them and talk to them. Whenever I come back from those kinds of conferences in the States it's a bit like when Christmas is over and you have that dip at the beginning of January, coming back to Britain is a bit like that, because suddenly you don't have those conversations, you don't have those networks, they are just not here in the same way. (Black Caribbean and White, male)

Several interviewees talked about wanting to 'give something back' to their country of origin, either where they were born or where they had family connections.

...that attachment is also in my own mind associated with the need to give back to the continent. I think some of us are quite pained by the fact that the continent still remains labelled with all sorts of words that relate to being underdeveloped, when in fact a very large pool of academics and very highly educated and experienced people are living out in the diaspora. I think at some point we have an obligation to come back and give back to the continent. (Black African, male)

I see the change in the academic world in China. And in particular in the last few years the resources for research in education has rapidly increased. And also China has opened the doors, really wants to catch up with the international academic society in all aspects. And young people really need guidance, need some proper guidance to catch up with the international standards. (Chinese, female)

What Might Attract BME Academics Back to the UK Higher Education Sector?

Several people stressed that although it was important to have policies in place, they would need to see clear visible signs of change for the inclusion of BME staff in the academy, in order for them to return to the UK.

I feel the number one thing, and this would work for me, is if I had a really clear sense that there was an institution that _valued_ the presence of racialised faculty. Meaning that they problematized the fact that there weren't people there and that they had a mandate to _have_ to attract people. And I still look at websites to see if I can see that. I think that's what would be primary. I'd have to know that there was a change that was supported by the institution itself, that it thought it was problematic and wanted to address it. So that is number one. And no weird things like a Diversity Report . That's problematic. It really would have to be reflected in: Research Institutes; programmatic language that you have programmes that you are now trying to address issues with. (Black Caribbean, female)

I think on a very simple level, the sense that academic life is more diverse would make you certainly think, well, I can come and go, I can do this. It would certainly make you think that. That there were just as many opportunities for you there as away. (Black Caribbean and White, female)

A sense of belonging in the UK, and being included in networks even whilst working overseas, would contribute to BME academics maintaining their links to the UK with the possibility of returning in the future.

…And as institutions internationalise, maybe they are going to think more creatively – I could give a Skype lecture. Those things would begin to pull you back. Research collaborations would pull you back, if you were in a research network and you were working with others, those kinds of things I think

would. And I am certain that people would have to feel that there was an opening to take the chance. (Black Caribbean and White, female)

Some respondents suggested a broadening of the curriculum to give value to the study of race and ethnicity as a valued subject area in the UK higher education sector as an attraction.

A university would have to have the broad enough shoulders to set up a unit. There should be something like 'Centre for Black British Studies'. What's wrong with that? I mean, there is nothing wrong with that. And that could embrace mainstream scholars as well, not black academics only. So, a Centre for Black British Studies. It's like a snowball effect. If there was one Black British Centre there would be others then. (Black, male)

If we are to develop things in the UK it cannot just be – here we have a Centre in London. I think it would be great if it was also a sense of how black studies, diaspora studies, postcolonial studies is linked to Leeds, Bradford, Sheffield, and various places around the UK rather than being institutionalised or support for a growing space for black British intellectuals in London. (Black Caribbean and White, male)

The survey findings suggest that BME academics are more likely than non-BME academics to consider a move overseas for employment. The destination of preference is the USA or the Far East. This urge to seek new employment crosses boundaries of gender, age and experience. Whilst many reject the idea of a move overseas it is the push and pull factors that are of interest and were explored in the interviews.

The interviews with BME academics shed light on aspects of their experiences in UK HE institutions, why they consider moving overseas, and what might retain them, or attract them back. A striking aspect of the experiences of the interviewees is the recurrent theme of feeling an 'outsider' and not belonging. This is reinforced by lack of access to career development opportunities and in particular informal opportunities such as their mentoring and advice. The attraction to migrate overseas, or the 'pull factors' is based on a number of academic and personal issues. The reports of the value given to race and ethnic studies in the US was noteworthy and could lead to the development of inclusive curricula in the UK higher education sector.

Conclusions

Our research suggests that greater change is needed in UK higher education for the retention of BME staff. This change has to take place in specific areas such as the prioritisation of race equality; higher education institutions valuing diversity; developing inclusive curricula; addressing micro-aggressions, inequalities and subtle forms of racism; recruitment and promotion; coaching and mentoring; addressing workload and development issues and networking and addressing isolation issues for BME academics. We suggest that higher education institutions must be proactive in the inclusion of BME academics at all levels, particularly in relation to the acknowledgement of racism and indeed how to tackle it. Senior leaders must prioritise race equality within their institution and within the sector as a whole. One of the ways this could take place is for institutions to engage with the Race Equality Charter mark which would demonstrate the institution's commitment to race equality, inclusion and diversity. A further addition to this would be making training on unconscious bias compulsory and active bystander strategies as embedded elements of training. We suggest that, 'there is a systematic perception that race equality is not being prioritised within the sector, which is representative of a culture that is pushing BME academics away, and preventing them from returning. Ensuring that race equality is prioritised within the sector in meaningful ways is not easy, but is the first step to instigating systemic, long-term culture change' (Bhopal et al. 2015: 18). Whilst the issues we highlight here have been constantly reported in research on race and inequality, we argue that it is time for real change in the sector. Furthermore, the issues we report are not isolated to a single institution, rather they exist in the higher education sector itself. If institutions are serious about tackling inequalities in higher education, then they must address inequalities in their own organisations and examine how they can move towards an agenda that demonstrates equity and social justice.

References

Bhopal, K. (2014). *The Experience of BME Academics in Higher Education: Aspirations in the Face of Inequality*. Stimulus Paper. London: Leadership Foundation for Higher Education.

Bhopal, K., & Jackson, J. (2013). *The Experiences of Black and Ethnic Minority Academics, Multiple Identities and Career Progression*. Southampton: University of Southampton EPSRC.

Bhopal, K., Brown, H., & Jackson, J. (2015). *Academic Flight: How to Encourage Black and Minority Ethnic Academics to Say in UK Higher Education*. London: ECU.

Equality Challenge Unit (ECU). (2014a). *Evaluating the Effectiveness and Impact of the Athena SWAN Charter*. London: ECU.

Equality Challenge Unit (ECU). (2014b). *Equality in Higher Education: Statistical Report, Part 1: Staff*. London: ECU.

Equality Challenge Unit (ECU). (2015) *Equality in Higher Education: Statistical Report*. London: ECU.

Jones, C. (2001). Black Women in Ivory Towers: Racism and Sexism in the Academy. In P. Anderson & J. Williams (Eds.), *Identity and Difference in Higher Education* (pp. 147–161). Farnham: Ashgate.

Jones, C. (2006). Falling Between the Cracks: What Diversity Means for Black Women in Higher Education. *Policy Futures in Education, 4*(2), 145–159.

Manfredi, S., Grisoni, L., Handley, K., Nestor, R., & Cooke, F. (2014). *Gender and Higher Education Leadership: Researching the Careers of Top Management Programme Alumni*. London: Leadership Foundation for Higher Education.

Morley, L. (2013). The Rules of the Game: Women and the Leaderist Turn in Higher Education. *Gender and Education, 25*(1), 116–131.

Morley, L. (2014). Lost Leaders: Women in the Global Academy. *Higher Education Research and Development, 33*(1), 114–128.

Pilkington, A. (2011). *Institutional Racism in the Academy, A Case Study*. Stoke on Trent: Trentham Books.

Savigny, H. (2014). Women, Know Your Limits: Cultural Sexism in Academia. *Gender and Education, 26*(7), 794–809.

University and College Union (UCU). (2012). *The Position of Women and BME Staff in Professorial Roles in UK HEIs*. London: UCU.

Part III
Outsiders Within the Academy: Surviving the 'Sheer Weight of Whiteness'

8

'Are You Supposed to Be in Here?' Racial Microaggressions and Knowledge Production in Higher Education

Azeezat Johnson and Remi Joseph-Salisbury

Introduction

> Remi: *Having arrived early to work on a Monday morning, I keyed in the security code and entered the staff room. I photocopied the papers for the seminar sessions I would deliver later that day. As I stood waiting for the final copies to print, a member of the cleaning staff entered the room. 'Are you supposed to be in here?' she asked in an accusatory tone. Slightly stunned, I simply responded 'yes'.*

Despite often being imagined as a utopian space beyond racial inequality, the academe is deeply implicated in maintaining and perpetuating the conditions that give rise to racial microaggressions

A. Johnson
Queen Mary University of London, London, UK
e-mail: azeezat.johnson@qmul.ac.uk

R. Joseph-Salisbury (✉)
The University of Manchester, Manchester, UK

© The Author(s) 2018
J. Arday and H. S. Mirza (eds.), *Dismantling Race in Higher Education*,
https://doi.org/10.1007/978-3-319-60261-5_8

143

(Henry 1994; Stockdill and Danico 2012; Turney et al. 2002). Thus, as we theorise racial microaggressions as abstract phenomena occurring *out there*, we live with the pernicious effects of that which we theorise in a space that vehemently denies its racist underbelly (Back 2004; Stockdill and Danico 2012; Tyrer 2004). In this chapter we draw upon auto-ethnographic accounts and the experiences of other racialised academics in order to illustrate some of the ways in which white supremacy is perpetuated within Higher Education (HE). In placing ourselves at the centre, we provide a counter-narrative to the pervasive myth that HE is somehow beyond the perpetuation of racial inequity. This is what is encapsulated in the racial microaggression recalled in the chapter's epigraph. This interaction summarises the questions at the heart of our positionalities within HE—are we as scholars of colour supposed to be here? On what and whose terms is our presence acceptable (or perhaps tolerable)? How are the answers to these questions negotiated?

As we consider these questions and develop an understanding of the processes that shape our experiences, we draw upon what George Yancy (2008) terms an *episteme of Blackness*—a way of knowing that is developed experientially, collectively and intergenerationally. In developing this episteme of Blackness we draw from Critical Race Theory (CRT), Black Feminism and Postcolonial Theory: as Yancy points out, this episteme has been essential to Black survival. Through our conversations with each other and amongst other doctoral students, we have developed and continue to develop an episteme of Blackness that allows us to better understand, navigate and negotiate our position within the academe. Once we recognise that lived experiences of Blackness engender a unique and valuable source of knowledge (Solorzano and Yosso 2002), we are better placed to recognise the way that race operates in the chapter's epigraph specifically, and our lives generally. It is perhaps this episteme that allows Gulam (2002: 10) to observe such 'perceptional differences' between Black and white academics views on race in HE.

Thus, we work to disrupt the *epistemologies of ignorance* (Mills 2007; Dotson 2011), or the 'structured blindness' that occlude an understanding of the normalised racist structures that shape lived experiences outside and inside of the academe (Yancy 2008: 22). We charge that approaches to scholarship that centre whiteness have been unwilling and unable to see academic knowledge as a particular institutionalised (and therefore legitimised) branch of knowledge production. This works to silence and ignore knowledge produced outside of the confines set up by these institutions, perpetuating the cycle of epistemic violence. We understand that HE generally, and 'traditional' social science specifically, are characterised by these epistemologies of ignorance. So whilst the very notion of an episteme of Blackness may seem anathema to traditional social science, we believe it has the potential to offer an important and timely corrective. This is particularly important for those of us trying to find a way to negotiate these spaces where our very presence is questioned.

As in the epigraph, an episteme of Blackness is particularly useful in developing an understanding of racial microaggressions. This is an important part of the endeavour we undertake in this chapter. For that reason, we use the first section to define racial microaggressions as a theoretical concept. In the second section we consider knowledge production in the academe and how we as scholars of colour are faced with the threat of being fixed as a spectacle. Before moving into the third section, we ask, what role does this threat play in reproducing/representing the academe as *the* legitimate space of knowledge production? In the concluding section we look at ways in which we may subvert and speak back to the racial processes that threaten to define our experiences.

So before discussing our own experiences in more depth, let us first define what is invoked by the racial microaggressions concept.

Defining Racial Microaggressions

It was the African American psychiatrist Chester Pierce (1969) who first theorised the concept of racial microaggressions. According to Pierce (1969), racial microaggressions are a form of systemic, everyday racism. Often subtle and seemingly innocuous in nature, racial microaggressions threaten to 'keep those at the racial margins in their place' (Pérez Huber and Solorzano 2015: 298; Rollock 2012). Racial microaggressions do not occur in abstraction from white supremacist racial structures, they are inextricably linked to those structures. Not only does white supremacy 'provide the ideological foundations that justify' racial microaggressions (Pérez Huber and Solórzano 2015: 303), but, in turn, racial microaggressions, mediated by institutional racism, act to reinforce those very ideological foundations (Pérez Huber and Solorzano 2015). In part, it is the obfuscation of this symbiosis that enables microaggressions to seem relatively innocuous. Derrick Bell (1993: 6) observes that invisibility and normality make 'discriminatory acts more oppressive than ever'. Similarly, Chester Pierce (1974: 520) argues that microaggressions are 'only micro in name' and given their incessancy, produce a cumulative threat to the wellbeing of people of colour.

As racism manifests in increasingly normalised and subtle forms (Bell 1993; Delgado and Stefancic 2012), the concept of racial microaggressions provides a useful analytical tool that responds to the changing face of racism (Sue 2010). As Nicola Rollock (2012: 517) puts it, the concept allows us to move beyond 'a narrow and unsophisticated version of racism which is seen to exist only in overt forms'. It is perhaps for this reason that the concept has gained traction in the popular discourse of recent years. In 2014, first on US university campuses, but quickly followed by UK campuses, students of colour utilised the concept of racial microaggressions in order to bring attention to the everyday forms of racism they face on university campuses.[1] The concept has also been used in a plethora of CRT-informed education research (Constantine et al. 2008; Ek et al. 2010; Kohli and Solórzano 2012; Pittman 2012; Rollock 2012; Solorzano et al. 2000). Our chapter continues in this tradition.

As we have suggested, in isolation, racial microaggressions can be difficult to identify, and even more difficult to challenge; this is their very nature (Sue 2010; Sue et al. 2008). Nevertheless, as Chester Pierce (1988: 33) argues, 'all blacks must have a firm theoretical grasp of racism in order to dilute its crippling effects'. Recognising epistemes of Blackness as a legitimate site of knowledge offers an entry point for us to develop the firm 'theoretical grasp' of our experiences: this is essential to our ability to navigate HE. Thus as we return once more to the episode that opens this chapter, we see this instance not in

---

[1]The 'I too am Oxford' campaign was one such campaign (see Edds 2014).

abstraction from, but always situated in a wider context of systemic and institutional white supremacy (Pérez Huber and Solorzano 2015). The racial microaggression is therefore always able to tell us something about the wider context in which it occurs. The university space renders Remi *a body out of place*, and thus, engenders the possibility for this micro-aggressive act. To be clear, it is the constitutive conditions that make this interaction racially significant. Moreover, the microaggression acts to re-entrench those very conditions, to remind us of our marginal position. The microaggression is always in iteration with institutional and macro white supremacy.

What follows are a series of vignettes that describe just some of our experiences. Through these vignettes we weave an analysis that situates the racial microaggressions in their broader context and allows us to consider how, as scholars of colour, we are visible as spectacle in the academe. Finally, having identified the racial processes that implicate us, we consider some of the work we have done to dilute and subvert the effects of white supremacy in these spaces that perpetuate our marginalisation.

The Whiteness of Academia: Can We Teach Here?

Remi: *I arrived at the seminar room five minutes early to make sure the PowerPoint and videos for the session were set up before the students arrived. The session in the room had just ended and the students were packing up. I entered the room and spoke to my colleague who had led that session. As we conversed, one of the students in the room, with piercing incredulity shouted 'Do **you** teach here?'*

The incredulity of this student when questioning Remi's ability to 'teach here' illustrates how easily our bodies are rendered as out of place. As we have suggested, our absence from these spaces (see Shilliam 2016) is intertwined with how white supremacist racial structures sustain themselves on the micro-level. Through this process, white bodies are neutralised and recognised as belonging within these spaces, 'while others are marked out as trespassers, who are, in accordance with how both spaces and bodies are imagined (politically, historically and conceptually), circumscribed as being 'out of place'' (Puwar 2004: 8).

Much like the suspicion that lingers in the question that framed this chapter, as a Black mixed-race man, Remi's marked body is, for the white gaze, more intelligible as the Black male trespasser (or criminal) than as an academic (Yancy 2008). In the parallels between the episodes, we may begin to see how racial microaggressions pose a cumulative burden that we as scholars of colour must face. In this second episode, Remi is reminded of the first and the threat to his legitimacy in the academe is reinforced. This is particularly insidious when it is our legitimacy as knowledge holders that is called into question: 'do you teach here?' might be interpreted as a metonym for the more intrusive and challenging metacommunication: '*can* you teach here?' The racialisation of Black bodies as hypervisible works to position us as too specific to be able to act as 'objective' or 'universal' producers of knowledge.

Our Blackness within these academic spaces works to remind us of how often we become known (and, in part, need to know ourselves) through this role of an objectified Other (Yancy 2008). And yet this is not reflected in the way in which academics speak of racism: so much of the academic discourse on racism locates the language of racism as 'out there' on the everyday researched bodies. As Les Back (2004: 4) argues,

> For many academics the face of racism is that of the moral degenerate, the hateful bigot. So it is unthinkable that such an ugly word could be directed at a genteel, education and liberal don such as themselves.

This logic is of course extendable from the individual professor to the university as an institution. Little is done to understand how racist discourses inform the way in which academia, as a central site of knowledge production, constructs those everyday spaces, and which bodies are seen as knowledge-able in the first place.

The way in which our abilities as researchers are questioned when marked as part of the researched object has been discussed by scholars like Nirmal Puwar (2004: 45) who reflects on a particular encounter

Levi-Strauss had whilst doing research in New York Public Library. Levi-Strauss 'was thrown by the sight of a feathered Indian with a Parker pen' within this space of knowledge development.

> What he sees before his eyes is 'odd' for Levi-Strauss because, for him, the specialist in the image before him does not fit the 'authentic' image of an Indian. As Chow says, 'what confronts the Western scholar is the discomforting fact that the natives are no longer staying in their frames.' (Puwar 2004: 45)

Through this interaction, Levi-Strauss' whiteness is neutralised whilst the "Indian" becomes highlighted and fetishised. The assumed neutrality of this whiteness within a space of learning and as an assumed holder of knowledge is unconsciously yet undoubtedly stained onto the research created through Levi-Strauss and re-created/perpetuated through scholars using and reusing his work within the walls of academia. It is these same academics and texts which are centred in the academic canon without a critical understanding of how whiteness is maintained as neutral; this neutrality of whiteness is simply a different aspect of the systems of power that we are also in the process of studying.

It is within this context that we find ourselves questioning our role within these systems where our melanin is highlighted whilst whiteness is neutralised. Despite becoming a part of the academe as researchers and doctoral students, we know ourselves as apart from these institutions as our bodies trouble the expectations associated with knowledge holders. Our presence within these institutions marks a deviance from the bodies that are seen to occupy the academe as well as the way in which knowledge has been produced. We see our outsiderness manifest at every level of the academe from the curriculum (e.g. #WhyisMyCurriculumWhite, see Peters 2015), to the professorate (e.g. #WhyisntmyprofessorBlack, see Black 2014; Jahi 2014), to the architecture (e.g. #RhodesMustFall, see Elgot 2016). These are the conditions that breed racial microaggressions and threaten to determine our positionalities. Thus we encounter these spaces of knowledge production where our Blackness is part of the spectacle: we are the oddity of the 'feathered Indian with a Parker pen,' attempting to produce research which moves us beyond this position of fetishised spectacle.

The Academic Native Informant

Azeezat: *I remember deciding to come back to university because I desperately wanted to learn more and give back to the Black Muslim women who had taught me how to be and cared for me. Yet when entering the academe I kept feeling that I was being asked to describe and objectify our life experiences for the purposes of overwhelmingly white audiences. What is my role in this?*

This question of whether we belong here requires us to look around and think about what belonging here would mean when so many racialised people are absented as knowledge-holders within this space. This is what Azeezat refers to: what happens when the knowledge produced about our bodies is shared to a majority white audience, reaffirming the distance between racism and our racialised experiences as happening 'out there' rather than 'in here'?

When doing research within the context of these power dynamics, Azeezat is concerned with perpetuating the assumption of the 'natives […] staying in their frames' (Chow cited in Puwar 2004: 45). It is within this context that Khan (2005) and Villenas (1996) found themselves doing work on their own communities and attempting to move through their role as hypervisible academics of colour speaking to primarily white audiences. Specifically, Khan questions her positioning as a researcher living in the USA but doing work about *zina* laws[2] in Pakistan:

As I perform the native and speak about zina laws, I am inviting the viewer back to the familiar position that Islam is once again crushing women. I am therefore suspect. I am suspect to myself: can I do ethical research? Others are also suspicious of me: is she authentic enough? Will she betray us? Although the "good native" connotes a different person to

---

[2]This refers to the illegality of extra-marital relationships.

each of these positions, they all want to know if I am going to be a good girl. (Khan 2005: 2028)

The 'overwhelmingly white' audiences that Azeezat speaks to as a racialised academic informs the way research is created, as well as the tools used to create this research. When we use these ways of knowing to describe our bodies, knowledge-holders remain neutralised bodies through the logic of white supremacy. This positioning is distinguishable from the lived experience of our Blackness within which our bodies are always marked as objects to know. This forces us into a position outlined by W.E.B. Du Bois (2007 [1903]) where we are located between the subjective Self and the objectified Other. Within this logic of double-consciousness, we as racialised academics know ourselves through this relationship to a (white) Self whose subjecthood is defined in contrast to our racialised status as objectified Other. We can never be situated as a Self and the (Black) Other has been used to fix us as racialised spectacle: not as knowledge producers but objects of knowing. In trying to produce knowledge out of this contradiction, it is no surprise that we have difficulties in claiming a voice from this precarious in-between state.

However, this contradiction is not new and has been discussed by Black feminists across disciplines (Collins 1990; hooks 1989; Lorde 1996; Nayak 2015; Noxolo 1999). They all point to how spaces of knowledge production outside of those legitimised by the academe have been essential in developing a way of knowing about our Blackness beyond that of a racialised spectacle. As Black women have historically been excluded from academic institutions, Black feminist scholarship referred to kitchens, hair salons, everyday conversations, musicians, poets and writers as key to understanding how processes of racialisation can be understood in different forms.[3] This Black feminist tradition has included 'searching for its expression in alternative institutional locations and among women who are not commonly perceived as intellectuals' (Collins 1990: 14).

---

[3]At the time of writing this chapter, Beyoncé released a visual album which centred experiences of women across the Black diaspora, leading to a flurry of commentary from Black feminist intellects unpacking this popular cultural artefact (e.g. Harris-Perry 2016; Mock 2016; Oluo 2016).

It is these ways of knowing which challenge the invisibility and centrality of white supremacy in these legitimised spaces of knowledge production. One such example could be seen in the politics behind intersectionality, a term coined by Kimberlé Crenshaw (1989) dispelling the way social categories are assumed to not interact. On the surface, in centring women of colour, Crenshaw worked to illustrate how race, gender and class must be understood in relation to one another. More importantly, Crenshaw works to create new parameters, changing the way in which social categorisations are constituted.

However, this does come without its own problems. Alexander-Floyd (2012) and Bilge (2013) both pointed to how the political impetus behind intersectionality is emptied out from the term in order for it to be used in mainstream feminist research (also see Rodriguez and Freeman 2016). The explicitly Black feminist standpoint which created intersectionality is kept off-stage whilst the term is redeployed for 'the positivist dictates of traditional disciplines' (Alexander-Floyd 2012: 14). This is what happens when a few racialised persons are let into the walls of academia without the knowledge produced by these institutions being challenged. Indeed, there must be a critique of the creation of those walls which keep our bodies 'out' in the first place (Joseph-Salisbury 2016). How do we move beyond the superficial inclusion of our bodies (and the use of buzzwords like 'diversity') and towards the possibilities in the different critical knowledges that we could use when examining the society around us? How do we appreciate what hooks (1994: 4) describes as, 'the difference between education as the practice of freedom and education that merely strives to reinforce domination'?

Navigating Microaggressions, Subverting the Ivory Tower

Azeezat: After my 1st year as a PhD student struggling to belong within this overwhelmingly white space, I remember two (white) academics encouraging me to claim my representation and voice within this space as it would help me to see the change I wanted to see. I remember this catching me off-guard: how do we claim our voices within a space that is and was in no way built with our bodies in mind?

This question of how to claim our voice within the academe has led us to this search for the episteme of Blackness. For Yancy (2008), these epistemes create the space to speak back to deficit thinking. It is a position from which we challenge academia, and understand its role as one of the critical sites where white supremacy is reproduced. Epistemes of Blackness thus provide us with the language to understand how our Blackness has been defined as spectacle to this normalised whiteness. Once recognising this, we can open up dialogues which challenge the way knowledge produced by the academe is centralised and legitimised.

Like Stockdill and Danico (2012), it has been our conversations with each other, and with other students and academics of colour that have enabled us to move beyond accusations of 'being too sensitive' and resist individual deficit explanations. As Carmichael and Hamilton (1967: 5) note, to realise the way that race operates 'and to attempt to deal with it does not make one a racist or overly preoccupied with race; it puts one in the forefront of a significant struggle'. Thus, these conversations are essential to our survival (Yancy 2008). When we presented some of our experiences as part of an organised panel discussion, we were struck by the appreciation and understanding with which we were met. Several delegates of colour approached us to regale us with tales of similar experiences in their own institutions and to thank us for having opened up a space to refute deficit explanations and acknowledge our shared racialised struggles.

These conversations also provide a necessary break in the distinctions made between racism 'out there' and racism 'in here.' Our collective challenge to the structures enabling white supremacy to function (and flourish) within the academe includes challenging the dichotomy set up when we are asked to distance ourselves from our personal experiences of racialisation and mimic unmarked (i.e. white) knowledge producers. It includes forming connections to these different spaces of knowledge production that we have been taught to see as secondary to the tools and theories developed within the ivory tower: our Blackness requires us to speak across this divide, and to recover our own racialised experiences as part of knowledge on how these systems perpetuate themselves rather than 'data' to be mined. We do not see this experientially-felt knowledge as a failure to live up to the standard set by knowledge holders within the walls of the ivory tower: rather, we use this to decentralise the way knowledge is legitimised through the academe (Joseph-Salisbury 2018).

We are wary of any research which claims to have dismantled the inequalities which pervade academic institutions. For example, within the social sciences, Rose (1997) has expressed why 'reflexive' feminist researchers who claim to have uncovered and challenged power relationships between the interviewer and the interviewee are performing a modern-day 'goddess-trick' where all can be known by the all-seeing researcher. This is not our desire, and runs counter to our understanding and experiences of micro-aggressions. Indeed, as we have argued, by their very nature microaggressions are not always explicit and therefore not always discoverable in order to be dismantled. The forces which guard the way the academe perpetuates itself are beyond the ability of any one researcher to overcome. What we are interested in is how we find a place to be within these institutions that, as Azeezat points out, were 'in no way built with our bodies in mind.'

Because of the magnitude of these structures, we must be realistic about the labour involved in this endeavour and how it may run counter to the perpetuation of the academe as it exists currently. We have both had to prioritise developing this episteme of Blackness (through the use of emotional, intellectual and physical labour) over our academic careers. However, if we really want a chance to belong here on terms that have not been pre-defined against us, this work is a priority. This work has provided us with a form of nourishment and an ability to speak back to the isolation often felt as a racialised spectacle within the ivory tower. As Baldwin stated, 'the place in which I'll fit will not exist until I make it' (Pierpont 2009). An episteme of Blackness opens up the opportunity for us to begin making this space by challenging the way knowledge has been produced to construct us as out of place.

Whilst we recognise the possibilities in epistemes of Blackness for surviving in HE, we also know that Baldwin's call to create the spaces in which we'll fit includes seeing leaving the academe as a viable option. Indeed, whilst attempts to transform HE from within perhaps appears as *the* option for subverting standards of knowledge production, non-participation might also prove to be a vital choice. Once recognising that developing these epistemes of Blackness exists across different spaces of knowledge production, to assume that such work must be done within these HE institutions is to perpetuate the assumption that knowledge must be produced within the academe in order to be legitimate. Non-participation might mean a refusal to collude in the academe's perpetuation of white supremacy.

This option of leaving the academe also speaks to recognising (as has been discussed) the cumulative threat racial microaggressions can pose to our wellbeing (see Pierce 1974; Sue 2010). If we understand the academe as a space that creates fertile conditions for microaggressive acts (whilst simultaneously lacking the requisite conditions for critique) then it is perfectly reasonable for people of colour to opt to leave the academe. Whilst certainly under-discussed, increasing attention is being paid to the threat that life as an academic can pose to an individual's stress, anxiety and mental health (Shaw and Ward 2014). The racialised structures that shape the academe, manifest in the pernicious threat of racial microaggressions, can only compound these issues. Thus, as we grapple with the decision of whether we will continue in the academe, we might recall the words of Audre Lorde (1988: 27), 'caring for myself is not self-indulgence, it is self-preservation, and that is an act of political warfare'. The option of leaving, the ability to reject the ivory tower is often starkly missing from these conversations and thus we are led to believe that survival is the only option. We must reject this false logic and recognise that academia is not the only space for the production of legitimate knowledge. In casting a critical eye we know this to be a fallacy; too often the knowledge produced by the academe is hampered by an inability to recognise the racial conditions that produce particular forms of knowledge. bell hooks (1995: 235) argues that,

> The desire to share knowledge while centralizing black folks and our struggle for self-determination, without excluding non-black audiences, requires different strategies from those intellectuals normally deploy to disseminate work. [... We] know that we must use lectures, radio, television, and conversation in diverse settings to share information.

Perhaps the different strategies that hooks refers to are more likely to come from outside of the academe. We do not know whether our futures will be inside or outside of the academe but refuse to see the academe as our only option.

Concluding Remarks: Are We Supposed to Be Here?

To conclude, we return to answer the question posed in the opening epigraph, 'are you supposed to be in here?'

> No, we, as people of colour, are not supposed to be in this space that renders our bodies out of place and we thank you for the incessant reminders. However, as we cultivate an episteme of Blackness that allows us to understand and confront the academe for what it does to racialise and objectify our bodies, we develop tools to survive and thrive, or to leave and reject these spaces as they currently exist. Our goal is not to find a way to belong here. We aim to find a way to thrive beyond here.

Whilst we offer no blueprint for success, we believe that—whether from inside of outside—our focus must remain firmly on destabilising the academe's position as *the* legitimate producer of knowledge.

Acknowledgements Thanks to Maryam Jameela and Muna Abdi for reading drafts of this chapter. We would also like to thank the community of doctoral students and academics who have supported us and enabled us to find spaces to survive within these institutions—they have helped us to find the words needed to write this paper.

References

Alexander-Floyd, N. G. (2012). Disappearing Acts: Reclaiming Intersectionality in the Social Sciences in a Post-black Feminist Era. *Feminist Formations, 24*(1), 1–25.

Back, L. (2004). Ivory Towers? The Academy and Racism. In I. Law, D. Phillips, & L. Turney (Eds.), *Institutional Racism in Higher Education* (pp. 1–6). Stoke on Trent: Trentham Books.

Bell, D. A. (1993). *Faces at the Bottom of the Well: The Permanence of Racism.* New York: Basic Books.

Bilge, S. (2013). Intersectionality Undone. *Du Bois Review: Social Science Research on Race, 10*(2), 405–424.

Black, L. N. (2014). *Why Isn't My Professor Black? On Reflection* [Online]. Runnymede Trust. Available from http://www.runnymedetrust.org/blog/why-isnt-my-professor-black. Accessed 7 Sept 2016.

Carmichael, S., & Hamilton, A. (1967). *Black Power: The Politics of Liberation in America*. New York: Random House LLC.

Collins, P. H. (1990). *Black Feminist Thought: Knowledge, Consciousness, and the Politics of Empowerment*. London: Routledge.

Constantine, M. G., Smith, L., Redington, R. M., & Owens, D. (2008). Racial Microaggressions Against Black Counseling and Counseling Psychology Faculty: A Central Challenge in the Multicultural Counseling Movement. *Journal of Counseling and Development: JCD, 86*(3), 348.

Crenshaw, K. (1989). Demarginalizing the Intersection of Race and Sex: A Black Feminist Critique of Antidiscrimination Doctrine, Feminist Theory and Antiracist Politics. *University of Chicago Legal Forum, 139*–167.

Delgado, R., & Stefancic, J. (2012). *Critical Race Theory: An Introduction*. New York: New York University Press.

Dotson, K. (2011). Tracking Epistemic Violence, Tracking Practices of Silencing. *Hypatia, 26*(2), 236–257.

Du Bois, W. E. B. (2007 [1903]). *The Souls of Black Folk*. New York: Oxford University Press.

Edds, R. (2014). 65 Students of Colour Share Their Experiences of Life at Oxford University [Online]. *Buzzfeed*. Available from https://www.buzzfeed.com/robinedds/students-of-colour-share-their-experiences-of-life-at-oxf?utm_term=.ppLnxZDlK#.tbbj6QmEq. Accessed 25 Aug 2016.

Ek, L. D., Cerecer, P. D. Q., Alanís, I., & Rodríguez, M. A. (2010). "I Don't Belong Here": Chicanas/Latinas at a Hispanic Serving Institution Creating Community Through Muxerista Mentoring. *Equity & Excellence in Education, 43*(4), 539–553.

Elgot, J. (2016). 'Take It Down!': Rhodes Must Fall Campaign Marches Through Oxford [Online]. *The Guardian*. Available from https://www.theguardian.com/education/2016/mar/09/take-it-down-rhodes-must-fall-campaign-marches-through-oxford. Accessed 7 Sept 2016.

Gulam, W. A. (2002). Black and White Paradigms in Higher Education. In I. Law, D. Phillips, & L. Turney (Eds.), *Institutional Racism in Higher Education*. Stoke: Trentham Books.

Harris-Perry, M. (2016). A Call and Response with Melissa Harris-Perry: The Pain and the Power of 'Lemonade' [Online]. *Elle*. Available from http://www.elle.com/culture/music/a35903/lemonade-call-and-response/. Accessed 25 Aug 2016.

Henry, M. (1994). Ivory Towers and Ebony Women: The Experiences of Black Women in Higher Education. *Changing the Subject: Women in Higher Education* (pp. 42–57). Milton Park: Taylor & Francis.

hooks, b. (1989). *Talking Back: Thinking Feminist, Thinking Black.* Boston, MA: South End Press.

hooks, b. (1994). *Teaching to Trasgress: Education as the Practice of Freedom.* London: Routledge.

hooks, b. (1995). *Killing Rage: Ending Racism.* London: Penguin Books.

Jahi, J. (2014). *Why Isn't My Professor Black?* [Online]. UCL Events and Reviews Blog. Available from https://blogs.ucl.ac.uk/events/2014/03/21/whyisntmyprofessorblack/. Accessed 7 Sept 2016.

Joseph-Salisbury, R. (2016). *Reducing 'Drop-Out' Rates for Black Students Means Institutional Transformation, Not Individual Support* [Online]. Novara Media. Available from http://wire.novaramedia.com/2016/08/reducing-drop-out-rates-for-black-students-means-institutional-transformation-not-individual-support/. Accessed 25 Aug 2016.

Joseph-Salisbury, R. (2018). Confronting my duty as an academic of colour in times of explicit racial violence. In A. Johnson, R. Joseph-Salisbury, & E. Kamunge (Eds.), *The Fire Now: Anti-racist Scholarship in Times of Explicit Racial Violence.* London: Zed Books.

Khan, S. (2005). Reconfiguring the Native Informant: Positionality in the Global Age. *Signs, 30*(4), 2017–2037.

Kohli, R., & Solórzano, D. G. (2012). Teachers, Please Learn Our Names!: Racial Microaggressions and the K-12 Classroom. *Race Ethnicity and Education, 15*(4), 441–462.

Lorde, A. (1988). *A Burst of Light.* Ann Arbour, MI: Firebrand Books.

Lorde, A. (1996). The Master's Tools Will Never Dismantle the Master's House. *The Audre Lorde Compendium: Essays, Speeches and Journals* (pp. 158–161). London: Pandora.

Mills, C. (2007). White Ignorance. In S. Sullivan & N. Tuana (Eds.), *Race and Epistemologies of Ignorance.* Albany: State University of New York Press.

Mock, J. (2016). *'Lemonade' Is Beyoncé's Testimony of Being Black, Beautiful & Burdened* [Online]. Janet Mock. Available from http://janetmock.com/2016/04/26/beyonce-lemonade-testimony-black-women-burden/. Accessed 25 Aug 2016.

Nayak, S. (2015). *Race, Gender and the Activism of Black Feminist Theory: Working with Audre Lorde.* Hove: Routledge.

Noxolo, P. (1999). *'Dancing a Yard, Dancing Abrard': Race, Space and Time in British Developmental Discourses.* Unpublished PhD thesis, Nottingham Trent University.

Oluo, I. (2016). Beyoncé's Lemonade Is About Much More Than Infidelity and Jay Z [Online]. *The Guardian*. Available from https://www.theguardian.com/commentisfree/2016/apr/25/beyonce-lemonade-jay-z-infidelity-emotional-project-depths. Accessed 25 Aug 2016.

Pérez Huber, L., & Solorzano, D. G. (2015). Racial Microaggressions as a Tool for Critical Race Research. *Race Ethnicity and Education, 18*(3), 297–320.

Peters, M. A. (2015). Why Is My Curriculum White? *Educational Philosophy and Theory, 47*(7), 641–646.

Pierce, C. (1974). Psychiatric Problems of the Black Minority. *American Handbook of Psychiatry* (2nd ed., pp. 512–523). New York: Basic Books.

Pierce, C. M. (1969). *Is Bigotry the Basis of the Medical Problems of the Ghetto?* New York: Meredith.

Pierce, C. M. (1988). Stress in the Workplace. In A. Coner-Edwards & J. Spurlock (Eds.), *Black Families in Crisis: The Middle Class* (pp. 27–34). New York: Brunner/Mazel.

Pierpont, C. R. (2009, February 9). Another Country. *The New Yorker*. Available from http://www.newyorker.com/magazine/2009/02/09/another-country. Accessed 25 Aug 2016.

Pittman, C. T. (2012). Racial Microaggressions: The Narratives of African American Faculty at a Predominantly White University. *The Journal of Negro Education, 81,* 82–92.

Puwar, N. (2004). *Space Invaders: Race, Gender and Bodies Out of Place.* Oxford: Berg.

Rodriguez, J., & Freeman, K. (2016). 'Your Focus on Race Is Narrow and Exclusive': The Derailment of Anti-racist Work Through Discourses of Intersectionality and Diversity. *Whiteness and Education, 1*(1), 69–82.

Rollock, N. (2012). Unspoken Rules of Engagement: Navigating Racial Microaggressions in the Academic Terrain. *International Journal of Qualitative Studies in Education, 25*(5), 517–532.

Rose, G. (1997). Situating Knowledges: Positionality Reflexivities and Other Tactics. *Progress in Human Geography, 21*(3), 305–320.

Shaw, C., & Ward, L. (2014). Dark Thoughts: Why Mental Illness Is on the Rise in Academia. *The Guardian Higher Education Network* [Online]. Available from https://www.theguardian.com/higher-education-network/2014/mar/06/mental-health-academics-growing-problem-pressure-university. Accessed 10 Sept 2016.

Shilliam, R. (2016). *Black Academia 1.2.* [Online]. Robbie Shilliam. Available from https://robbieshilliam.wordpress.com/2016/07/10/black-academia-1-2/. Accessed 25 Aug 2016.

Solorzano, D., Ceja, M., & Yosso, T. (2000). Critical Race Theory, Racial Microaggressions, and Campus Racial Climate: The Experiences of African American College Students. *Journal of Negro Education, 69,* 60–73.

Solorzano, D. G., & Yosso, T. J. (2002). Critical Race Methodology: Counter-Storytelling as an Analytical Framework for Education Research. *Qualitative Inquiry, 8*(1), 23–44.

Stockdill, B. C., & Danico, M. Y. (2012). The Ivory Tower Paradox: Higher Education as a Site of Oppression and Resistance. In B. C. Stockdill & M. Y. Danico (Eds.), *Transforming the Ivory Tower: Challenging Racism, Sexism, and Homophobia in the Academy* (pp. 1–30). Hawaii: University of Hawaii Press.

Sue, D. W. (2010). *Microaggressions in Everyday Life: Race, Gender, and Sexual Orientation.* Hoboken: Wiley.

Sue, D. W., Capodilupo, C. M., & Holder, A. (2008). Racial Microaggressions in the Life Experience of Black Americans. *Professional Psychology: Research and Practice, 39*(3), 329.

Turney, L., Law, I., & Phillips, D. (2002). *Institutional Racism in Higher Education: Building the Anti-racist University: A Toolkit.* Leeds: Centre for Ethnicity and Racism Studies, University of Leeds.

Tyrer, D. (2004). The Others: Extremism and Intolerance on Campus and the Spectre of Islamic Fundamentalism. In I. Law, D. Philips, & L. Turney (Eds.), *Institutional Racism in Higher Education* (pp. 35–48). Staffordshire: Trentham Books.

Villenas, S. (1996). The Colonizer/Colonized Chicana Ethnographer: Identity, Marginalization, and Co-optation in the Field. *Harvard Educational Review, 66*(4), 711–732.

Yancy, G. (2008). *Black Bodies, White Gazes: The Continuing Significance of Race.* Lanham: Rowman & Littlefield.

9

Being Black, Male and Academic: Navigating the White Academy

Jason Arday

Achieving a goal or an objective for any human being is the pinnacle of visualising a dream and being able to see this come to fruition. As someone diagnosed on the autistic spectrum with a strand of autism referred to as Global Development Delay (GDD) who learned to read and write at the age of 18, I often think about my journey within education. These thoughts are then followed by what this journey represents when I consider my chosen career path... academia. Upon reflection, there is a self-deprecating aspect of me which often queries whether I have the characteristics, capabilities and credentials traditionally associated with being an academic. Perhaps, my experiences in education and in some ways the deficit position I started from contribute to this particular view, in addition to the professional experiences I have encountered in academia. Interestingly, the 'hidden' part of my journey as an autistic learner is very different from my outward facing presence and journey as a Black Male. Something that cannot remain hidden.

J. Arday (✉)
University of Roehampton, London, UK
e-mail: Jason.arday@roehampton.ac.uk

© The Author(s) 2018
J. Arday and H. S. Mirza (eds.), *Dismantling Race in Higher Education*,
https://doi.org/10.1007/978-3-319-60261-5_9

Negotiating this professionally has always been difficult, as I am overtly aware that my presence as a Black Male academic powerfully disrupts the normativity and centrality of Whiteness within academia.

Whilst disrupting these patterns of normativity are essential towards advocating greater diversification and equality for Black and Minority Ethnic (BME)[1] staff within academia, this does often come at a personal cost. During my time in academia, I have more often than not felt isolated and marginalised. There had always been a feeling that survival needed to resemble keeping my head below the parapet and ensuring that I did not draw attention towards myself. The feelings that accompany these experiences ultimately result in a disposition that 'I do not belong here' or 'I am not good enough to be here'. Often these feelings are compounded by racialised experiences which reassert hegemony, normativity, Whiteness, power and privilege (Leonardo 2002). A prominent and more insidious vehicle for maintaining these oppressive cultures has been the racial micro-aggression (Pérez Huber and Solorzano 2015). This effective 'tool of Whiteness' reminds us how racism can be conveyed through subtle occurrences of subordination (Leonardo 2002; Picower 2009). Negotiating and grappling with my presence as a Black Male in academia has been difficult because you are reminded through verbal and symbolic occurrences that you are different from your White counterparts in many cases you are perceived as inferior (Cordova 1998; Ladson-Billings 1998). This becomes a reoccurring narrative which eventually affects and erodes confidence. These feelings become a burden on one's psyche and I have always been aware of the potential effects of this on my mental facilities.

My recent reflection on these experiences through my research and verbal recollections have allowed me to begin conceptualising the effects of racial discrimination and marginality on Black Male academics. The patterns of exclusion which facilitate these experiences can be difficult to articulate or conceptualise due to the irrationality which often ensues

---

[1]Black and Minority Ethnic (BME) and People of Colour are used interchangeably throughout this chapter to refer individuals experiencing racism or discrimination in the Academy or society. This term is also used to describe individuals from Black, Asian, Middle-Eastern (Asia), Mixed-Heritage or Latin American ethnic backgrounds.

when racism is confronted by BME academics. These reflections have also prompted and ignited a desire to confront racism despite the imbalance of power and hegemony which pervades within higher education. Challenging this becomes pertinent particularly in a professional context where causal racism within academia is fluid and commonplace. I offer my story as a cathartic outlet for the racialised experiences I have encountered during my journey in academia; as a way of better understanding these experiences and how racism continues to endure within academia to the detriment of Black Male academics.

In this chapter, I draw upon three personal narratives which illuminate my experiences of navigating the White Academy as a Black Male academic. I will employ the counter-narrative as a semi-biographical instrument to unpack the following experiences; attempting to gain employment opportunities within the Academy; and negotiating staff and students perceptions of me as a Black Male within academia. The counter-narrative is a tool of Critical Race Theory (CRT) which seeks to explore and challenge the prevalence of racial inequality within society (Cordova 1998; Solorzano and Yosso 2002). This chapter will conclude with future considerations for greater diversification within Higher Education and exploring my own position as a practitioner and researcher of race and social justice discourse within the Academy.

Gaining Entry into the Ivory Tower

The centrality and all-encompassing nature of Whiteness makes it extremely difficult to penetrate within academia (Ansley 1997; Gillborn 2015; Shilliam 2015). The normativity of this supremacy has meant that the Academy continues to remain the province of the White Middle classes, with recruitment processes often resembling academic appointments made through conscious biases (Alexander and Arday 2015; ECU 2015). A process which continues to be the most prominent disabler of diversity. Upon recalling my experiences of attempting to gain employment within academia; I am reminded of the countless times I have walked into an interview situation where a normally all-White panel are astounded to see a Black Male applicant. At this point, I am already mindful that several racial ascriptions are taking place in the mind of the interviewees which potentially boarder on an ignorant disposition. This is contradictory to the footnote that nowadays precedes most job advertisements in academia… 'We value a diverse workforce and would particularly welcome applications from BME candidates where we are currently underrepresented'. The continued dearth of BME academics within the sector suggests this statement to be a tokenistic response to increased calls for greater diversification of academic staff (Ahmed 2012; Bhopal 2014). At the end of all interviews, I have always taken the opportunity to claim a small semblance of control and redistribute the power dynamics that so often do not work in the favour of BME applicants. The questions I pose always query two fundamental aspects; 'Is your staff and student population diverse?' the common response to this being… 'No'. This is followed by interrogating the interview panel further; 'What is your university doing to promote greater diversification of staff and students?' By this point there is a slight sadistic thrill gained from observing (in most, not all cases) a clearly non-cognisant panel squirm on race-related politics and issues. For a short period, the discomfort encountered whilst answering these questions provides a brief source of amusement for what quite frankly will often result in an unsuccessful interview. In many cases, I am rarely provided with the reasons as to why I was unsuccessful, compounding the disappointment further and making this harder to comprehend. Conveying this experience to others is difficult, particularly White colleagues who often view my interpretations of these 'racialised' encounters as subjective, interpretive and without an evidence base. The wall of fragility which I encounter has become an expected and obvious reaction towards discussing or disseminating experiences of racial inequality within academia or society more generally (McIntosh 1992; Shilliam 2015).

My experiences illustrate the multi-dimensional reach of Whiteness and how it can be utilised to continually facilitate processes which perpetrate racial inequality (Picower 2009). These processes ensure that BME academics continue to operate on the periphery of our overwhelmingly White institutions (Casey 1993). Universities by and large are often lauded as a microcosm of society and a hub for multiculturalism and diversity (Alexander and Arday 2015). I have always found it interesting how universities interpret 'diversity and equality' as they have always been wedded to the idea of meritocracy, which is somewhat of a fallacy upon examining the current landscape. Research (Arday 2017a; Alexander and Arday 2015; Andrews 2016; ECU 2015; Shilliam 2015) suggests that in fact universities are deepening and perpetuating inequitable cultures which reinforce poor diversification and racial inequality. This becomes contradictory of the egalitarian utopia espoused by universities, especially when they continue to create inequitable systems through recruitment processes which appear to disadvantage BME applicants (Bhopal 2014). Clearly, these systems have not been penetrative because there remains an impenetrable 'glass-ceiling' which ensures that the centrality of Whiteness pervades at the expense of BME academics (Ahmed 2012).

This narrative and these barriers become entrenched within the mind as a BME academic. You apply for jobs aware that there are inequitable external factors beyond your control. You also become cognisant of your presence as a potential tokenistic gesture playing lip-service to the mantra… 'We are an equal opportunities employer'. You are effectively faced with a situation where it becomes difficult to approach these interview experiences with any kind of optimism, because you immediately become aware of two main factors; will they be able to look past the colour of my skin and will the interview panel most likely be all white? For many BME academics continuously in this situation you are fighting against a systemic and institutional problem which reinforces the paucity of faculty of colour within the sector. This problem is deeply engrained within universities, with its roots firmly entwined within discriminatory cultures (Andrews 2016). As David Lammy MP former Higher Education minster stated in *The Guardian* in response to British universities employing no Black academics in top roles:

This is absolutely shocking. I am appalled that higher education is so deeply unrepresentative of the country. Universities talk about widening participation and fair access but the complete lack of diversity in senior positions sends out an absolutely dreadful message to young people from ethnic minorities who find themselves wondering whether university is for them or not. (David Lammy MP for Tottenham, Former Higher Education Minster, *The Guardian*, 2017)

HESA figures from 2015–2016 compound some of the arguments presented within this chapter. The 2015–2016 figures show universities employed 3,205 Black people as academics, 1,805 in secretarial roles and 1,410 in 'elementary occupations', including cleaners, porters and security guards (HESA 2016). Comparatively, HESA found 158,000 white staff in academic posts and fewer than 70,000 performing clerical or manual labour. Unsurprisingly, this all points to a reoccurring and enduring narrative… BME staff continue to be under-represented in less senior and senior levels within higher education (Bhopal 2014; ECU 2015). Under the Equality Act 2010, universities have a duty to ensure equal opportunities for those who may be discriminated against or under-represented. However, monitoring and accountability for senior university stakeholders who do not prioritise diversification of academic staff remains problematic as there are no formal penalties or sanctions, despite the introduction of the ECU Race Equality Charter which specially focuses on improving racial equality practices in higher education (ECU 2015).

Having been overlooked for several senior academic posts despite being suitably qualified, I am often reminded of my first experience applying for a job in higher education 8 years ago. I was unsuccessful during this application, but was proud to have been shortlisted. I asked the interviewer for some feedback on my interview and was really perplexed by their retort, which was, 'unfortunately, Jason… sometimes your face does not fit'. At this point, I had not aligned this potentially to experiencing racism or being treated differently. As the saying would suggest, familiarity breeds contempt… particularly when you find yourself on the end of these types of comments regularly. The language of rejection or covert racism as I would see it became more refined against a backdrop of diplomatic jargon, 'on this occasion Jason, you were great, but just not what we were looking for at this time'. I was often left with feelings of why do I even bother? The thing I have always taken away from these disappointing experiences is that I am fortunate to be able to use my work as a vehicle to disseminate these encounters. Professionally, I have experienced more disappointment than success, which is commonplace in academia.

For an academic of colour, this disappointment can be continuous and unrelenting. Perhaps, an important aspect for me now as a Black Male academic which I was unware of before entering the Academy is the dynamics and subtle nuances of racism and how this penetrates society and its major institutions. Being able to navigate racism within higher education, particularly when attempting to gain employment requires resilience. Significantly, what these experiences do provide are opportunities for BME academics to consider how they may circumnavigate racial inequality whether they are successful or unsuccessful during interview and recruitment processes (Leonardo 2016; Rollock 2016).

Negotiating Staff and Students Perceptions of Me as a Black Male in Academia

Penetrating the walls of the ivory tower and gaining employment is difficult, but perhaps something more difficult than this is negotiating staff and student perceptions which reside against a backdrop of normative Whiteness and dominant Eurocentric curricula (Pérez Huber and Solorzano 2015). My own engagement in negotiating staff and student perceptions of me as a Black Male academic have often been surprising, particularly with regards to the judgements placed upon your professional capabilities (Ahmed 2012; Mirza 2017; Puwar 2004). Upon reflecting on some of these experiences, I am reminded of the constant indifferent treatment to my White contemporaries. Working within these binaries of racism can be enlightening due to becoming aware of how this overt instrument manifests itself in varying insidious ways. For myself and the majority of BME academics this insidious racism derives from the racial micro-aggression. Racial micro-aggressions are often utilised as 'tool of Whiteness' to accentuate deficiency or to demonstrate that Blacks are not as capable as their White counterparts (Cordova 1998; Leonardo 2002; Picower 2009; Sue 2010).

My encounters with this form of racism always resembled a questioning of my capabilities as an academic. The unsurprising caveat to these experiences came from the solitary position I have always adopted as the only or one of few Black members of faculty. Very often I found myself in situations where I was continuously under surveillance, an aspect that became quite upsetting as I soon came to realise that this type of surveillance was not extended to my White colleagues. Andrews (2016) reminds us that often inequitable academic environments and cultures are sustained by those that have the power and privilege to ensure this. The gap between compliance and enforcement becomes a real and prevalent issue for the BME academic attempting to comply and not destabilise the establishment (Adams 2017; Shilliam 2015). Moreover, there is an awareness of who maintains the power and privilege, whilst recognising the vulnerability of your position as a Black academic at the behest of senior White administrators who have the authority to make your position become untenable (Ahmed 2012; Apple 2004; ECU 2015). Effectively, operating on the margins has become a normalised disposition for BME academics, which has made us susceptible to feelings of marginalisation, isolation and inequity (ECU 2015; Ladson-Billings and Donnor 2008; Mirza 2017). During my time in higher education, I have always been thought of as deficient or not as capable, and I proffer this without a sense of paranoia, hyper-sensitivity or cynicism. At this juncture, I recall two particular incidents which with the passing of time I have come to accept as part of the symbolic acts of violence which permeated my everyday professional life.

The first recollection, points to a discussion with a previous colleague after a period of student feedback in which the cohort of students suggested that I had been a real asset to the module, something my colleagues at the time found quite hard to digest. A colleague then referred to me as a 'dark horse'… stating that, 'I did not know someone like you was capable of such things'. This comment was preceded by 'Let's be honest, the only reason students like you is because you are Black, and Black is the new cool, also you give everyone hugs and high-fives'. Interestingly, the gravity of such an overtly ignorant and racist comment was accepted as a source of humour by my White colleagues at the time. As the only person of colour in the room, I felt undermined, degraded and humiliated, with my mouth arrested in disbelief, subconsciously mindful that a flippant or curt response could potentially place me in a position of further vulnerability. Unfortunately, what I soon came to realise is that while these comments are instantaneous; the residual effects of these racial micro-aggressions are enduring and a constant reminder that you are perceived as professionally inadequate (Ignatiev and Garvey 1996; Ladson-Billings 1998; Lipsitz 1998; Mirza 2017).

The second recollection, draws upon an encounter with a series of students who all held a similar viewpoint in relation to being assured of my professional capabilities. During my time in academia, I have become very aware of how taken aback students are to be taught by a Black Male. There is a recognition that my presence challenges and disrupts their views of what they perceived Black Males to be, or as one student put it to me once, 'Are you into Rap music…? No offence but you look like you should be a Rapper instead of a Lecturer'. To which the group responded with rapturous laughter. Mindful of my place as a minority ethnic individual, there are times where you visibly weigh up the consequences of challenging and confronting such ignorant comments. This internal conflict undermines and erodes confidence, as you begin to observe this erosion reflecting back as you observe yourself in the mirror.

These racialised experiences reach a crescendo, when students ask you for your help, meanwhile making a clear judgement upon your capabilities which place your racial identity before your professional competence. Frequently, I encountered the same experience which resembled providing students with support or advice on how to complete a piece of coursework or navigate their way through a module; they then discuss their encounter with me to a White colleague, to validate whether the information provided was accurate or inaccurate. With my credibility and competence validated by a White colleague, the students then gain a sense of gratification knowing that this affirmation ensures that the information provided was correct. As a BME academic, you often find yourself in situations where staff and students are both complicit in your racialised experiences. For me this realisation, really emphasised the scale, hegemony and normativity of Whiteness and the reluctance to embrace ethnic difference. Ultimately, contributing to further feelings of operating on the periphery of an institutionally racist society (Alexander 2017; Gillborn 2008).

Racism is ingrained within the Academy. As Leonardo (2016) states the elevation and positioning of those with the power and privilege is reliant on this inequity and imbalance. An imbalance BME academics continue to be disadvantaged by. I offer my experiences not to extract sympathy or awe, but to highlight the cumulative effect of these occurrences and demonstrate how eventually they lead BME academics to lose confidence; question their own capabilities; or sadly leave the Academy altogether.

Many of the narratives provided collide with the notion of racial equality. Inequitable cultures are sustained by the insidious and covert nature of the racial micro-aggression (Rollock 2012). The burden that accompanies BME academics resembles invisibility and hyper-surveillance by both staff and students, with errors being exaggerated and exploited; and praise being reduced to fortuitous episodes or occurrences. To assimilate yourself within these cultures, comes at a physical and mental cost; an aspect of your suffering that you de-compartmentalise everyday within your professional working life in an attempt survive (Arday 2017a; Stovall 2006). Keeping some semblance of yourself becomes crucial and integral in BME academics attempts to survive the Academy. As Williams (1991) states the loss of oneself within the landscape of Whiteness, can be hard to retrieve. Unfortunately, this personal, mental and physical cost is one that many BME academics endure for the entirety of their professional careers within academia. The enduring nature of racial discrimination within the Academy shows minimal signs of relenting, unless senior university stakeholders and policy-makers actively attempt to disrupt these cultures with penetrative interventions (Arday 2017b; ECU 2015).

Conclusion

Throughout this chapter, a counter-narrative approach has been adopted to elicit racialised experiences of navigating the Academy as a Black Male academic. Understanding oppressive, patriarchal regimes is difficult because their foundations thrive on an unequal distribution of power. The function of Whiteness will always be used to as an instrument to sustain hegemony, supremacy and inequality (Kincheloe and Steinberg 1997; McIntosh 1990). The point of departure which subsequently occurs at this juncture recognises that sustained and penetrative efforts are needed to ensure greater diversification in higher education which are accommodating and inclusive of BME academics (Ahmed 2012; Arday 2017b). Achieving this requires a continuous integration of racist and inequitable cultures within the Academy. As generational and temporary custodians of the Academy we have a collective responsibility to dismantle racism and create a sector that is reflective of our multi-cultural and diverse society (Alexander 2017; Rollock 2016). Establishing legitimacy for BME academics within the Academy will always remain problematic because of the subordinated view of people of colour. However, disrupting racial inequality is integral if we are to collectively realise a more inclusive and diverse Academy.

Upon reflecting on this, there is something that has always comforted me even through the most difficult of experiences during my professional tenure in the Academy. Often, I am presented with the 18 year old Jason, and I remember the sense of euphoria that overwhelmed me once I had learned how to read and write… For me this was my Everest. At no stage, during that point did I ever entertain the idea that I could go from that particular milestone to gaining a PhD 12 years later and working in academia.

In July 2017, I was presented with a dream, in which I was talking to my 18 year old self… the day which preceded this was quite a stressful one in which I had encountered racism within the workplace. My 18 year old self, said to my older self… 'Do you know what Jason, I know this is hard but you have achieved something great, against great odds… you have set out to do something and you have overcome every obstacle in achieving that particular feat'. As I awoke, I thought to myself despite the traumatic, racialised experiences I have encountered professionally, I am one of the lucky few in this world that get to truly do something that while difficult, they enjoy.

Moreover and perhaps more pertinently, I am able to use my voice to speak to the inequality I have witnessed and experienced. Perhaps, sometimes in the mist of these negative experiences, I must remember those BME individuals that do not have a platform to discuss their encounters of racism; those who are continuously silenced, subordinated and marginalised without an outlet for their frustration. If nothing else, having the opportunity to provide this counter-narrative as a Black Male reminds me of how fortunate I am to be able to tell my story. It is my hope that this story may provide some solace or resolve in navigating racism in all of its institutions forms.

References

Adams, R. (2017). *British Universities Employ No Black Academics in Top Roles, Figures Show.* Available at https://www.theguardian.com/education/2017/jan/19/british-universities-employ-no-black-academics-in-top-roles-figures-show.

Apple, M. W. (2004). *Ideology and Curriculum* (3rd ed.). New York: RoutledgeFalmer.

Ahmed, S. (2012). *On Being Included: Racism and Diversity in Institutional Life.* Durham and London: Duke University Press.

Alexander, C. (2017). Breaking Black: The Death of Ethnic and Racial Studies in Britain. *Ethnic and Racial Studies.* https://doi.org/10.1080/01419870.2018.1409902.

Alexander, C., & Arday, J. (2015). *Aiming Higher Race, Inequality and Diversity in the Academy.* London: Runnymede Trust (Runnymede Perspectives), AHRC and London: Runnymede Trust (Runnymede Perspectives), Common Creative.

Andrews, K. (2016). *Black Studies University Course Long Overdue.* Available at https://www.theguardian.com/commentisfree/2016/may/20/black-studies-university-course-long-overdue/.

Ansley, F. L. (1997). White Supremacy (and What We Should Do about It). In R. Delgado & J. Stefancic (Eds.), *Critical White Studies: Looking Behind the Mirror.* Philadelphia, PA: Temple University Press.

Arday, J. (2017a). *University and College Union (UCU): Exploring Black and Minority Ethnic (BME) Doctoral Students' Perceptions of a Career in Academia: Experiences, Perceptions and Career Progression.* London: Creative Commons.

Arday, J. (2017b). *Confronting Racial Inequality in the Academy.* Available at http://www.universityworldnews.com/article.php?story=20170418113613343/.

Bhopal, K. (2014). *The Experiences of BME Academics in Higher Education: Aspirations in the Face of Inequality.* Stimulus Paper. London: Leadership Foundation for Higher Education.

Casey, K. (1993). *I Answer with My Life: Life Histories of Women Teachers Working for Social Change*. New York: Routledge.

Cordova, T. (1998). Power and Knowledge: Colonialism in the Academy. In C. Trujillo (Ed.), *Living Chicana Theory*. Berkeley, CA: Third Woman Press.

Equality Challenge Unit. (2015). *Equality in Higher Education: Statistical Report, Staff and Students*. Available at http://www.ecu.ac.uk/publications/equality-higher-education-statistical-report-2015/.

Gillborn, D. (2008). *Racism and Education: Coincidence or Conspiracy?* London: Routledge.

Gillborn, D. (2015). Racism as Policy: A Critical Race Analysis of Education Reforms in the United States and England. *The Educational Forum, 78*(1), 26–41.

HESA. (2016). *Staff in Higher Education: Staff by Ethnicity 2015/2016*. Available at https://www.hesa.ac.uk/data-and-analysis/publications/staff-2015-16.

Ignatiev, N., & Garvey, J. (1996). Abolish the White Race. In N. Ignatiev & J. Garvey (Eds.), *Race Traitor*. New York and London: Routledge.

Kincheloe, J., & Steinberg, S. (1997). Addressing the Crisis of Whiteness: Reconfiguring White Identity in a Pedagogy of Whiteness. In J. Kincheloe, S. Steinberg, N. Rodriguez, & R. Chennault (Eds.), *White Reign*. York and London: Routledge.

Ladson-Billings, G. (1998). Just What Is Critical Race Theory and What's It Doing in a Nice Field Like Education? *International Journal of Qualitative Studies in Education, 11*(1), 7–24.

Ladson-Billings, G., & Donnor, J. (2008). The Moral Activist Role of Critical Race Theory Scholarship. In N. K. Denzin & Y. S. Lincoln (Eds.), *The Landscape of Qualitative Research*. Los Angeles, CA: Sage.

Lammy, D. (2017). *British Universities Employ No Black Academics in Top Roles, Figures Show*. Available at https://www.theguardian/education/2017/jan19/british-universities-employ-no-black-academics-in-top-rolesfigures-show.

Leonardo, Z. (2002). The Souls of White Folk: Critical Pedagogy, Whiteness Studies, and Globalization Discourse. *Race Ethnicity & Education, 5*(1), 29–50.

Leonardo, Z. (2016). The Color of Supremacy. In E. Taylor, D. Gillborn, & G. Ladson-Billings (Eds.), *Foundations of Critical Race Theory in Education* (2nd ed.). New York: Routledge.

Lipsitz, G. (1998). *The Possessive Investment in Whiteness*. Philadelphia, PA: Temple University Press.

McIntosh, P. (1990). White privilege: Unpacking the Invisible Knapsack. In B. Schinder (Ed.), *An Anthology: Race in the First Person*. New York: Crown Trade Paperbacks.

McIntosh, P. (1992). White Privilege and Male Privilege: A Personal Account of Coming to See Correspondences Through Work. In R. Delgado & J. Stefancic (Eds.), *Women's Studies, in Critical White Studies: Looking Behind the Mirror*. Philadelphia, PA: Temple University Press.

Mirza, H. S. (2017). One in a Million: A Journey of a Post-colonial Woman of Colour in the White Academy. In D. Gabriel & S. A. Tate (Eds.). *Inside the Ivory Tower: Narratives of Women of Colour Surviving and Thriving in Academia*. London: Trentham UCL Press.

Pérez Huber, L., & Solorzano, D. G. (2015). Racial Micro-Aggressions as a Tool for Critical Race Research. *Race Ethnicity and Education, 18*(3), 297–320.

Picower, B. (2009). The Unexamined Whiteness of Teaching: How White Teachers Maintain and Enact Dominant Racial Ideologies. *Race Ethnicity & Education, 12*(2), 197–215.

Puwar, N. (2004). Fish In and Out of Water: A Theoretical Framework for Race and the Space of Academia. In I. Law, D. Phillips, & L. Turney (Eds.), *Institutional Racism in Higher Education*. Stoke on Trent: Trentham Books.

Rollock, N. (2012). Unspoken Rules of Engagement: Navigating Racial Micro-Aggressions in the Academic Terrain. *International Journal of Qualitative Studies in Education, 25*(5), 517–532.

Rollock, N. (2016). *How Much Does Your University Do for Racial Equality?* Available at https://www.theguardian.com/higher-education-network/2016/jan/19/how-much-does-your-university-do-for-racial-equality/.

Shilliam, R. (2015). *Black Academia in Britain. The Disorder of Things.* Available at https://thedisorderofthings.com/2014/07/28/black-academia-in-britain/.

Solorzano, D., & Yosso, T. J. (2002). Critical Race Methodology: Counter-Storytelling as an Analytical Framework for Education Research. *Qualitative Inquiry, 8*(1), 23–44.

Stovall, D. (2006). Forging Community in Race and Class: Critical Race Theory and the Quest for Social Justice in Education. *Race Ethnicity & Education, 9*(3), 243–259.

Sue, D. W. (2010). *Micro-Aggressions in Everyday Life: Race, Gender, and Sexual Orientation*. Hoboken, NJ: Wiley.

Williams, P. J. (1991). *The Alchemy of Race and Rights*. Cambridge, MA: Havard University Press.

10

Black Bodies 'Out of Place' in Academic Spaces: Gender, Race, Faith and Culture in Post-race Times

Heidi Safia Mirza

Introduction: Affective 'Eduscapes' in Post-race Times

In this chapter, I ask how can we 'affectively' navigate the intersections of gender, race, faith and culture in our rapidly changing places of higher education. In so called 'post-race times' it is argued that, in contrast to the 'colour line' that defined the twentieth century, the embodiment of 'race' through skin colour is now no longer an impediment to educational and economic opportunities in the twenty first century (Nayak 2006; Lentin 2014; Goldberg 2013; Kapoor et al. 2013). The pernicious discourse of 'white hurt' that accompanies the multicultural backlash that characterises this particular 'post-race' moment sees equality for people of colour as an unfair advantage rooted in political correctness (Lentin 2016). It is now believed, in the political landscape, that those who are the 'really left behind' and truly discriminated

H. S. Mirza (✉)
Goldsmiths College, University of London, London, UK
e-mail: heidi.mirza@gold.ac.uk

© The Author(s) 2018
J. Arday and H. S. Mirza (eds.), *Dismantling Race in Higher Education*,
https://doi.org/10.1007/978-3-319-60261-5_10

against are the displaced white majority (Gilroy 2012; Bhambara 2016). In a visceral political 'colour-blind' climate where 'race' is deemed 'off the agenda', new patterns of insidious racism and deep inequalities are evolving in the 'affective' learning landscapes, or 'eduscapes' of our seemingly cosmopolitan but inherently white elitist universities (Caluya et al. 2011). In the commodified global industry of higher education, the challenge for our institutions in 'post-race' times is to move beyond the entrenched equalities discourse where institutional diversity is seen as 'good business sense' achieved through 'targeting' the bodies of raced and gendered 'others' to 'get them in the door'. 'Real' diversity in democratic societies has to be a moral and legal imperative which fundamentally changes our pedagogy and moves us towards a decolonised practice that embraces 'other ways of knowing' and being for all.

As a woman of colour and a Black feminist academic, living in this 'post-race' moment means constantly asking questions about what shapes the worlds of profound difference that I witness for racialised staff and students in the 'hideously white' places I teach and work (Bhopal and Jackson 2013). The task of being an embodied raced and gendered researcher is not easy and the notion of 'embodied intersectionality' (Mirza 2009a) that I draw on in this chapter is a useful concept I developed to enable me to excavate the 'affective' processes of exclusion and marginality that I encounter daily on my journeys in and through academia (Mirza 2017). I focus on the racialised institutional 'flashpoints' of recruitment, retention and progression which Black and Minority Ethnic students encounter on a teacher education course. I take a situated 'embodied' journey into the micro-institutional practices that feed the systemic institutional structures that maintain endemic patterns of racist exclusion in higher education in these so called 'colour-blind', 'post-race' times.

Telling Stories: Embodying Intersectionality in Research

The research study I discuss here looks at white tutors' accounts of their 'best practice' when teaching and engaging with Black and Minority Ethnic (BME) students on a Post Graduate Certificate of Education

(PGCE) course (Mirza and Meetoo 2012). The best practice stories that frame this chapter highlight some of the specific ways in which tutors approached issues of visible race, faith and gendered difference when supporting Black and Minority Ethnic students during their study.

The research was carried out in a higher education institution (HEI) that provides initial teacher training. The HEI was situated in a large multicultural city in England, and though the student body was ethnically diverse, all of the 23 tutors we interviewed, except one, were white. The tutors engaged with the process of data collection and openly shared their views in interviews, focus groups and questionnaires, describing what they see as crucial cultural and learning issues for Black and Minority Ethnic students. In contrast the discussion group of diverse students focused on their academic wellbeing. In particular making 'affective' links between tutors understanding of their gender, race, faith and disabilities, and their ability to progress and stay the course.

Due to the sensitive nature of 'race' research, we drew on a Critical Race Theory (CRT) perspective which advocates storytelling and the use of composite characters to conceal and protect the participants' identity (Gillborn 2008; Solórzano and Yosso 2002). Thus while each 'best practice' case is complex and located in the specific circumstances narrated by the tutors, in its reconstruction their narrations do not represent any single tutor, or student, or event. Similarly the two researchers on the project were women of colour which had implications for the interaction between the researcher and the researched. In post-race times when race is an 'absent present' (Lentin 2016; Mirza 2015) what will be revealed in interviews to a white researcher will be different than to a person of colour. In the case studies white tutors often told us 'happy' and successful stories of overcoming racism (Ahmed 2009, 2012). While such narrative exchanges may seemingly reflect the respondent's interpretation of the racial and gendered dynamics of their social world as they see it, we were always aware that their retelling was embedded in the embodied discursive practices that shape their social world (Applebaum 2008). Situated as 'outsiders within' academia (Collins 2000; Simmonds 1997) we recognised in the tutor's narrative accounts, an 'affective link' between structural institutional process (i.e. access and progression) and the 'identity affects' (of how a subject 'feels' and experiences the social world).

As an analytic framework embodied intersectionality draws on the concept of intersectionality, which is concerned with understanding the 'matrix of domination in which cultural patterns of oppression are not only interrelated, but are bound together and influenced by the intersectional systems of society' (Collins 2000: 42). The notion of embodied intersectionality uses the malleability of the concept of intersectionality (Crenshaw 1989, 1991; Brah and Phoenix 2004) and takes it a stage further (Mirza 2009a). In this study it provides a way to methodologically operationalise intersectionality by mapping the 'affect' of equality discourses as lived in and through the raced and gendered embodied subjectivities of the tutors and the students they teach. That is, it looks at how the external materiality of the Black and Minority Ethnic student's situatedness (i.e. the political, economic and social structures that produce inequality) is constituted, reconfigured and lived through their corporeal representation as seen by the white tutors (i.e. as 'undeserving', 'needy', or 'oppressed' racialised others). In this way it illuminates how intersectional 'othering' is then organised into systematic social relations and practices. It is at the intersection of the material external world and the embodied interior world that the identity of the racialised, sexualised, marginal subject comes into being.

'Getting In and Getting On': A Journey into the Heart of Whiteness

The research investigated the micro-institutional everyday practices that reproduce racism by identifying the 'flashpoints' in an organisation that lead to discriminatory practices for Black and Minority Ethnic teacher trainees. One such everyday institutional 'flashpoint' resides in the recruitment and admissions process where we found systemic patterns of racist exclusion. The tutor's best practice narratives revealed the ways in which certain 'black bodies', such as the bodies of African Caribbean young men were perceived as 'space invaders' when they did not represent the 'racial somatic norm' within elite white institutions (Puwar 2004). Keith, one such African Caribbean young man, who had ambitions to be a science teacher was told by a tutor when attempting to apply to a high status HEI, 'Don't bother to apply, African Caribbean students have difficulty in getting in'. However, when Keith breaks through the admissions barrier with the help of an access workshop and a sympathetic mentor he finds, as many of the BME students did, that he has to pay a high personal price for his 'assimilation' into 'the institutional heart of whiteness'.

Keith's story is not an unfamiliar tale of 'embodied 'lacking', 'personal happenchance' and 'assimilated redemption' that unfolds for many Black and Minority Ethnic students. First Keith was 'protectively' warned not to apply as he was seen—like *all* other African Caribbeans to inherently 'lack' the cultural and academic capital to enter the competitive academic spaces of elite whiteness. Many students may fall at this first hurdle where institutional gatekeepers police the boundaries of what is an 'acceptable or unacceptable' body and which 'type' of body has the right racial credentials to be allowed to enter the hallowed halls of white privilege. Many of the BME students in our study said they did not feel they would stand much of a chance of getting into elite universities, with comments including 'it is way too out of my league'. Their decisions tended to be moulded by an embodied sense of who they are and their expected 'place' in relation to how their race, class, and gender would be perceived. Many saw the 'old' sandstone and redbrick universities as more traditional and strictly catering to more middle class white students and therefore less accessible to them coming from non-traditional educational backgrounds. They often commented on how their familiarity with an HEI influenced their decision, especially if friends and family had gone before. Research shows BME students tend to stick to what they know is achievable and culturally comfortable, and in the light of exorbitant tuition fees, Black and minority working class students reduce their costs by not leaving home and going to a local university, often with a lower market value (Reay et al. 2005; Reay 2017; Smith 2007).

Nirmal Puwar explains how cultures of exclusion operate within the contested social space of higher education (2004). She suggests that Black bodies 'out of place' in elite white institutions are perceived as 'space invaders' when they do not represent the "racial somatic norm" within white institutions. She writes, '*Social spaces are not blank and open for anybody to occupy. Over time, through processes of historical sedimentation, certain types of bodies are designated as being the "natural" occupants of specific spaces…Some bodies have the right to belong in certain locations, while others are marked out as trespassers who are in accordance with how both spaces and bodies are imagined, politically, historically and conceptually circumscribed as being "out of place"* (Puwar 2004: 51). Such 'somatic' processes of exclusion in higher education are difficult to unpack as they are underscored by the embodied intersectional dynamics of race, class and gender. Reay et al. (2005) shed light on these processes of exclusion suggesting young working class and minority ethnic people can engage in affective self-exclusion when making university choices saying, "what's a person like me doing in a place like that" (161). Processes of exclusion work through having "a sense of one's place which leads one to exclude oneself from places from which one is excluded" (Reay et al. 2005: 91). For Black and Minority Ethnic students it is a painful journey of what they must 'give up' of themselves in order to belong. Reay (2017) and Reay et al. (2009) show how Black and working-class survivors in elite universities learnt to navigate the hostilities of higher education through reflexively incorporating dominant white middle-class academic dispositions into their own working class habitus. By taking part in the workshop Keith gained the cultural and academic capital necessary to 'pass' into 'the heart of whiteness'. Kathleen Casey describes how Black student's innocent expectations and eager quest for knowledge can take them on an unexpected journey 'to another place' where they are transformed by the consuming, monolithic power of whiteness: "*young black (wo)men set off into the white world carrying expectations of mythic proportions … their odysseys, they believe, will transform their lives … but separated from their cultural communities these young (people's) passages turn out to be isolated individual journeys into the heart of whiteness*" (Casey 1993: 132).

Ultimately, in the tutor's best practice narrative Keith was redeemed through his 'assimilation' into a white HEI, facilitated by his 'white saviour' (the mentor). To be 'acculturated', lose your cultural markers, to learn to 'act white' (Fordham 1996) and 'fit in' is important for

Black and Minority Ethnic students, as 'standing out' can invoke deep feelings of need, rejection and anxiety within the 'white other'. Black and Minority Ethnic students can be benignly or exotically different but not too racially sexually and religiously different as such radical difference is taken as a rejection of the institutional 'host's society's gift of the multicultural embrace' (Ahmed 2012). Thus to be unassimilated or 'stand out' in an institution invites a certain type of surveillance that appears benign but can be deeply distressing for Black and ethnicised students. For example Patricia Hill Collins (1998: 38) shows how middle-class African American women in higher education are "watched" to ensure they remain "unraced" and assimilated when they enter desegregated institutional spaces of whiteness in the increasingly devalued public sphere from which they were hitherto barred. As the Black feminist Patricia Williams (1991: 74) explains as a Black person you can so easily 'loose a piece of yourself' when navigating the traumatic everyday incursions into your selfhood on the journey 'into the heart of whiteness'.

'Staying the Course': Equalities and the Sheer Weight of Whiteness

Equal opportunities is not always about equality in white institutions, and Sam's case demonstrates the contradictions of policies aimed at creating an equitable 'level playing field' for students of colour. A post-race 'colour-blind' approach to equalities, in which everyone is 'treated the same' whatever their background, was evident in the case of Sam, a Nigerian engineer. Sam was a mature student, who after a long period of unemployment and volunteer youth work, desired to teach young people mathematics. Though bringing a wealth of 'non-traditional experience' to the teaching profession, Sam was given no extra support when he was struggling to complete the course. On one hand Sam as a mature student suffered from the racialised misrecognition of the 'African black male other' (Fanon 1986). On the other his hypervisibility engendered a conscious colour-blind approach among his tutors that cut him adrift in a hostile learning environment.

Whether their views were radical or conservative most of the tutors outwardly expressed a social justice ethos and wanted to be more effective in supporting their Black and Minority Ethnic students through their programmes of learning. However many demonstrated a reluctance to take explicit 'positive action' to support a struggling Black or minority ethnic student. They often felt this amounted to unfair 'special pleading' on the grounds of 'racial disadvantage' that would ultimately lead to a 'dilution of quality' and 'lowering standards' on the course. It was common for white tutors to talk about 'merit' and 'ability' as an objective, value free 'antiracist' arbiter of true equality, without any regard for the caste, class and white privilege that structure access to such opportunities.

Sam's story is a tale of the racialised consequences of liberal equity policies and a student's resilience to overcome the structural systemic racism it engenders. Sam was caught up in the complex web of disadvantage inherent in the liberal approach to equal opportunities. On one hand it recognises the need to 'level up the playing field' of opportunities to ensure people from excluded or disadvantaged ethnic minority or other protected groups can compete on equal terms with more privileged groups. On the other hand certain policies like 'positive action' which are intended to either prevent discrimination or make up for the accumulated effects of past discrimination do not tackle the underlying structural causes of racism (Bhavnani et al. 2005; Essed 1991). Thus while numerical targets and policies can be set if there is evidence of under-representation of minority ethnic groups within various levels of an organisation, professional interventions based on such race equality initiatives are imbued with contradictions inherent in their racialised development. For example, while one tutor celebrated and embraced Sam's 'difference' as a positive attribute to facilitate his access, another tutor interpreted equity as treating everyone the same in a colour-blind way. Sam fell into the gap between the two interpretations of equity (of outcome) and equality (of access) that circulates in our policies in HE institutions.

Sara Ahmed (2012) argues equality policies and diversity documents alone cannot remove racism from the institution. These documents constitute 'non-performative' institutional 'speech acts'. Thus a university making a public commitment to diversity, or admission that they are non-racist and 'for equality', becomes a 'speech act' that work precisely by *not* bringing about the effects it intends. She explains having a 'good' race equality policy gets translated into an institution *being good at race equality*—'as if saying is doing'. For example newer universities which are seen as 'diversity led' (as they have many students from ethnic minorities and lower socioeconomic backgrounds) present themselves as 'being diverse' without having to do anything. Simply 'being diverse' means new universities need not commit to 'doing diversity'. The significant disparity between universities' policy commitments and the experiences of BME students such as Sam suggests deep ongoing institutional barriers and discriminatory practices in the higher education sector.

There are many costs to 'just being there' for Black and Minority Ethnic students in higher education and a Sam's 'price' was high. Black and Minority Ethnic students are more likely to leave university before completing their course than any other group and least likely to get a good degree (Universities UK 2016; Richardson 2015). The most influential reasons for leaving are unmet expectations about higher education. While financial and family difficulties, institutional factors (such as poor teaching), and wrong subject choice also feature, ethnic minority students additionally reported the feeling of isolation or hostility in academic culture (Connor et al. 2004; Bhopal et al. 2013). These are worrying findings, as they signal the fact that many Black students do not feel they 'belong'. Bodies that are visually recognised as raced and gendered clearly carry unequal value depending on their position in space and place (Skeggs 1997). Sam's embodied experience as a Black African man 'out of place' is articulated in Franz Fanon's classic analysis of the colonial racialisation of the Black body which he poignantly argues is '*sealed into the crushing object hood of the skin*'. As Fanon writes, "*Not only must the black man be black, he must be black in relation to the white man. The Black man does not know at what moment his inferiority comes into being through the other. In the white world the man of colour encounters difficulties in the development of his bodily schema - a slow composition of me as a body in the middle of a spatial and temporal world-such seems to be the schema. It does not impose itself on me; it is rather a definitive structuring of the self and the world- definitive because it creates a real dialectic between my body and the world*" (Fanon 1986: 11).

There appears to be two antagonistic forces at play in higher education which frames Sam's intersectional raced, gendered and classed embodied experience. One moves unconsciously and haphazardly towards what Stuart Hall has called 'multicultural drift' (Hall 2000) with its eclectic 'grab bag' of solutions for achieving equality through the end goal of 'assimilated difference' (Lentin 2016). The other remains the 'sheer weight of whiteness' which in HE institutions is overt and impenetrable (Back 2004; Alexander and Arday 2015). Gillborn (2008) argues whiteness is a position that involves the maintenance of white interests and white privilege. It does so by excluding non-whites and denying that white people are racialised. By asserting white supremacy is only claimed by extremists groups, whiteness assumes the 'business-as-usual' silent domination which sustains the symbolic violence of everyday racism. This whiteness is evident in the 'soft' unchallenging anti-racist/multicultural position taken up by white student teachers and tutors (Lander 2011). For example Wilkins and Lall (2010) found racist comments aimed at Black and Minority Ethnic student teachers were perceived as 'unwitting prejudice' rather than racist. A comment such as 'did you have an arranged marriage' was normalised rather than been seen as racist because of the assumed 'unintentionality' of the comment. Solomon et al. (2005) found student teachers rejected notions of white privilege as did Aveling's (2006) study in which the examination of whiteness led to student hostility, defence and denial.

'Threatening Bodies': Navigating Institutional Gendered Religious Racism

The story of Kusbah, a young Muslim woman trainee teacher on her school placement illuminates how the intersectional complexities of gender, race and religion is lived in, on and through the Muslim female body and has real consequences for how she is perceived and the opportunities to progress that are therefore open to her. The overt racism which Kusbah experienced as a veiled Muslim woman shows the multiple ways macro geopolitical discourses of anti-Islamic hostility in Britain and its production of the raced and gendered Muslim female body operates through institutional structures in higher education to 'affectively' reproduce racialised gendered divisions that inhibit the academic progression.

Kusbah's story is one of embodied racialised religious 'threat' and the racist gendered physical and psychological containment it invokes. Visible Muslim women wearing the veil, such as Kusbah, openly face hostile reactions in a climate of State sanctioned gendered Islamophobic discrimination (EHRC 2016). The scholarly interventions of postcolonial critical race feminists shows how the Muslim female body has become a symbolic battlefield in the war against Islam and the perceived Muslim enemy 'within' (Razack 2008; Razack et al. 2010). In the West's ideological 'War Against Terror' the ubiquitous 'Muslim woman' has come to symbolise the 'barbaric Muslim other' in our midst. The visibility of patriarchal community and group cultural practices such as forced marriage and honour crimes conveniently contribute to the Western 'Orientalist' construction of the racialised Muslim other's barbaric customs and cultures (Said 1985). This is articulated through Muslim women being pathologised as voiceless victims of their 'backward' communities who are in need of 'saving' by the enlightened 'West' (Abu-Lughod 2002).

The tutors 'best practice' narrative of Kusbah shows how Muslim female students come to be stereotyped as either 'passive or oppressed'. Paul, her white male placement tutor was exceptionally hard on a Kusbah because he believed *all* Muslim women make poor teachers and she needed 'saving' from herself and given a dose of tough love so she could make 'the grade'. Paul believed he had a legitimate right— authority even, to comment and judge Kusbah as a weak and acquiescent 'Muslim woman'.

Research shows Muslim young women in schools are often subject to white western teachers' essentialised expectations about what it means to be a 'true' and 'good' Muslim young woman (Mirza and Meetoo 2018). Their lives in the classroom are structured by both openly expressed gendered religious racism, as well as the more subtle forms of covert bodily regulation of their sexuality through the policing of their behaviour and dress. The teachers' perceptions of the young women wearing the veil

were bounded by popular concerns about their agency and what they perceived to be their cultural and familial disempowerment and restricted
scope for choice. The hyper-surveillance Kusbah was subjected to by
Paul in the cultural and social space of the school amounted to a form
of 'infantilisation' of her agency and ability (Puwar 2004). Here not only
was Kusbah pigeonholed as being Muslim and female but she was also
seen by Paul as less capable of being in authority—with 'pupils walking all
over her'. She was viewed suspiciously and had to work harder for recognition outside of the confines of stereotypical expectations. The constant
doubt about her skills and the disciplinary measures she was disproportionately subjected to affected her career progression as she was being
failed by Paul in her teaching practice.

Paul saw Kusbah's Islamic practices and beliefs through the western
normative assumptions about Muslim female docility and complicity
with patriarchal conservative cultural values. However a Muslim wom-
en's agency and acts of faith are rarely seen within the broader political and social environment. As Sara Ahmed (2004) explains the figure
of the veiled Muslim woman challenges the values that are crucial to
the multicultural nation, such freedom and culture, making her a symbol of what the nation must 'give up' to be itself. Muslim women are
conscious of the 'disjunction' between how they see themselves and how
they are racially constructed as a 'female Muslim other' in Britain (Khan
2016). The embodied experience of being a British Muslim woman 'out
of place' is articulated by the postcolonial feminist writer Lata Mani.
She writes, 'The disjunctions between how I saw myself and the kind of
knowledge about me that I kept bumping into in the West opened up
new questions for social and political inquiry' (1989: 11).

For Kusbah being a Muslim woman was a crucial aspect of her sense
of self and ethnic belonging. It was through her religious disposition
that she expressed her embodied gendered religious agency. For many
Muslim women the headscarf (hijab) is not a symbol of oppression but
experienced as a 'second skin' (Mirza 2013). Personal embodied acts
of piety such as wearing the hijab are an 'identity affect' which enables
them to move beyond the simplistic cultural constructions of Muslim
women in the media that negates Muslim female agency (Haw 2009).
In contrast to the more outwardly collective masculine expressions

of Muslimness, in which Islam has been mobilised as a political and nationalistic power resource in civil society, Muslim women like Kusbah express their faith as a private transcendental spiritual space from which they derive an inner strength. Saba Mahmood (2005) seeks to explain this form of embodied gendered religious agency through acts of piety or taqwa. She argues Muslim women's religious disposition, such as obedience to God brings spiritual rewards in and of itself to the women. She suggests that in order to understand Islamic female forms of moral subjectivity and embodied spiritual interiority, we must move beyond western imperialist notions of libratory emancipation and the deterministic binaries of resistance/subordination by which Muslim female subjectivity and agency is so often judged.

Conclusion: Finding 'Safe Spaces' in Post-race Times

In this chapter I take a Black feminist embodied approach to evaluating the intersectionality of race, faith and gender as it manifests itself in our overwhelmingly dominant white places of teaching and learning in post-race times. By interrogating the micro-institutional practices that maintain endemic patterns of racist exclusion in higher education the three 'best practice' narratives of the tutors that frame this chapter illuminate what I call racialised institutional 'flashpoints'. These are moments when Black and Minority Ethnic students on a teacher education course come up against systemic institutional gendered and racialised discrimination. 'Embodied intersectionality' as a concept gave me the theoretical tools to help me make sense of the PGCE tutors narratives and unpack the ways in which gender, race, religion, and other social divisions were simultaneously experienced as lived realities on and through the Black male and Muslim female bodies of Keith, Sam and Kusbah. All three students were constructed as 'bodies out of place' in the 'best practice' equality narratives of the tutors. In each case the students embodied raced and gendered human agency framed their struggle for life chances and determined their academic well-being and progress through the course.

The experience of racism was not uncommon during the student's course and tutors reported having to deal directly with incidents around gendered race faith based ethnic and cultural differences. Teacher educators often asked us in interviews, 'tell us how to tackle cultural, faith-based and familial tensions without being racist or patronising?' Generally, and somewhat surprisingly for a university with a 'diverse' student make-up, tutors were not confident and received very little training and support about issues to do with multiculturalism, bilingualism, inclusive pedagogy and practice. Topics such as talking about Islam and ethnic and religious difference were consciously avoided in classroom discussions. While supporting Black and Minority Ethnic students through their teaching practice was a core concern of tutors, many felt 'multiculturalism', with its inclusive emphasis on accommodating different cultures and religions can conflict with their 'neutral' professional aim of supporting *all* students to achieve their potential.

The white tutors were united in wanting more open dialogue in their institutions about tackling issues of racism that went beyond simple compliance with the law, they however found little time to do so. They expressed a desire to challenge their professional practice by developing an inclusive classroom pedagogy underpinned by culturally relevant curricula and desired a 'safe space' for open and frank dialogue about tackling issues of racism at a personal and professional level. However decolonising taken-for-granted knowledges and entrenched 'ways of being' inherent within our institutional walls requires not only deep self-reflection, but an intellectual and institutional 'safe space' to develop critical consciousness. This is not easy to achieve and as Gaine (2001) asserts—if it did 'not hurt' then it did 'not work' alluding to the cognitive conflict associated with race awareness training, that without there would be no true shift in understanding the privileges of whiteness. However in the latest incarnation of bureaucratic anti-racist training, concerns about systemic institutional racism in 1990s has given way to lessons in addressing individual 'unconscious bias' (ECU 2015). Such workshops are never 'safe spaces' for people of colour who are so often invited to 'tell their story'. As Leonardo and Porter (2010) eloquently argue, in an inherently violent colonial racial order, race dialogue in white privileged settings means in reality, 'Blacks disappear to give way to educating whites'.

As committed researchers and practitioners, if we are serious about the political project of decolonising higher education, we first need to ask ourselves, 'what are our principles of anti-racist professional and academic engagement, and how do we arrive at them?' If we are to achieve '*real*' equality of outcome for Black and Minority Ethnic people *in* our places of higher learning, the challenge for intersectional inclusion in 'post-race' times is to move the discourse beyond targeting the bodies of raced and gendered others as proof of an institutions commitment to diversity. In post-race times, where 'race' is off the political agenda, to achieve a more diverse and equitable higher education system, there must be an honest dialogue on gender, race, faith and culture that goes beyond the 'performativity' of 'race equality' in our institutions—where saying you are *for* race equality does not mean you *do* race equality! My hope is always, that with visionary leadership our universities can be 'brave places of possibility', opening up radical movements for achieving 'real' race equality which respects and embraces the humanity of every person. The task is not easy, and as history shows, movements for racial justice are fraught with messy and hard fought struggles between the powerful and those who are deemed less than human. The sustainability and success of such movements are predicated on an 'unsafe' steep and honest learning curve for all those involved.

References

Abu-Lughod, L. (2002). Do Muslim Women Really Need Saving? Anthropological Reflections on Cultural Relativism and Its Others. *American Anthropologist, 104*(3), 783–790.

Ahmed, S. (2004). *The Politics of Emotion*. Durham and London: Duke University Press.

Ahmed, S. (2009). Embodying Diversity: Problems and Paradoxes for Black Feminists. *Race Ethnicity and Education, 12*(1), 41–52.

Ahmed, S. (2012). *On Being Included: Racism and Diversity in Institutional Life*. Durham: Duke University Press.

Alexander, C., & Arday, J. (Eds.). (2015). *Aiming Higher: Race Inequality and Diversity in the Academy*. London: Runnymede Trust and London School of Economics.

Applebaum, B. (2008). 'Doesn't My Experience Count?' White Students, the Authority of Experience and Social Justice Pedagogy. *Race, Ethnicity and Education, 11*(4), 405–414.

Aveling, N. (2006). Hacking at Our Very Roots: Rearticulating White Racial Identity Within the Context of Teacher Education. *Race, Ethnicity and Education, 9*(3), 261–274.

Back, L. (2004). Ivory Towers? The Academy and Racism. In I. Law, D. Phillips, & L. Turney (Eds.), *Institutional Racism in Higher Education* (pp. 1–13). Stoke on Trent: Trentham Books.

Bhambara, G. (2016, November). Class Analysis in the Age of Trump (and Brexit): The Pernicious New Politics of Identity. *The Sociological Review.* https://www.thesociologicalreview.com/blog/the-crisis-of-multicultural-ism-and-the-global-politics-of-trumpism.html.

Bhavnani, R., Mirza, H., & Meetoo, V. (2005). *Tackling the Roots of Racism: Lessons for Success.* Bristol: Policy Press.

Bhopal, K., & Jackson, J. (2013). *The Experiences of Black and Minority Ethnic Academics: Multiple Identities and Career Progression.* Southampton: University of Southampton.

Brah, A., & Phoenix, A. (2004). Ain't IA Woman? Revisiting Intersectionality. *Journal of International Women's Studies, 5*(3), 75–86.

Caluya, G., Elspeth, P., & Shvetal, V. (2011). 'Affective Eduscapes': The Case of Indian Students Within Australian International Higher Education. *Cambridge Journal of Education, 41*(1), 85–99.

Casey, K. (1993). *I Answer with My Life: Life Histories of Women Teachers Working for Social Change.* New York: Routledge.

Collins, P. H. (1998). *Fighting Words: Black Women and the Search for Justice.* Minneapolis: University of Minnesota Press.

Collins, P. H. (2000). *Black Feminist Thought: Knowledge Consciousness and the Politics of Empowerment* (2nd ed.). London: Routledge.

Connor, H. Tyers, C., Modood T., & Hillage, J. (2004). *Why the Difference? A Closer Look at Higher Education Minority Ethnic Students and Graduates.* DfES Research Report 552. http://www.dfes.gov/research.

Crenshaw, K. W. (1989). Demarginalising the Intersection of Race and Sex: A Black Feminist Critique of Antidiscrimination Doctrine, Feminist Theory and Antiracist Politics. *University of Chicago Legal Forum,* (1), 139–167. Article 8.

Crenshaw, K. W. (1991). Mapping the Margins: Intersectionality, Identity Politics, and Violence Against Women of Color. *Stanford Law Review, 43*(6), 1241–1299.

ECU. (2015). *Unconscious Bias and Higher Education.* London: Equality Challenge Unit.

EHRC. (2016, August). *Healing a Divided Britain: The Need for a Comprehensive Race Equality Strategy.* London: Equality and Human Rights Commission.

Essed, P. (1991). *Understanding Everyday Racism: An Interdisciplinary Theory.* London: Sage.

Fanon, F. (1986). *Black Skin White Masks* (3rd ed.). London: Pluto Books.

Fordham, S. (1996). *Blacked Out: Dilemmas of Race, Identity and Success at Capital High.* Chicago: University of Chicago Press.

Gaine, C. (2001). 'If It's Not Hurting It's Not Working': Teaching Teachers about 'Race'. *Research Papers in Education, 16*(1), 93–113.

Gillborn, D. (2008). *Racism and Education: Coincidence or Conspiracy?* London: Routledge.

Gilroy, P. (2012). My Britain Is Fuck All: Zombie Multiculturalism and the Race Politics of Citizenship. *Identities: Global Studies in Culture and Power, 19*(4), 380–397.

Goldberg, D. T. (2013). The Post-racial Contemporary. In N. Kapoor, V. Kalra, & J. Rhodes (Eds.), *The State of Race* (pp. 15–30). Basingstoke: Palgrave Macmillan.

Hall, S. (2000). The Multicultural Question. In B. Hesse (Ed.), *Un/Settled Multiculturalisms.* London: Zed Books.

Haw, K. (2009). From Hijab to Jilbab and the 'Myth' of British Identity: Being Muslim in Contemporary Britain a Half-Generation on. *Race Ethnicity and Education, 12*(3), 363–378.

Kapoor, N., Kalra, V., & Rhodes, J. (Eds.). (2013). *The State of Race.* Basingstoke: Palgrave Macmillan.

Khan, A. (2016, December 6). Sorry Louise Casey but Women Are Held Back by Discrimination. *The Guardian.* https://www.theguardian.com/commentisfree/2016/dec/06/louise-caseydiscrimination-muslim-women-bradford.

Lander, V. (2011). Race, Culture and All That: An Exploration of the Perspectives of White Secondary Student Teachers About Race Equality Issues in Their Initial Teacher Education. *Race, Ethnicity and Education, 3*(14), 351–364.

Lentin, A. (2014). Post-race, Post Politics: The Paradoxical Rise of Culture After Multiculturalism. *Ethnic and Racial Studies, 37*(8), 1268–1285.

Lentin, A. (2016, December 6). The 'Crisis of Multiculturalism' and the Global Politics of Trumpism. *The Sociological Review.* https://www.

thesociologicalreview.com/blog/the-crisis-of-multiculturalism-and-the-glob-al-politics-of-trumpism.html.

Leonardo, Z., & Porter, R. K. (2010). Pedagogy of Fear: Toward a Fanonian Theory of 'Safety' in Race Dialogue. *Race Ethnicity and Education, 13*(2), 139–157.

Mahmood, S. (2005). *The Politics of Piety: The Islamic Revival and the Feminist Subject*. Princeton: Princeton University Press.

Mani, L. (1989). Multiple Mediations: Feminist Scholarship in the Age of Multiple Mediations. *Inscriptions, 5*, 1–23.

Mirza, H. S. (2009a). *Race, Gender and Educational Desire. Why Black Women Succeed and Fail*. London: Routledge.

Mirza, H. S. (2009b). Plotting a History: Black and Postcolonial Feminisms in New Times. *Race Ethnicity and Education, 12*(1), 1–10.

Mirza, H. S. (2013). 'A Second Skin': Embodied Intersectionality, Transnationalism and Narratives of Identity and Belonging Among Muslim Women in Britain. *Women's Studies International Forum, 36*, 5–16.

Mirza, H. S. (2015). 'Harvesting Our Collective Intelligence': Black British Feminism in Post-race Times. *Women's Studies International Forum, 51*, 1–9.

Mirza, H. S. (2017). 'One in a Million': A Journey of a Post-colonial Woman of Colour in the White Academy. In D. Gabriel & S. Tate (Eds.), *Inside the Ivory Tower, Narratives of Women of Colour Surviving and Thriving in British Academia*. London: Trentham Press.

Mirza, H. S., & Meetoo, V. (2012). *Respecting Difference: Race, Faith and Culture for Teacher Educators*. London: IOE Press.

Mirza, H. S., & Meetoo, V. (2018). Empowering Muslim Girls? Post-feminism, Multiculturalism and the Production of the 'Model' Muslim Female Student in British Schools. *British Journal of Sociology of Education, 39*(2), 227–241. https://doi.org/10.1080/01425692.2017.1406336.

Nayak, A. (2006). After Race: Ethnography, Race and Post-race Theory. *Ethnic and Racial Studies, 29*(93), 411–430.

Puwar, N. (2004). Fish In or Out of Water: A Theoretical Framework for Race and the Space of Academia. In I. Law, D. Phillips, & L. Turney (Eds.), *Institutional Racism in Higher Education*. Stoke on Trent: Trentham Books.

Razack, S. (2008). *Casting Out: The Eviction of Muslims from Western Laws and Politics*. Toronto: University of Toronto Press.

Razack, S., Smith, M., & Thobani, S. (Eds.). (2010). *States of Race: Critical Race Feminism for the 21st Century*. Toronto: Between the Lines Press.

Reay, D. (2017). *Miseducation: Inequality Education and the Working Classes.* Bristol: Policy Press.

Reay, D., Crozier, G., & Clayton, J. (2009). 'Strangers in Paradise'? Working-Class Students in Elite Universities. *Sociology, 43*(6), 1103–1121.

Reay, D., David, M., & Ball, S. (2005). *Degrees of Choice: Social Class, Race and Gender in Higher Education.* Stoke on Trent: Trentham Books.

Richardson John, T. E. (2015). The Under-Attainment of Ethnic Minority Students in UK Higher Education: What We Know and What We Don't Know. *Journal of Further and Higher Education, 39*(2), 278–291.

Said, E. (1985). *Orientalism: Western Concepts of the Orient.* Harmondsworth: Penguin.

Simmonds, F. (1997). My Body Myself: How Does a Black Woman Do Sociology? In H. S. Mirza (Ed.), *Black British Feminism.* London: Routledge.

Skeggs, B. (1997). *Formations of Class and Gender: Becoming Respectable.* London: Sage.

Smith, H. (2007, December). Playing a Different Game: The Contextualised Decision-Making Processes of Minority Ethnic Students in Choosing a Higher Education Institution. *Race, Ethnicity and Education, 10*(4), 415–437.

Solomon, R. P., Portelli, J. P., Daniel, B. J., & Campbell, A. (2005, July). The Discourse of Denial: How White Teacher Candidates Construct Race, Racism and 'White Privilege'. *Race, Ethnicity and Education, 8*(2), 147–169.

Solórzano, D. G., & Yosso, T. J. (2002). Critical Race Methodology: Counter-Storytelling as an Analytical Framework of Education Research. *Qualitative Inquiry, 8*(1), 23–44.

Universities UK. (2016). *Working in Partnership: The Final Report of the Social Mobility Advisory Group.* London: Universities UK.

Wilkins, C., & Lall, R. (2010). Getting by or Getting on? Black Student Teachers' Experiences of Teacher Education. *Race Equality Teaching, 28*(2), 19–26.

Williams, P. J. (1991). *The Alchemy of Race and Rights: The Diary of a Law Professor.* Cambridge, MA: Harvard University Press.

11

White Privilege, Empathy and Alterity in Higher Education—Teaching About Race and Racism in the Sociology of PE and Sport

Michael Hobson and Stuart Whigham

Introduction

This autoethnographic account discusses our experiences of delivering lectures on race and ethnicity in physical education (PE) and sport to consider the extent to which our status as white HE practitioners reinforces and/or undermines white privilege in HE. As white males with research interests in other sociological phenomenon in the fields of PE and sport, namely social class (Michael) and nationalism (Stuart), we make no claim to be experts in the field of race. Instead, we attempt to position ourselves as part of the structures that reinforce the hegemonic status of whiteness within higher education (HE). Hereby, we explore our attempts to simultaneously develop critical consciousness

M. Hobson (✉)
St Mary's University, Twickenham, UK
e-mail: michael.hobson@stmarys.ac.uk

S. Whigham
Oxford Brookes University, Oxford, UK
e-mail: swhigham@brookes.ac.uk

© The Author(s) 2018
J. Arday and H. S. Mirza (eds.), *Dismantling Race in Higher Education*,
https://doi.org/10.1007/978-3-319-60261-5_11

in both our own praxis and that of the students that we work with (Ladson-Billings 1995), in order to both illuminate and challenge the often unacknowledged inherent power of whiteness in education and society more broadly (Leonardo 2004; Leonardo and Porter 2010). In this piece we unpick some of the frailties of our previous practice and provide a discussion of some of the principles we are currently considering in developing pedagogic strategies that attempt to develop an actively anti-racist stance.

Despite the fact that the undergraduate programmes we work on incorporate lectures on race and ethnicity as a part of the curriculum, such sessions are comparatively low-status in comparison to the development of sport-specific knowledge and pedagogical strategies in an applied context. Instead, lectures on race and ethnicity are viewed as an optional supplement for students with an interest in this topic, rather than a crucial aspect of developing effective pedagogical practitioners in the field of PE and sport. For example, within Michael's institution, students are offered the opportunity to learn about the practical application of disability sports techniques nearly thirty times over the space of three years, whereas bespoke lectures on race and ethnicity are only offered four times. This therefore illustrates that in our experience issues of race and ethnicity are often marginalised during the development of PE and sport practitioners, with a lack of emphasis on the importance of developing praxis which challenges the normative whiteness of these fields.

This chapter therefore aims to consider whether our past practice has provided a critical pedagogic voice, or if it has simply provided a platform for white academics to unconsciously reinforce the institutional whiteness of HE. In particular, we reflect upon the possibility for white academics such as ourselves to empathise with the racialised social experiences of BME students in our cohorts, and the potential risk that our practice simply offers tokenistic discussion of race which reinforce the current forms of inequality and white privilege, whilst violating the alterity of our students (Frank 2004; Levinas 1999). These risks to our students' alterity, and the resultant need for respect of their position as an 'other' whose experiences and emotions which can never be fully understood, thus demand that we, as white academics, critically reflect upon the potential unintended outcomes of our practice in this regard.

Given that academic discussion of race and racism in HE is underdeveloped across disciplines compared to other aspects of identity, such as gender, it can be argued that there is a requirement for pedagogy to instigate activism within the student body. To this end, we heed the arguments of Flintoff et al. (2015) who rightfully identify the benefits of exploring our personal experiences of white privilege within the domain of PE and sport. However, in line with the arguments of (Leonardo 2004; Leonardo and Porter 2010), we also reflect on how we have sought to develop our pedagogical practice when teaching about race and ethnicity in order to move beyond narcissistic accounts and discussions of our 'whiteness', and attempting instead to encourage our students from all racial and ethnic backgrounds to critically reflect upon the structural factors which continue to perpetuate white racial dominance in society. As a result, we hope to provide stimulus for fellow white academics to adopt pedagogical approaches that provide the impetus for activism and empowerment, whilst exploring the nature of normative behaviours associated with 'whiteness' in HE.

We adopt an autoethnographic methodological approach to inform our forthcoming discussion, centering our discussion around a series of reflective vignettes on critical events which epitomise our many shared ruminations on our 'whiteness' when delivering lectures on the topics of race and ethnicity. As has been argued elsewhere (Chang 2016; Ellis and Bochner 2000; Ellis et al. 2010), autoethnographic approaches facilitate an opportunity for researchers to both share and critically analyse past experiences with their audience, and this methodological approach has been shown to be fruitful in academic reflections on the nature of 'whiteness' (Magnet 2006; Pennington 2013; Toyosaki et al. 2009). Whilst colleagues and office-mates on the BA Physical and Sport Education degree programme at St. Mary's University, we spent a great deal of time informally reflecting upon our pedagogical practice together. As relatively inexperienced members of academic staff in our field these conversations were central in shaping our awareness of our own positionality within our field, and our practice when delivering content relating to race and ethnicity emerged as the most frequently discussed element of our teaching responsibilities. Indeed, it is the frequency of these reflective discussions which has motivated us to share our reflections with a wider audience.

To this end, we have selected four vignettes which concisely illustrate examples of incidents which have challenged our pedagogical practice as white academics, with each vignette followed up with a critical reflection on the respective incident by each author through engagement with academic literature from the fields of critical race theory, education and the sociology of sport. The concluding section brings our separate 'voices' back together for a collaborative reflection upon the potential implications of our respective experiences for white academics, particularly those who also strive to move beyond simply creating 'safe space' discussions of whiteness which fail to illuminate the engrained structural nature of white domination and racial injustice in our society (Leonardo and Porter 2010).

Am I Too White to Talk About Blackness?—Michael Hobson

Since the department's expert on race in sport (a black male) had left at the end of the previous semester I'd volunteered to take the session on race the first time. Yet as it grew nearer more worries ran through my head, with just over a third of the class of thirty from BME backgrounds. As a white male will I appear sincere to my students? Will I offend anybody? What if the group don't engage in discussion, or somebody says something ignorant or offensive? I'd prepared a lot for the session, thinking carefully about the tasks I planned to offer room for discussion but to limit the chance of causing offense. I'd even sent my slides to my former colleague to get his thoughts on what I'd prepared. Validation from a black peer seemed important for me to ease my anxieties. Nonetheless, I still felt on edge. An hour and half later and the session was complete and I felt a sense of relief; the discussions had been good, no one had appeared to take offense, and a few students even mentioned discussing the topic in their assignment. Now that I'd finished… this all seemed a bit dramatic.

During my initial experience of teaching in HE, I had embraced the relative comfort of teaching about the rules of sports, pedagogical models, and creative ways of transmitting knowledge. However, the incorporation of critical discussions of identity was something I did not appreciate the value of. The power dynamics associated with the content I taught were not was invisible to me, and as far as I was concerned using what I deemed to be fairly exciting and innovative approaches towards teaching should be enough to engage all learners regardless of race. However, through exposure to critical theory, my opinion began to change with the focus of my teaching increasingly being orientated towards the sociology of PE, and sport, moving away from the "what" and the "how" of teaching and coaching sport that preoccupied many of my colleagues. However, even as a sociologist I still felt a discomfort in discussing issues regarding race, I often lent towards discussing safer topics such as social class, policy or social theory. If I as a liberal, white sociologist felt unable to approach the topic of race this led me to question other people readiness to tackle such issues within HE.

In the years following the session discussed above, Morrison's (1992) analogy of 'the fishbowl' has become an extremely powerful metaphor for the invisibility of racism which has informed my thinking. She argues that white supremacy in society is present on a structural level that reflects the political system and power struggle in which it is embedded (Taylor 2016). Like a fishbowl, these structures transparently permit the order of life inside, however remain invisible to white protagonists whose lived experience renders them unable to view their own privilege within the system. Within HE the 'order of life' derives from the curricula, the hierarchy of disciplines, the heritage of establishments, the faculty and the student body (Gillborn 2008; Pilkington 2013); all of these are shaped by the historical and cultural developments of HE (Bathmaker et al. 2013). Recent critiques of HE in the UK have described the hierarchy as 'male, pale, and stale' (NUS 2016) with white middle-class males dominating the most influential positions, both ideologically within the curriculum (the dominance of dead white male theorists), and physically within the faculty. This has often left me wondering as a white male lecturing in HE, how to highlight and disrupt the structural inequalities and anxieties that reproduce white privilege within the discipline of PE and sport in HE.

Traditionally, the more vocationally-focused programmes such as the mass PE and sport degrees I teach on are viewed as being lower within the hierarchies of HE; however, these 'lower-status' courses often still demonstrate privileges to white students (Shay 2013). Through subtle implicit messages that are transmitted through daily practices of PE and sports programmes in schools and universities, invisible pedagogies are transmitted, subtly conveying idealised forms of knowing for students in order to successfully negotiate the terrain of PE and sport in HE (Fitzpatrick 2012; Aldous et al. 2014). Central to the construction of the correct way of knowing is desire for these programmes to reproduce 'people like us', a phenomenon that occurs in the recruitment of staff and the knowledge studied within courses (Alexander and Arday 2015). Archer (2007) notes the curriculum of education studies within HE has moved away from the critical discussions of society present during the 1970s, instead privileging understanding of the 'what' and the 'how' of teaching, while the who is sidelined to a number of labels and acronyms such as 'BME', English as an Additional Language (EAL) and Special Educational Needs and Disabilities (SEND). These technocratic practices are rooted in the development of practical competencies of transmission of skills, drills, and behaviour management (Dowling et al. 2015). This knowledge is viewed as neutral to race, gender, sexuality and other aspects of social identity, thus reproducing behaviour that demonstrates idealised forms of whiteness in PE and sport rather than illuminating its racialised nature (Hylton 2015).

Subsequently, this is reinforced through the lack of diversity regarding staff members within my institution. Within studies of HE, one influential factor for students from all social stratifications and ethnicities in their choice of institution is a sense of attending a university with other 'people like us' (Bourdieu 1990). However, while on the one hand my students from a BME background are becoming increasingly likely to experience others with similar cultural heritage in the student body (Alexander and Arday 2015; Gorard 2010), constituting approximately a third of our 300 students at St. Mary's, the experience of being taught by 'people like them' is not possible at my institution given our entirely white staff team. Seeing individuals that display similar tastes, mannerisms, and physical characteristics is considered highly influential in drawing students towards particular topics and institutions (Ball et al. 2002; Crozier et al. 2008; Reay 1998, 2001). This reinforces the notion that white academics act as custodians of knowledge who unconsciously reinforce a hierarchy of whiteness and 'other' BME students. This can result in BME students experiencing a disconnect from the faculty, and experiencing a sense of the university being a white space. In sum, this section is representative of the awakening of my critical consciousness regarding the inherent whiteness of our field within HE, and the need for more actively anti-racist pedagogical stances.

The 'Affective Domain' and Student Alterity in Higher Education—Stuart Whigham

6 months after leaving St Mary's, I receive a 'Jiscmail' mailing list email from my replacement as module leader on the second year sociology of sport and PE module. Curious, I read on to discover that they are appealing for guest lecturers to deliver particular sessions on the module relating to religion, sexuality, social inclusion, race and ethnicity in sport, arguing their privileged position as a "straight, white, atheist, PhD-educated" academic potentially prevents them from adopting a sufficiently "critical vantage" to deliver these topics. I immediately feel uncomfortable as this new set of eyes on the module content has confirmed a nagging feeling that I had discussed with my previous colleague Michael – my inability to truly empathise with my students when delivering these sessions from a similarly privileged standpoint. I feel a flush of embarrassed red coming over my face as I reflect on whether I have been doing my Black, Ethnic Minority, female, or LGBT students a disservice through my fudged attempts to empathise with their lived experiences, or whether I have simply missed a trick to enhance the quality of their learning experience by failing to enlist the help of academics with specialisms on these topics...

With Michael having considered his increased awareness of 'white privilege' in HE, my attention now turns to the manifestation of this privileged position when delivering educational content on race. In particular, I draw on the work of Bloom (1956) and Bloom et al. (1956) on the contrasting domains of learning, with specific reference to learning experiences in the 'affective domain', to reflect on the issues of empathy and alterity highlighted in my vignette. For Bloom, learning in the 'affective domain' involves the development of an individual's ability to understanding both their own emotions and those of others, thus being able to empathise with the values, experiences, attitudes and positions of others more effectively.

I have found the notion of learning in the 'affective domain' important when reflecting upon the issue of race and racism in HE. This approach moves beyond simply developing the 'cognitive domain' of knowledge that racism and racial stereotyping exists in society, to a more empathetic understanding of the experiences of individuals of a different race where the learning experiences focus on challenging racial attitudes by considering the subjective positions of others (Flintoff and Webb 2012). Through my knowledge of the structure of similar PE courses in the UK, it would appear that the inclusion of sociological content within PE degree programmes, and Initial Teacher Training programmes more widely, tends to have the explicit rationale of fostering this empathetic understanding of the impacts of social stratification on learners (Flintoff et al. 2015; Hylton 2015).

Whilst this use of sociological content to develop more empathetic and inclusive educational practitioners is undoubtedly a laudable goal at face value, I have found that the core assumptions of this approach to learning in the 'affective domain' are more problematic and, at times, potentially contradictory when applied in practice (Beard et al. 2007). For example, when teaching students about the potential barriers to progression to senior leadership positions within the field of sport or PE for Black students, or the potential falsehood of using sport as a means of social mobility for Black athletes, my understanding of the nature of racial discrimination is clearly limited by my lack of experience of such phenomena in practice.

However, these positional challenges may not always be fully appreciated by practitioners due to a lack of self-examination of the privileges afforded to them by their 'invisible' whiteness in the educational domain (Flintoff et al. 2015). My personal experience of these positional challenges has always prompted a certain degree of navel-gazing with regards to the delivery of content on the topic of race and my inability to empathise with the lived experiences of our Black and Minority Ethnicity students within both education and society more broadly. Given that I have never experienced the effects of overt, covert or institutionalised racism due to my whiteness, my ability to provide a fully authentic or appreciative account of the impacts of race in the contexts of education or sport is undoubtedly hampered by our own privileged racial characteristics.

Levinas' (1999) and Frank's (2004) arguments regarding the concept of 'alterity' is instructive for exploring the impact of my white privilege on student-teacher dynamics in the context of HE. Both theorists emphasise the importance of respecting the 'alterity' or 'otherness' of other individuals within social interactions, highlighting the risk of crudely violating the experiences and beliefs of others through well-intentioned attempts to empathise with others. In particular, Frank (2004: 115) argues that:

> to infringe on the other person's alterity – their otherness that precedes any attributes – is to commit violence against the other. Symbolic violence comprises the often subtle ways that alterity is challenged and violated.

The positional challenges faced by white practitioners in HE when covering content relating to race are fundamentally rooted in the violation of the alterity of Black and Minority Ethnicity students. Whilst my attempts to encourage learning through the 'affective domain' and the development of skills of empathy for white educational practitioners or students may have good intentions, I will always remain unable to provide an authentic and complete understanding of the lived experiences of other racial groups who occupy the 'liminal space of alterity' (Ladson-Billings and Donnor 2008; Rollock 2012). Furthermore, if the discussions I facilitate fail to critically examine the factors which support the structural nature of white domination in society, then we will simply revert back to the superficial 'safe-space' discussion of race denounced by Leonardo and Porter (2010: 148):

> ...the reason why safe-space discussions partly break down in practice, if not at least in theory, is that they assume that, by virtue of formal and procedural guidelines, safety has been designated for both white people and people of color. However, the term 'safety' acts as a misnomer because it often means that white individuals can be made to feel safe. Thus, a space of safety is circumvented, and instead a space of oppressive color-blindness is established. It is a managed health-care version of anti-racism, an insurance against 'looking racist'.

Race, Ethnicity and the Sociology of PE & Sport—A Case in Point?—Stuart Whigham

I'm pretty sure that at some point during my seminar on the topic of race and ethnicity in sport, the 'n-word' debate will be raised by a student for discussion, as has happened on every previous occasion. This time it happens in record speed, with the issue raised by a Black male student halfway through the lecture who asks my thoughts on whether it is racist for a white person to use the phrase – no ducking the issue in front of a full crowd. Following what can only be described as painful advanced caveating of my response (e.g. context of phrase, intent of phrase, lyrical repetition versus self-selected descriptive term, and so on), I finally bring myself to hesitantly offer a response that I do not believe that using the 'n-word' necessarily makes someone a racist in itself, but that instead displaying racist behavior and discriminatory attitudes makes someone a racist. Having avoided eye contact with all students as the uncensored 'n-word' leaves my mouth, I hope that my attempt to break the ice will lead to a more open debate on the semantics of the word (and not a formal complaint)… my answer appears to be met with approval by the original questioner and others, and the ensuing dialogue on the topic weighs up different stances on the phrase from students in a balanced and critical manner. However, I note that the only students to repeat the word uncensored are those who are black or mixed-parentage… the white students awkwardly fidget and stick to saying the 'n-word', possibly in an attempt to avoid the perceived risks that I appear to have taken…

Although a respectful appreciation of student alterity can begin to address some of the challenges faced by white HE practitioners when discussing topics relating to race, it is also abundantly clear that a number of other challenges remain for consideration. My attention now turns to the specific academic field in which my experiences lie, namely the sociology of PE and sport, to reflect upon how these challenges have presented themselves in practice.

Sociology of sport is said to suffer from 'double domination' (Bourdieu 1988: 153), creating the "specific difficulties that the sociology of sport encounters: scorned by sociologists, it is despised by sportspersons". This 'double domination' that inflicts the sociology of sport emanates from, first, the relatively low status of sport within the general field of sociology (Carrington 2015). This is due to perceptions about the triviality of sport as a social phenomenon. Secondly, there is a general dislike from the sporting profession due to the often critical arguments of sociologists about the nature of sport. Despite these spurious headwinds for the sociological study of sport and PE, the very nature of these activities are undoubtedly an extremely useful medium for examining the impact of race on society historically and contemporaneously with my students, given both the centrality of sports within global popular culture and the 'embodied' nature of sport which provides an explicit, highly visual representation of racial stratification within the sporting domain.

Indeed, sports and PE can be viewed as analogous examples for the wider effects of racial stratification within wider society, with phenomena such as the 'racial stacking' of playing positions, whereby leadership and decision-making positions have been historically dominated by white players in contrast to the over-representation of Black players in positions demanding power and pace. This phenomenon has thus been attributed to false perceptions of contrasting physical and intellectual capabilities of different racial groups based on misleading, biologically-deterministic 'evidence' (Azzorito and Harrison 2008; Entine 2001; Hoberman 1997; Hylton 2015; St. Louis 2003, 2004). Sport and PE have therefore acted as a useful medium to explore some of the wider impacts of race within education and society more broadly within my teaching practice in HE.

However, discussion of concepts such as racial stacking, the lack of representation of BME individuals in leadership positions, and the way in which BME sports people are stereotyped in the media fail to highlight notions of white privilege (Carrington 2010, 2013; Hylton 2015). The focus becomes on how seemingly distant organisations mistreat and misrepresent BME sports people. Although doing so may help my students developed an understanding of discrimination, this fails to develop an understanding of white privilege. Furthermore, my attempts to foster open discussion of racial terminology and slurs, such as in the example of my above vignette, can arguably only achieve the superficial, 'safe space' discussions which Leonardo and Porter (2010) are critical of. Nonetheless, Hylton's (2015) extensive critical reflections on the importance of pedagogical practices which support critical exploration of the nature of 'race talk' within the domain of sport and PE exemplify the fertile nature of these topics for developing critical practitioners. To this end, Hylton argues that "talking critically about these myths and stereotypes disrupts the calcifying of racial ideas that could potentially lead to new generations of PE educators and leaders in sport reproducing toxic racialised ideologies" (2015: 511); this is a position which we have attempted to embrace within our own teaching practice.

'Discrimination Ball'—Michael Hobson

As I sit in the office preparing for my forthcoming session on race in PE and sport, I flick through the pages of Fitzpatrick's Physical Education, Critical Pedagogy, and Urban Schooling, *and I'm inspired by the practices of Dan, a teacher working in an underprivileged community in New Zealand. I quickly grab a pen and paper and start jotting down notes, thinking about how I can adapt his practices. The end product is an invasion game similar to his, played in teams of five, where the rules are designed to explicitly 'privilege some students and marginalise others'. Rules stipulating that only certain players can run, hold the ball, or are allowed within particular areas of the pitch are enforced. Furthermore, only certain students are allowed to contribute to team-talks and other students are to act as coaches providing feedback to some students purely on their physical qualities, and others on their intelligence replicating racial stacking. Once the session comes around, I do my best to make sure that the white males in the group who are the most distinguished athletes are penalised the most, in the hope of provoking emotions of anger, frustration, and disheartenment. It is my hope that the group can spot the game is a metaphor for society, and consider adopting similar approaches in some of their future practices. However, I soon realise that while the game embodies inequality, it will take much more than a twenty-minute game of "Discrimination Ball" to challenge racial inequality.*

Although the above practice sets out to tackle social inequality, it has been argued that our academic discipline of PE and sport has traditionally reinforced social stratifications in relation to race, gender, social class and disability (Carrington 2010; Dowling et al. 2015; Flintoff 2014; Flintoff and Webb 2012). Sport has helped to perpetuate the eugenicist notion of 'the dangerous other' by depicting the Black body as animalistic, aggressive and hypersexual thus normalising white privilege (Fitzpatrick 2013; Shilling 2012). For Fernández-Balboa and Muros (2006), the traditional forms of practice associated with PE result in a central focus on the physical development of pupils through depositing skills, and physical competencies. This reinforces the notion that Black students are physical and not intellectual, reducing learning in PE and sport to an embodied form of 'banking', ignoring the repressive social and political contexts which remain unchallenged (Freire 1970). The emphasis on sport-specific knowledge, learning theory and instructional models in PE programmes within HE diverts attention from the racialised nature of the sporting domain, neutering the capabilities of students in terms of challenging the norms within sport, PE and education more broadly.

Reflecting upon my past experiences of teaching about race I often focused upon 'barriers faced by minority groups in PE and sport curriculum', and have come to realise that this can lead to further isolation or frustration for members of minority groups. At times the stereotypical perceptions expressed by white, middle-class peers can further patronise and pathologise students from 'non-traditional' backgrounds (Leonardo 2004). For example, when I have set assignments that ask students to discuss racialised barriers to participation in sport, this can result in white students 'othering' BME students, placing the emphasis upon non-whites as the problem for not meeting the norms of society. This potentially results in superficial discussions of issues such as religious fasting, religious clothing, sub-cultural groupings and cultural practices (Hylton 2015). In doing so students from white backgrounds fail to recognise their own racial privileges by considering themselves to be lacking of ethnicity.

While the practical activity mentioned in the vignette above encouraged students to empathise with the position of others, as with the assessment tasks too it failed to extend beyond the confines of the task and achieve Freire's (1970) desire for students to commit themselves to enacting social change by continually re-examining themselves, and challenging oppressive social practices. Freire's position resonates with Fernández-Balboa and Stiehl's (1995) contention that the study of critical topics in PE and sport is insufficient; it is therefore argued that there is a need for practitioners in PE and sport to embrace critical approaches to assessment and delivery, avoiding transmission of current inequalities and power dynamics within the study of PE and sport. Interventions such as the expanded use of staff and student biography within pedagogical practice have been argued to achieve this goal of embracing critical practice, thus creating a more reflexive and open environment which allows greater political and social agency for students and staff to re-examine themselves constantly (Camacho and Fernández-Balboa 2006; Fernández-Balboa 2009). One practice that we are therefore exploring which has potential to enhance awareness of white privilege is to set assignments that encourage students to reflect upon their own experiences of privilege and/or discrimination in the context of PE and sport. However, we recognise that this practice in itself may have limitations and is only one of a number of tools that can be deployed when developing an anti-racist pedagogy.

A Concluding Dialogue on Reflexive Whiteness and Pedagogic Practice in PE—Michael and Stuart

As white male academics teaching PE we both found the process of reflecting on our practice both challenging and somewhat disconcerting at times. How do we overcome the challenges of respecting student alterity when exploring issues of race in our teaching? We do not wish to be defeatist in tone. Instead, we argue that the self-reflections and navel-gazing recommended in Flintoff et al. (2015) work on collective biography relating to race in PETE can benefit white practitioners in our field, and HE more broadly. However, in order to maximise the potential benefits of reflexive processes, we need to move beyond introspection regarding our own discomforts or uncertainties when tasked to deliver such content by demonstrating a willingness to expose ourselves to vulnerability by embracing teaching methods which will critically explore the nature of racial privilege and discrimination in our chosen academic fields.

We therefore advocate the use of provocative teaching methods and critical questioning which can force reflexivity from all students and practitioners regarding issues of race and ethnicity throughout all of our practice, thus embracing the potential impact of exploring the uncomfortable or awkward realities of discussing these emotive and delicate social phenomena. Furthermore, we also advocate the integration of discussions of race and whiteness within other lectures we deliver, instead of isolating it to the few dedicated lectures within the curriculum. One tactile way to do so could be to ask the questions such as that presented by Hacker (1992) "how much compensation would somebody need to pay you to become black for the rest of your life?". Critical questions such as these help white students to understand the value that society places upon their whiteness and unpick the normative inequality experienced by BME students within the field of PE and sport.

References

Aldous, D. C. R., Sparkes, A. C., & Brown, D. H. K. (2014). Transitional Experiences of Post-16 Sports Education: Jack's Story. *British Journal of Sociology of Education, 35*(2), 185–203.

Alexander, C., & Arday, J. (2015). *Aiming Higher: Race, Inequality, Diversity and in The Academy*. London: The Runneymede Trust.

Archer, L. (2007). Diversity, Equality and Higher Education: A Critical Reflection on the Ab/Uses of Equity Discourse Within Widening Participation. *Teaching in Higher Education, 12*(5), 635–653.

Azzorito, L., & Harrison, L. (2008). 'White Men Can't Jump': Race, Gender and Natural Athleticism. *International Review for the Sociology of Sport, 43*(4), 343–367.

Ball, S. J., Davies, J., David, M., & Reay, D. (2002). 'Classification' and 'Judgement': Social Class and 'Cognitive Structures' of Choice of Higher Education. *British Journal of Sociology of Education, 23*(1), 52–72.

Bathmaker, A., Ingram, N., & Waller, R. (2013). Higher Education, Social Class and the Mobilisation of Capitals: Recognising and Playing the Game. *British Journal of Sociology of Education, 34*(5–6), 723–743.

Beard, C., Clegg, S., & Smith, K. (2007). Acknowledging the Affective in Higher Education. *British Educational Research Journal, 33*(2), 235–252.

Bloom, B. S. (1956). *Taxonomy of Educational Objectives: The Classification of Educational Goals; Handbook I: Cognitive Domain*. London: Longman.

Bloom, B. S., Krathwohl, D. R., & Masia, B. B. (1956). *Taxonomy of Educational Objectives: The Classification of Educational Goals; Handbook II: Affective Domain*. London: Longman.

Bourdieu, P. (1988). Program for a Sociology of Sport. *Sociology of Sport Journal, 5*(2), 153–161.

Bourdieu, P. (1990). *In Other Words: Essays Towards a Reflexive Sociology*. Cambridge, UK: Polity Press.

Camacho, A. S., & Fernández-Balboa, J. M. (2006). Ethics, Politics and Bio-pedagogy in Physical Education Teacher Education: Easing the Tension Between the Self and the Group. *Sport, Education and Society, 11*(1), 1–20.

Carrington, B. (2010). *Race, Sport and Politics: The Sporting Black Diaspora*. London: Sage.

Carrington, B. (2013). The Critical Sociology of Race and Sport: The First Fifty Years. *Annual Review of Sociology, 39*(1), 379–398.

Carrington, B. (2015). Assessing the Sociology of Sport: On Race and Diaspora. *International Review for the Sociology of Sport, 50*(4–5), 391–396.

Chang, H. (2016). *Autoethnography as Method*. London: Routledge.

Crozier, G., Reay, D., Clayton, J., Colliander, L., & Grinstead, J. (2008). Different Strokes for Different Folks: Diverse Students in Diverse Institutions—Experiences of Higher Education. *Research Papers in Education, 23*(2), 167–177.

Dowling, F., Fitzgerald, H., & Flintoff, A. (2015). Narratives from the Road to Social Justice in PETE: Teacher Educator Perspectives. *Sport, Education and Society, 20*(8), 1029–1047.

Ellis, C. S., & Bochner, A. (2000). Autoethnography, Personal Narrative, Reflexivity: Researcher as Subject. In N. K. Denzin & Y. S. Lincoln (Eds.), *The Handbook of Qualitative Research* (2nd ed., pp. 733–768). Los Angeles, CA: Sage.

Ellis, C., Adams, T., & Bochner, A. (2010). Autoethnography: An Overview. *Forum: Qualitative Social Research, 12*(1). Available at http://www.qualitative-research.net/index.php/fqs/article/view/1589/3095.

Entine, J. (2001). *Taboo: Why Black Athletes Dominate Sports and Why We're Afraid to Talk About It*. New York, NY: PublicAffairs.

Fernández-Balboa, J. M. (2009). Bio-pedagogical Self-reflection in PETE: Reawakening the Ethical Conscience and Purpose in Pedagogy and Research. *Sport, Education and Society, 14*(2), 147–163.

Fernández-Balboa, J. M., & Muros, B. (2006). The Hegemonic Triumvirate—Ideologies, Discourses, and Habitus in Sport and Physical Education: Implications and Suggestions. *Quest, 58*(2), 197–221.

Fernández-Balboa, J. M., & Stiehl, J. (1995). The Generic Nature of Pedagogical Content Knowledge Among College Professors. *Teaching and Teacher Education, 11*(3), 293–306.

Fitzpatrick, K. J. (2012). 'That's How the Light Gets in': Poetry, Self and Representation in Ethnographic Research. *Cultural Studies: Critical Methodologies, 12*(1), 8–14.

Fitzpatrick, K. (2013). Brown Bodies, Racialisation and Physical Education. *Sport, Education and Society, 18*(2), 135–153.

Flintoff, A. (2014). Tales from the Playing Field: Black and Minority Ethnic Students' Experiences of Physical Education Teacher Education. *Race, Ethnicity and Education, 17*(3), 346–366.

Flintoff, A., Dowling, F., & Fitzgerald, H. (2015). Working Through Whiteness, Race and (Anti) Racism in Physical Education Teacher Education. *Physical Education and Sport Pedagogy, 20*(5), 559–570.

Flintoff, A., & Webb, L. (2012). 'Just Open Your Eyes a Bit More': The Methodological Challenges of Researching Black and Minority Ethnic Students' Experiences of Physical Education Teacher Education. *Sport, Education and Society, 17*(5), 571–589.

Frank, A. (2004). *The Renewal of Generosity*. Chicago, IL: The University of Chicago Press.

Freire, P. (1970). *The Pedagogy of the Oppressed*. London: Continuum.

Gillborn, D. (2008) Racism and Education: Coincidence or Conspiracy? London: Routledge.

Gorard, S. (2010). Education Can Compensate for Society—A Bit. *British Journal of Educational Studies, 58*(1), 47–65.

Hacker, A. (1992). *Two Nations: Black and White, Seperate, Hostile, Unequal*. New York, NY: Scribner.

Hoberman, J. M. (1997). *Darwin's Athletes: How Sport has Damaged Black America and Preserved the Myth of Race*. New York, NY: Houghton Mifflin Harcourt.

Hylton, K. (2015). 'Race' Talk! Tensions and Contradictions in Sport and PE. *Physical Education and Sport Pedagogy, 20*(5), 503–516.

Ladson-Billings, G. (1995). "But That's Just Good Teaching!" The Case for Culturally Relevant Teaching. *Theory Into Practice, 34,* 159–165.

Ladson-Billings, G., & Donnor, J. (2008). The Moral Activist Role of Critical Race Theory Scholarship. In N. K. Denzin & Y. S. Lincoln (Eds.), *The Landscape of Qualitative Research* (pp. 279–301). Los Angeles, CA: Sage.

Leonardo, Z. (2004). The Color of Supremacy: Beyond the Discourse of 'White Privilege'. *Educational Philosophy and Theory, 36*(2), 137–152.

Leonardo, Z., & Porter, R. (2010). Pedagogy of Fear: Toward a Fanonian Theory of 'Safety' in Race Dialogue. *Race, Ethnicity and Education, 13*(2), 139–157.

Levinas, E. (1999). *Alterity and Transcendence* (M. B. Smith, Trans.). New York, NY: Columbia University Press.

Magnet, S. (2006). Protesting Privilege: An Autoethnographic Look at Whiteness. *Qualitative Inquiry, 12*(4), 736–749.

Morrison, T. (1992). *Playing in the Dark: Whiteness and the Literary Imagination*. Cambridge, MA: Harvard University Press.

National Union of Students. (2016). NUS HerStory Month—Where Are All the Women? Available at https://www.nus.org.uk/en/news/susuanaamoah-whereareallthewomen. Last Accessed 10 Feb 2017.

Pennington, J. (2013). Silence in the Classroom/Whispers in the Halls: Autoethnography as Pedagogy in White Pre-service Teacher Education. *Race, Ethnicity and Education, 10*(1), 93–113.

Pilkington, A. (2013). The Interacting Dynamics of Institutional Racism in Higher Education. *Race, Ethnicity and Education, 16*(2), 225–245.

Reay, D. (1998). 'Always Knowing' and 'Never Being Sure': Familial and Institutional Habituses and Higher Education Choice. *Journal of Education Policy, 13*(4), 519–529.

Reay, D. (2001). Finding or Losing Yourself?: Working-Class Relationships to Education. *Journal of Education Policy, 16*(4), 333–346.

Rollock, N. (2012). The Invisibility of Race: Intersectional Reflections on the Liminal Space of Alterity. *Race, Ethnicity and Education, 15*(1), 65–84.

Shay, S. (2013). Conceptualizing Curriculum Differentiation in Higher Education: A Sociology of Knowledge Point of View. *British Journal of Sociology of Education, 34*(4), 563–582.

Shilling, C. (2012). *The Body and Social Theory*. London: Sage.

St. Louis, B. (2003). Sport, Genetics and the 'Natural Athlete': The Resurgence of Racial Science. *Body and Society, 9*(2), 75–95.

St. Louis, B. (2004). Sport and Common Sense Racial Science. *Leisure Studies, 23*(1), 31–46.

Taylor, E. (2016). The Foundations of Critical Race Theory in Education. In E. Taylor, D. Gillborn, & G. Ladson-Billings (Eds.), *Foundations of CriticalRace Theory in Education* (2nd ed.). New York: Routledge and Taylor & Francis.

Toyosaki, S., Pensoneau-Conway, S., Wendt, N., & Leathers, K. (2009). Community Autoethnography: Compiling the Personal and Resituating Whiteness. *Cultural Studies ↔ Critical Methodologies, 9*(1), 56–83.

12

Access and Inclusion for Gypsy and Traveller Students in Higher Education

Kate D'Arcy and Lisa Galloway

In this chapter we consider the barriers in Higher Education for Gypsy and Traveller students in higher education in the context of wider society's understanding and attitudes towards Traveller communities and cultures.[1]

The structure of the chapter is as follows: we begin by providing an overview of the educational picture for Traveller pupils in the UK. This is followed by consideration of the barriers and opportunities within Higher Education by drawing on interviews with Gypsy and Traveller

---

[1]In this chapter we will refer to 'Travellers' when we refer to all groupings and refer to specific groups as and when relevant e.g. Galloway's research involved Gypsies and Irish Travellers.

K. D'Arcy (✉)
University of Bedfordshire, Luton, UK
e-mail: kate.d'arcy@beds.ac.uk

L. Galloway
University Centre, Blackpool and The Fylde College, Blackpool, UK
e-mail: lisa.galloway@blackpool.ac.uk

© The Author(s) 2018
J. Arday and H. S. Mirza (eds.), *Dismantling Race in Higher Education*,
https://doi.org/10.1007/978-3-319-60261-5_12

students and families as well as university staff. The chapter concludes by summarising the issues and providing some recommendations to improve access and inclusion in Higher Education.

This chapter is informed by the empirical research of the authors who have studied and worked in Higher Education. Kate D'Arcy worked in a Traveller Education service for many years and undertook research into primary—secondary transition (D'Arcy 2010a), on-line and vocational learning (ELAMP[2]) and the home and school education experiences for Traveller pupils (D'Arcy 2014). Her move to teaching in Higher Education meant she had the privilege of teaching and supervising two female Traveller students who were both the first in their families to attend university. Discussions with one current and one student who has just graduated informed this chapter. Lisa Galloway is a Programme Leader for Health and Social Care in a University setting and has over eighteen years' experience working with diverse groups of students within Further and Higher Education settings. She has been using an ethnographic research framework to explore the complexities, challenges, and opportunities for Traveller students. Her research was inspired by her own educational experiences as a child. The research utilised 46 interviews with men (26) and women (20) from the Gypsy and Irish Traveller community who are living on authorised and unauthorised sites in 'Westbrooke'.[3]

The Educational Picture: Early Barriers to Schooling

The term Traveller is used by the Department for Education (2010: 1) to include:

---

[2]ELAMP—Electronic and Mobility Project, see https://www.natt.org.uk/natt/the-work-of-natt/the-elamp-initiatives/.

[3]A pseudomn to protect the identity of the real geographical area under study.

Gypsies including Romanies, Romanichals, Welsh Gypsies/Kaale, Scottish Gypsies/Travellers; Irish Travellers, Minceir; Roma from Eastern and Central Europe.

As this definition suggests, some Traveller groupings have a distinctly common ethnic and linguistic heritage. Other groups who do not fall under the DfE Traveller terminology include Showmen, Circus people and Bargees, because they are not recognised ethnic minorities but travel for cultural and business purposes. While the term Traveller is often used interchangeably, the groups it comprises are quite distinct and should not be considered homogenous. Nevertheless, in English schools there are just two distinct ethnic groups used to register pupils' ethnicity—'Gypsy/Roma' or Irish Traveller. This data, collected since 2004, has been helpful in providing some evidence of Traveller pupils' access and achievement in schools.

Travellers' achievement in England has improved significantly at primary school level. Recent analysis of achievement data (ACERT 2013) indicates that gaps are closing for Irish Travellers at KS2[4] and Gypsy/Roma at GSCE level, but all Traveller groups start at a significant disadvantage. The Equality and Human Rights Committee (2016) confirmed that the educational attainment of Gypsy, Roma and Traveller children in England had improved between 2008/2009 and 2012/2013; however, the attainment gap between Gypsy and Roma children, and White pupils appears to have increased and Irish Traveller exclusions remain high whilst Gypsy/Roma exclusions have fallen. For all other groups of children attendance has improved but Traveller attendance remains significantly lower (Wilkin et al. 2010). The picture for secondary-school Traveller students is less positive. There is a significant body of literature highlighting the barriers that may prevent young people from different Traveller communities from remaining and achieving in mainstream education. The main barriers include racism, bullying, discrimination, negative teacher attitudes and inconsistent or inadequate support

---

[4]In the UK the national curriculum is taught in schools and this is organised into blocks of years called 'key stages' (e.g. KS2) and at the end of each key stage children are formally assessed.

(Lloyd and Stead 2001; Lloyd and McClusky 2008; Wilkin et al. 2010; Foster and Norton 2012). Traveller pupils have the lowest school attendance rate of all ethnic minority groups (DfES 2005; Equality and Human Rights Commission 2010). Traveller boys also have the highest school exclusion rate of all ethnic groups (Foster and Norton 2012). Within mainstream school Traveller children are more likely to be identified as having a Special Education Need (SEN[5]) (DfES 2005; Wilkin et al. 2010).

There continues to be a lack of understanding and respect towards Traveller pupils. Consequently, expectations of these students are often low and the rate of drop-out during the secondary school phase is high (Derrington and Kendall 2004; Wilkin et al. 2009). A previous longitudinal study tracking the progress of 44 Traveller students (Derrington and Kendall 2004) found that more than two-thirds had left school before the end of Key Stage 4. Wilkin et al. (2010) studied the national data and reported that this showed 'a steady and disproportionate decline in the progression of Traveller pupils from one year group to the next throughout Key Stages 3 and 4...' By Year 11, only 50.9% of Gypsy, Roma and Traveller pupils were recorded on school rolls compared with 92.4% of non-Gypsy.

Derrington (2007) suggests that Traveller students in school resort to specific coping strategies to deal with cultural dissonance and social exclusion and these maladaptive strategies can be summarised as *fight, flight and playing White*. *Fight* describes the physical and verbal retaliation to racial abuse. Research has shown that this often results in their own exclusion from school even though they started out as the victim. (Lloyd et al. 1999; Ofsted 1999; Derrington 2007). *Flight* refers to Travellers' low attendance and self-imposed exclusion. *Playing White* describes the concealment of one's ethnicity or denying one's heritage and is a fairly common institutional response adopted by pupils Travellers to cope with deep-rooted racism (Derrington 2007).

---

[5]A statement of Special Educational Needs (SEN) sets out a child's perceived needs and the help they should receive. It is reviewed annually to ensure that any extra support given continues to meet a child's needs.

The educational literature (Padfield 2005; Lloyd and Mccluskey 2008; DCSF 2008) suggests that parents and pupils from Traveller communities can be hesitant to disclose their ethnicity on official documentation such as school enrolment and data collection forms. Wilkin et al. (2010) reported that within primary and secondary school Traveller pupils are considerably more likely to change their ethnic ascription than pupils in other minority groups. Their analysis at individual pupil level revealed that almost 70% ascribed themselves differently over their period in school. Interestingly, around 50% of pupils changed their ascribed ethnicity when they moved from primary to secondary school.

Acting White: Ascription and Entry into Higher Education

This strategy of hiding one's identity is also a factor for those who progress to Further and Higher education. For example, one university Traveller student explained that she chose not to disclose her ethnicity at the UCAS application stage for fear that this might jeopardise both her chance of gaining a place and her future experience at the chosen institution.

> *I never put down that I was a Traveller at university because you never know what will happen, you put it down but you don't know whether you will be a successful candidate because of that? There are probably a lot more Travellers that have not come forward. I did not put down that I was a Traveller at college but I am very open with it. I have a Traveller background but it does seem to – well in schools it does seem to have an —well bullying in school and labelling from teachers so I just thought, well I am doing all right as I am.* (Jasmine 2015)

Such reasoning regarding ascription explains one of the challenges in determining the actual number of Traveller students in Higher Education in the UK.

This evidence highlights the reality of Derrington's *playing White* theory. Traveller students are *playing White* to cope in school and

Table 12.1 Numbers of UK domiciled students with an ethnicity of Irish Traveller or Gypsy or Traveller at UK Higher Education providers

Ethnicity	Higher Education provider				
	English provider	Welsh provider	Scottish provider	Northern Irish provider	Total
Irish Traveller	0	0	0	5	5
Gypsy or Traveller	120	10	20	0	150
Total	120	10	20	5	155

avoid racism and discrimination. One consequence of ongoing racism and discrimination is that we cannot ascertain the exact number of Traveller pupils in schools. Nor can we observe whether or not schools and local authorities are improving access, inclusion and outcomes for Traveller pupils (Wilkin et al. 2010). The same can be said for data analysis at Further and Higher education; we do not effectively monitor ethnicity and therefore we cannot assess Traveller students' educational access or outcomes. According to Galloway (2016) data analysis from Westbrooke suggest that the use of category '*other*' in enrolment ascription data is vague. We cannot draw any conclusions as to who the '*other*' actually are. Additionally, there are those who identify as mixed, such as Scottish, Irish and Welsh Travellers.

According to the 2013/2014 Higher Education Statistics Agency's[6] student record, the numbers of UK domiciled students with an ethnicity of Irish Traveller or Gypsy or Traveller at UK Higher Education providers were (Table 12.1).

Once again Traveller students can only ascribe as being Gypsy or Traveller OR Irish Traveller. This limited categorisation shows how the state treats 'ethnicity' as an essential defining characteristic. The reality is that individuals negotiate their identity very differently. This was reflected within the data collected and discussed in key work on identity (Acton and Mundy 1999). This negotiation is often situated both within an individual's perception of identity and imposed externally as an adult explains:

---

[6]https://www.hesa.ac.uk/.

I am Gypsy, I have both Irish and Sinti heritage, but I am always classed as an Irish Traveller by outsiders, actually, by everyone. It's just easier. (Bell 2016)

Some students are from distinct Travellers groups, but they may choose not to ascribe due to fear of discrimination and exclusion (D'Arcy 2014). At Westbrooke, one Gypsy/Traveller explained why they do not identify at enrolment:

I didn't tick the box, neither did my friend. I don't want teachers looking at us any differently or thinking like they did at school that we need special classes. That's what happens when we say we are Traveller. (Smith 2016)

According to Westbrooke university equality and diversity data records, there had not been any student with a stated ethnicity of 'Gypsy or Irish Traveller' since 2012/2013 when there was just one. In fact, according to the data the college only ever had two students with that ethnicity (Galloway 2015). Galloway's research confirms that students simply do not ascribe, and this may further confirm the complex issues of ascription and identity as representative of the overall lack of data for these communities as in other service sectors.

Others acknowledge that they come from a Traveller family background but have not been brought up as a Traveller, hence may not feel that they 'fit' into the ethnic categories the state provides:

I did not talk about having a Traveller background in the first year- it did not occur to me. My nan [who was a Traveller] died after my 1ˢᵗ year and I thought about it then – how I missed out on understanding about my heritage so I was reading a lot about Travellers. In school they used to throw the word Pikey around. At a social gathering I was referred to as 'Gypsy' girl and then they were really embarrassed – another girl I told said "oh you are a Gyppo". It did not affect me personally but if I had struggled in school with bullying/racism abuse, only to get to university and heard that – that could really hurt me. The use of the word 'Gypsy' interests me – I was talking to people about Romany Gypsies – other people tried to correct me, but I am using a word that my dad gave me ... (Rose, current HE student)

At Westbrooke College there are similarly low ascription rates and students tend to identify as White British rather than Irish Traveller or Gypsy or Traveller. The classroom setting reveals a far higher figure but students choose not to identify formally and *play White*, for fear of discrimination. One 19 year old female student stated she changed her surname on college forms so she would not be perceived as a Gypsy, she explained:

> Being *a Gypsy means people think you are dirty and you thieve. My family are well known in this town; we are on an illegal site so I know I would be looked down on.* (Mathews 2016)

Traveller Students' Perceptions and Experiences of Pre-Higher Education

Among the sample of students interviewed there were a range of different educational journeys and perceptions of life-long learning. Talking to students it was clear that they are influenced by close family and that there is a lack of information about the range of educational opportunities available to them. This directly impacts on their perception of Higher Education as a limited opportunity afforded to others in society (Galloway 2016).

Jasmine (an ex-Higher Education student) did attend school from her early years. She went right through school, and, as she suggests, attitudes from her family varied about her journey into Higher Education:

> *I went to Kindergarten, my school was very old fashioned it was Church of England. We lived in small village and all my siblings went to primary school. My oldest brother went to upper school and did GCSE and started at college–he felt really different. He did not like it. We were used to very small classrooms in school – in primary school there were only 8 children in my whole year. I am the only one who has gone right through education in my family, but also my wider family. I am the first one to go to college and university. They have mixed views. They all finished and had children so they ask things like 'what did you do that for?' …' it might not get you anywhere'. Others were really supportive. My immediate family were really supportive that I was going to university and the first one in the family.*

These types of comments reflect a self-identification of underachievement and concern about Travellers' own ability to fit in and succeed in mainstream establishments. Their perceived position can be compared to the experiences of the white working class. Reay (2009) proposed that the prevalent 'common-sense' view of the white working classes is that they themselves are to blame for their underachievement, that it is about cultural deficits, lack of ambition, and the wrong sorts of attitudes that hamper their inclusion and social mobility. Similarly, Bourdieu's earlier work on 'Habitus' and 'Social Capital' confirms that habitus is produced and perpetuated in cyclical form by an individual's position in the social structure. The impact of such social positioning is critical and can be to some extent self-limiting on life opportunity. The reproduction of the social structure, along with class, gender and cultural positions in society results from what Bourdieu describes as the habitus of individuals (Costa and Murphy 2015). The reasons for poor Traveller achievement in education are, as Le Bas states, cultural and complex (Le Bas 2014). Le Bas (2014) is a Gypsy poet, artist and journalist and speaks from his own experiences and as an author on human rights and asserts that there is an interplay of persecution and racism, family self-sufficiency and a mistrust of traditional routes in society.

However, the complexity of challenges in education for Travellers is not widely understood and Travellers themselves, like the White working class, are blamed for withdrawal from school, lack of progress and achievement. Galloway's interviews with lecturers across several universities revealed that they all held similar perceptions of Gypsy and Travellers' needs. Although there was recognition of human rights and equality, and a desire to uphold legislation, the common view was that education is not desired by the Traveller community:

Gypsies don't do education, don't they all have trades? (Norcliffe 2016)

Assumptions and stereotypes, perhaps due to a lack of understanding, impact on educational aspirations and opportunities for the students. Negative media reporting regarding Traveller communities and programmes such as the Channel 4 'Big Fat Gypsy Wedding' programme simply perpetuate these barriers. Foster (2012) reports that the programme caused a real, measurable impact and long-term harm:

Harm is on a number of levels, including physical and sexual assault, racist abuse and bullying, misinformation and hostile questioning, resulting in damage to the self-esteem of children and withdrawal from school.

Lecturers in the focus groups stated that the only time that they had seen Gypsies was on this programme *'but I am sure that this was a clear misrepresentation, I would not know how these groups actually do live'* (Michelle 2016).

Findings from Galloway's research indicate that both university staff and Gypsy/Travellers themselves have low expectations of education. Among university staff there was a majority perception that education was not for Gypsy/Travellers and this view was also reflected among some Westbrooke families. College and university were seen to be completely inaccessible due to the qualifications required, especially among families who have problematic interactions with school or whose children have dropped out. Young Gypsy/Travellers (aged 17 and 18) stated:

Isn't college for people who have exams? (Tom 2016)

You can't get into college if you haven't done schooling. (Howarth 2016)

Moreover, the older generation spoke of their fears that education was a mechanism both to assimilate their people and to further increase their social exclusion. These fears are also reflected within the literature on social class and the rejection of education as an irrelevant resource (Bhopal 2009; Myers et al. 2010). Reay (2009: 78) confirms:

The White working class are at far greater risk of losing themselves in education, rather than finding themselves.

In Westbrooke many adults felt there could be a loss of 'our ways' if young people were to engage with education in any form, with the exception of primary school as there was a clear value in learning to read and write. These concerns are valid for a community who have experienced years of exclusion from mainstream institutions, and where discriminatory policies and practices have often attempted to simply assimilate and exterminate their cultures (Liégeois 1998).

> *Why would I want to be like you? How can a gorja ever be a role model? No teachers are Travellers, are they?* (Joey 2016)

Attitudes from the younger generation were somewhat different. There was intense interest in college from the younger people (18–22 years of age) across the Westbrooke sample, and a strong focus on aspirations for university:

> *I'm not sure what I have to do to get there, but there's a few of us would like to show that Gypsies aren't thick; we are clever, we have laptops and iPads and smart phones, like they do ….* (Levi 2016)

> *Why can't we learn and do well? I might go to Oxford like that girl did, the show family wasn't it?* (Sherri, age 18)

Resolve like this was reflected in Jasmine's experience:

> *The day my tutor told me at school- 'you will never get anywhere in life' - I came home and cried to my mum. But it makes you think 'I can do it', if you put your mind to it, it makes you want it more. People that say – you are never going to do it- you can say – 'I proved you wrong'…*

The fact that Jasmine was told early on by a teacher she would not make it to university, made her more determined to go and succeed in university.

> *I look at my degree certificate pretty much every day- just to say 'I have done it'. When I was in upper school - they learn you are from Traveller background and they say 'oh you will never make it'- and I did make it so I feel like going back and telling them. It is such a big achievement, you can feel really proud, deep down without being too big-headed about it…I would encourage anyone to go. I tell my brothers you should go and do it - the experience is amazing. You learn so much from other people …not just from going yourself. If there is something you want to do - don't let anything hold you back- do it! I encourage as many people as I can – go to university it is really good.*

I never was put off. I did not have the confidence in school and college to speak to people, I was really quiet. But having to talk to others and be at university and be independent…it brings it out in you. So when I had to go for my job assessment day I had confidence to do it. You learn life skills doing a degree.

On the other hand, Rose's story reflected some of the struggles in Higher Education, but these were not directly related to her ethnicity or background, but confidence and class:

I settled in university but struggled a lot, I failed first year and was behind in all course work had to take a year out. I had to retake the second year – then failed that second year because did not complete course work and attend all exams. I have just completed the second year.

I was not confident. Especially having a year out – I had always found school easy and then losing motivation. I expected it to come naturally and it was scary …

Not feeling like you belong in a way that it is not expected of you, is the biggest barrier. In university I felt at odds with wealthy peers – I have felt out of place because of class. Young people need positive role models who go to university too who encourage them, but they don't need to be Travellers. People need to ask for help at university, ask for support- especially mental health.

Rose also felt that positive encouragement regarding education was necessary to promote access and ascription. In Westbrooke the need for positive encouragement and support was also reflected:

We need role-models, that what we need, someone to mentor our young people to do well in life…I think that's what's missing, people who understand and can provide some help. (Edge—lecturer)

Documenting experiences and views of education highlights the subjective and often contradictory nature of education and how educational journeys are influenced by a wide range of factors. This is worthy of consideration. Traveller communities are not homogenous and nor are their educational needs and desires. Nevertheless, what cannot be denied is that they almost all continue to experience discrimination and this limits their educational opportunities. Three quarters of the main case study sample in Westbrooke felt that the perceptions of Gypsies and Travellers are still seen as 'bad' in our society and that education merely reflects the common problems they experience with, such as poor access to health care, unequal planning status and inappropriate council policy towards providing pitches on sites.

A current example of the negative effect of legislation upon Traveller communities can be seen in the recent announcement of Government changes to Gypsy and Traveller planning guidance, called Planning Policy for Traveller Sites (PPTS). This policy includes a change to the definition of Gypsy and Traveller status for the purposes of planning policy:

> *Persons of nomadic habit of life whatever their race or origin, including such persons who on grounds only of their own or their family's or dependants' educational or health needs or old age have ceased to travel temporarily, but excluding members of an organised group of travelling Show people or circus people travelling together as such… (FFT[7])*

Friends, Families and Travellers (FFT 2015) point out that the definition previously covered those Gypsy or Travellers who stopped travelling permanently. Travellers in Westbrooke were concerned about this policy as they felt they might need to travel a percentage of every year in order to keep their Traveller status. If so, this will impact on schooling and the opportunity to progress to Higher Education.

The consequences of this change could deteriorate access to and inclusion in education. This goes against the recommendations on good practice in improving outcomes for Travellers in the past decade (Cemlyn et al. 2009; DCSF 2009; Robinson and Martin 2008) but as one of the adult participants in Westbrooke stated:

> *Why would that be a surprise when they have cut all the services on site, no education workers come on here now, only social workers. (Jackson 2016)*

---

[7]http://www.gypsy-traveller.org/wp-content/uploads/2015/10/Changes-to-planning-for-Gypsies-and-Travellers-website-leaflet.pdf.

Conclusion: Working Towards Inclusion

There are clearly a number of complex issues at stake in considering access and inclusion in Higher Education for Traveller students. The next section will draw out the key issues discussed in this chapter in order to consider how these can inform improvements to participation in Higher Education. The main issues include:

1. Ascription to an ethnic category that identifies the student as being of Gypsy, Roma or Traveller heritage.
2. Support and information for Gypsy/Traveller students and staff and those working with Travellers.
3. Awareness of teaching staff and wider society regarding Gypsy/Traveller cultures and communities.

Currently, we cannot ascertain the exact number of Traveller pupils in schools or Higher Education as parents and pupils from Traveller communities continue to be hesitant to disclose their ethnicity. Centuries of discrimination have meant that Travellers are rightly cautious in declaring their ethnicity for fear of the consequences. Capturing accurate data for effective ethnic monitoring of all educational outcomes is an important starting point to enable academics and teachers to understand the profile of Travellers in Higher Education. Nevertheless, the benefits of collecting this data may be less obvious for the Travellers themselves.

Traveller education services have been hard hit by recent funding cuts, the Independent newspaper reported that half of 127 authorities have either abolished their Traveller education service or drastically cut staff levels (Doherty 2011). Cuts to the Access and Inclusion Unit in Westbrooke have meant the closure of any on site provision and E-learning for compulsory school aged children. A national initiative (ELAMP) had supported distance learning using developing technologies (Marks 2010[8]; D'Arcy 2010b).

---

[8]http://www.natt.org.uk/wp-content/uploads/2015/12/Home-Access-on-the-Move.pdf.

Nevertheless, Westbrooke college have adopted their own creative E-learning strategies (online teaching sessions, materials and Skype) to reach those students who cannot attend including Travellers. These initiatives have proved successful for the local college and university, allowing students who had to be absent to complete their work and achieve good results. Two Travellers worked on-line to meet all their deadlines successfully (Galloway 2016).

Westbrooke also held a recent 'Friends and Family' event. All students were invited to bring in their families to see the university and meet staff. This event proved pivotal in recognising the contribution families make to the student's journey and ultimate achievement by supporting and understanding, providing emotional and often financial and practical support. During this event three Traveller families were present and spoke in their own language (Cant/Roma), showed photos of their families and told staff and students of their fears and also their hopes for their family members who attend currently.

Teacher training and awareness raising has been an ongoing recommendation in the school educational literature (Wilkin et al. 2010). However, the reality of teacher education is often that student teachers focus on the technicalities of teaching rather than the needs of those they teach in any depth. One lecturer (2016) stated:

> *I did ask about meeting diversity and we did one module on it, but we were really looking at those cultures that there are more of in our locality, so class and poverty and disability issues in the main. There was no mention of Travellers at all.*

Similarly, when undertaking staff induction, another lecturer mentioned that the 'quick fix' half day training does mention those affected under the Equality Act but '*does not delve into the needs of those learners or how we might encounter them and how best to plan for them; half a day is not enough*' (Day 2016).

The focus on Traveller inclusion and the need for better outcomes is not new. Better strategic directives, policy and action to improve those outcomes are still called for. Prejudice and discrimination towards Travellers continues, media portrayals are often damaging and Travellers continue to be marginalised and misunderstood. Policy makers and professionals continue to write about and on behalf of the lives of those affected rather than writing with. The need to secure narrative detail and engage with those at the focus of such debate is crucial. As this chapter has shown, particularly through the voices of interviewees, Traveller communities want to access to Further and Higher education and the creation of safe spaces and opportunities to engage with Traveller families is not an impossible feat. All that is needed is the institutional and political will to do so.

References

ACERT. (2013). *Why Do Gypsies, Roma and Travellers Underachieve?* Data Provided by the DFE.

Acton, T., & Mundy, G. (1999). *Romani Culture and Gypsy Identity*. Hatfield: University of Hertfordshire Press.

Bhopal, K. (2009). *What about Us? Gypsies, Travellers and White Racism in Schools*. British Education Research Association (BERA) Annual Conference 2009. Keynote Symposia: Race, Ethnicity and Education, Manchester, UK, 02–05 Sept 2009.

Cemlyn, S., Greenfields, M., Burrett, S., Matthews, Z., & Whitwell, C. (2009). *Inequalities Experienced by Gypsy and Traveller Communities: A Review* (Research Report 12). Equality and Human Rights Commission.

Costa, C., & Murphy, M. (Eds). (2015). *Bourdieu, Habitus and Social Research; The Art of Application*. London: Palgrave Macmillan.

D'Arcy, K. (2010a). *How Can Early Years Services Improve Access and Inclusion into Early Years Settings and Primary Schools for Gypsy, Roma and Traveller Children?* Practitioner-led Research Report, pp. 1–14. CWDC. Available at http://dera.ioe.ac.uk/2693/1/Microsoft_Word__PLR0910005D_Arcy_HYL.pdf.

D'Arcy, K. (2010b). *Electronic Learning and Mobility Project, Strand B, Final Report*, pp. 1–16. NATT. Available at http://www.natt.org.uk/sites/default/files/documents/Final_Strand_B_report.pdf.

D'Arcy, K. (2014). *Travellers and Home Education: Safe Spaces & Inequality*. London: Trentham and IOE Press.

Department for Children, Schools and Families. (2008). *Attendance Advice for Travellers Children*. National Strategies.

Department for Children, Schools and Families. (2009). *Moving Forward Together: Raising Gypsy, Roma and Traveller Achievement. The National Strategies, Booklet 1: Introduction*. London: DCSF.

Department for Education and Skills. (2005). *Ethnicity and Education: The Evidence on Minority Ethnic Pupils* (Research Topic Paper RTP01-05). Nottingham. Available at https://www.education.gov.uk/publications/eOrderingDownload/DFES-0208-2006.pdf. Accessed Sept 2010.

Derrington, C. (2007). Fight, Flight and Playing White: An Examination of Coping Strategies Adopted by Gypsy Traveller Adolescents in English Secondary Schools. *International Journal of Educational Research, 46*(6), 357–367.

Derrington, C., & Kendall, S. (2004). *Gypsy Traveller Students in Secondary Schools*. Stoke-on-Trent: Trentham Books.

Doherty, M. (2011, August 1). Cuts Threaten Traveller Children's Schooling. *The Independent*. http://www.independent.co.uk/news/uk/politics/cuts-threaten-traveller-childrens-schooling-2330282.html.

Equality and Human Rights Commission. (2010). *England's Most Disadvantaged Groups: Gypsies, Travellers and Roma. A Review Spotlight Report (1 of 4) from How Fair Is Britain? The First Triennial Review*. Manchester: Equality and Human Rights Commission.

Foster, B. (2012). *Bigger, Fatter, Gypsier*. Report to the Advertising Standards Authority.

Foster, B., & Norton, P. (2012). Educational Equality for Gypsy, Roma and Traveller Children and Young People in the UK. *The Equal Rights Review, 8*, 85–112. http://www.equalrightstrust.org/ertdocumentbank/ERR8_Brian_Foster_and_Peter_Norton.pdf.

Friends, Families and Travellers. (2015). What we do—Policy. Available at https://www.gypsy-traveller.org/what-we-do/policy-2/.

Galloway, L. (2015). *Not All Who Wander Are Lost; A Study of Travellers in FHE*. Scholarly Symposium 'Westbrooke'.

Galloway, L. (2016). *'If You Ask Me ...'*. Scholarly Journal 'Westbrooke'.

Le Bas, D. (2014, January 22). Yes, Gypsies Lag in Education, but the Reasons Are Complex and Cultural. *The Guardian*. https://www.theguardian.com/commentisfree/2014/jan/22/gypsies-lagging-education-gypsies-travellers.

Liégeois, J. (1998). *School Provision for Ethnic Minorities: The Gypsy Paradigm. Gypsy Research Centre*. Hatfield: University of Hertfordshire Press.

Lloyd, G., & McClusky, G. (2008). Education and Gypsy Travellers: Contradictions and Significant Silences. *International Journal of Inclusive Education, 12*(4), 331–345.

Lloyd, G., & Stead, J. (2001). The Boys and Girls Not Calling Me Names and the Teachers to Believe Me: Name Calling and the Experiences of Travellers Children in School. *Children and Society, 15,* 361–374.

Lloyd, G., Stead, J., Jordan, E., & Norris, C. (1999). Teachers and Gypsy Travellers. *Scottish Educational Review, 31,* 48–65.

Marks. (2010). THE E-LAMP PROJECTS: 2003–2010. Available at: https://view.officeapps.live.com/op/view.aspx?src=%3A%2F%2Fwww.sheffield.ac.uk%2Fpolopoly_fs%2F1.24145!%2Ffile%2Felamp.doc.

Myers, M., McGhee, D., & Bhopal, K. (2010). At the Crossroads: Gypsy and Traveller Parents' Perceptions of Education, Protection and Social Change. *Race, Ethnicity and Education, 13*(4), 533–548.

Ofsted. (1999). *Raising the Attainment of Minority Ethnic Pupils—School and LEA Responses* (HMI Ref: 170). London: Crown Copyright.

Padfield, P. (2005). Inclusive Educational Approaches for Gypsy/Traveller Pupils and Their Families: An 'Urgent Need for Progress'? *Scottish Educational Review, 37*(2), 127–144.

Reay, D. (2009). Making Sense of White Working Class Educational Underachievement. In *Who Cares About the White Working Class?* (pp. 22–28). London: Runnymede Trust, Runnymede Publication.

Robinson M., & Martin K. (2008). *Approaches to Working with Children, Young People and Families for Traveller, Irish Traveller, Gypsy, Roma and Show People Communities—A Literature Review.* Children's Workforce Development Council.

The Equality and Human Rights Committee. (2016). *England's Most Disadvantaged Groups: Gypsies, Travellers and Roma, an Is England Fairer?* Review Spotlight Report (1 of 4).

Wilkin, A., Derrington, C., & Foster, B. (2009). *Improving the Outcomes for Gypsy, Roma and Traveller Pupils, Literature Review* (Research Report DCSF-RRO77). London: DCSF.

Wilkin, A., Derrington, C., White, R., Martin, K., Foster, B., Kinder, K., et al. (2010). *Improving the Outcomes for Gypsy, Roma and Traveller Pupils: Final Report* (Research Report DFE-RR043). London: Department for Education.

13

Islamophobia in Higher Education: Muslim Students and the "Duty of Care"

Tania Saeed

Introduction

Muslims in western countries are caught in a discourse of "securitisation" where their religious identities have turned them into potential terrorists. Such a discourse has promoted an atmosphere of Islamophobia, where Muslims are discriminated against because of their religious affiliation, where the hijab has become a signifier of oppression, and the bearded Muslim man reduced to a fundamentalist and a terrorist. Awan and Zempi (2015) in their research have illustrated how Muslims tend to experience more Islamophobia in the aftermath of a terrorist attack by terrorist groups claiming to act in the name of Islam, or is fuelled by media and political rhetoric around the 'dangerous Muslim' perceived to be a potential recruit for terrorist organisations like the Islamic State of Iraq and Syria or the Levant (also known as Isis, Isil or Daesh) (see Feldman and Littler 2014; Saltman and Smith 2015;

T. Saeed (✉)
Lahore University of Management Sciences, Lahore, Pakistan
e-mail: tania.saeed@lums.edu.pk

© The Author(s) 2018
J. Arday and H. S. Mirza (eds.), *Dismantling Race in Higher Education*,
https://doi.org/10.1007/978-3-319-60261-5_13

233

Hoyle et al. 2015). This sense of insecurity is reflected in government legislation, especially the counter terrorism strategies of western governments that aim to root out extremism, in particular "Islamist" extremism from their midst. The UK is one such western country where social institutions, from universities to community centres have been regulated since the tragedies of July 7, 2005 to "prevent" radicalisation of mostly young Muslims (see HM Government 2006, 2011a, b). The more recent piece of legislation, the Counter Terrorism and Security Act 2015 has taken this regulation one step further by imposing a "statutory duty" on educational institutions to inform on students "vulnerable" to radicalisation (HM Government 2015a, b). Such a local context has further promoted a culture of insecurity about the Muslim identity. Such insecurity breeds Islamophobia, where Muslims have to constantly defend their right to practice their religion without prejudice. This context is also prevalent in educational institutions (BIS 2011; Tyrer and Ahmad 2006), where Muslims continue to feel monitored, "studying under siege" (Saeed and Johnson 2016), with university officials looking out for "vulnerable" students.

Given such a context, universities then, not only have to uphold the "statutory duty" to ensure that no student is vulnerable to radicalisation, but also a welfare duty towards Muslim students to prevent Islamophobia on university campuses. While recent scholarship on Muslim students has focused on Islamophobia or securitisation within universities (see Durodie 2016; O'Donnell 2016; Davies 2016; Coppock and McGovern 2014; El-Haj et al. 2011), there is an urgent need to examine the kind of welfare provisions that are in place to support students who may become victims of Islamophobia in such a securitised context. This chapter enters this discussion on Islamophobia within the university by examining university welfare support that is provided to Muslim students who have experienced Islamophobia. Building on a study of Muslim student experiences of Islamophobia undertaken by the author between 2010 and 2012, the chapter highlights how Muslim students are often reluctant to report incidents of Islamophobia, either lacking confidence in the welfare procedures within universities, or afraid of standing out. These narratives have implications for university welfare protocols and its duty towards equality and social inclusion, highlighting the need to reinforce a no tolerance policy on Islamophobia, which is often tolerated or ignored.

Universities, Terrorism and Student Welfare

Cases such as those of Umar Farouk Abdulmutallab, an alumnus of a British university who attempted to blow up a plane headed to the US, or Roshonara Chaudhry a university drop out who attacked an MP by stabbing him in retaliation for the war on Iraq underline the potential danger of students turning towards terrorism (BBC News 2010, 2011). With Isis the most recent terrorist organisation to attract Muslims including young British Muslims (though a minority within the British Muslim community), the Muslim student radical has become more dangerous. Suhaib Majeed "a physics undergraduate at Kings College London" and Tarik Hassane "a medical student who split his time between London" and a "university in Sudan" were inspired by Isis and convicted of terrorism in March 2016 for planning "to commit a drive-by shooting using a moped and a firearm" in London (BBC News 2016a). These incidents become the impetus for counter terrorism strategies that focus on educational institutions to prevent radicalisation of its students. Under the Counter Terrorism and Security Act 2015 higher educational institutions are "expected to carry out a risk assessment for their institution which assesses where and how their students might be at risk of being drawn into terrorism. This includes not just violent extremism but also non-violent extremism, which can create an atmosphere conducive to terrorism and can popularise views which terrorists exploit" (HM Government 2015b: 5). The "risk assessment" seems to be more at risk of simplifying a complex problem of radicalisation, a problem that continues to baffle academics and security experts (Kundnani 2012, 2015; Githens-Mazer 2010). The counter terrorism duty also takes on the guise of a "duty of care" (see Saeed and Johnson 2016), that looks into "institutional policies regarding [...] campus and student welfare, including equality and diversity and the safety and welfare of students and staff" (HM Government 2015b: 5). While the government has attempted to provide training to university staff and personnel in carrying out the duties set under its Prevent agenda, innocent Muslims nonetheless are trapped within the security discourse.

Mohammad Umar Farooq, a student at Staffordshire University was accused of being a terrorist after he was caught reading a book on terrorism related to his postgraduate degree (Ramesh and Halliday 2015). Rizwaan Sabir was arrested and held in custody with a friend for ten days by the police after he downloaded the Al Qaeda manual that is freely available in bookstores across the UK for his research (Townsend 2012). In both cases it was the university that alerted the relevant authorities about their students' "suspicious" behaviour. The reaction to Malia Bouattia the "first black woman" and Muslim to be "elected president of the National Union of Students" further testifies to the atmosphere of intolerance and suspicion that exists across universities. Bouattia has "been accused of being an extremist for campaigning against this government's Prevent agenda", a campaign that has been supported by academics, and human rights activists, yet "when a Muslim woman speaks out on this, it seems she is suddenly a danger, and a matter of national concern" (Bouattia 2016). Muslim students at universities are not alone in being wrongfully suspected of terrorist behaviour. In schools Muslim children have also been suspected of being vulnerable to terrorism. A ten-year-old student who misspelt "terraced house" by calling it a "terrorist house" was questioned "by Lancashire Police." According to the Muslim Council of Britain "dozens of" such "cases" have been reported to them (BBC News 2016b, also see Saeed 2016a).

With Muslims being perceived as a potential threat, their actions in schools and universities are constantly under a security microscope. Such students continue to face both direct and indirect Islamophobia from university staff, or fellow students. In a larger context where Islamophobic crime for London alone has witnessed an increase of 51.9% between April 2015 and 2016 (Mayor's Office for Policing and Crime 2015), such experiences are also becoming more common in educational institutions, especially after the introduction of the Counter Terrorism and Security Act 2015. These experiences further bring into question the university's duty towards equality and social inclusion.

According to Kimura (2014) universities may claim to be committed to equality but there remains a stark difference between "being diverse and doing diversity" (Ahmed 2006a as cited in Kimura 2014), and "actually achieving equality amongst different groups" (2014: 529). The notion of "achieving equality" becomes problematic in a context where a particular group is singled out because of their religious beliefs, as being a potential threat. The challenge for universities in a securitised British context is to ensure that all students are treated equally, where Muslim students despite being the object of a security discourse are not singled out for being Muslim, where Islamophobes and racists are not only *not tolerated* but also reprimanded.

Methodology

This chapter explores findings from a larger narrative study undertaken in 2010–2012 that examined experiences and responses to Islamophobia and the British state's security agenda in universities across England. The focus of the research were forty Muslim women between the ages of 19–28, who were contacted through student Islamic societies and Pakistani student societies in their universities. The research also included a small scale survey of fifty-five male and female Muslim students undertaken at a national conference organised by a Pakistani student organisation that included Muslim students with a Pakistani heritage from across the UK. In addition, a representative of the Federation of Student Islamic Societies (FOSIS) was also interviewed in 2011, as well as welfare officers at different universities. The author followed the ethics guidelines set by the University of Oxford in undertaking this research, ensuring that participants' anonymity was guaranteed through the use of pseudonyms, and that participants were given the time to review information about the study, and the opportunity to ask questions, as well as the discretion to opt out of the study at any point during the research. While the sample is small, the findings from the research are indicative of important trends concerning Muslim student welfare that may have relevance for other universities across the UK.

Islamophobia in Higher Educational Institutions

Tabussum: *I think the kind of Islamophobia that we are dealing with is not the kind you see with the BNP, or the English Defence League [...] What it is, is an institutional attitude towards the perception of the potential threat that Muslim students might be potential terrorists especially after the UCL incident. [...] Actually members of the Islamic society came forward and said we are really really worried, is the university going to start monitoring us. So we met with them, so it was in a sense Islamophobia from an institutional perspective as opposed to an individual perspective. So what we did was we managed to convene a meeting with the head of student services, myself, head of the equality and diversity unit and talked through some of the issues that were worrying them and from that we managed to assure them but also make sure that their voice was heard, and make sure that we were supporting Muslim students in the right way.*

Interviewer: *What were the major concerns raised?*

Tabussum: *About being monitored, about being watched. [...] It was just fear around that, and being treated differently, and being treated as suspects when they haven't done anything wrong. Which is of course Islamophobia, but an intelligent approach to Islamophobia instead of the Daily Mail, Sun kind of Islamophobia.* (Tabussum, South East1, Racism and Equality Advisor)

The nature of Islamophobia that university students confront in their day to day existence is this "institutional attitude" or an "intelligent approach to Islamophobia" where students internalise the fear of being watched (see Saeed 2016b). Tabussum's discussion on Islamophobia in universities was before the introduction of the Counter Terrorism and Security Act 2015 and its "statutory duty" to inform on "vulnerable students". The "institutional attitude" under the new security agenda has been formalised, where in the name of "welfare" students are to be monitored in case they display vulnerability towards radicalisation. The majority of these students are Muslims. However, while universities and student organisations such as the National Union of Students (NUS) have challenged this statutory duty under the campaign "students not suspects",[1]

---

[1]See https://www.nusconnect.org.uk/articles/students-not-suspects-join-us-to-up-the-fight-against-prevent.

and universities like Tabussum's have attempted to work with Muslim students, there continues to be a disconnect with students feeling targeted for being Muslim.

In the survey for this study for instance students were asked if their university "tolerates Islamophobia more than other forms of discrimination". 43% of the participants agreed with the statement, with 80% believing that Muslim men with beards and Muslim women with veils "are treated with greater suspicion of radicalisation." Stemming from this belief was also their inability to report incidents of Islamophobia, with many citing varied reasons such as:

I don't think there is anyone I know who I can report to (Female, postgraduate, 21–25 years),

Because I believe that nothing will be done (Male, undergraduate, 17–20 years),

I will never get into the victim mentality (Male, undergraduate, 21–25 years),

Not sure they care (Male, graduate, 25–30 years)

I do not like to cause a fuss just because some person cannot be bothered to educate themselves about why Muslims do certain things and dress a certain way rather I feel sorry for them in that they are so ignorant that to make themselves feel better they have to attack or make people who are different feel inferior. (Female, undergraduate, 21–25 years)

The myriad of responses to the presence of Islamophobia in universities, the lack of reporting, and the welfare provisions that are in place suggest a disconnect between the university and the students, who are either unaware of the services, or are reluctant to access them believing nothing will be done. Tehmina, as a member of her university's Student Union has encountered this problem of under-reporting,

I mean for example I've been SU officer now. I'm not saying that I'm a fantastic officer but I am more approachable, more familiar with the students, and the Islamic societies [...] However I don't think many of the students, or even lecturers going through Islamophobia would really know where to go with that. I think a lot of the statistics, many people don't report the incidents but the cases that I hear of, or the students I've had conversations with, or the unions I have spoken to, they told me it goes unreported there isn't directly anyone they can go to. Or if they do make a big song and dance about it they can be seen as extreme or radical. (Tehmina West Midlands1, 19, Undergrad Social Sciences, British)

Tehmina's observation highlights three important points which have also been raised by other participants: the level of approachability for such services; lack of knowledge about these services; and the fear of standing out. Another problem is also the student's own inhibition at reporting the event, which often requires bureaucratic paperwork, as well as lack of time on the part of the student who just 'can't be bothered' to chase up such complaints. Faiza who encountered Islamophobia during an exam by invigilators, one of whom asked her to remove her niqab in front of an entire room full of students for identification (see Saeed 2016b), did not report it precisely because she wanted to avoid all the 'fuss' and did not want to get into the bureaucratic process of making the complaint. Faiza's university has a high percentage of Muslim students, especially with a South Asian heritage. However, only a few number of students wear the niqab. Faiza's university welfare personnel who was interviewed was confident that sufficient welfare procedures were in place for any student who may encounter any form of discrimination. She was at the same time confident that such forms of discrimination did not exist in her university.

Diane: *We have contacts with all the societies [...] we also arrange meetings with them.*

Interviewer: *Have the societies ever reported any problems?*

Diane: *Nothing at all.* (Diane, West Yorkshire2, University Welfare, 2011)

Both the university policy documents that she shared and the welfare website of the university have a clear policy against any form of discrimination, and has provided faith advisors for Muslim students. Given the large Muslim population of the university, three faith advisors are available, a separate male and female one, as well as an academic member of staff. The contact information for these advisors is clearly provided on the university website. Despite such a strong welfare team there continues to be a communication gap between students and their university's welfare advisors. The students are also hesitant about contacting the student Welfare officer. Nadia, the head sister of the Islamic Student society at the same university is often approached by young women with matters concerning discrimination or welfare. While she communicates these matters further to the Welfare officer she nonetheless encourages the complainants to speak to the relevant authority:

I think most students don't even know that is available and don't even know how approachable these people are. The most approachable person in the whole student union is a Polish guy, the academic affairs officer. Even the black student officer was with us for the prayer rooms and if it wasn't for him we wouldn't have the prayer rooms. He got us an hour free for jummah[2] time every Friday. He got us so many things and if ever I have an issue I could go to him [...]

He is Polish. He is fantastic and I would tell so many people to go to him because he will sit down and he will actually make time for you. But people are like how is he going to understand [...] I'm like this is the mentality you have got to get yourself out of. He can help you. (Nadia, West Yorkshire2, 20, Undergrad Law, British)

The disconnect between students and welfare facilities in universities is more complex than a matter of non-reporting on the part of the students, or universities assuming that policies in place would mean that students would make use of them. The problem faced by students and welfare services at West Yorkshire2 are quite similar to problems in other universities. While many students might dismiss their experience of Islamophobia, there are others who clearly do speak to Islamic society members about their experiences. However, unless the Islamic societies take the matter further, often such experiences remain under reported. The reason for under reporting can also vary depending on

---

[2]Friday afternoon prayers.

the socio-political climate, a point reiterated by Tabussum's discussion of "intelligent Islamophobia" especially in the aftermath of the Abdulmutallab incident. However, in Tabussum's case, with welfare officers who were trying to understand the realities of Muslim students the university was quick to allay the fears of the Islamic society, and was more supportive in understanding their position, thereby managing to clearly engage with Muslim students and support them. Yet the same racism and equality advisor also acknowledged the need to advertise their services more to students, and to further pour resources into encouraging Muslim students to come forward with any complaints about Islamophobia. In the same university for instance, there were students who did not report incidents of Islamophobia that they had experienced with other students, despite the provision of such services. They would either accept it as part of a socio-political context that problematises their Muslim identity, or look the other way. Other participants have also highlighted similar reasons. Often unsure about the intentions of the Islamophobe, students are quick to dismiss or provide explanations for the acts of discrimination, from ignorance to misunderstanding. In situations where students perceive hostility but never directly experience it, there is an added fear of being perceived as paranoid or overly sensitive, or 'making a big deal' about Islamophobia which again prevents young people from coming forward and filing a formal complaint. In order to bridge that gap between the university and students, the participants were questioned about the possibility of including an Islamophobia officer that was entirely dedicated to providing support against such discrimination. The students predominantly rejected this idea. The FOSIS representative captures the problem with such a proposition:

> *I would disagree with assigning an Islamophobia officer. You don't want to create the victim mentality that the whole world is against you. Definitely there are people who are against you but the more [...] you think you are victims the more you segregate yourself [...] we have officers, welfare or black student officers or anti-racism.* They are there to help students, whether they are that effective I am not entirely sure. The NUS is trying to give training around *Islamophobia for student officers [...] also a lot of Hindus*

and Sikhs actually get treated similarly because of the ignorance since they are brown which is really unfortunate. They are also getting the same language and verbal abuse and at times physical abuse as well. There are elements of hostility towards the Muslim community. (FOSIS Representative, 2011)

Faiza a Muslim student who wears the niqab, had experienced Islamophobia and did not report the incident to the university. She also agreed that a welfare officer assigned to deal with Islamophobia alone would be ineffective. Such an idea would instead further create separation within the student body.

The more we separate I think the more people would direct hate towards us because you know we are already different and then if we have separate, separate jobs it would only worsen things, make things worse. It would peak these attitudes you know what I mean.

Interviewer: *What should be done to prevent them?*

Faiza: *I don't think you can prevent these attitudes, that would only make it worse. Making things exclusive to Muslims would only worsen their situation. People's attitudes would be I don't know why do they need separate this, separate that separate.* (Faiza, West Yorkshire2, 22, Undergrad Humanities, British)

Diane, the Welfare staff member at the same university also echoed similar sentiments about greater division. Given that West Yorkshire2 has a large population of Muslim students, predominantly with a Pakistani heritage, having separate officers would not have been a sufficient solution to the problem of such specific discrimination, and would result in what she calls,

A different form of racism […] taking one race out, which ever race it is and putting additional focus will have a different impact […] it feels to me a process of sort of greater separation rather than greater acceptance or acknowledgment. (Diane, West Yorkshire2, University Welfare, 2011)

Participants echoed similar sentiments throughout the research. The question that arises then is what can universities do to create an atmosphere of no tolerance against Islamophobia, where Muslim students can go up to university welfare officials and report an incident of Islamophobia without feeling like they stand out? One of the solutions proposed for university welfare is to build the capacity of existing welfare officers instead of creating separate positions. As the FOSIS representative mentions, training is being provided to Student Unions, but the capacity of the university to deal with Islamophobia effectively also needs to be communicated to students, especially in the present day context of a security agenda that imposes a "statutory duty" on universities that is akin to monitoring and surveillance of Muslim students. There is an additional need to address Islamophobia against non-Muslim students, especially Hindus and Sikhs who may be mistaken for being Muslim.

Since the emphasis of student narratives was not so much on lack of facilities rather than lack of information about these facilities, there is a need for universities to be more vocal about its no tolerance policy, whether by holding workshops for different student societies or having an orientation every year on different types of discrimination that may exist in universities and the protocols in place to report such incidents. However, student societies also need to be more proactive in promoting information about such welfare provisions in universities. Ahmed for instance is a member of his university's Student Union and believes that his university which has an internationally diverse student population is well equipped to deal with any incident of Islamophobia:

Interviewer: *Is there university support for anyone who experiences Islamophobia?*

Ahmed: *Absolutely from my personal conversation with the director at this school [...] the dean for undergraduate studies, the chaplain, we have people in (my university) who are terrific on Islamophobia. They recognize that it is a problem and they I am sure, this hasn't been tested yet, but I am sure if there was an Islamophobic incident where a student was attacked for just being a Muslim they would be quite strict in terms of following all procedures that are in place. There is also good support in terms of counselling services.*

Interviewer: *Do students know about this?*

Ahmed: *It is not very well publicized I think. It could be better publicized in that sense.* (Ahmed, London3, Student Union Anti Racism Officer)

Rukshanda clearly illustrates the problem of such lack of awareness about university provisions. Her example provides insights into welfare and Islamophobia related problems that may directly interfere with a student's academic work:

> *I think the laws in the university are really good. I know one of the postdocs, she is British Pakistani and she was doing her postdoc in one of the groups and she was the only Muslim there. Her boss had an issue with her praying. He would say that you spend this much time when you go pray and would ask her if she makes up for the wasted time in the lab later. Then Ramzan³ came, and of course the fasts in Ramzan were long so her progress went down and her boss was also unhappy about that. But being a British she knew her rights so she went to HR, she complained about that man and she resigned from that job, and found a new job. I also know some Pakistanis who had issues with their supervisors and they put up with it for months until someone told them that they had the option of changing supervisors. But of course if students don't know about these provisions then of course they will continue to suffer.*
>
> *[...]*
>
> Interviewer: *Do you think other students in your university know who to talk to?*
>
> Rukshanda: *I don't think so.* (Rukshanda, London2, 28, Science Grad, Overseas)

Whether the best solution to the problem that Rukshanda cites was resigning or changing jobs for the student is debatable, what is obvious in this incident however is that any welfare protocol is irrelevant if it is not effectively communicated to students. There is also a problem of accountability, where appropriate actions should be taken against Islamophobia.

> *I think first of all people need to feel like something is going to be done. I think mostly people feel like nothing will be done whether it is a university [...] Or if it is you have to go through all these boards. If they made it easier if you didn't have to go through a million and one boards and sit down*

---

³Islamic month of fasting.

directly and speak to someone and have it dealt with there and then people would be more willing to do it. If people were generally more approachable and were part of the student life. (Nadia, West Yorkshire2, 20, Undergrad Law, British)

In Nadia's university the welfare officers are also trying to get students of psychology involved with issues related to welfare to meet the needs of students who may have been victims of discrimination. However, universities need to go one step further and have protocols in place to reprimand Islamophobes, so students also have faith in a system that ensures their protection no matter what their religious belief. Ahmed's Student Union for instance has been a success story in this regard, being one of the first Student Unions that gave a 'a code of practice' to student societies and groups which instructs them to take action against 'any kind of misconduct,' which includes 'Islamophobia'. The success of his Student Union might be the result of greater involvement of Muslim students in student politics that resulted in students like Ahmed raising awareness about the problems faced by Muslim students, and a more proactive response from his university that is actively aiming to create an inclusive university environment.

Conclusion: Muslim Student Welfare, Counter Terrorism and the University

In a socio-political context where universities will continue to be drawn into the British state's security agenda, Muslim students will feel further targeted because of their religious beliefs. While the more recent threat of Isis and its appeal to a minority of Muslims, some of whom are students cannot and should not be ignored, stigmatising an entire Muslim student community within the university is also not the solution. However, while the UK government and higher educational institutions attempt to balance between security, equality and their duty of care towards all students, this chapter has illustrated that an atmosphere of distrust and insecurity exists within university campuses (also see Saeed and Johnson 2016). It is important to note that the study explored in this chapter was undertaken in 2010–2012 before the introduction of the "statutory duty" under the counter terrorism agenda of 2015. Given media reports of students as young as ten being suspected of radicalisation, while others questioned for reading course related books on terrorism at a university library, the paranoia about Muslim students has only gained further traction. There is an urgent need for universities to revisit and review their policies and protocols on racism and Islamophobia, to ensure that no student is unfairly treated because of his or her religious belief.

This chapter has highlighted the challenges that university personnel need to address to ensure that their university truly is a place where all students are treated equally and without prejudice. While students may be reluctant to report incidents of Islamophobia, lack of knowledge about the incident is also no excuse for an institution that has a "duty of care" towards all its students. There is a need on the part of the university to actively challenge the belief that no action will be taken against an Islamophobe if found guilty; to raise awareness about welfare facilities that can adequately address any form of discrimination or racism against Muslim students; to challenge the fear of individuals being labelled "victims" especially in cases where the reporting of an incident can prevent similar incidents in the future. A more proactive approach may range from workshops for all student societies, not just welfare officers that trains students to deal with incidents of discrimination ranging from Islamophobia to Anti-Semitism to any form of racism or religious discrimination. There is also a need to spread awareness during orientation week about the protocols in place for reporting on incidents of discrimination and Islamophobia.

The security context has created greater obstacles for universities to celebrate diversity, equality and inclusion within university campuses. However, these obstacles can be overcome by universities taking an active role in implementing anti-racist, anti-Islamophobic policies, where Muslim and non-Muslim students alike have faith in a university welfare system that is unbiased, and dedicated to meeting the needs of all its students.

References

Awan, I., & Zempi, I. (2015). *We Fear for Our Lives: Offline and Online Experiences of Anti-Muslim Hostility.* Birmingham City University, Nottingham Trent University and Tell MAMA.

BBC News. (2010, November 3). Woman Jailed for Life for Attack on MP Stephen Timms [Online]. *BBC News.* Available from http://www.bbc.co.uk/news/uk-england-london-11682732. Accessed 3 May 2011.

BBC News. (2011, October 12). Profile: Umar Farouk Abdulmutallab [Online]. *BBC News.* Available from http://www.bbc.co.uk/news/world-us-canada-11545509. Accessed 12 July 2012.

BBC News. (2016a, March 23). IS-Inspired 'Drive-By' Terror Plot: Two Students Guilty. *BBC News.* Available from http://www.bbc.com/news/uk-35884915. Accessed 4 May 2016.

BBC News. (2016b, January 20). Lancashire 'Terrorist House' Row 'Not a Spelling Mistake'. *BBC News.* Available from http://www.bbc.com/news/uk-england-lancashire-35354061. Accessed 4 May 2016.

BIS Research Paper Number 55. (2011). *Amplifying the Voice of Muslim Students: Findings from Literature Review.* Department for Business Innovation and Skills.

Bouattia, M. (2016, April 24). I'm the New NUS President—And No, I'm Not an Antisemitic Isis Sympathiser. *The Guardian.* Available from http://www.theguardian.com/commentisfree/2016/apr/24/new-nus-president-not-antisemitic-isis-sympathiser. Accessed 5 May 2016.

Coppock, V., & McGovern, M. (2014). 'Dangerous Minds'? Deconstructing Counter-Terrorism Discourse, Radicalisation and the 'Psychological Vulnerability' of Muslim Children and Young People in Britain. *Children and Society, 28,* 242–256.

Davies, L. (2016). Security, Extremism and Education: Safeguarding or Surveillance? *British Journal of Educational Studies, 64*(1), 1–19.

Durodie, B. (2016). Securitising Education to Prevent Terrorism or Losing Direction? *British Journal of Educational Studies, 64*(1), 21–35.

El-Haj, T. R. A., Bonet, S. W., Demerath, P., & Schultz, K. (2011). Education, Citizenship, and the Politics of Belonging: Youth from Muslim Transnational Communities and the "War on Terror". *Review of Research in Education, 35,* 29–59.

Feldman, M., & Littler, M. (2014). *Tell MAMA Reporting 2013/14: Anti-Muslim Overview, Analysis and 'Cumulative Extremism'.* Teesside: Teesside University Press.

Githens-Mazer, J. (2010). *Rethinking the Causal Concept of Islamic Radicalisation. Political Concepts: Committee on Concepts and Methods Working Paper Series.* Montreal: International Political Science Association.

Her Majesty's Government (HM Government). (2006). *Terrorism Act 2006.* UK: Crown.

Her Majesty's Government (HM Government). (2011a). *Prevent Strategy.* UK: Crown.

Her Majesty's Government (HM Government). (2011b). *CONTEST the United Kingdom's Strategy for Countering Terrorism.* UK: Crown.

Her Majesty's Government (HM Government). (2015a). *Counter-Terrorism and Security Act 2015.* Available from http://www.legislation.gov.uk/ukpga/2015/6/notes/contents. Accessed 28 Mar 2015.

Her Majesty's Government (HM Government). (2015b). *Prevent Duty Guidance for Higher Education Institutions in England and Wales.* UK: Crown.

Hoyle, C., Bradford, A., & Frenett, R. (2015). *Becoming Mulan? Female Western Migrants to ISIS.* London, UK: Institute for Strategic Dialogue.

Kimura, M. (2014). Non-performativity of University and Subjectification of Students: The Question of Equality and Diversity in UK Universities. *British Journal of Sociology of Education, 35*(4), 523–540.

Kundnani, A. (2012). Radicalisation: The Journey of a Concept. *Race & Class, 54*(2), 3–25.

Kundnani, A. (2015). *A Decade Lost. Rethinking Radicalisation and Extremism.* London, UK: Claystone.

Mayor's Office for Policing and Crime. (2015). Crime Figures. Latest Crime Figures for London. Available from http://www.met.police.uk/crimefigures/. Accessed 5 May 2016.

O'Donnell, A. (2016). Securitisation, Counterterrorism and the Silencing of Dissent: The Educational Implications of Prevent. *British Journal of Educational Studies, 64*(1), 53–76.

Ramesh, R., & Halliday J. (2015, September 24). Student Accused of Being a Terrorist for Reading a Book on Terrorism. *The Guardian.* Available from http://www.theguardian.com/education/2015/sep/24/student-accused-being-terrorist-reading-book-terrorism. Accessed 4 May 2016.

Saeed, T. (2016a). Muslim Narratives of Schooling in Britain: From "Paki" to the "Would-Be Terrorist". In M. M. Ghaill & C. Haywood (Eds.), *Education, Neo-liberalism and Muslim Students: Schooling a 'Suspect Community'.* London, UK: Palgrave Macmillan.

Saeed, T. (2016b). *Islamophobia and Securitization. Religion, Ethnicity and the Female Voice (Palgrave Politics of Identity and Citizenship series)*. London, UK: Palgrave Macmillan.

Saeed, T., & Johnson, D. (2016). Intelligence, Global Terrorism and Higher Education: Neutralising Threats or Alienating Allies? *British Journal of Educational Studies, 64*(1), 37–51.

Saltman, E. M., & Smith, M. (2015). '*Till Martyrdom Do Us Part' Gender and the ISIS Phenomenon*. London, UK: Institute for Strategic Dialogue.

Students Not Suspects Campaign. (2017). Available from https://www.nusconnect.org.uk/articles/students-not-suspects-join-us-to-up-the-fight-against-prevent. Accessed 7 Dec 2017.

Townsend, M. (2012, July 14). Police 'Made Up' Evidence Again Muslim Student [Online]. *The Guardian*. Available from http://www.guardian.co.uk/uk/2012/jul/14/police-evidence-muslim-student-rizwaan-sabir. Accessed 16 Feb 2013.

Tyrer, D., & Ahmad, F. (2006). *Muslim Women and Higher Education: Identities, Experiences and Prospects. A Summary Report. Liverpool John Moores University and European Social Fund*. Oxford: Oxuniprint.

Part IV

Seize the Day! The Irresistible Rise of
Decolonising Movements

14

Why Is My Curriculum White? A Brief Genealogy of Resistance

Michael Adrian Peters

Introduction

In a recent story by Minna Salami (2015) in *The Guardian* entitled 'Philosophy has to be about more than white men', the following claim is made, 'The campaign to counter the narrow-mindedness of university courses is gathering pace because philosophy should investigate all human existence'.[1]

Salami makes reference to a 20-minute video with the title *Why is My Curriculum White?* made by University College London (UCL) students who propose responses to this question pointing out the lack of awareness

---

[1]Minna Salami is the founder of the MsAfropolitan blog, which covers Africa and the diaspora from a feminist perspective. I would like to thank Tina Besley from drawing my attention to this story and for discussing the underlying issues. I would also like to acknowledge the helpful editorial comments of Heidi Mirza who reminds me of my own white privilege as a scholar and the contributions of women of colour to Black activism.

M. A. Peters (✉)
University of Waikato, Hamilton, New Zealand
e-mail: michael.peters@waikato.ac.nz

© The Author(s) 2018
J. Arday and H. S. Mirza (eds.), *Dismantling Race in Higher Education*,
https://doi.org/10.1007/978-3-319-60261-5_14

253

that the curriculum is white comprised of 'white ideas' by 'white authors' and is a result of colonialism that has normalised whiteness and made blackness invisible. This is a fundamental educational challenge that has not been addressed by the educational establishment, nor by the majority of philosophers including philosophers of education, most of whom are white men and women. Racism rarely figures on philosophy of education conference agendas and papers discussing the ethics of education that tend to talk in general and abstract terms neglecting issues of race or gender.

Salami wrote a blog rather than a philosophy paper making the argument that 'we should not dismiss white, western, or male thinking simply on the premises that it is white, western, or male' while at the same time acknowledging, by reference to Michael McEachrane's (2014) statement, 'Modern philosophical concepts of personhood, human rights, justice and modernity are deeply shaped by race'.[2]

My purpose is to take seriously the issues that she and UCL students are making. In view of the events in Ferguson, USA, where social unrest and a series on ongoing protests began the day after the shooting of Michael Brown (9 August 2014), it is necessary to raise the question again of the roots of US racism and racism in general. This is exactly the topic of The Stone interviews conducted by George Yancy of prominent American philosophers.[3] Yancy's latest interview features 'Noam Chomsky on the Roots of American Racism'.[4]

Chomsky provides a brief history in terms of slave labour camps, a major factor in American's success and current wealth, the harsh criminalisation that followed after the end of slavery and the new Jim Crow that neoliberalism under Reagan initiated in the 1970s as part of the 'drug war'. Chomsky says:

---

[2]See McEachrane's (2014) *Afro-Nordic Landscapes: Equality and Race in Northern Europe*. Salami also makes reference to Dirk J. Louw's 'Ubuntu: An African Assessment of the Religious Other' at http://www.bu.edu/wcp/Papers/Afri/AfriLouw.htm.

[3]The Stone features the writing of contemporary philosophers for the *New York Times* moderated by Simon Critchley.

[4]See http://opinionator.blogs.nytimes.com/2015/03/18/noam-chomsky-on-the-roots-of-american-racism/?_r=1. George Yancy is himself a philosopher who works on 'critical philosophy of race, critical whiteness studies, and philosophy of the Black experience' as he say on his university webpage (http://www.duq.edu/academics/faculty/george-yancy). His latest edited collection is *White Self-Criticality beyond Anti-Racism: How Does It Feel to Be a White Problem?* (2014).

The national poet, Walt Whitman, captured the general understanding when he wrote that "The nigger, like the Injun, will be eliminated; it is the law of the races, history… A superior grade of rats come and then all the minor rats are cleared out." It wasn't until the 1960s that the scale of the atrocities and their character began to enter even scholarship, and to some extent popular consciousness, though there is a long way to go. (Yancy and Chomsky 2015)

Yet Ferguson demonstrates that Obama's 'post-racial America' is a kind of mythology that persists despite the critical scholarship of Yancy and Chomsky and many others, including Black women scholars (Green and Mabokela 2001).[5] Part of the problem is what scholars call 'internal colonisation,' a psychological state that Césaire, Fanon, and Malcolm X knew too well meant that the dominant ideology had become internalised and thus part of the psychological make-up of the oppressed. This notion of 'internal colonisation' was first recognised by the movement called Négritude.

The Concept of Négritude

Négritude was a literary movement by French-speaking African and Carribean writers that philosophically established the fact and value of Black selfhood and identity during the 1930–1950s as a counternarrative to French colonial rule. Aimé Césaire's *Discourse on Colonialism* (Orig. Fr 1955) and his *Cahier d'un retour au pays natal* composed in 1939 and translated as *Return to My Native Land* (1969), is a lyric and sustained narrative long poem (over 1055 lines in the original French) that became the anthem for the Négritude movement and helped lay

---

[5]In this regard see James Anderson's AERA lecture, 'A Long Shadow: The American Pursuit of Political Justice and Education Equality', that explores the historic and inseparable relationship between the right and freedom to vote and the pursuit of education equality. Video, transcript, and slides at http://www.aera.net/Newsroom/AERAHighlightsE-newsletter/AERAHighlightsOctober2014/JamesDAndersonDeliversEleventhAnnualAERA BrownLecturetoRecordAudience/tabid/15698/Default.aspx.

the foundations for the emergence of Postcolonial studies in the 1970s. Reminiscent of W.E.B. Dubois' (1903) *The Souls of Black Folk* in that it explores the notion of Black selfhood, Césaire explores identity through the metaphor of trying on masks and utilises uncompromising language that emulates a virulent self-hatred. Fanon's (1952) *Black Skin, White Mask* also used the device of the mask to explore the psychology of racism under colonialism focusing on the divided self-perception of the Black subject who had lost his (sic) culture. In the 1986 Pluto Press edition of the English translation by Charles Lam Markmann, Homi Bhabba notes in his Foreword 'Remembering Fanon: Self, Psyche and the Colonial Condition' how Fanon's ideas are effectively "out of print" in Britain with little acknowledgement except through mythical means as the avenging angel of Black revolutionary activity.

Léopold Sédar Senghor, one of the founders of the movement and an African political leader, was a poet and intellectual who with Aime Césaire and Leon Damas built the Négritude movement. Senghor in the late 1920s went to France to prepare himself to enter the École Normale Supérieure. In the 1930s he became one of the main voices for the concept of negritude and after WWII entered politics in Senegal breaking from French socialism to build his own party that rested on Muslim support. He became the first president of an independent Senegal in 1960 and held the post until 1980. He published his first collection of poetry in 1945 and continued to write and publish poetry through his life and presidency. His poetry focused on the Black experience of the natural and social worlds in a lyrical and sensual form that he thought characterised Black sensibilities. His *Liberté 1: Négritude et Humanisme* (1964a) part of a five volume collection, contains some of his early speeches and provides background to the emergence of Black African culture. His *On African Socialism* (1964b) takes issue with classical Marxism to emphasise Marxism as a humanism and the Marx of the *Economic and Philosophical Manuscripts* of 1844. As Barbara Celarent (2013: 302) comments:

> He wants his hearers not to reject the Negro-African heritage for a Europeanized materialism, for Marx's "terribly inhuman metaphysics, an atheistic metaphysics in which mind is sacrificed to matter, freedom to the determined, man to things". (*On African Socialism*, p. 76)

Senghor tended to avoid Marxism and anti-Western ideology that was characteristic of this time in Africa. The African Studies Center at Leiden that provides an introduction to his work and a list of his publications, writes of Senghor:

> As co-founder of the Negritude movement, Senghor tried to awaken African consciousness and dispel feelings of inferiority. The term 'Negritude' embraces the revolt against colonial values, glorification of the African past, and nostalgia for the beauty and harmony of traditional African society. The concept is defined in contradistinction to Europe. According to Senghor, the African is intuitive, whereas the European is more Cartesian. This statement led to numerous protests, with Sartre even declaring that Negritude was "an antiracist racism". Senghor's poetry often displayed what he called "this double feeling of love and hate" regarding the "white" world. Though his African nationalism emerged in his poetry and his politics, he refused to reject European culture. (ASCLibrary 2016)

Little known, Anténor Firmin, a Haitian anthropologist wrote a book *De l'égalité des races humaines* (On The Equality of the Human Races), published in 1885 in response to Arthur de Gobineau's work *Essai sur l'inégalité des races humaines* (Essay on the Inequality of the Human Races, 1853–1855) which proclaimed the superiority of the white race arguing in one of the earliest examples of scientific racism that civilisations based on "mixed races" will fail. Firmin together with Henry Sylvester Williams, a Trinidadian lawyer, and Bénito Sylvain organised the first Panafrican conference in London in 1900, a conference attended by W.E.B. DuBois who was made responsible for writing the general report. Some five similar conferences were held during the twentieth century that eventually led to the African Union.

As is also well known, the Harlem Renaissance originally named "The New Negro Movement", constituted the rebirth of African-American arts that began in the 1920s lasting through the 1930s strongly influenced the Négritude philosophy with the flowering of music, fashion, dance, poetry, drama, art and literature. The Harlem Renaissance was partly the result of the Great Migration out of the South to the new Black neighbourhoods in the North in places like Manhattan. There were race riots in 1919 as tensions grew over economic competition for jobs. New drama such as *Three Plays for a Negro Theatre* rejected the stereotypes of the Black and white minstrel show tradition. New Black newspapers and academic journals were launched. Religion played a strong role with the ideology of inclusion and Islam and Black Judaism came to Harlem to promote social and racial integration as well as a Panafricanism. All Black productions of theatre and opera of, for example, Gershwin's *Porgy and Bess*, saw art, theatre and music as a means of artistic self-expression but also a way of expressing dimensions of human equality.

The Emergence of Black Studies

The groundwork for Black studies was established and laid down at the turn of the century with works by Du Bois like *The Philadelphia Negro* (1898). It took Du Bois until 1941 to present a program for Black studies to the Annual Conference of the Presidents of Negro Land-Grant Colleges and the first program did not appear until twenty-five years later (see the W.E.B. Du Bois Research Institute at Harvard established in 1975, http://hutchinscenter.fas.harvard.edu/dubois).

Afro-American studies departments emerged in the 1960s after student activism, although the reconstruction of African-American history began in the late nineteenth century. The origins cannot be separated from the Civil Rights context. Students for a Democratic Society at Berkeley held a conference in 1966 called 'Black Power and its Challenges' inviting Black civil rights leaders. Then came the demand for Black Studies:

> The black freedom movement, in both the civil rights phase (1955–1965) and Black Power component (1966–1975), fostered the racial desegregation and the empowerment of black people within previously all-white institutions. The racial composition of U.S. colleges changed dramatically. In 1950 approximately 75,000 blacks were enrolled in colleges and universities. In the 1960s three quarters of all black students attended HBCUs.[6] By 1970, approximately 700,000 blacks were enrolled in college, three quarters of whom were in predominantly white institutions. (Land and Brown 2017)[7]

---

[6]HBCU—Historical Black Colleges and Universities.
[7]Historical Black Colleges and Universities. http://education.stateuniversity.com/pages/1742/African-American-Studies.html.

Black Studies was also strengthened through the growth of Black Legal Studies and Critical Legal Studies in the 1970s that drew heavily of changes to the political culture occurring during the counter culture of the 1960s. Critical Legal Studies explored how the practices of legal institutions, legal doctrine, and legal education worked to buttress dominant white culture and rule of law devoid of hidden class and race interests. Critical race studies applied critical theory to the intersections of race, law, and power providing a critique of liberalism and revisionist accounts of American civil rights law. Critical race theory and critical pedagogy also pursued these issues theorising the notion of whiteness as property. As Delgado and Stefancic (2006: 2) comment:

> Although CRT began as a movement in the law, it has rapidly spread beyond that discipline. Today, many in the field of education consider themselves critical race theorists who use CRT's ideas to understand issues of school discipline and hierarchy, tracking, controversies over curriculum and history, and IQ and achievement testing.[8]

Even with these movements for justice and social change, recent surveys would suggest that little progress has been made in eliminating systematic or institutional racism in the US (see http://education.stateuniversity.com/pages/1742/African-American-Studies.html).

The Civil Rights Movement

The Civil Rights movement was a movement to end segregation and racial discrimination in the USA during the initial period from 1954 to 1968 that focussed on nonviolent protest and campaigns of civil disobedience. This was an age of protest with mass mobilisation which replaced litigation and was perhaps ignited with the famous case of Brown vs The Board of Education in 1954, which was the beginning of the end of segregation of schools. This case was a landmark decision of the US Supreme Court which overturned the Plessy vs Fergusson

---

[8]See http://www.huffingtonpost.com/2015/02/07/college-student-survey-race_n_6632854.html.

case of 1896 that mandated state segregation and held that as long as there were separate facilities for races segregation did not violate the 14th Amendment that stated an equal protection under the law provision. The Supreme Court decision came at a time strongly influenced by the new international agencies emphasis on equality and the UNESCO document *The Race Question* (1950) that was an attempt to clarify the false claims of scientific racism especially in view of the experience of Nazi racism. Claude Levi-Strauss and Ashley Montagu, alongside a group of authors, expressed a concern for human dignity and the equality of all citizens before the law declaring that Homo sapiens was one species, that 'race' was a classificatory concept that provided no support for 'pure races' or reproduction between persons of different races. The Brown vs The Board of Education Supreme Court decision found no place for 'separate but equal':

> Segregation of white and colored children in public schools has a detrimental effect upon the colored children. The effect is greater when it has the sanction of the law, for the policy of separating the races is usually interpreted as denoting the inferiority of the negro group. A sense of inferiority affects the motivation of a child to learn. Segregation with the sanction of law, therefore, has a tendency to [retard] the educational and mental development of negro children and to deprive them of some of the benefits they would receive in a racial[ly] integrated school system…

> We conclude that, in the field of public education, the doctrine of "separate but equal" has no place. Separate educational facilities are inherently unequal. Therefore, we hold that the plaintiffs and others similarly situated for whom the actions have been brought are, by reason of the segregation complained of, deprived of the equal protection of the laws guaranteed by the Fourteenth Amendment. (Legal Information Institute 2017)

The Civil Rights movement about which much has been written was a nonviolent movement to gain legal equality before the law, to uphold the 15th Amendment of the Constitution, and to secure Constitutional rights of African Americans thus ending the era of state mandated segregation especially focusing on equality of opportunity and equality of access to public institutions including education and the right to vote.

It is impossible to capture all the elements, personalities and events of the civil rights movement in an essay of this kind; the historical sources include much contemporary Black history and primary sources collections including streaming videos and oral histories.[9] From a broad philosophical viewpoint the aim of the movement was to achieve equal citizenship:

> In contemporary political thought, the term 'civil rights' is indissolubly linked to the struggle for equality of American blacks during the 1950s and 60s. The aim of that struggle was to secure the status of equal citizenship in a liberal democratic state. Civil rights are the basic legal rights a person must possess in order to have such a status. They are the rights that constitute free and equal citizenship and include personal, political, and economic rights. No contemporary thinker of significance holds that such rights can be legitimately denied to a person on the basis of race, color, sex, religion, national origin, or disability. Antidiscrimination principles are thus a common ground in contemporary political discussion. However, there is much disagreement in the scholarly literature over the basis and scope of these principles and the ways in which they ought to be implemented in law and policy. (Altman 2013)

Critical Race Theory and Black Legal Studies

It is a sobering thought that Critical Race Theory, which emerged from the discipline of law only in the 1970s, was developed by a range of critical theorists because they thought that the civil rights movements of the 1960s had effectively stalled. As Richard Delgado and Jean Stefancic (2006: 2) in their Introduction to *Critical Race Theory* write:

> Critical race theory sprang up in the mid-1970s, as a number of lawyers, activists, and legal scholars across the country realised, more or less simultaneously, that the heady advances of the civil rights era of the 1960s had

---

[9]For primary sources of the civil rights Movement See http://www.findingdulcinea.com/guides/Education/US-History/Civil-Rights-Movement.pg_01.html.

stalled and, in many respects, were being rolled back. Realizing that new theories and strategies were needed to combat the subtler forms of racism that were gaining ground, early writers such as Derrick Bell, Alan Freeman, and Richard Delgado … put their minds to the task. They were soon joined by others, and the group held its first conference at a convent outside Madison, Wisconsin, in the summer of 1989.

Kimberlé Williams Crenshaw (2011), the Black feminist critical race legal scholar, looking back on twenty years of critical race theory, begins: 'Today, CRT can claim a presence in education, psychology, cultural studies, political science, and even philosophy. The way that CRT is received and mobilised in other disciplines varies, but it is clear that CRT has occupied a space in the canon of recognised intellectual movements that few other race-oriented formations have achieved' (pp. 1256–1257). She mentions the texts by Du Bois, Joyce Ladner (*The Death of White Sociology*), Robert Guthrie (*Even the Rat Was White*), Tukufu Zuberi and Eduardo Bonilla-Silva and Toni Morrison (*Playing in the Dark*), that contested the academy had 'disciplined knowledge about race' (p. 1257) and goes on to explore what ignited CRT in law. It is indeed salutary to understand how CRT emerged as an intellectual movement and Crenshaw (2011) is at pains to point out that CRT was not simply 'a philosophical critique of the dominant frames on racial power. It was also a product of activists' engagement with the material manifestations of liberal reform' (p. 1253). She also remarks how 'liberal visions of race reform and radical critiques of class hierarchy failed in different ways to address the institutional, structural and ideological reproduction of racial hierarchy' (p. 1253). Crenshaw (2011) provides a clear picture of the movement's origins and political formation beginning with the 1989 conference and the way in which CRT became 'interdisciplinary, intersectional, and cross- institutional' (p. 1253). What is important about Crenshaw's (2011) paper is the questioning of Obama's post-racial ideology and the, then, 'configuration of racial power' and 'the entrapment of civil rights discourse more broadly' (p. 1347). It reminds us how quickly the framework of racial power changes and how, even under the first African-American administration, viewed by some as fulfilling the dream of Martin Luther

King Jr. the ideological dimensions of 'post-racial' policies increasingly
became exposed during Obama's two terms, especially after the Great
Recession where Blacks and other minorities lost heavily in the housing
and job crises. '*Black Lives Matter*' the social movement for racial justice
formed during Obama's administration goes beyond the 'extrajudicial
killings of Black people by police and vigilantes' to '(re)build the Black
liberation movement' (http://blacklivesmatter.com/). The movement
began in 2013 when George Zimmerman was acquitted of shooting a
Black teen, Trayvon Martin. The movement organised street demon-
strations following the deaths of Michael Brown in Ferguson and Eric
Garner in New York city. One of the editors of this volume comments
that these were started and organised by queer Black women, who have
been written out of herstory (http://blacklivesmatter.com/herstory/).
Race relations in the post-election climate of Donald Trump's administration seemed destined to deteriorate as Trump intensifies racial divisions and politically exploits racism, appointing top advisors who have
been criticised for their association with, and condonement of, white
supremacist groups.

Anti-racist Education

Anti-racist education differed strongly from multicultural education,
designed to eliminate the practice of classifying people according to
their skin colour or racial identity. Anti-racist education in Britain and
the US criticised the liberal assumptions of multiculturalism by uncov-
ering and dismantling the hidden power structures that were responsible for inequality and racism in institutions. Educational institutions,
in particular, it is claimed play a fundamental role in reproducing
white privilege and schools are seen as places where racism and stereotypes against ethnic and minority groups take place through a variety
of means. The curriculum and pedagogy have been analysed as sites for
this kind of reproduction that takes place through misinterpretations of
history and the 'othering' of minorities, shaping both white and non-
white subjectivities and identities. Gillborn (2006) focusing on the UK
argues 'conventional forms of anti-racism have proven unable to keep

pace with the development of increasingly racist and exclusionary education policies that operate beneath a veneer of professed tolerance and diversity', especially in the context of 'conservative modernisation' and the resurgence of racist nationalism which if anything has increased under austerity programs since Gillborn wrote his essay. He concludes by suggesting 'Racism is complex, contradictory, and fast-changing: it follows that anti-racism must be equally dynamic' (p. 26).

Gillborn's analysis is entirely salutary. After 50 years of struggle in the form of multiple movements, it is heartbreaking and extremely frustrating for Blacks, for indigenous peoples, for minority groups and for society as a whole that there has been so little progress or that social change has been resisted, destabilised, and under- mined. At the same time, it is encouraging that a new generation of students and scholars is actively pursuing 'whiteness as ideology' as with the UCL Collective.

Why Is the Curriculum White?

The UCL collective remarks:

> Although often treated as something biological, fixed or even benevolent, 'race' is an ideologically constructed social phenomenon. Therefore, when we talk about whiteness, we are not talking about white people, but about an ideology that empowers people racialised as white. (New Urban Collective 2015)

To the question 'why is the curriculum white?' they provide eight answers (summarised here):

1. To many, whiteness is invisible.
2. A curriculum racialised as white was fundamental to the development of capitalism.
3. Because its power is intersectional.
4. The white curriculum thinks for us; so we don't have to.
5. The physical environment of the academy is built on white domination.

6. The white curriculum need not only include white people.
7. The white curriculum is based on a (very) popular myth.
8. Because if it isn't white, it isn't right (apparently).

Even if one disagrees with the statement of these reasons it is clear that there is a general philosophical problem concerning the curriculum and that efforts to resolve it so far have been only partially effective. One of the difficulties has been that western philosophy itself has been part of the problem rather than part of the solution. Of all disciplines, it has seemed most resistant to taking race seriously and only recently have Black philosophers begun to deconstruct and dismantle the ideology of 'whiteness' as it affects our institutions in education, in government, in the academy and in the law.

A combination of philosophical critique and activism is required. *Rhodes Must Fall* is another example of an anti-racist protest movement. It began in 2015 at Cape Town University campaigning for the removal of the statue of Cecil Rhodes which was regarded as an inappropriate symbol of a colonial era based on the exercise of racial colonial power. Rhodes is seen as a racist, a symbol of colonialism and as someone who prepared South Africa for the introduction of the apartheid system. While the movement began as a protest by students and staff against institutional racism at the University of Cape Town it developed into a wider student movement designed to decolonise higher education across South Africa and also at Oxford University, where Rhodes was a benefactor. *Rhodes Must Fall in Oxford* (n.d.) states its aims as:

> *Rhodes Must Fall in Oxford (RMFO)* is a movement determined to decolonise the institutional structures and physical space in Oxford and beyond. We seek to challenge the structures of knowledge production that continue to mould a colonial mindset that dominates our present.

Our movement addresses Oxford's colonial legacy on three levels:

1. Tackling the plague of **colonial iconography** (in the form of statues, plaques and paintings) that seeks to whitewash and distort history.
2. Reforming **the Euro-centric curriculum** to remedy the highly selective narrative of traditional academia—which frames the West as sole

producers of universal knowledge—by integrating subjugated and local epistemologies. This will create a more intellectually rigorous, complete academy.

3. Addressing the **underrepresentation and lack of welfare provision** for Black and Minority Ethnic (BME) amongst Oxford's academic staff and students (Bold in original).

The 'structures of knowledge production' includes the disciplines and the curriculum, the physical space of the university campus, and its symbolic colonial representations. We might also add to this characterisation by mentioning the political economy of a publishing world dominated by Anglo-American interests and English as the global academic language even for China and other Asian countries. This is to recognise the strategic nature of academic journals, the uneven distribution of academic journal nature, and the emergence of big data distribution and bibliometric systems that determine international rankings (Peters et al. 2016). Of all the disciplines, philosophy, perhaps is the oldest and one of the most influential in promoting colour-blindness and 'whiteness' at the expense and recognition of Black consciousness, identity, responsibility and action.

White Philosophy

I have used the term 'white philosophy' to designate the notion of colour-blind philosophy which in my view,

> has special application to American philosophy for its extraordinary capacity to ignore questions of race and for its incapacity to recognize the centrality of the empirical fact of blackness and whiteness in American society and as part of the American deep unconscious structuring politics, economics and education. (Peters 2011: 145)

I traced the development of American pragmatism especially in the work of Stanley Cavell and Richard Rorty (and also John Dewey) to show how race is all but peripheral in the development of the American philosophical canon. I also charted the beginning of Cornel

West's challenge to white philosophy crystallising in the late 1980s beginning with his book *The Evasion of American Philosophy* (West 1989). Paradoxially, as I remark in the paper, 'West himself names Wittgenstein, Heidegger and Dewey as those philosophers who set us free from the confines of a spurious universalism based on a European projection of its own self-image' (p. 153).

The recognition of the whiteness of philosophy and its effects is a complex matter. In education, it is important to recognise with critical pedagogy scholars like Henry Giroux, Michael Apple, and Peter McLaren, sociologists like Gillborn, Barry Troyna, and Fazal Rizvi, and feminist scholars of colour such as Aileen Moreton-Robinson, Gloria Ladson-Billings and Heidi Safia Mirza to name only a few, that the curriculum is an *official* selection that structures knowledge in ways that privilege a particular construction of knowledge and the history of knowledge. It is no longer surprising to us after establishing new awareness sensitivities to past knowledge that some of the most eminent philosophers of the nineteenth and twentieth centuries—Nietzsche, Heidegger, Wittgenstein—were strongly racist, at least at some points of their lives. American philosophers on the whole have been largely agnostic on the question of racism. Only in the 1990s does the question come up for study and review.

The lack of recognition of cultural context, of contexualism in general, in curriculum theory was perpetrated in philosophy of education by Paul Hirst and R.S. Peters' forms of knowledge thesis that focused on propositional knowledge and admitted no historical understanding of evolving forms of knowledge let alone their cultural embeddedness and variation (White 2005).

Park (2014) gives an account of the development of philosophy as an academic discipline in the late eighteenth and early nineteenth centuries. During this period, European philosophy influenced by Kant formulated the history of philosophy as a March of progress from the Greeks to Kant. It was an account that demolished existing accounts beginning in Egypt or Western Asia thus establishing an exclusionary canon of philosophy. Hegel's account of world history was strongly racist and imbued European philosophy with a prejudicial history we are still trying to escape from. These two philosophers contributed so much to a contemporary understanding of modernity as fundamentally Western (Peters 2014).

Roy Martinez (2010) as the basis for his collection *On Race and Racism in America* asks: "Given the racial complexity of the United States—not to mention the racism of its foundations and its persistence—why is it that the most influential white philosophers have not addressed the issue of race, its social construction and myth, and the problems it raises on a daily basis?" More recently, Ason Stanley and Vesla Weaver (2014) in the *New York Times* Stone forum ask "Is the United States a 'Racial Democracy'?" where *racial democracy* is defined as

> one that unfairly applies the laws governing the removal of liberty primarily to citizens of one race, thereby singling out its members as especially unworthy of liberty, the coin of human dignity. (Stanley and Weaver 2014)

Referring to the increase of statistics for Black imprisonment since the 1970s—an astonishing 517% increase from 1966 to 1997—Stanley and Weaver conclude that the system that has emerged in the last few decades in the US is a *racial democracy*.

Sean Harvey (2016) and other historians have mapped closely the influence of "race" in early America and the way a basically contestable philosophical idea provided foundations for American institutions.

> "Race," as a concept denoting a fundamental division of humanity and usually encompassing cultural as well as physical traits, was crucial in early America. It provided the foundation for the colonization of Native land, the enslavement of American Indians and Africans, and a common identity among socially unequal and ethnically diverse Europeans. Longstanding ideas and prejudices merged with aims to control land and labor, a dynamic reinforced by ongoing observation and theorization of non-European peoples. Although before colonization, neither American Indians, nor Africans, nor Europeans considered themselves unified "races," Europeans endowed racial distinctions with legal force and philosophical and scientific legitimacy, while Natives appropriated categories of "red" and "Indian," and slaves and freed people embraced those of "African" and "colored," to imagine more expansive identities and mobilize more successful resistance to Euro-American societies. (Harvey 2016, n.p.)

A critical question for me as a white male philosopher is whether the Western tradition in philosophy has the intellectual resources within to transform itself and come to terms with the historical effects and traces of racism that are invested in our institutions and in our knowledge traditions. I think it has—*as a teacher I have to believe this*—but we are only at the very beginning of this process of transformation and the UCL collective and *Rhodes Must Fall* have initiated student-led movements that have the potential to provoke and demand curriculum change.

References

Altman, A. (2013). Civil Rights. In E. N. Zalta (Ed.). *The Stanford Encyclopedia of Philosophy* (Summer 2013 Edition). https://plato.stanford.edu/archives/sum2013/entries/civil-rights/.

ASCLibrary. (2016). *Léopold Sédar Senghor.* http://www.ascleiden.nl/content/webdossiers/leopold-sedar-senghor. Accessed 8 Mar 2017.

Celarent, B. (2013, July). Review of Liberté 1: Negritude et Humanisme and On African Socialism. *American Journal of Sociology, 119*(1), 299–305.

Crenshaw, K. (2011). Twenty Years of Critical Race Theory: Looking Back to Move Forward. *Connecticut Law Review, 43*(5), 1253–1352.

Delgado, R., & Stefancic, J. (2006). *Critical Race Theory: An Introduction.* New York: New York University Press.

Gillborn, D. (2006). Critical Race Theory and Education: Racism and Anti-racism in Educational Theory and Praxis. *Discourse: Studies in the Cultural Politics of Education, 27,* 11–32.

Green, A., & Mabokela, R. (2001). *Sisters of the Academy: Emergent Blck Women Scholars in Higher Education.* Sterling, VA: Stylus.

Harvey, S. (2016). Ideas of Race in Early America, American History. *Oxford Research Encyclopaedias.* http://americanhistory.oxfordre.com/view/10.1093/acrefore/9780199329175.001.0001/acrefore-9780199329175-e-262.

Land, R., & Brown, M. (2017). *African-American Studies—The Foundations of African-American Studies, The Emergence of African-American Studies Departments.* http://education.stateuniversity.com/pages/1742/African-American-Studies.html. Accessed 8 Mar 2017.

Legal Information Institute. (2017). *Brown v. Board of Education.* https://www.law.cornell.edu/supremecourt/text/347/483. Accessed 8 Mar 2017.

Martinez, R. (Ed.). (2010). *On Race and Racism in America: Confessions in Philosophy*. University Park: Penn State University Press.

McEachrane, M. (Ed.). (2014). *Afro-Nordic Landscapes: Equality and Race in Northern Europe*. London: Routledge.

New Urban Collective. (2015). *Facebook*. https://www.facebook.com/NewUrbanCollective/posts/807471629336069. Accessed 8 Mar 2017.

Park, P. (2014). *Africa, Asia, and the History of Philosophy: Racism in the Formation of the Philosophical Canon, 1780–1830 (SUNY Series Philosophy and Race)*. New York: SUNY Press.

Peters, M. A. (2011). White Philosophy in/of America. *Pragmatism Today*. Available at http://www.pragmatismtoday.eu/index.php?id=2011summer1.

Peters, M. A. (2014). Eurocentrism and the Critique of 'Universal World History': The Eastern Origins of Western Civilization. *Geopolitics, History, and International Relations, 1,* 63–77.

Peters, M. A., Jandrić, Petar, Irwin, Ruth, Locke, Kirsten, Devine, Nesta, Heraud, Richard, et al. (2016). Towards a Philosophy of Academic Publishing. *Educational Philosophy and Theory, 48*(14), 1401–1425. https://doi.org/10.1080/00131857.2016.1240987.

Rhodes Must Fall in Oxford. (n.d.). https://rmfoxford.wordpress.com/. Accessed 8 Mar 2017.

Salami, M. (2015). Philosophy Is More than White Men. *The Guardian*. https://www.theguardian.com/education/commentisfree/2015/mar/23/philosophy-white-men-university-courses. Accessed 8 Mar 2017.

Senghor, L. (1964a). *Liberté 1: Negritude et Humanisme*. Paris: Éditions du Seuil.

Senghor, L. (1964b). *On African Socialism* (M. Cook, Trans.). New York: Praeger.

Stanley, A., & Vesla Weaver. (2014). Is the United States a 'Racial Democracy'? *New York Times Stone Forum*. https://opinionator.blogs.nytimes.com/2014/01/12/is-the-united-states-a-racial-democracy/?_php=true&_type=blogs&_r=0.

West, C. (1989). *The American Evasion of Philosophy*. Madison: University of Wisconsin Press.

White, J. (2005). Reassessing 1960s Philosophy of the Curriculum. *London Review of Education, 3,* 131–144.

Yancy, G., & Chomsky, N. (2015). *Noam Chomsky on the Roots of American Racism*. http://opinionator.blogs.nytimes.com/2015/03/18/noam-chomsky-on-the-roots-of-american-racism/?_r=1.

15

The Black Studies Movement in Britain: Becoming an Institution, Not Institutionalised

Kehinde Andrews

Exclusionary Knowledge

The overwhelmingly white make-up of academia is a crisis whose implication runs far beyond the university. Critics of schooling have for a long time drawn on Paolo Freire's idea of the *banking* concept, where students are handed down elite knowledge from the teachers and meant to absorb it uncritically (Freire 1999). With recent government moves to embed the 'classics' and 'rigorous' examinations back into schooling these critiques of top down, oppressive knowledge will continue to find amply sources to support them. However, if the critique of this oppressive learning solely focuses on schooling it is easy to miss where the elite knowledge that is filling the *empty receptacles* of the children is produced. Academia is the zenith of the schooling system, creating the elite knowledge being fed to the children. Freire's critique of the schools is not just of their learning styles, but also of the content of the knowledge that is

K. Andrews (✉)
Birmingham City University, Birmingham, UK
e-mail: kehinde.andrews@bcu.ac.uk

© The Author(s) 2018
J. Arday and H. S. Mirza (eds.), *Dismantling Race in Higher Education*,
https://doi.org/10.1007/978-3-319-60261-5_15

being passed down. A central reason why knowledge remains exclusive is because the places that are producing it are exclusionary clubs of white privilege. Inclusive knowledge can never be created in exclusionary places.

The impact of this exclusionary knowledge is that it is then passed down through the school system and also fed out to wider society. It is knowledge produced in universities that informs social policy, media discourse (at least to some extent), and how society understands the events and changes that occur. University is certainly not the only producer of knowledge, but is a powerful and foundational one that impacts the whole of society.

The Whiteness of academia then presents as a serious impediment to social progress. Alternative voices become marginalised by the lack of their presence, and the lack of those voices solidify further marginalisation of the alternatives. The difficulty in securing jobs in British academia has led to an exodus of Black (African and African Caribbean) scholars to the United States in search of opportunities (Christian 2005). This creates a vacuum of knowledge, a silence from voices that can shed an alternate light on how we understand the world.

It is not that Black people all think differently than those whose skin is white, or that there is a common Black perspective on society that is lost. To the contrary, there is a plurality of ideas and concepts that cross and overlap any notion of racial difference. The issue here is that by marginalising whole groups of people we lose the perspectives that are drawn from very different experiences. It is one thing to theorise about racism and diversity from a privileged position, and quite another to do so when you have had to live with the experiences of the racism you are writing about.

The paucity of Black representation in the British academia explains the banality of much of the theory of race and racism emerging from Britain, including empty concepts like the ever popular *superdiversity*. There is a reason that Black British scholars rely on US scholars for theory and ideas, it is because in Britain we even have to defend our right to Blackness. In the British context, defined by anti-racist coalitions, blackness is defined in an apparently political sense to denote all those who are not white (Andrews 2016a). Having to constantly justify your existence demonstrates the level to which academic knowledge is exclusionary. Also it exemplifies the extent to which the academy is removed from the social world. Modood (1994) complained of how 'political blackness' marginalised British Asians because Blackness is generally used to refer to those of African descent. Nothing has changed since then but there is still debate about the nature of Blackness.

The debate over Blackness is important because it speaks to the importance of the inclusion of voices from different groups in society. The reticence of British academia to embrace Blackness, in African ancestry, is due in large part to an uneasiness about the concept of race. In British sociology race is placed in 'scare quotes' to denote that it is not a real concept (Alexander 2002). This is due to race being seen as a social construction that has been used to oppress and dominate different groups. British academia has focused on trying to see the connections beyond difference, hence uniting under the unified experience of racism, in political blackness. British scholars have taken the disavowal of race further, specifically critiquing the idea of identity politics as narrow and divisive. When Black scholars break into British academia the prior debates often frame their interventions, for example authors such as Gilroy (2002) critique the essentialism at the heart of Black politics and yearns for a more fluid and complex form of identity.

The problem with the British account of race and Blackness is that it is based on a Eurocentric, top down approach to understanding difference. It is certainly true that Europeans built a regressive concept of racial difference that they used to justify their slaughter and oppression of hundreds of millions of dark skinned people in creating the West (Niro 2003). However, it is clearly inadequate to assign the only meaning of difference to the concept of Western race. At the same time that Europeans were conceiving the phenotypical differences that they encountered with peoples across the globe, those people were also creating their own understandings. The differences were not used by those in Africa, Asia or the Americas to concoct a racial hierarchy but that does not mean that the 'natives' did not see colour. The reality is that seeing difference is not the problem, the issue is when hierarchies become assigned to those variances.

It is Eurocentric and entirely disempowering to imagine that oppressed people simply internalised the racist categories of the West and use these as the basis for their identity politics. When Blackness is embraced it is not based on the Western concept of race. Rather Blackness is an identity that can be linked back through centuries of struggle and resistance that predate European involvement on the African continent (Andrews 2018). Blackness is a concept linked to radical movements for social change and is first used to identify those of African descent by people of African descent during the 1960s. Malcolm X (1971: 91) was one of the first to declare the importance of Blackness, proclaiming that 'there is a new type of Negro on the scene. This type doesn't call himself a Negro. *He calls himself* a Black man. He doesn't make any apology for his Black skin' (*emphasis* added). Embracing Blackness was an important step because slavery had taught the descendant of Africa to hate their skin, a key part of Black radical becoming has been to follow Garvey's message that the 'Black skin is not a badge of shame, but rather a glorious symbol of greatness' (Cronon 1969: 4).

Blackness represents as entirely the opposite to oppressive constructs of Western race and is a concept central to resisting racism. Blackness is not a category assigned from above, it is a grassroots identity of radical becoming that is an essential part of resistance. When we look at Blackness through the lens of those who created it then we understand that academia's tiptoeing around difference is actually harmful to social progress. It is only when we incorporate a range of perspectives in producing knowledge that we can come to such insights.

Black feminist thought is one such school of thought that would have been impossible without the broadening of knowledge in US universities. Patricia Hill Collins (2000) outlines the importance of including different standpoints when producing knowledge. Hill Collins does not see the marginalisation of Black and in particular female voices from the academy as being a benign issue of diversity, she condemns the academy because:

the shadow obscuring Black women's intellectual tradition is neither accidental nor benign. Suppressing the knowledge produced by any oppressed group makes it easier for dominant groups to rule because the seeming absence of an independent consciousness in the oppressed can be taken to mean that subordinate groups willingly collaborate in their own victimisation. (5)

This critique of academia as an institution raises the fundamental question as to what role the university plays in society. It is often taken for granted that the university is a force for social justice, where critical thought can be used to challenge the status quo. However, if we place the university in its social context, if anything, we quickly realise that the opposite is true.

The University Is Racism

Deepa Naik, a British scholar-activist summed up the role of racism succinctly during a National Union of Students Black Student Conference in 2015 perfectly. In the context of questioning the myriad of statistics demonstrating the institutional racism of universities she questioned why people were surprised of the lack of change. She explained very simply that 'the university is not racist, the university *is* racism'. Her argument was that academia is not infected by institutional racism that can be overcome through the correct treatment, rather the university is a central source of producing the very racism that contaminates society. If university is the disease then it cannot be the cure.

In Ivan Illich's (1973) *Deschooling Society* he argues that the role of universal schooling is the opposite of the stated noble aims to provide equal opportunities for all those in society. The role of schooling, for Illich, is to hand out credentials to the elite that justify their superior status in society. When all children have the same so-called opportunities to gain the necessary qualifications, then those who fail do not deserve the rewards available in society. The problem with this meritocratic principle is that all children are not given an equal chance; though schooling is universal it is anything but equal and class is a key determiner of success. However, the illusion of equal opportunity cements inequality into the system by providing the justification for it. This system of *credentialisation* creates situations that lock disadvantaged groups out of middle class success. I was recently talking to a student who had graduated with a first class degree in business and finance and was unable to even apply for a graduate job in any of the top firms because they required applicants to have over 300 UCAS points from their *A-level* equivalents. The pre-university credentials were actually more important that their achievements in higher education.

Universities rely on the same credentials as employers to determine who can access the courses. In fact, the universities insistence on these credentials is a key reason why they are so powerful, with consistently over forty percent of those leaving further education entering university (Ilochi 2015). The university degree has become the latest credential for success in society, being the gateway to graduate jobs and professional careers.

Higher education is also arranged into a hierarchy that reinforces the system of hierarchy. A degree from the elite universities is worth more on the job market than from a less prestigious institution. To access this higher credential, requires better qualifications on entry, again privileging the privileged. The result is that academia works to reinforce class and racial disadvantages in society. This is not an accident, it is by design.

It is only the last few decades that universities have opened up to the masses. In the sixties around less five percent of people went to university (Coughlan 2010). They were the bastions of the privileged, the elite, those with academic minds who could cope with the necessary intellectual burden. The massification of higher education opened up the sector to women, the working classes and ethnic minorities, however, it did so in manner that entrenched rather than challenge them. For instance, Black students are actually slightly overrepresented in British universities, however they are heavily populated in the new, less prestigious universities (Bow Group 2012). In a credentialised system it is not a surprise then that Black Students find themselves significantly less likely to find a job after graduation (Zwysen and Longhi 2016). There is so-called access to higher education though acts that mask the racial inequality that the students are facing.

Not only does the university form an integral part of the exclusionary school system, it also produces the knowledge that is the foundation of racism itself. When accounting for the roots of racism there are many sources that are popular to cite. Some of the key culprits are: rampant, evil capitalists who wanted to enslave and colonise the world (Williams 1975); the church and its poisonous doctrine; the mendacious media in the service of global capitalism; and racial 'science' in that justified that provided evidence for the superiority of Europeans (Niro 2003). Only in the case of science do we touch on identifying universities as a key source of the problem. In terms of creating and justifying the devastating Western concept of race is perhaps the universities and their intellectuals who are the most foundational.

The Swedish biologist Carl Linneaus offers perhaps the most succinct description of European race in his classification of the human species into different groups in the second edition of *Systema Natura in* 1740:

> Eurpaues albus: ingenious, white, sanguine, governed by law, Americus rubescus; happy with his lot, liberty loving, tanned and irascible, governed by custom, Asiatic luridus; yellow, melancholy, governed by opinion, Afer Niger; crafty, lazy, black, governed by arbitrary will of the master (Niro 2003: 1965)

The intellectual justification of European biological superiority is absolutely essential in providing a basis for genocide, slavery and colonialism, particularly in an age or so called scientific reason. Africans were treated in the law as cattle because they were understood to be no more evolved than livestock. In the Western system the intellectual cannot be separated from the university, they are bred, incubated and birthed by academia. It is no coincidence that there remains a university names after Linneaus in Sweden due to the centrality of his work to the current world system and also the symbiotic relationship of universities and intellectuals.

It is indisputable that universities produce the knowledge that was necessary for western conquest and this continued into the twentieth century. Movements such as eugenics have their origin in the university, and it was the academically sanctioned racial science that was used to justify the genocide of the Jews in Nazi Germany (ibid.). Even after the Second World War universities continued to have a regressive role in regards to knowledge and racism. The infamous Tuskegee study, where African Americans were purposely left with untreated syphilis to study the effect ran till 1972, out of a historically Black university no less (Gray 1998). The reputation of sociology in the US to be oppressive on racial issues was so bad that Joyce Ladner (1973) brought together the collection *The Death of White Sociology*. As explained earlier the sociology of race and ethnicity in the UK has remained so detached from the people it is writing about that its negligence can only be called regressive.

Given this deplorable history it speaks to the mythology surrounding the progressive nature of universities that we would expect anything other than racism from the academy. I am writing this from a university, so would hope it is possible to produce critical work within the institution. However, the progressive and critical work that is produced in academia is largely in spite, rather than because of, the institution and is also dramatically reduced because of it.

The academic industrial project frames all of the work inside of the academia (Smith 2007). Our academic careers are defined by writing for publications that only other academics can access; speaking at conferences that only other can afford to (or would be interested in) attending; teaching to students who are paying to be in the institution and; carrying out soul deflating admin tasks to fulfil the overwhelmingly bureaucratic institutional model. Academia is a bubble, its own self-sustaining and self-referential eco-system that essentially exists parallel to the social world. To progress within it, the demands easily fill a sixty hour week leaving little time to engage outside of the bubble. Therefore even those of us who profess to be critical are severely limited in terms of the scope of our work to be fully engaged in society. The academic bubble, the alternative universe that it creates, is an essential tool for the maintenance of the current social order. It means that the knowledge produced cannot be that from or fundamentally connected to those projects for social transformation.

In his presidential address to the American Sociological Association in 2004 Michael Burawoy (2005) attempted to answer the critiques of the discipline by calling for a *public sociology*. He clothed his appeal in the Marxist tradition outlining his own eleven theses of public sociology and drawing on Gramsci in his distinction between the *traditional* and *organic* intellectual. For Burawoy the traditional public sociologist engages with the public from the university in the form of public profile; whereas the organic public sociologist is much more rooted in the social movements or organisations they are research-ing. However, Burawoy's invocation of Marxist thought, in particular Gramsci, draws attention to the limits of academic engagement with social change.

The meaning of the traditional intellectual was entirely different for Gramsci (1971), who saw the role of the traditional intellectual as regressive in capitalist society. He saw the traditional intellectual as removed from the interests of the workers and oppressed, who gener-ated their own organic intellectuals. In a Gramscian framework it is impossible for an academic to be an organic intellectual because they (we) are bourgeois functionaries of an oppressive State. In order to be organic intellectuals we would have to leave the comfort of the ivory tower and join the ranks of the workers.

The Marxist framework, and certainly the idea that the university is itself racism, essentially argues that academia cannot be redeemed, that to engage in it is to be complicit in reproducing racism and oppres-sion. The mythology of the progressive university can be seen to be in the form of what I term the *psychosis of Whiteness* (Andrews 2016c). This refers to the myths that Western society needs to create in order to maintain the social order. Whiteness becomes seen as progressive by distorting the memory of the history and the present to re-create the West in benevolent terms. Without this mythology the reality of oppressive racial relations would be revealed and people would no longer support the status quo. Therefore we delude ourselves to remain comfortable with the fruits of exploitation. The idea of the progres-sive university is a foundation stone of this psychosis, allowing us to imagine that we are engaged in critical, socially transformative, even Marxist, work when it reality we are complicit in reproducing and benefiting from an oppressive system. If this is the case then the uni-versity can surely provide no platform for challenging racism, and this piece is Exhibit A in proving the power of the psychosis. However, perhaps once we accept the nature of universities perhaps there is a way to utilise them.

Becoming an Institution, Not Institutionalised

A core purpose of the university is to maintain social, and therefore racial, disadvantage. However, the same is true of Western society in general. It is almost impossible to be in the West without being complicit in its project. Therefore, simply leaving and joining a so-called social justice organisation is no solution. Due to the status of university knowledge, academia remains (though even this is changing) a profession where there is at least some autonomy over the content of our research and activities. I cannot think of another job where I could spend as much time writing and speaking about Black radicalism or being involved in community organisation. The uncomfortable reality about the regressive role of university is that it is a system what we all too often willingly participate in. The REF, admin and teaching loads make for excellent excuses not to engage but if we are brutally honest social transformation is actually against our interests. The status quo works well for those in a profession whose average salary puts us comfortably in the upper echelons of global income. The challenge for the academic who wants to be engaged in social change is to be in the institution without being institutionalised. Ordinarily this is impossible because of the institutional constraints. The regimentation and surveillance of school teaching make it much more difficult to operate outside of the confines of the institution. Universities at least offer the potential to develop critical work.

When Black Studies emerged in the US universities it had a radical edge. Nathan Hare (1972: 33) argued that:

> Black education must be education for liberation, or at least for change... All courses - whether history, literature, or mathematics - would be taught from a revolutionary ideology or perspective. Black education would become the instrument for change.

Hare refers to the movement for Black Studies as a 'battle' and it involved a grassroots movement to force US campuses to open up to the discipline. At Hare's university, San Francisco State, the struggle involved protests, sit-ins and support from organisations such as the

Black Panther Party. The protests even involved a four month long student wide strike from November 1968 to March 1969. A protest at Cornell University involved the occupation of the Willard Straight Hall student accommodation building, which escalated to the point that the students armed themselves for protection (Rojas 2007). Establishing Black Studies was a political act, supported by communities because it was seen as a progressive step that could improve the lives of African Americans.

Due to the nature of community support and activist roots of the discipline, from the outset Black Studies aimed to be organically linked to local communities, as Hare explained (1972: 33):

> crucial to Black studies, Black education, aside from its ideology of liberation, would be the community component of its methodology. This was designed to wed Black communities, heretofore excluded, and the educational process, to transform the black community.

The roots of this organic connection are important for two reasons. Firstly, the discipline would not have emerged without the support of Black communities, who galvanised the campaign. Therefore the academics who spearheaded Black Studies had to be organic intellectuals, rooted in the communities they were working with. The second reason for the importance of the community is that Black Studies spoke to so many because it set out to transform the accepted knowledge base. The movement was far more substantial than simply asking for more Black people to be hired, it insisted on recognising previously excluded knowledges.

Key to the exclusions of the university is the demarcation of so called *academic* versus *popular* knowledge (Fals-Borda and Rahman 1991). The elite knowledge produced in the academy is given privilege, reinforcing the academic bubble. When African American students were permitted onto university campuses they encountered courses where the knowledges taught were exclusively white, and the lack of Black academics (because of racism) in the university canon meant that their voices were excluded (Hare 1972). Black Studies aimed to change that by including so-called popular knowledge on the same level as that produced in the ivory tower. This is essential to producing liberatory knowledge because it opens up academia to the organic intellectuals who have been so been influential in activism and social change, not simply to be studied but to shape theory and create new concepts of understanding (Staples 1973).

Black Studies therefore did not seek legitimacy from established scholarship and set out to provide a new set of paradigms based on scholars and activists from the African Diaspora. Of course, academics whose contributions had been overlooked because of racism were given prominence in the discipline. A figure like WEB DuBois is the perfect example of a scholar who was written out of the sociological canon for no other reason than prejudice. However, Black Studies was just as likely to draw on the work of Malcolm X, Marcus Garvey, Ida B Wells or Claudia Jones. This democratisation of knowledge was central to organically connecting into movements for racial justice. Black Studies did not try to change the whole institution, the aim was to use the university and its resources in order to support broader movements. For a time it provided a blueprint for breaking outside of the academic industrial complex.

The problem with the legacy of Black Studies in the US, however, is that though it established itself as institution it quickly became institutionalised and divorced from the more radical roots from which it arose. As Hare warned in 1972 Black Studies has morphed into African American Studies or Africana Studies, which both represent limits on the disciplines former more radical nature. African American studies tends to, though does not exclusively, focus the discussion on learning about the history and experiences within the nation state. One of the key principles of early Black Studies was the linking of the America struggle into the global one of freedom in the Diaspora. As Malcolm X (1964) complained that of the civil rights movement 'whether they know it or not, are confining themselves to the jurisdiction of Uncle Sam'.

Africana Studies offers insights based on Afrocentricity and a different cultural base to Eurocentric scholarship (Asante 2003). The issue with how the discipline has developed, however, is the focus on cultural forms which can lead to omitting the political resistance that was at the heart of the movement for Black Studies (Andrews 2016b). In fact, Maluana Karenga's, who is the inspiration for African Studies, United Slaves (US) organisation actually engaged in gun battles with the Black Panther Party, who criticised US as being cultural nationalist (Thompson 2006). The charge of cultural nationalism was levelled by the Panthers who saw the embrace of culture at the expense of political programme. As Warren (1990: 26) explains 'culture is crucial to revolution, but it is not revolution', and it is not always clear that Africana Studies achieves, or seeks, an organic connection to a politics of racial justice.

The developments of Black Studies into the nationally oriented African American Studies, and cultural focused Africana Studies attest to the difficulty of maintaining a politically oriented programme in academia. I am not arguing that either of these endeavours are not worthwhile, simply that they fit into the institutional mechanisms of the university in a way that Black Studies never intended. As Black Studies has integrated into the institutions it has largely been institutionalised into the academic industrial project. Whilst it still presents alternative bases of knowledge that are vitally important it no longer has the activist edge, rooted in a politics of resistance organically connected to Black communities.

It may be the case that maintaining that organic connection was never possible, that being inside meant becoming part of the system and replicating its exclusions. This has to be a possibility that we are prepared for; that the university cannot be redeemed as a space for organic intellectualism rooted in resistance. In fact, if we see the university as an institution that produces racism in the same way as the police force then we begin to see the potential impossibility of what we are trying to achieve. In building Black Studies we must always remember that the struggle is outside the university and we are attempting to utilise the resources of the plantation to further our movements for liberation. If we find as Lorde (1984: 110) warns that 'the master's tools will never dismantle the Master's house' then we cannot be afraid to abandon the academy to achieve liberation.

Blueprint for Black Studies

In order to attempt to subvert the system we need to be clear about our key principles from the outset because the road to neoliberalism is paved with good intentions. The foundation for the work that we are building in British academia is based on the following themes that must always be embedded.

First and foremost is that our goal must be liberation. Not equality. Not social justice. Not equal opportunities. Liberation. The complete liberation of all of those in the African Diaspora worldwide. This is not a semantic issue about wording, but goes to the heart of the philosophy of Black Studies. The aim is not simply to get Black people in Britain good jobs and opportunities. In fact, the first thing to accept when we embrace a politics of liberation is that any success in Western society is done on the back of the Black and the poor worldwide. Malcolm X (1963) used the metaphor of the plantation to distinguish between the House and Field Negro. In the present context the House is the West and the Field is the developing world where Black people literally catch hell. It is not enough to make our lives more comfortable in the Western House, we must be working and theorising for the complete liberation of those in the global Field. To do so changes our point of emphasis, our understanding of society.

In order to be focused on liberation we must also be organically connected into movements outside of the academy. This means being directly engaged theoretically and in practice in the process of liberation. There is no space for the free floating academic in Black Studies. Our research questions must change from diagnosing the problem to helping to provide the solutions. It is not good to say that previous social movements have failed to work, we must be asking how they can work in the future. This organic connection outside of academia is also essential in terms of knowledge and by drawing on those scholars who are given no recognition because they were not legitimised by an institution. It also means drawing on the lessons of educational movement outside of academia, like the Black supplementary school movement that has 50 years of knowledge and experience in the field of Black Studies to offer (Andrews 2013).

We also have to be keenly aware that Blackness has been used in essentialist ways that exclude or proscribe the participation of those who are not male, heterosexual or able bodied. Liberation, means leaving no one behind. Therefore, we must root our work in intersectional forms of knowledge and practice (Crenshaw 1991). Blackness, and therefore

Black Studies, is not a monolith. It is broad church that is meant, and will need to, bring us all together to achieve liberation.

There is no guarantee that by rooting our work in these principles that we will not succumb to institutionalisation within the academic industrial project. However, we have launched the endeavour and it will certainly not be successful without the support from academics, students and wider communities. In order to resist institutional pressures Black Studies must be more than a subject students can pay to study. It must be a movement connected into a wider politics of resistance of the African Diaspora. We invite all those who are interested in liberation to join us as we attempt establish the Black Studies movement in Britain.

References

Alexander, C. (2002). Beyond Black: Re-thinking the Colour/Culture Divide. *Ethnic and Racial Studies, 25*(4), 552–571.

Andrews, K. (2013). *Resisting Racism: Race, Inequality and the Black Supplementary School Movement.* London: UCL Institute of Education Press.

Andrews, K. (2016a). Changing the Nature, Not Just the Face of the Academy. In K. Andrews & L. Palmer (Eds.), *Blackness in Britain* (pp. 203–214). London: Routledge.

Andrews, K. (2016b). The Problem of Political Blackness: Lessons from the Black Supplementary School Movement. *Ethnic and Racial Studies.* https://doi.org/10.1080/01419870.2015.1131314.

Andrews, K. (2016c). The Psychosis of White: The Celluloid Hallucinations of Amazing Grace and Belle. *Journal of Black Studies.* https://doi.org/10.1177/0021934716663880.

Andrews, K. (2018). *Back to Black: Retelling the Story of Black Radicalism for the Twenty-First Century.* London: Zed Books.

Asante, M. (2003). *Afrocentricity: The Theory of Social Change.* Chicago: African American Images.

Bow Group. (2012). *Race to the Top: The Experience of Black Students in Higher Education.* http://www.bowgroup.org/sites/bowgroup.uat.pleasetest.co.uk/files/Race%2520to%2520the%2520Top%2520-%2520Bow%2520Group%2520-%2520Elevation%2520Networks%2520(April%25202012)_0.pdf.

Burawoy, M. (2005). 2004 American Sociological Association Presidential Address: For a Public Sociology. *British Journal of Sociology, 56*(2), 259–294.

Christian, M. (2005, March 4). Why Do We Go Abroad? There Are No Opportunities for Us in Britain. *Time Higher Education*.

Coughlan, S. (2010). Majority of Young Women in University. *BBC News*. http://news.bbc.co.uk/1/hi/education/8596504.stm.

Crenshaw, K. (1991). Mapping the Margins: Intersectionality, Identity Politics, and Violence Against Women of Color. *Stanford Law Review, 43*(6), 1241–1299.

Cronon, E. (1969). *Black Moses: The Story of Marcus Garvey*. Madison: The University of Wisconsin Press.

Equality Challenge Unit. (2009). *The Experience of Black and Minority Ethnic Staff Working in Higher Education*. London: Equality Challenge Unit.

Fals-Borda, O., & Rahman, M. A. (1991). *Action and Knowledge: Breaking the Monopoly with Participatory Action Research*. London: Intermediate Technology Publications.

Freire, P. (1999). The Banking Concept of Education. In D. Bartholomae & A. Petrosky (Eds.), *Ways of Reading*. New York: Bedford/St. Martin's.

Gilroy, P. (2002). *The Black Atlantic: Modernity and Double Consciousness*. London: Verso.

Gramsci, A. (1971). *Selections from the Prison Notebooks*. London: Lawrence and Wishart.

Gray, F. D. (1998). *The Tuskegee Syphilis Study: The Real Story and Beyond*. Montgomery: NewSouth Books.

Hare, N. (1972). The Battle for Black Studies. *The Black Scholar, 3*(9), 32–47.

Hill Collins, P. (2000). *Black Feminist Thought: Knowledge, Consciousness, and the Politics of Empowerment*. London: Routledge.

Illich, I. (1973). *Deschooling Society*. Harmondsworth: Penguin Education.

Ilochi, C. (2015). *Participation Rates in Higher Education: Academic Years 2006/7–2013/14 (Provisional)*. London: Department of Business, Innovation and Skills. https://www.gov.uk/government/uploads/system/uploads/attachment_data/file/458034/HEIPR_PUBLICATION_2013-14.pdf.

Ladner, J. A. (Ed.). (1973). *The Death of White Sociology: Essay on Race and Culture*. Baltimore: Black Classic Press.

Lorde, A. (1984). *Sister Outsider*. Berkeley: The Crossing Press.

Malcolm, X. (1963, November 10). *Message to the Grassroots*. Speech at the Negro Grass Roots Leadership Conference, Michigan.

Malcolm, X. (1964, April 3). *The Ballot or the Bullet*. Speech at Cory Methodist Church in Cleveland, Ohio. Hartford Web Publishing. http://www.hartford-hwp.com/archives/45a/065.html.

Malcolm, X. (1971). *The End of White World Supremacy: Four Speeches*. New York: Merlin House.

Modood, T. (1994). Political Blackness and British Asians. *Sociology, 28*(4), 859–876.

Niro, B. (2003). *Race*. Houndmills: Palgrave Macmillan.

Rojas, F. (2007). *From Black Power to Black Studies: How a Radical Social Movement Became an Academic Discipline*. Baltimore: The John Hopkins University Press.

Smith, A. (2007). Social-Justice Activism in the Academic Industrial Complex. *Journal of Feminist Studies in Religion, 23*(2), 140–145.

Staples, R. (1973). What Is Black Sociology? Toward a Sociology of Black Liberation. In J. A. Ladner (Ed.), (1998) *The Death of White Sociology: Essay on Race and Culture* (pp. 161–172). Baltimore: Black Classic Press.

Thompson, J. (2006). *Double Trouble: Black Mayors, Black Communities, and the Call for a Deep Democracy*. Oxford: Oxford University Press.

Warren, N. (1990). Pan-African Cultural Movements: From Baraka to Karenga. *The Journal of Negro History, 75*(1/2), 16–28.

Williams, E. (1975). *Capitalism & Slavery*. London: Andre Deutsch.

Zwysen, W., & Longhi, S. (2016). *Labour Market Disadvantage of Ethnic Minority British Graduates: University Choice, Parental Background or Neighbourhood?* Sussex: Institute for Social and Economic Research. https://www.iser.essex.ac.uk/research/publications/working-papers/iser/2016-02.pdf.

16

"Free, Decolonised Education"—A Lesson from the South African Student Struggle

Adam Elliott-Cooper

In October 2015, I travelled to South Africa for the first time, visiting Witwatersrand University in Johannesburg, the University of Cape Town (UCT), and Rhodes University in Grahamstown. Rhodes was my first stop, and I knew relatively little about an institution I would soon find out had been renamed by students 'The University Currently Called Rhodes'. As we pulled up, my eyes were drawn to the grand, whitewashed archway over the entrance to the university's campus. On it, in thick, dark spray-paint, stood the words 'Black Power'. As in many universities across the country, Rhodes students occupied campus buildings, marched on management meetings and struggled in solidarity with university staff. Earlier that year, RhodesMustFall, a UCT campaign against a statue of the British colonialist, turned into a movement against the imperialism that Cecil Rhodes represented. For the first time since the anti-apartheid movement, South African students were grabbing international headlines, as they struggled for universal access

A. Elliott-Cooper (✉)
King's College London, London, UK
e-mail: adam.elliott-cooper@kcl.ac.uk

© The Author(s) 2018
J. Arday and H. S. Mirza (eds.), *Dismantling Race in Higher Education*,
https://doi.org/10.1007/978-3-319-60261-5_16

to an education that did not reproduce the imperial logic their parents' generation fought to dismantle. As researchers, teachers and students, particularly those based in the old centre of Empire, how can we ensure that our work is used to dismantle colonialism and its legacies?

"A Proper Degree of Terror"

In 1811, John Graham, a Scottish colonel in the British Army, led a coalition of British regulars and Boer commandos into the eastern frontier region of what was then the Cape Colony (now part of South Africa's Eastern Cape Province). The area was then inhabited by the amaXhosa, and Graham's task was to clear the land of people in preparation for white settlement. In a letter to George III, he informed the King that the amaXhosa people had been pushed beyond the Cape Colony's frontiers using a 'proper degree of terror'. Such terror consisted of shooting women and children who attempted to flee, and destroying crops in order to starve out any survivors. The land was renamed Grahamstown and, like much of the colony, it implemented a system of rule that subjugated Black Africans, eventually formalised through apartheid (Maclennan 1986).

It would be nearly a century until a large endowment from the Rhodes Trust in 1904 enabled the establishment of the university which goes by the same name. Rhodes University was an all-white institution during the period of apartheid. During the 1950s it was briefly affiliated to Forte Hare (a higher educational institution for Black Africans), but these ties were quickly severed by the ruling apartheid government. Today, 54% of Rhodes' undergraduate population is Black (despite Blacks constituting 86% of the population of the Eastern Cape), and 38% is white (whites constitute only 4.7% of the province's population).

When I visited Rhodes University in 2015, I was struck by how spaces were contested by colonial and decolonial symbols. A large, heavy wooden door led into an imposing old social science building; the words Black Pain were spray-painted across one side. It was here in 2015 that the students had begun their occupation, demanding changes to the curriculum, an end to the outsourcing of university workers, the end of financial barriers to education and, of course, a change in the name of the university. Calling itself the Black Students Movement, this multiracial campaign's primary demands can be encapsulated in its two most iconic slogans: Rhodes Must Fall and Fees Must Fall. The relationship between imperialism and capitalism is vividly portrayed throughout South Africa's history, and in many ways present-day universities there are a post-colonial microcosm of its legacies. In addition to demands for a new curriculum, protests were aimed at reductions in per capita funding and increases in fees which excluded most Black students. The protests were met with violent repression, with rubber bullets and stun grenades accompanying mass arrests (Manyathela 2016).

A Proper Degree

In 1788, the Association for Promoting the Discovery of the Interior Parts of Africa was founded in London, to help map the areas of the continent that Britain knew relatively little about. This organisation was a precursor of Britain's Royal Geographical Society (RGS, founded in 1830 as the Geographical Society of London). It is within the discussions among RGS members that British geography developed debates around the ways in which the discipline is implicated in Empire. However, it took over half a century for geography to become established as an academic discipline; the first readership in geography was established in 1887 at the University of Oxford. In 1893, Peter Kropotkin addressed a Teachers Guild conference in Oxford, asserting that geography "must teach us, from our earliest childhood, that we are all brethren, whatever our nationality" (Williskey 2000: 144). Some earlier utterances, however, were less egalitarian. An 1852 letter to the president of the RGS reads:

> Geography lays open to the Government and to the Capitalist the hidden resources of the remote parts of this great Empire, and teaches the one how to govern at the least cost, and the other to apply profitably the surplus capital and labour of the Country which thru' the RGS may be made known sooner than thru' any other means. (ibid: 141)

Such ideas were uncontroversial in nineteenth-century Britain. Thirty-two years later came the Conference of Berlin (1884–1885), in which the European powers carved up the African map among themselves. Britain accrued a larger portion than most, a bounty that swelled significantly following its 1899 invasion of one of the inland regions of what is now eastern South Africa (Pakenham 1979). But while the Empire accrued land, resources and labour, the prestige of imperial expansion and acquisition also necessitated a philosophy which could justify the intense levels of violence, dispossession and genocide left in its wake.

Why Is My Curriculum White?

In 2014, Nathaniel Coleman, an early career scholar in University College London's (UCL) Department of Philosophy, began a project on the critical philosophies of race. I joined Dr. Coleman in the September of that year. As a doctoral student in a geography department, I had never considered myself a philosopher. One thing I quickly learned about philosophy was that it is not necessarily interested in providing the right answers, but more in asking useful questions. In this case, the questions had to do with the ideas that were used to justify imperialism, and the contradictions between the progressive ideals of the enlightenment and the enslavement, genocide and exploitation which accompanied it. This contradiction was reconciled through the racist myth that Europe is, and always has been, the intellectual and moral leader of the world. Looking at the content of the teaching in contemporary educational institutions, we saw this myth being reproduced across almost every discipline, leading us to ask one simple question: Why is my curriculum white?

This question immediately exposes the embeddedness of racial thinking within academia. Many people associate whiteness with what people are, rather than seeing it as an idea that shapes actions and thoughts. This led to queries not only about the relevance of the question, but whether it makes sense. However, the question implicitly states that whiteness is an idea, and one upon which the curriculum is premised. The assertiveness of the question cut through tired debates on diversity and representation that at best result in putting Black faces in high places, or peppering a reading list with a darker face or an exotic name. Rather, the question seeks to challenge the fundamental assumptions of academic knowledge production, critically reflect on canonised thinkers, and introduce multiple histories and theories that are too often rendered alternative, optional or invisible.

The project was launched with a student-led film named after the question we were asking: Why Is My Curriculum White?[1] We also ran a series of public events, including a tour of UCL highlighting the issues in an institution that now designates itself London's Global University. There was interest from a range of media outlets. In a matter of months, the question had sparked debates, events and similar projects across the country. One of the reasons for its success was that the question resonated with students who found university education far from universal and often insufficiently critical of the thinking that was covered on their courses. And importantly, the campaign compelled debates to focus on the legacies of Empire, the social constructions of race, and the hegemony of racist thinking in Europe and its former colonies. The message we brought to campuses across the country was simple: If the electronic components in our computers come from Central Africa, the wood in our tables is extracted from Latin America and the clothes we wear to our lectures are manufactured in South Asia, then it's clear that the economic relations that existed under British colonialism are being reproduced today. Learning in spaces which are, in a very material way, monuments to imperialism simply highlights the de facto exploitative relationship with the formerly colonised world. This inequality is normalised and legitimised by racism, and one way of beginning to unlearn and dismantle these structures is by incorporating the moral and intellectual contributions colonised people make to global knowledge production.

In July 2015, Why Is My Curriculum White? campaigners at UCL came together with two other campus-based campaigns, the UCL rent strike and the fossil fuel divestment campaign Fossil Free UCL. A direct action

---

[1]UCL: Why Is My Curriculum White? https://www.youtube.com/watch?v=Dscx4h2l-Pk, (accessed 21 Nov 2017).

involving smoke flares, loudspeakers and drums disrupted the university's Open Day, marching through corridors and atriums before converging on the front quadrangle outside the university's main entrance. Activists on the day linked issues such as the struggle against the neoliberal capitalism of London's housing, the exploitation of the Global South by fossil fuel companies, and the whiteness which underpins British academia. As disgruntled university management and security staff looked on, unsure how to respond, teenagers asked their parents why this wasn't on the Open Day programme. The campaign had progressed from an intellectual endeavour to a public debate, an impetus for concrete change and part of a popular student movement. It was not long before international links of solidarity were forged with Black student campaigns in Holland, the US and Rhodes Must Fall in South Africa.

Conclusion

Academia in Britain today often frames decolonisation as something which, if it needs to happen, is required elsewhere. Unlike South Africa, or other settler colonies such as the United States, the geographical disjuncture between Britain and its colonies can often lead to a conceptual disjuncture between Britain and post-colonialism (Hall 1991). But while imperialism's afterlife isn't as viscerally present as it is other post-colonial nations, as the historic centre of Empire it remains vital that British geography joins a global movement towards decolonisation. This must begin with correcting the most powerful false assumption of the post-colony— that Europe is, and has long been, the intellectual and moral leader of the world. While the victories of anti-racism and anti-imperialism mean that articulating such an assumption is instinctively frowned upon, it remains the conventional wisdom underscoring the citations, curricula, canons and recruitment patterns across geography's academic institutions.

The past president's address by Audrey Kobayashi at AAG[2] (2013) was titled 'Dialecta Interrupta: The Idea of 'Race' in the Discipline of Geography'. She provided a radical intervention into both the conference and the

[2]The American Association of Geographers (AAG).

Association, telling us that "the idea of race in geography represents a contested and unfinished discourse, in a dialectic that has had many inter-ruptions". Kobayashi urged geographers to reflect critically upon the his-tory of the discipline, and how this history has situated the discipline today. Such critical self-reflection is wholly necessary for comparable researchers, teachers and students of all disciplinary backgrounds here in Britain if we are to unlearn the Eurocentric assumptions of colonial thought.

The student movements in South Africa are one example of the inter-ruptions that necessitate the decolonisation of knowledge production. South African universities rely on African land and African workers, making their default relationship with Black peoples one of extraction and exploitation. While the resources of the Global South can appear geographically distant to academics based in Britain, this nation's impe-rial history means that our intellectual culture is not too distant from that which is being struggled against on campuses in Britain's former colonies. British academia was (and remains) a vital component in shap-ing the imperial ambitions of nation states. But it is also well placed to highlight the links between spaces and places divided by physical-ity, yet interconnected through militarism, appropriation and ideology (Godlewska and Smith 1994). The campaigns described in this chap-ter have built on the struggles of previous generations, placing us at a historical crossroads. There is no middle, benevolent way forward. We can either attempt to ignore, and thus implicitly reproduce, the imperial logics that have influenced the shape of British academia since the dawn of Empire, or we can actively rethink and dismantle imperialism's after-life, by unlearning the unjust global hierarchies of knowledge produc-tion upon which much of the Empire's legitimacy was based.

References

Godlewska, A., & Smith, N. (1994). *Geography and Empire*. London: Blackwell.

Hall, S. (1991). Old and New Identities, Old and New Ethnicities. In A. D. King (Ed.), *Culture, Globalisation and the World System: Contemporary Conditions for the Representation of Identity*. Minneapolis: University of Minnesota Press.

Kobayashi, A. (2013). *Dialecta Interrupta: The Idea of 'Race' in the Discipline of Geography*. AAG (The American Association of Geographers) Past Presidential Address 2013.

Maclennan, B. (1986). *A Proper Degree of Terror: John Graham and the Cape's Eastern Frontier*. Johannesburg: Raven Press.

Manyathela, C. (2016). Fresh Rounds of Stun Grenades, Rubber Bullets Fired at Protesting Wits Students. *Eye Witness News*. http://ewn.co.za/2016/10/04/Police-fire-fresh-round-of-stungrenades-and-rubber-bullets-at-protesting-Wits-students. Accessed 7 Nov 2016.

Pakenham, T. (1979). *The Boer War*. London: Abacus.

Williskey, J. (2000). *Learning to Divide the World: Education at Empire's End*. Minneapolis: University of Minnesota Press.

17

Decolonising Oxford: The Student Movement from Stuart Hall to Skin Deep

Anuradha Henriques and Lina Abushouk

In recounting our particular trajectory of decolonial student activism at Oxford University, what we hope to do in this chapter is to emphasise that any attempt to analyse and quantify the successes and failures of student-led movements must recognise that there are no 'finished' conversations. These narratives of the various Oxford-based movements, in particular the 'I, too, am Oxford campaign', the BME conference, Skin Deep and the Rhodes Must Fall Oxford (RMFO) movement, are examples of particular types of political interventions which occurred at a specific historical conjuncture. In these 2014–2016 campaigns, what we find are iterations of an ongoing struggle, which must continue to grow, adapt and respond to changing times and historical contexts.

A. Henriques (✉)
Wadham College, Oxford, UK
e-mail: anu@skindeepmag.com

L. Abushouk
Sarah Lawrence College, Bronxville, NY, USA
e-mail: lina@skindeepmag.com

J. Arday and H. S. Mirza (eds.), *Dismantling Race in Higher Education*,
https://doi.org/10.1007/978-3-319-60261-5_17

Linking Histories: Oxford Students Then and Now

In an essay entitled the 'Life and Times of the First New Left', the famed cultural theorist, sociologist, activist and one-time Oxford student, Stuart Hall reflects on the founding of the New Left Review back in the 1950s and the significance of having such a journal emerge from a conservative institution like Oxford. Hall writes,

> How and why did this happen then—and why, of all places, partly in Oxford? In the 1950s universities were not, as they later became, centres of revolutionary activity. A minority of privileged left-wing students, debating consumer capitalism and the embourgeoisement of working-class culture amidst the 'dreaming spires', may seem, in retrospect, a pretty marginal political phenomenon. Nevertheless, the debate was joined with a fierce intensity, self-consciously counterposed to the brittle, casual confidence of Oxford's dominant tone, set by the attempts of the 'Hooray Henries' of its time to relive *Brideshead Revisited*. In fact, Oxford also contained its rebel enclaves: demobbed young veterans and national servicemen, Ruskin College trade unionists, 'scholarship boys' and girls from home and abroad. Although they were unable to redefine its dominant culture, these outsiders did come to constitute an alternative—not to say beleaguered—intellectual minority culture. This was the *NLR* constituency.[1]

At the time of his arrival in Oxford, Hall's political sensibilities and inclinations were primarily anti-imperialist. Marxism would come later as Hall began to engage more regularly with leftist politics at the University. Hall explains,

> I was sympathetic to the left, had read Marx and been influenced by him while at school, but I would not, at the time, have called myself a Marxist in the European sense. In any event, I was troubled by the failure of

---

[1]Hall, Stuart. "The Life and Times of the First New Left", *New Left Review 61* (Jan/Feb 2010): 181.

orthodox Marxism to deal adequately with either 'Third World' issues of race and ethnicity, and questions of racism, or with literature and culture, which preoccupied me intellectually as an undergraduate.[2]

What is particularly significant about Hall's recounting of his early days at Oxford is that almost seventy years later, his experience rings true for the types of politics that many politically engaged students of colour come to university with. Although today their politics are more often anti-racist as opposed to explicitly anti-imperialist. As it was in the 1950s, the left in Oxford continues to be a heterogeneous outfit that encompasses a wide range of views, making it hard to say what 'the [student] left is' definitively committed to.

There are, however, a few generalising statements that one can make: the student left is majority white, and while many are sympathetic to, and a small minority even seriously committed to anti-racist, decolonial and anti-imperial politics, for the most part the left has had limited engagement with these struggles since the end of Apartheid in South Africa in 1994. Moreover, whilst most in the student left are committed to wider societal structural change, that has not successfully translated to a sustained demand or consistent agitation for structural change within Oxford itself. Some of this certainly has to do with the fact that the student left has not been able to put forth a coherent programme for radical transformation that students can get behind. But in large part the inability of the student left to redefine the University's dominant culture has more to do with banal realities such as the fact that students are generally only in university for three to four years, they tend to be separated by colleges and degree programs, and there exists no real sense of institutional memory which means that many student organisations either end up repeating work that has already been done by their predecessors, or are too invested in claiming for themselves the coveted title of 'first...' to continue with the work that others have already started.

---

[2]Hall, Stuart, "The Life and Times of the First New Left", *New Left Review 61* (Jan/Feb 2010): 179.

Skin Deep: Capturing the Legacy of Decolonial Voices

It is with this in mind that one should think about the emergence of Skin Deep, which was realised in its first iteration as an online platform created in January of 2014 on Facebook for Oxford students of colour. Much like how the New Left Review emerged for Stuart Hall and his fellow Oxonians as a space to articulate their frustrations, debate solutions and refine their nascent ideas as young Marxist intellectuals who were just beginning to come into political maturity, Skin Deep became a space in which students of colour could centre their voices and experiences at a predominantly white and academically conservative institution.

It would be disingenuous to suggest that Skin Deep had any real political or activist motivations from its inception. It was created primarily out of a sense of alienation that one of us, Anuradha Henriques, felt within the University and a sense that other students probably felt similarly. The initial online discussion forum (which is now called Race Matters) emerged at a time when there were few spaces in Oxford whose primary aim was to give matters surrounding race, racial representation and racial identity a platform. At its core, the goal of Skin Deep was to allow for the exploration of why racial equality is paramount, and how we can and should challenge the ways in which race is represented in the media, literature and education.

Skin Deep created a virtual space that existed outside of the ethno cultural societies like the Afro-Caribbean Society, whose concerns had over the years shifted from being political to primarily being concerned with providing entertainment, networking and helping prospective students apply to Oxford and enrolled students connect with job recruitment agencies. It also remained distinct from the Campaign for Racial Awareness (CRAE), a student union led campaign that gained prominence in 2012 when it published the much needed *100 Voices Campaign 2: Black and Minority Ethnic Students of Oxford Speak Out.*[3]

[3]Tuck, Stephen, and Henry L. Gates. 2014. *The Night Malcolm X Spoke at the Oxford Union: A Transatlantic Story of Antiracist Protest.* Oakland: University of California Press. Print, p. 202.

Given that Oxford is a majority white institution, it was inevitable that Skin Deep, despite primarily being targeted at students of colour, would begin to reflect that. The very nature of online and open discussion spaces is such that curatorial control is all but impossible, meaning that the forum soon shifted to being a space where Black and brown members were often called upon by the growing number white members of Skin Deep to explain and justify the frustrations that had arisen from their experiences within the institution. If the intention was for Black and brown students to be part of a space that existed independently from the institution, where they could discuss issues of representation within and outside of Oxford, then the space quickly became unable to accommodate that goal. The demand that students of colour continue to explain and justify their lived realities and their desires for reform in a majority white institution detracted from the meaningful actions that could have been galvanised in that online space.

Skin Deep magazine, which was first published six months after the establishment of the Facebook discussion forum, emerged out of a desire to produce an intellectual and artistic product that addressed themes and issues that were of concern to students of colour, away from explanations and qualifications that were demanded on the online forum. The magazine would accompany other established leftist magazines that enjoyed wide readership within the University, such as Cuntry Living (a feminist zine) and the newly released No Heterox* (a magazine for LGBTQ issues). The print publication would serve as an avenue for students to develop an archival project that chronicled the experiences and reflections of students of colour. Through the curation of a print publication, we felt we would be able to raise contemporary issues that affected students of colour within a global context, whilst simultaneously contributing to the institutional memory of decolonial and antiracist organising within our institution. It was not so much a critique of the institution itself, but rather an attempt to capture the voices and experiences of previous generations, which were reflected in the pieces written on the work and legacies of Stuart Hall, Maya Angelou and Gabriel Garcia Marquez, all of whom had passed away that year.

The magazine became a termly publication, each addressing a particular theme: Roots/Routes (Issue 2), Terrorising the Masses (Issue 3), Theorising from Outside (the Academy) (Issue 4). For example here is an extract from the introduction of Root/Routes (Issue 2):

> The colonial garden was pruned to the point of predictability. No weeds were allowed to grow, no "exotic" flowers were allowed to bloom, and no other garden was to be imagined. The garden was a project that could not accommodate a diversity of vision and growth. In our efforts to uproot this imaginative roadblock, we challenge you to plant your roots and to find new routes out of this dull and deceptively beautiful garden. We seek not to build a better garden, but a more engaging and inclusive one.

I, Too Am Oxford: 'Speaking Back'

The inspiration for I, Too, Am Oxford campaign, was a Buzzfeed article entitled "63 Black Harvard Students Share Their Experiences In A Powerful Photo Project".[4] That it was shared on Skin Deep just two months after it was started is a testament to the fact that even in the early days of the forum, members were concerned with translating what was happening at the level of discourse on the platform into concrete and impactful action in the real world. To date, the 'I, too, am Oxford' campaign is perhaps the most important political action to have emerged from that space. The Buzzfeed article inspired much excitement amongst students of colour on the platform and a call for spontaneous organising occurred. As a movement, the 'I, too, am….' campaign required very little in terms of actual planning. All that was necessary was a few whiteboards, some marker pens for students to take it in turn to write out their messages and a willing photographer—none of which were hard to source in a network of a few hundred students. In the comments section a time was agreed upon and students were expected to show up in front of the Radcliffe Camera, a building that

---

[4]Vingiano, Ali, "63 Black Harvard Students Share Their Experiences in A Powerful Photo Project", *BuzzFeed*, 2014, Viewed 6 May 2017. http://bzfd.it/2qLFl5k.

has come to signify Oxford as an institution. The broad spectrum of political affiliations and opinions that students of colour came from is evidenced by the range of sentiments that were expressed in the photo series. Some of what was written spoke to personal or social experiences and interactions, whereas others commented directly on issues with curriculum and institutional structures that needed to be addressed. For some students of colour it was the first time they were given the opportunity to speak back, and (re)claim the campus. We created a tumblr page for the campaign in which we uploaded all the photographs that had been taken by the various students. Shortly thereafter, we created a twitter account to share the link and tweet at various media outlets that we thought might be interested in the campaign. The aim was to get word out as far and wide as possible in the hopes that public pressure might encourage the institution to take the concerns raised by students more seriously. Buzzfeed UK, a subsidiary of the media outlet that had first published the I, too, am Harvard photographs, was one of the first media outlets to release an article on the campaign. Of course, both the tumblr and the subsequent article were shared on the Skin Deep platform, where the campaign garnered a great deal of support and also some criticism. Separately from the platform, many of the students who participated in the campaign also made it a point to change their profile pictures on their various social media profiles as a way to both share what they'd done and to promote the campaign. Examples of I, too, am Oxford whiteboard messages:

On Afro-Caribbean Society: How would you feel if I started a 'white society'. Look around, Oxford is white society.

All the post-colonial and other critical theories you study does not entitle you to speak for me or over me.

No, my family did not have to flee the Sudan… Sorry I don't have a more "exotic" African story

Yes, I have the right to be offended when you confuse me with the only other black girl in my year.

If you 'don't see race', how don't we see that in the admissions statistics?

Why are only 0.4% of UK professors black? #InstitutionalRacism

"Are you here on an access scheme?"

"You're such a bounty!" Valuing education does not make me less black or more white.

Don't use 'where are you from' as a euphemism for 'explain to me why you're not white.'

Even if I was religious, Muslim Land is not a place I can just swim back to.

Of course you got in, you fill both Black and Asian quotas.

I am the voice of Africa #AllAfricansAreBlack #AfricaIsACountry #BeCarefulIMakeUpStories

Oh you're from Ghana! My cousin's nanny is from Kenya.

It has been noted elsewhere (see Tuck and Louis Gates Jr. 2014)[5] that the launch of the 'I, too, am Oxford' tumblr coincided with the Race Summit, a CRAE organised initiative that brought administrators, faculty and student representatives together "to address the existence of racism at Oxford, and how they can work towards creating a more just and inclusive student experience".[6] While a happy coincidence, and hopefully one that helped to bolster the arguments being made at the Summit, the reality is that few of the students that partook in the campaign were aware of what was going on with regards to issues of anti-racism, access and curricular reform at the University level. The choice of date arose more from a practical concern—to get the message out before term was up—rather than a symbolic one. Any other interpretation would suggest that the campaign had long term reform goals and a clear sense of how to realise them at an institutional level, when in actuality many students saw this as a one-off event that allowed for them to share misconceptions of what life in Oxford was like for BME students.

[5]Tuck, Stephen G. N, and Henry Louis Gates. 2014. *The Night Malcolm X Spoke at the Oxford Union*. Oakland: University of California Press.
[6]University Oxford University Student Union. n.d. *Press Release for Race Summit*, Viewed 6 May 2017, from https://ousu.org/pageassets/whatson/newsracesummit_pressrelease2.pdf.

For those of us who would continue to agitate and organise around these issues, it became increasingly obvious that a coherent political movement could not have occurred from this particular campaign. What it did do was bring people together, with no particular or overt political agenda, to give an informed expression to ideas and frustrations that were simmering amongst students of colour.

The BME Conference: Dissidence in an Era of Diversity

As a follow up to the campaign, during the following term (Trinity), we led a group of students in organising a conference titled "The BME conference: Dissidence in an Era of Diversity". The conference was a concerted effort to engage with a more specific and formulated political agenda. It was an attempt to build a coalition with other student movements around the UK, such as the 'Ain't I A Woman' collective at SOAS and the SOAS's iteration of 'I, too, am….', as well as to interrogate the methodologies and share experiences of organising student led campaigns in the age of new media and the usefulness of American activist methods in British institutions. Professor Patricia Daley (one of the few Black Professors at Oxford) and Professor Elleke Boehmer who are part of the Geography and English departments in Oxford respectively, addressed questions of curricular reform and representation within the faculty and student body. The inclusion of faculty in the conference was crucial to ensuring that these conversations were being had at several levels and spheres within the university and for us, as students, it helped us get a better understanding of how to frame demands for curricular reform across the disciplines.

Most importantly, the conference helped establish student-faculty alliances, which are crucial to any long-term and sustained effort for institutional reform in higher education. Students come and go and the movements they start rise and fall, but the faculty are the ones who remain and are put in charge of instituting the changes that students demand. Hence it was crucial for students in Wadham College, following the BME conference, to establish the colleges' first people of colour and diversity officer in the student union, alongside the implementation of a Tutor for Race and Racial Equality on the college governing body. Given the many student lifetimes that faculty live out in institutions, their institutional memory is far longer and in some ways far more realistic than that of the student-body. Ensuring that student-faculty networks and alliances are in place, means that students can continue to agitate, protest and organise for transformation without concession and guarantee that someone inside the institution will take up their struggle and try to implement those changes. It is worth noting here that in our particular context the academics who were invested in institutional reform and supporting student-led activist initiatives were unfortunately in the minority. As you can imagine, there are indeed a large number of academics who are keen to ensure that the university and its curriculum are preserved in a way that they recognise and feel reflects their specific, Eurocentric understanding of a 'world class' institution.

The conference, on reflection, allowed for what the campaign had not, which was for us, as students and now activists, to think strategically about developing a political and academic decolonial and anti-racist initiative, led by the students and centring curricular reform. The hope was that the focus on these issues would effectively address the structures of whiteness and the colonial systems that were upheld by the institution. What became evident fairly quickly, however, was that the conference was a far less 'sexy' platform for students. Organising the conference did not create the same kind attention or mobilisation that the 'I too, am Oxford' campaign had encouraged. What did emerge from the conference, however, was the idea to create a print publication of Skin Deep, the first edition of which came to fruition in June 2014.

The guiding influence of academics who were working both in and outside of Oxford at that time and the assistance they gave in helping structure the conversations around decoloniality and the histories of global decolonial movements cannot be overstated. Dr. Nathaniel Tobias ~~Coleman~~, a former student of Merton College, Oxford, was at that time working as an academic at University College London and organising events and teach-ins that raised important questions such as: "Why Isn't My Professor Black?" and "Why Is My Curriculum White?"—both of which are titles of talks that he had given. Whilst he was in Oxford for an event, he was invited by a small group of student activists of colour to meet to discuss the shared issues that students and academics were facing in both UCL and Oxford. Crucially, he invited us to consider organising around a specific decolonial struggle with which we were already familiar: Rhodes Must Fall, which had gained significant momentum in early 2015 in the University of Cape Town (UCT), South Africa. The context from which the resistance in Cape Town emerged was clearly very distinct from the Oxford context, but there were particular grievances about representation, curriculum reform, and access to quality higher education for students of colour that resonated on both campuses.

Rhodes Must Fall Oxford (RMFO): In the Footsteps of Malcolm X

It's difficult to say whether RMFO would have emerged were it not for the mobilisation that occurred around the 'I, too, am Oxford' campaign. Certainly, members of that campaign who were still pursuing their studies both at the undergraduate and postgraduate level at Oxford went on to participate and indeed lead the actions of RMFO. Of course, this movement was not entirely home-grown, given that it primarily began as a solidarity campaign with Rhodes Must Fall South Africa. Moreover, the arrival of Rhodes Scholars to Oxford, who had been part of the movement at UCT, meant that new tactics and a new type of vocabulary was introduced into the rhetoric of anti-racist discourse in Oxford. Indeed, prior to RMFO, no student movement in recent memory had utilised and centred the term 'decolonial', or considered what its implications might mean in the physical and architectural context of Oxford. It was from these early conversations with Dr. ~~Coleman~~ in the spring of 2015 that student activists in Oxford were able to make the link with their South African counterparts. We were able to identify with the significance of the deep colonial ties that run through the history of Oxford as an institution, and how these ties continue to influence economics, curriculum and power structures within the university. What Rhodes Must Fall in Oxford necessarily facilitated was a transnational discussion around structural transformation which would force the university, an institution which is highly resistant to change, to be self-reflective and consider learning from both its British and international students.

The aims, gains and successes of RMFO have been widely documented both by members of the group and the media. Therefore, to give a brief account here would be both futile and unfair to the complex and vibrant history of this ongoing movement. That said, it is worth thinking through how differently 'I, too, am Oxford' and RMFO were received by the University, the media and the public. In large part, because the difference in treatment speaks to how readily institutions of higher education, and the media and public by extension, are willing to engage with and admit shortcomings when it comes to issues of 'diversity', which can be easily remedied by greater representation, a few workshops on micro-aggressions perhaps featuring one or two more BME students on the university brochure. Whereas 'decolonisation', as iterated by RMFO, demanded the removal of statues, the acknowledgement of past wrongs and the rewriting of a whitewashed colonial history that defined both national culture and the ways in which the humanities and social sciences were being taught at the University. The former is inoffensive, superficial and affordable to implement, whereas the latter requires serious existential and epistemological considerations and comes at the expense of alienating wealthy donors and spending a great deal on architectural restructuring.

Therefore, it is unsurprising that the University opted to delay responding to the demands of RMFO in the hope that the students who were putting pressure on the university to address issues of institutional racism, global economic structures, and colonialism would do what most students do when their time at University has come to an end: leave, never to be heard from again. Yet, despite all of this, we can be encouraged by the fact that RMFO activists, like Malcolm X fifty years before them, debated in the most hostile institution within the university—the Oxford Union—and won.

From Roots to Routes: Towards a Global Student Movement

It is perhaps wise at the end to return to the words that we began with by way of Stuart Hall, 'and why, of all places, partly in Oxford?' There can be no doubt that these movements emerged at a particular juncture in global student of colour activism. The 'I, too, am' movement is part of a long history of American student activism, influencing discussions and activism around race in the United Kingdom. The RMF movement begins where the decolonisation movements of the twentieth century left off, bringing the question of decolonisation both to the academy and home to the metropole.

In order to create sustainable student movements that force a shift from the much more convenient position of political apathy and docility, which continues to be associated with privileged leftist politics, we must continue to document and archive the decolonial struggles that have taken place and build on the long history of student-led activism within the academy. In this way, we can disrupt the cycle and limitations of time frames offered by an undergraduate or postgraduate degree, and build on the roots laid down by those before us, whilst informing the routes of those who will inevitably come after. Student activists must continue to reflect on the benefits of seeing their work in a global context, and understand what can be gained from recognising that a particular struggle should be in constant conversation with global struggles and solidarity movements.

Part V

Brick Walls and Tick Boxes: The 'White-Washing' of Equality and Diversity Policies

18

The Heart of Whiteness: Racial Gesture Politics, Equity and Higher Education

Nicola Rollock

Gesture Politics

>...any action by a person or organisation done for political reasons and intended to attract public attention but having little real effect (Cambridge English Dictionary (undated))

Early in 2016, I gave a talk to an audience of academics, professional staff and students as part of an event to celebrate the launch of a university equality network. At the end, as is customary in most presentations, the Chair (a senior member of the university) stood to give closing remarks and invite questions from the floor. Thanking me for my contribution, she observed, "our universities would certainly look very different if you were in charge". The comment stayed with me. If, for a moment, we were to take the statement seriously rather than assume it to be a mere polite throwaway remark, what then was it about the content of

N. Rollock (✉)
Goldsmiths, University of London, London, UK
e-mail: N.Rollock@gold.ac.uk

© The Author(s) 2018
J. Arday and H. S. Mirza (eds.), *Dismantling Race in Higher Education*,
https://doi.org/10.1007/978-3-319-60261-5_18

my presentation that made her come to this conclusion? Further if my perspective, along with others who work in the field and share a similar analytical lens, had the potential to make such impact why was change not more forthcoming? Indeed why do we continue to encounter resistance to our proposals to advance racial justice? I share these ruminations not as an exercise in academic self-aggrandisement but rather as means to reflect upon why, despite a well-established record of equalities legislation in the UK, despite the policies, guidance documents and professed commitments of higher education institutions, and the supposedly liberal, inclusive ideals of many academics, meaningful change on race equality might be labelled at best slow and at worse, abysmally static. With such questions in mind, this chapter focuses on the wider institutional context and hegemonic practices in which race inequalities persist. It draws attention to the ways in which universities engage with and attempt to address racial disparities. Drawing on examples from empirical research, personal communications from colleagues in the UK and overseas and, my experience advising on race equality, I posit that institutional initiatives to address race inequalities often fail to engage seriously with the fundamental aspects of race and racism. Instead, it is argued that they tend to embrace a range of limited short-term strategies that while giving the *appearance* of serious engagement, in effect, make little substantial, long-term difference to the experiences, outcomes and success of students and faculty of colour.

What Is Race Inequality and What Does It Look Like in Our Universities?

> Being African American in a predominantly white institution is like being an actor on stage. There are roles one has to perform, storylines one is expected to follow, and dramas and subplots one should avoid at all cost. [It is like] playing a small but visible part in a racially specific script. Survival is always in question. (Carbado and Gulati 2013: 1)

It is precisely this script that interests me given that as faculty of colour we are seldom the authors or playwrights determining the roles, content or direction of what happens on the academic stage.

Gender is important here. To be a woman of colour within mainly white institutions is to occupy an identity which is diametrically distinct from the white male leaders who make the decisions within those spaces. And for women of colour specialising in race within higher education, this is a space which is often surreal, frustrating and exhausting (Ahmed 2009; Maylor 2009). This particular state of double consciousness (Fanon 1967) is characterised by the careful, oscillating dance between a white academy that largely avoids, limits or shuts down any meaningful debate on race and, the endless pained accounts of people of colour who work or study within this arena. I am struck by how many—a large number of whom are strangers—come to me, fuelled by some awareness of my work, to share their experiences. They contact me by email or pull me aside at conferences, seminars and talks within and outside of the academy to speak in hushed, pained tones about what has happened to them within the ivory towers. Students speak of lecturers whose course content dismisses or subjugates their identity or history, of white supervisors who seek to minimise or altogether alter the content of postgraduate research where race is the focus. Administrative staff describe being forever stuck at the same grade or of their contributions being overlooked by dismissive line managers and, academic staff share endless examples of incidents in which colleagues repeatedly question their competence and expertise. I have lost count of the number of these conversations I have been part of but note that at the heart of each is the desire to be treated with respect and with courtesy and, an expectation of a fair opportunity to progress and succeed.

It is not uncommon for the observations that I set out above to be dismissed by the 'scriptwriters' as anecdotal, as individual perception or as the attention-seeking cries of a disgruntled few. However a small but growing body of literature and empirical research has shown these experiences to be part of the norm for faculty of colour within universities in the UK (e.g. Ahmed 2009; Bhopal et al. 2015; NUS 2015; Leathwood et al. 2009; Mirza 2006; Rollock 2011, 2012) mirroring the experiences of their US counterparts (e.g. Carbado and Gulati 2013; Harris and Gonzalez 2012; Smith et al. 2006; Yoshinaga-Itano 2006). Given such evidence, it should come as no surprise that UK faculty of colour are more likely, when compared with their white colleagues, to consider leaving the country to work at overseas institutions (Bhopal et al. 2015) believing the opportunities for progression to be better, though still not ideal, elsewhere. For this too has been something about which faculty of colour have long whispered—before the empirical research gave it formal legitimacy—and dreamt about during those conversations at the margins of UK institutional spaces. For people of colour in such places, there is recognition that racism can go beyond the overt, crude reckonings of random individuals or disenfranchised Far Right groups. Instead, we are subject to what Pierce (1970: 472) describes as the "offensive mechanisms" of racial microaggressions:

> …racial microaggressions are a form of systemic, everyday racism used to keep those at the racial margins in their place. They are: (1) verbal and non-verbal assaults directed toward People of Color, often carried out in subtle, automatic or unconscious forms; (2) layered assaults, based on race and its intersections with gender, class, sexuality, language, immigration status, phenotype, accent or surname; and (3) cumulative assaults that take a psychological, physiological, and academic toll on People of Color. (Perez Huber and Solorzano 2015: 302)

Such acts, subtle though they may be in their manifestation, nonetheless speak to an implicit belief held by many white people that their experience and knowledge is inherently and unquestionably better than that held by people of colour. Racial microaggressions serve to remind people of colour that they are somehow different and less than whites. Much of the power of microaggressions is in their persistence and subtlety. Race or racism does not need to be explicitly named for this form of racial inequality to occur. Consider, for example, the following scenario:

Scenario 1

A white female academic joins a university as a new member of staff. She is assigned to a teaching team where the team leader is a female faculty of colour who has been at the university for ten years. On receiving students' coursework, the team leader sends an email to the teaching team which summarises university's practice with regard to marking and states the deadline for submitting grades. The new member of staff fails to complete the marking in line with the request and when prompted by the team leader responds with a curt, two-line email emphasising her extensive experience of working in higher education and her track record of marking. She refuses to address the team leader's concerns and insists that, in her view, she has already completed the marking according to university guidelines.

There are two critical issues that must be incorporated in the reading of the above incident. First, the absence of any *explicit* mention of race does not mean that race is absent from the equation. In recognising and challenging the whiteness of universities, it is necessary to explore how they become and remain that way. The task is to identify (and deconstruct) those hegemonic practices which form the natural, unquestioned fabric of the academy and enable its cultural preservation:

> Domination is a relation of power that subjects enter into and is forged in historical process. It does not form out of random acts of hatred, although these are condemnable, but rather out of a patterned and enduring treatment of social groups. *Ultimately, it is secured through a series of actions, the ontological meaning of which is not always transparent to its subjects and objects.* (Leonardo 2009: 77, emphasis added)

Looking then to the scenario, we may reasonably assume that the employee who has been at the institution the longest will have a better knowledge of university procedures. However, a critically reflexive and racially just analysis would also seek to understand the dynamics of power and how the racial identities and experiences of the actors might have given rise to the incident which occurred. A racially just perspective would demand, for example, that we ask whether the new employee would respond in the same way if the team leader were a white woman or indeed a man of colour.

Recognising and naming race, even if as a possibility, *must* co-exist with a second fundamental consideration, namely, the wider evidence on race. Here questions about what is known about the workplace experiences of people of colour and, in particular, women of colour are essential. By coupling a consideration of race *with* the research evidence, we can begin to move away from a colourblind approach and better acknowledge the way in which power relations, "forged in historical process" as Leonardo (2009: 77) reminds us, operate along axes of race (and other identities) within UK universities.

Yet it is precisely because such acts are carried out with no apparent "ontological meaning" (Leonardo 2009: 77) that such incidents tend to go uninvestigated or are trivialised by white power-holders in these very institutions. This, despite empirical evidence about the experiences of faculty of colour and recent large-scale studies documenting the persistence of racism in UK workplaces (Business in the Community 2015; Ashe and Nazroo 2016).

Let us hold onto these considerations as we return to our analysis of the scenario. By acting in the way that she has, the new employee also provides insight into the ways in which whiteness and white privilege operate. Entitlement and privilege operate to position as superior and more legitimate experience obtained prior to arriving at the university despite the fact that it does not complement practices at the new place of work. The team leader is also left with a predicament. Irrespective of the reasons for the new employee's behaviour, the coursework must be marked to time and according to university protocol. If this does not occur, it is the team leader and not the new member of staff who will be held responsible.

Let us take the scenario one step further and assume that the team leader reported the matter to senior colleagues believing that they would intervene and demand co-operation. Instead it is dismissed as being a "teaching related" issue that she should manage herself. This serves to legitimise the poor behaviour of her white colleague (thus reinforcing and sanctioning whiteness) and, because she has to now mark them herself, causes a delay in returning grades to the students. Complaints ensue and are reflected in the student evaluations, which are submitted later in the year. The external examiner and the same senior colleagues to whom the team leader had reported the incident, express serious concerns about the students' comments and seek explanation. It is the faculty of colour who is in their sights and *not* the intransigence of the white colleague. The team leader is left feeling frustrated, alienated and unsupported while the white colleague still has not been reprimanded (Harris and Gonzalez 2012).

It is experiences like the one set out in the above scenario that others share with me time and time again. In my 2011 article on racial microaggressions in the academy, I employ counternarrative (Delgado 2000) to articulate the semi-fictional experiences of Jonathan, one of few faculty of colour at a high profile university (Rollock 2011). The article describes how a colleague took issue with Jonathan's preference for opening windows in their shared office as opposed to using the air conditioning system and so approached Human Resources to issue a formal complaint against him. While it may seem trivial and possibly incredulous, the incident in fact draws on a real-life event. None of the key actors with the power to shape how the event unfurled (Jonathan's line manager, the HR manager) took account of the possible role of race. Jonathan ended up being informally reprimanded just two weeks into a new role. Several years later, in real life, the name of the same colleague with whom Jonathan had shared an office would surface in a race discrimination case.

I share these accounts as a means by which to demonstrate the insidious ways in which power through racial discrimination operates within the academy. Seemingly slight or even trivial acts serve to position faculty of colour at the margins of institutional spaces which continue to ignore, downplay or deny their experiences and the salience of race. Yet if we are to understand why the sector remains plagued by such low numbers of senior faculty of colour[1] (Equality Challenge Unit 2015) and why their experiences are largely negative, then it is imperative that we move beyond colour blindness and take seriously the experiences of this group.

The first step in this process is honest conversation.

The Fallacy of Honest Race Talk?

I keep trying new ways to make them see what they clearly do not want to see, what perhaps they're incapable of seeing... (Bell 1992: 142)

---

[1]An analysis of the most recent data from higher education information database (HEIDI) published by the Higher Education Statistical Agency (HESA) reveals that there were 75 UK Black professors in 2014/2015.

Derrick Bell is one of the founders of Critical Race Theory, an approach that offers a radical lens through which to make sense of and ultimately challenge racial injustice in society (Delgado and Stefancic 2001; Ladson-Billings 1998; Rollock and Gillborn 2011). While I ended the previous section with a call for white colleagues to move beyond colour blindness this, in fact, is to overlook some of the fundamental constraining aspects of racial politics and white dominance. Attempts to speak honestly with white colleagues about race are fraught with risk and challenge irrespective of the weight of additional evidence or new analyses that is brought to bear in the discussion:

> …by sharing their real perspectives on race, minorities become overt targets of personal and academic threats. It becomes a catch-22 for them. Either they must observe the safety of whites and be denied a space that promotes people of color's growth and development or insist on a space of integrity and put themselves further at risk not only of violence, but also risk being conceived of as illogical or irrational. Thus, white privilege is at the center of most race dialogues, even those that aim to critique and undo racial advantage. (Leonardo and Porter 2010: 140)

Prioritising the growth and progression of people of colour means disclosing to white colleagues when they are complicit in racist acts, which is seldom welcomed. It also means revealing that they, as whites, are racial beings (a fact which they know but seldom publicly acknowledge) implicated within and benefiting from the nature of a racially ordered society (Leonardo 2009). Most whites react against such revelations through actions such as denial, tears, guilt, defensiveness or anger (Picower 2009; Yoshinaga-Itano 2006). There are moments during my career where, drawing on research evidence, I have spoken truth about the experiences of people of colour and have been publicly shouted down, positioned as "challenging" or, patronisingly, as being "refreshingly frank". For as Ahmed (2009) reminds us:

> To speak of racism [within universities] is to introduce bad feeling. It is to hurt not just the organisation, re-imagined as a subject with feelings, but also the subjects who identify with the organisation, the 'good white diversity' subjects, to whom we are supposed to be grateful. (p. 46)

This is precisely because such words are viewed as a disruption to the dominant narrative in which whiteness is supposed to remain invisible and where people of colour are pathologised and positioned as inherently deficient and responsible for their own lack of progression. The unnamed requirement is that those working in the field of race equality collude with this norm or at least do not disrupt it and make white colleagues uncomfortable. As Leonardo and Porter (2009: 139) state "...pedagogies that tackle racial power will be most uncomfortable for those who benefit from that power".

As such, honest race conversation between whites and people of colour remains marred with difficulty. The two groups begin from fundamentally different starting points, investments and aspirations. However, Leonardo (2009) warns against coming to the conclusion that because whites evade, deny and fight against genuine racial analysis of education, they simply lack knowledge about race. For to think thus, would mean being seduced by the idea that *acquiring* knowledge via a few hours of 'unconscious bias' training (currently a la mode in UK higher education institutions) or a one-off invited session with a race expert will be sufficient to enable white colleagues to begin to move beyond whiteness and commit, genuinely, to the racial justice project. It would mean that once educated—once made race conscious—whites will set about proffering analyses and implementing initiatives that truly equate to equity for people of colour. Such radical acts are rare.

The Tale of the Emperor's New Clothes or, Racial Gesture Politics and the Myth of Race Equity in Higher Education

Many years ago, I was assigned a mentor—an older white female academic—as part of a university programme to support the development of junior Black and Minority Ethnic staff.[2] During our first meeting,

---

[2] I have long had reservations about the blanket, unquestioned use of mentoring programmes in higher education because they are often predicated on the notion that the mentee is lacking is some way and are seldom accompanied by wider imperatives for institutional or structural

in a local coffee shop, my new mentor asked about my professional aspirations. I liked academia I said, however, I was struck by the fact that there were only (at that point) 17 Black female professors across the entire sector. 'Oh' she said, 'you mustn't let that dissuade you or get you down'. In thinking that the figures could have only served to disincentivise me, she missed my point. My actual thinking was, if there are just 17 Black female Professors across the entire UK, what had their specific barriers to progression been and how might I too learn to navigate them? Later, sat before my computer in my office, I reflected that despite her well meaning, I did not want to do the work of educating my mentor about my views on success and survival as a woman of colour. I sent her an email to thank her for her time, making the excuse that mentoring was something about which I needed to give further thought and to which I might return in the future.

Since then, I have become increasingly interested in and concerned by the ways in which institutions respond to and engage with race and the issues raised by staff, students and faculty of colour. Of course, the first point to note is that within the current sociopolitical context, it is unusual to name race, racism or racial injustice so explicitly. Such language is politely subsumed within palatable umbrella terms such as *equality, diversity, inclusion* or, the clumsy all-encompassing acronym BAME (Black, Asian and minority ethnic). Race or racism is seldom named or foregrounded thus serving to maintain a racially sanitised norm which benefits whites and marginalises faculty, staff and students of colour. In this context, attempts to explicitly name or foreground race and racism are silenced or reworked and rebranded in an effort to preserve the institutional image as neutral, colourblind and progressive. These acts of brand management do not challenge whiteness rather are preoccupied only with protecting it whether through inadequate forms of action or, as with the senior colleagues in the scenario above, inaction and avoidance.

---

change. The notion of sponsorship, where the sponsor facilitates introductions to key individuals, share potential networking and job opportunities, is infinitely more attractive (Schwabel 2013) and aligns with research which demonstrates the powerful role that social and cultural capital plays in facilitating social mobility (e.g. see Ball 2003; Bourdieu 1986).

Ahmed's (2012) research examining engagement with racism and diversity in higher education institutions is relevant here. In one example, she describes how an anonymous college responded to newspaper coverage revealing that international students had experienced racist attacks on campus and, their complaint that the college lacked any means for dealing with such incidents:

> The college spokeswoman said, "This could not be further from the truth. The college prides itself on its levels of pastoral care". (p. 144)

In analysing this response, Ahmed makes the following observation:

> The response [of the college] not only contradicts the students' claims (…) but also promotes or asserts the good will of the college. (…) Pastoral care is tied to an organizational ideal as being good: we do not have a problem (with racism, with responding to those who experience racism?) *because we care for these students*. The response to a complaint about racism and how the college handles the complaint thus takes the form of an assertion of organizational pride (…) *The response to the complaint enacts the very problem that the complaint is about.* (p. 144, emphasis added)

I noted similar processes at work during my role as Chair of one of the Equality Challenge Unit's panels assessing university submissions for the race equality charter. The charter exists to support the success and progression of Black and Minority Ethnic staff and students. Universities who were not successful in receiving an award tended to be those who were unable to offer, for example, a coherent account of staff and student experience in their institution. They also tended to view the process as a public relations' exercise, downplaying or attempting to gloss over inconsistencies rather honestly proposing how they might address them (Herbert 2016; Rollock 2016). By contrast, those institutions that did well were able to provide a clear narrative—irrespective of how revealing this was of their own failings—about the experiences of their staff, faculty and students of colour and could describe their plans to facilitate change.

So what are universities actually doing when confronted by data on race inequality? The following semi-fictional scenarios, again drawn from different sources, give some insight.

Scenario 2

A faculty within a large university carries out research to determine how many staff are from Black and Minority Ethnic backgrounds and their level of seniority. There are just five such staff and none is at Reader or Professorial level. The faculty compares its figures to other faculties in the same university and finds fewer Black and Minority Ethnic staff in each. It congratulates itself on standing heads and shoulders above other departments and concludes that it does not need to take any action to address the representation of these staff.

Scenario 3

A university finds that over a five-year period, Black and Minority Ethnic staff are more likely to leave or take up voluntary redundancy compared with their white counterparts. The institution explains this by saying that it has a global workforce and no workforce is static. When questioned specifically about the racial disparity, it argues that it has equality policies in place and all staff are treated equally.

What should be apparent in each case is the shallowness of strategies allegedly implemented to address racial disparities. These "performative contradictions" (Ahmed 2012: 144) may give the appearance of engaging seriously with race but in fact are no more than what I term *racial gesture politics*, i.e.:

Racial gesture politics refers to (individual or collective) words, policies or behaviours, which ostensibly address racial disparities but in reality maintain a racially inequitable status quo.

If we accept that racial gesture politics persist as the norm in higher education institutions (and indeed elsewhere) despite evidence from experts that their conceptual and analytical framework is problematic and in some cases regressive, then we must obviously question whether the intention to change is genuine and whether, and indeed how, the racial justice project might actually be realised.

Beyond White Dominance

In 2008, I was commissioned by Runnymede (a UK-based race equality thinktank) to carry out the first independent review to assess whether the Government had met the criminal justice recommendations of the Lawrence Inquiry[3] (Rollock 2009). I carried out detailed secondary research, attended meetings at the Home Office, spoke with senior members within the police service, interviewed Stephen Lawrence's mother Doreen, read and analysed a substantial body of academic, government, and think-tank literature which had been published during the preceding 10 years. I found that the majority of the Inquiry recommendations had been met or were well on their way to being achieved. However, there were two recommendations—one relating to racial disproportionality in stop and search and, the other to the representation and retention of Black and Minority Ethnic officers—where there had been relatively little progress. I was surprised. After all, this was a period in recent British history where the term *institutional racism* had gained traction within print and broadcast media and, wider public and political consciousness. This was a period characterised by the fast-tracked implementation of the Race Relations (Amendment) Act 2000. This was a period where, under the Act, public bodies had to demonstrate how they were promoting equal opportunities and good relations between different ethnic groups. Funding was made available for conferences, training schemes, for new posts and projects that centred explicitly on advancing race equality. It seemed that race was finally on the political agenda. Yet despite this, my findings revealed that 10 years on disparities remained on the two key recommendations that focused on race and policing. It led to my posing different questions about my own understanding of racial justice: if unprecedented attention, commitment, resources and legislation had not made a difference to those recommendations, then what would and what

---

[3]The Lawrence Inquiry was published in 1999. It was announced in 1997 by the Labour Government with a remit to investigate the circumstances (including failed police investigation) surrounding the racist murder of Black teenager Stephen Lawrence (see Macpherson 1999; Rollock 2009). For a summary timeline of events stemming from his murder in 1993 see http://www.bbc.co.uk/news/uk-26465916.

were the actual barriers to change? I concluded that while considerable effort had been made to address racial disparities and improve the experiences and outcomes of Black and Minority Ethnic groups, there had been relatively little attention paid to exploring and challenging the attitudes, beliefs and practices of those in positions of power or to understanding how those positioned at the top of the racial hierarchy benefit from being there. In other words, while some important changes had been made to the script (to continue Carbado and Gulati's analogy), the scriptwriters essentially remained the same and remained unchallenged in their practice and the culture they perpetuated.

In returning attention to higher education, there remains a sense in which students, staff and faculty of colour must depend on the white majority for their eventual (possible) understanding and commitment to improving race outcomes. Yet if whites benefit from the current racial order then we must ask whether the changes we demand from our places at the margins, are likely to be forthcoming. Indeed, in knowing and accepting this, we must also ask how we as students and faculty of colour might move to a more humanising existence beyond merely hoping that whites might relinquish their privilege and power. It is in this context that campaigns such as #RhodesMustFall[4] must be understood. To position the campaign, as some have,[5] as merely focused on the removal of a single statue at the University of Oxford (albeit of an individual profoundly associated with the oppression of people of colour) is to miss the point of the students' and activists' demands (Espinoza 2016). Collective action, agency and self-determination serve as the bedrock of a movement which stipulates that the curriculum in its very broadest sense (i.e. taught provision, campus landscape, institutional culture, representation of staff and

---

[4]The #RhodesMustFall campaign began, in 2015, at the University of Cape Town, South Africa. Stimulated by the actions of Chumani Maxwele (who threw faeces on the statue of British colonialist Cecil Rhodes located on the campus), Black students demanded greater representation of a history and individuals that spoke to their Black African experiences. Their actions were later followed by campaigners at the University of Oxford, England, https://www.theguardian.com/news/2015/nov/18/why-south-african-students-have-turned-on-their-parents-generation.

[5]Lord Patten, the Chancellor of the University of Oxford (where the statue is located) dismissed the actions of the campaigners, announcing on a primetime BBC news programme that students who did not like the presence of the statue should study elsewhere (Espinoza 2016).

faculty of colour) is not simply diversified by the addition, for example, of a few more faculty or students of colour (an act of racial gesture politics) but instead is *decolonized*. In other words, that white structures, policies and decision-making processes are deconstructed and fundamentally reworked with principles of racial equity at the core (Olusoga 2016; Rhodes Must Fall Community Facebook page, undated). In the decolonised institution, whites are cognizant of the ways in which they have facilitated racial injustice; low expectations of faculty and students of colour are challenged and penalised; whistle-blowing policies exist to root out and eradicate racial microaggressions. Racial justice is a named, embedded and enacted normality of institutional life.

In closing, I return to the scholarship of Derrick Bell (1992). He invites us to embrace a 'both, and' positioning with regard to the racial justice project. On one hand we must accept the permanence and futility of racism—my experiences carrying out the research for the *Stephen Lawrence Inquiry 10 Years On* report were formative in this regard—and at the same time, we become empowered from the very knowledge of its permanence.[6] It is with this knowledge that we can begin to pay greater attention to how we might forge a healthy existence within the 'racial fantasyland' (Mills 1997: 18) of higher education as well as continue to challenge and deconstruct the racially unjust status quo.

References

Ahmed, S. (2009). Embodying Diversity: Problems and Paradoxes for Black Feminists. *Race, Ethnicity & Education, Special Issue Black Feminisms and Postcolonial Paradigms: Researching Educational Inequalities, 12*(1), 41–52.
Ahmed, S. (2012). *On Being Included: Racism and Diversity in Institutional Life*. Durham and London: Duke University Press.
Apple, M. (2004). *Ideology and Curriculum* (3rd ed.). Abingdon, Oxon, and New York: Routledge.

---

[6]In acknowledging this permanence, Bell does not suggest relinquishing the fight for racial justice or, indeed, becoming demoralised by it. It is the very awareness of this permanence and embeddedness that lends perspicuity to the strategies and work required to deconstruct it.

Ashe, S., & Nazroo, J. (2016). *Equality, Diversity and Racism in the Workplace: A Qualitative Analysis of the 2015 Race at Work Survey.* Manchester: Business in the Community.

Ball, S. (2003). *Class Strategies and the Education Market: The Middle Classes and Social Advantage.* Abingdon, Oxon, and New York: Routledge.

Bell, D. (1992). *Faces at the Bottom of the Well: The Permanence of Racism.* New York: Basic Books.

Bhopal, K., Brown, H., & Jackson, J. (2015). *How to Encourage Black and Minority Ethnic Academics to Stay in UK Higher Education.* London: Equality Challenge Unit.

Bourdieu, P. (1986). The Forms of Capital. In J. Richardson (Ed.), *Handbook of Theory and Research for the Sociology of Education* (pp. 241–258). New York: Greenwood.

Business in the Community (BiTC). (2015). *Race at Work Report.* London: Business in the Community.

Carbado, D., & Gulati, M. (2013). *Acting White? Rethinking Race in "Post-racial" America.* Oxford: Oxford University Press.

Delgado, R. (2000). Storytelling for Oppositionists and Others: A Plea for Narrative. In R. Delgado & J. Stefancic (Eds.), *Critical Race Theory: The Cutting Edge* (2nd ed., pp. 60–70). Philadelphia, PA: Temple University Press.

Delgado, R., & Stefancic, J. (2001). *Critical Race Theory: An Introduction.* New York: New York University Press.

Equality Challenge Unit. (2015). *Equality in Higher Education Statistical Report.* London: Equality Challenge Unit.

Espinoza, J. (2016, January 16). Oxford University Students Who Don't like Cecil Rhodes Should 'Think About Being Educated Elsewhere', Says Chancellor. *Daily Telegraph.* http://www.telegraph.co.uk/education/educationnews/12096928/Oxford-University-students-who-dont-like-Cecil-Rhodes-should-think-about-being-educated-elsewhere-says-hancellor.html. Last Accessed.

Fanon, F. (1967). *Black Skin, White Masks.* London: Pluto Books.

Harris, A. P., & Gonzalez, C. G. (2012). Introduction. In G. Gutierrez y Muhs, Y. Flores Niemann, C. G. Gonzalez, & A. Harris (Eds.), *Presumed Incompetent: The Intersections of Race and Class for Women in Academia.* Colorado, USA: Utah State University.

Herbert, C. (2016). Race Equality: Start the Conversation to End the Frustration. *Equality Challenge Unit Blog.* http://www.ecu.ac.uk/blogs/race-equality-start-the-conversation-to-end-the-frustration/. Last Accessed 1 Apr 2016.

Ladson-Billings, G. (1998). Just What Is Critical Race Theory and What's It Doing in a Nice Field Like Education? *International Journal of Qualitative Studies in Education, 11*(1), 7–24.

Leathwood, C., Maylor, U., & Moreau, M. (2009). *The Experiences of Black and Minority Ethnic Staff Working in Higher Education.* London: Equality Challenge Unit.

Leonardo, Z. (2009). *Race, Whiteness and Education (Critical Social Thought Series).* London and New York: Routledge.

Leonardo, Z., & Porter, R. (2010). Pedagogy of Fear: Toward a Fanonian Theory of 'Safety' in Race Dialogue. *Race Ethnicity & Education, 13*(2), 139–157.

Macpherson, W. (1999). *The Stephen Lawrence Inquiry.* London: Crown Copyright. Available at https://www.gov.uk/government/uploads/system/uploads/attachment_data/file/277111/4262.pdf. Last Accessed 1 Apr 2016.

Maylor, U. (2009). Is It because I'm Black? A Black Female Research Experience. *Race Ethnicity & Education, 12*(1), 53–64.

Mills, C. (1997). *The Racial Contract.* New York: Cornell University Press.

Mirza, H. S. (2006). The In/Visible Journey: Black Women's Lifelong Lessons in Higher Education. In C. Leathwood & B. Francis (Eds.), *Gender and Lifelong Learning* (pp. 137–152). London: Routledge.

National Union of Students (NUS). (2015). *Race Matters: A Report on the Experience of Black Staff in the Student Movement.* London: National Union of Students.

Olusoga, D. (2016, January 7). Topple the Cecil Rhodes Statue? Better Rebrand Him a War Criminal. *The Guardian.* http://www.theguardian.com/commentisfree/2016/jan/07/cecil-rhodes-statue-war-criminal-rhodes-must-fall. Last Accessed 1 Apr 2016.

Perez Huber, L., & Solorzano, D. G. (2015). Racial Microaggressions as a Tool for Critical Race Research. *Race Ethnicity & Education, 18*(3), 297–320.

Picower, B. (2009). The Unexamined Whiteness of Teaching: How White Teachers Maintain and Enact Dominant Racial Ideologies. *Race, Ethnicity and Education, 12*(2), 197–215.

Pierce, C. (1970). Black Psychiatry One Year After Miami. *Journal of the National Medical Association, 62*(6), 471–473.

Rhodes Must Fall in Oxford Community Facebook Page. https://www.facebook.com/Rhodes-Must-Fall-In-Oxford-1599672910303410/. Last Accessed 1 Apr 2016.

Rollock, N. (2009). *The Stephen Lawrence Inquiry 10 Years On.* London: Runnymede Trust.

Rollock, N. (2011). Unspoken Rules of Engagement: Navigating Racial Microaggressions in the Academic Terrain. *International Journal of Qualitative Studies in Education, 25*(5), 517–532.

Rollock, N. (2012). The Invisibility of Race: Intersectional Reflections on the Liminal Space of Alterity [Special Issue: Critical Race Theory in England]. *Race Ethnicity & Education, 15*(1), 65–84.

Rollock, N. (2016, January 19). How Much Does Your University Do for Racial Equality? *The Guardian Higher Education Network.* http://www.theguardian.com/higher-education-network/2016/jan/19/how-much-does-your-university-do-for-racial-equality. Last Accessed 1 Apr 2016.

Rollock, N., & Gillborn, D. (2011). Critical Race Theory (CRT), British Educational Research Association Online Resource. Available Online at www.bera.ac.uk/wp-content/uploads/2014/03/Critical-Race-Theory-CRT-.pdf?noredirect=1. Last Accessed.

Schwabel, D. (2013, September 10). Sylvia Ann Hewlett: Find a Sponsor Instead of a Mentor. *Forbes.* http://www.forbes.com/sites/danschwabel/2013/09/10/sylvia-ann-hewlett-find-a-sponsor-instead-of-a-mentor/#2208e98e1da6. Last Accessed 1 Apr 2016.

Smith, W., Yosso, T. J., & Solorzano, D. G. (2006). Challenging Racial Battle Fatigue on Historically White Campuses: A Critical Examination of Race Related Stress. In C. A. Stanley (Ed.), *Faculty of Color: Teaching in Predominantly White Colleges and Universities.* Boston, MA: Anker Publishing Company.

Sue, D. W., Capodilupo, C. M., & Holder, A. M. B. (2008). Racial Microaggressions in the Life Experience of Black Americans. *Professional Psychology: Research and Practice, 39*(3), 329–336.

Yoshinaga-Itano, C. (2006). Institutional Barriers and Myths to Recruitment and Retention of Faculty of Color: An Administrator's Perspective. In C. A. Stanley (Ed.), *Faculty of Color: Teaching in Predominantly White Colleges and Universities.* Boston, MA: Anker Publishing Company.

19

Rocking the Boat: Women of Colour as Diversity Workers

Sara Ahmed

Diversity work is work. This statement is an important starting point because diversity work is often not visible let alone valued as work. In this chapter I am thinking of diversity work in two senses. Diversity work is the work we do when we aim to transform institutions, often by trying to open them up to populations that have hitherto been excluded. Diversity work is also the work we do when we do not quite inhabit the norms of an institution. These two senses often meet in a body: those who do not quite inhabit the norms of an institution are often given the task of transforming these norms. Women of colour tend to be diversity workers in both senses. We find ourselves members of diversity committees and equality task forces. As women we might be asked to be on ATHENA SWAN committees working on gender equality. As people of colour, we find ourselves on race equality task forces, and BME staff networks. We also have work to do because we do not inhabit the norms of the institution. If you are a diversity worker

S. Ahmed (✉)
Cambridgeshire, UK

© The Author(s) 2018
J. Arday and H. S. Mirza (eds.), *Dismantling Race in Higher Education*,
https://doi.org/10.1007/978-3-319-60261-5_19

in both senses, however, the both tends to be obscured, as if 'doing diversity' is just about 'being diversity,' as if being is all we have to do. For diversity workers, being is never 'just being,' there is much you have to do to be.

We can start here: with the work we have to do to be. We know so much about institutions from trying to transform them. We know so much about institutions because they have not been built to accommodate us. As I will explain in due course, we often end up 'rocking the boat' just by turning up or by speaking up. In this chapter I draw on my experiences as a woman of colour academic. My inspirations include Chandra Talpade Mohanty (2003), M. Jacqui Alexander (2006), and Heidi Mirza (2015) who offer powerful critiques of uses of diversity within the academy as a way of building feminist of colour and Black feminist counter-institutional knowledge. I am also inspired by the monumental collection, *Presumed Incompetent: The Intersections of Race and Class for Women in Academia* (Muhs et al. 2012), which by offering reflections by women of colour students and faculty on their experiences within the academy gives us important new insights into how the academy works. I will be sharing some data I collected as a member of a team working on diversity and leadership during 2002–2004 including interviews with diversity practitioners and diversity leaders or managers, which I first presented in my book *On Being Included: Racism and Diversity in Institutional Life* (2012) and then again in the middle section of *Living a Feminist Life* (2017). I will also be sharing some of my own experiences as a diversity worker including my experiences of challenging institutional whiteness and institutional racism as well as, more recently, my participation in an effort to challenge sexual harassment as an institutional problem.

I used to think I was generating data on diversity work. I have come to realise that diversity work *generates its own data*. I have been collecting stories of diversity and equality within universities since my arrival within universities. And I would even claim that women of colour are ethnographers of universities; we are participating, yes, but we are also observing, often because we are assumed not to belong or reside in the places we end up.

Being Diversity

Universities often describe their missions by drawing on the languages of diversity as well as equality. But using the language does not translate into creating diverse or equal environments. Commitments might even be made because they do not bring something about. I have called this dynamic *non-performativity*: when something is named without coming into effect or when something is named in order not to being something in effect.

Equality and diversity can be used to create the appearance of being transformed. What are the consequences of how diversity becomes an appearance? In her important book *Space Invaders*, Nirmal Puwar notes how 'in policy terms, diversity has overwhelmingly come to mean the inclusion of people who look different' (2004: 1). Some of us come to embody diversity; we appear different, because of whom we are not, which means we allow an organisation to appear different. For women of colour this means that we often come to embody the promise of inclusion within universities. To embody a promise requires labour. I still remember when we began our research project on diversity, how the organisation that funded us kept wanting to photograph us (for further discussion see Ahmed 2012). We were the only team that included women of colour. By representing us they could represent themselves as being more diverse than they were. Being a happy symbol of diversity can be hard work, especially if your experiences of the organisation are not happy. The smile you provide masks more than organisational failure; it can also mask your own experience of that failure.

Creating the appearance of diversity can become an official policy. In one interview with staff from a Human Resources department of an elite university, we discussed a research project they had recently commissioned into how external communities perceived their university. This data is typically called perception data; many organisations collected such data in the period that immediately followed the Race Relations Amendment Act (2000), often as an explicit strategy in developing their new race equality policies.[1] In this case the research findings were that the university was perceived as 'white' as well as 'male dominated.' The response from human resources was to identify the perception as wrong, and to suggest they needed to 'correct the perception.' Diversity becomes about changing images of whiteness rather than changing the whiteness of organisations. In practice, changing the image of the organisation as 'white' as well as 'male dominated' means that women of colour within organisations have to be pictured more. We know the picture: those happy smiling colourful faces that are instantly recognisable as images of diversity. That this work of repicturing an organisation falls unevenly on those who inhabit organisations is very important. *The further away you are from the norm the more you have to appear.* It might be assumed that being a symbol of diversity, being diversity, does not require doing very much at all. But being a symbol of an organisation is how you end up working for an organisation by enabling it to appear in a way that is not consistent with how you experience the organisation.

Diversity then often creates a happy impression; it is how an organisation appears welcoming to those who appear different by drawing upon those who appear different. Diversity can appear as an invitation, an open door, translated into a tagline: minorities welcome! Come in, come in. To be welcomed is to be positioned as not yet part, a guest or stranger, the one who is dependent on being welcomed, the one whose arrival is conditional on the will of those who are already here (the word welcome, a 'friendly greeting,' derives from will, 'one whose coming suits another's will'). Even when diversity appears as will, as a welcome given to those who embody diversity, it does not mean they expect us to turn up. What happens when a person of colour turns up? Oh how noticeable we are in the sea of whiteness. Here is one account: 'When I enter the room there is shock on peoples' faces because they

---

[1]This is important. Many public sector organisations (including councils and hospitals as well as universities) completed intensive research projects into how local ethnic minority communities perceived them in the aftermath of the RRAA (2000). Research into race inequality can create race inequality as some communities are required to give more of their time and energy than others.

are expecting a white person to come in. I pretend not to recognise it. But in the interview there is unease because they were not expecting someone like me to turn up. So it is hard and uncomfortable and I can tell that they are uneasy and restless because of the way they fiddle and twitch around with their pens and their looks. They are uncomfortable because they were not expecting me—perhaps they would not have invited me if they knew 1 was Black and of course 1 am very uncomfortable. 1 am wondering whether they are entertaining any prejudice against me.' They are not expecting you. Discomfort involves this failure to fit. A restlessness and uneasiness, a fidgeting and twitching, is a bodily registering of an unexpected arrival. I *pretend not to recognise* it: diversity work can be the effort not to notice the bother caused by your own arrival. There is pretense involved; this is not about pretending to be something you are not but pretending not to notice that you are not what they expect.

Not fulfilling an expectation is often how we learn about expectations. Or maybe once they have appointed one person, they feel they have done enough. I remember one time a woman of colour was being considered for a job in my department. Someone said in a departmental meeting with concern, 'but we already have Sara,' is if having one of us was more than enough; as if we replicated each other. There was a murmured consensus that she would not provide anything different from what was already provided by me. Diversity: how we become providers. There was no such concern about other areas; there was no concern that having more than one white man doing political economy would be a replication of what we already had, for instance. Concern; no concern; how things stay the same by seeing others as the same. When you embody diversity, you fulfil a policy commitment. Your body becomes a performance indicator. You become a tick in a box; you tick their boxes. By being a tick it is then as if they have nothing left to do once they have hired you. But you have more to do when there is only one of you.

If your appointment becomes a form of compliance, a means by which an organisation can say it has done enough, you can end up feeling that you are fulfilling someone else's agenda. You can end up being perceived as somebody who has only arrived because she brings diversity. When you are not who usually appears, you can seem not at home or not quite at home; the one who is a stranger. In my earlier work I explored how a stranger often appears as a body out of place; as the one whose arrival is noticeable (Ahmed 2000). Only some arrivals appear as arrivals; to be at home as to appear as if you were always here. We can become strangers within universities, even when we have been here for some time.

Diversity work: a catalogue of incidents. We are at a departmental meeting with incoming students. We are all talking about our own courses, one after the other, each coming up to the podium. Someone is chairing, introducing each of us in turn. She says, this is Professor *so-and-so*. This is Professor *such-and-such*. On this particular occasion, I happen to be the only female professor, and the only professor of colour in the room (the latter was not surprising because at the time I was the only professor of colour in the department). When it is my turn to come up, the Chair says: 'This is Sara'. I am the only professor introduced without using the title professor. What do you do? What to do? Diversity work is how we fill this gap or hesitation. If you ask to be referred to by the proper name, you are insisting on being given what was simply given to others; not only that, you are heard as insistent, as or even for that matter as self-promotional (as insisting on your dues). Maybe some have to be self-promotional because others are promoted by virtue of their membership of a social group. Not only do you have to become insistent in order to receive what was automatically given to the others; but your insistence confirms the improper nature of your residence. We do not tend to notice the assistance given to those whose residence is assumed. An assumption is assistance.

We have to fight against ideas and expectations about how academics appear. You walk into a lecture room with a white male professor. You feel the gaze land on him; you recede into the background, perhaps they assume you are his assistant. You have to work just to appear as a lecturer, an academic, a professor. We are returning to my starting point: diversity work is work. There is so much assistance we do not receive because our residence is not assumed. When we are included it is as if we have been 'given' something special; if they arrive on merit (that fantasy of arrival that transforms structural advantage into individual achievement), we arrive through diversity. And then: we are expected to be grateful for the good fortune of our arrival. So happiness becomes not only how we must appear, *but how we must narrate the very terms of our inclusion.*

What does this 'must' mean in practice? One time after giving a talk on whiteness, a white male professor in the audience said, 'but you're a professor!' You can hear the implication of this but: but look at you Professor Ahmed, look how far you have gone! How easily we can become poster children for diversity, how easily we can be held up as proof that women of colour are not held up. It is as if by virtue of our own arrival, we bring whiteness to an end. When women of colour become professors this is not the only kind of reaction we receive, from white male professors or from others. Heidi Mirza describes another kind of reaction: "a white male professor leaned into me at the celebration drinks and whispered bitterly in my ear, 'Well they are giving Chairs to anyone for anything these days'" (Mirza 2017: 43). These seem to be quite different reactions to the woman of colour professor, affectively and otherwise. In the first, the singular brown body becoming shiny happy evidence of inclusion. In the second, when a brown body arrives, her body is not elevated as value. She comes to embody the loss of value: when she can be a professor, anybody can. Different reactions can share a premise. In both cases diversity becomes a fiction: it is how whiteness is anxiously celebrated (as inclusive) or how whiteness is bitterly mourned (as loss).

Another time, I was at a reception. A white male professor (who was also a senior manager) came up to me, and asked me very crossly why I was always 'going on' about being a feminist killjoy. He murmured something about there being lots of women in senior management at the college. The implication was: there was nothing to complain about; we should be happy and grateful for the support given to our own progression. The same manager was also overheard complaining about students who were complaining about sexual harassment. I will return to complaint in the next section; but we can just note here how feminist complaint becomes a form of institutional disloyalty. You are not being affected in the right way. Not be happy and positive is to become difficult; to become a problem. You are not doing diversity in the right way.

You are not doing diversity in the right way: this sentence is a judgement that has consequences. We learn about diversity by learning these consequences. Being diversity means not doing diversity in some ways. You are supposed to be compliant, manageable, before you can become a manager. One woman of colour manager describes the narrowness of the requirements are:

> I think with a person of colour there's always a question of what's this woman is going to turn out like... they're nervous about appointing people of colour into senior positions....Because if I went in my Sari and wanted prayer time off and started rocking the boat and being a bit different and asserting my kind of culture I'm sure they'd take it differently.

Some forms of difference are heard as assertive, as 'rocking the boat,' as if you are only different because you are insistent on being different. The pressure not to 'assert your culture' is lived as a demand to pass or to integrate. Note how this pressure can be affective: you experience the potential nervousness as a threat; you try and avoid the nervous glance by not fulfilling its expectation. Maybe you don't wear a sari; you don't want prayer time off, and so on. Or maybe if you do these things, because not doing them is not an option, then you find others ways of not rocking the boat. I have called this labour of not rocking the boat *institutional passing*. Institutional passing would then include the work you do to pass *through* by passing *out* of an expectation: you try not to be the angry woman of colour, the trouble maker, that difficult person. You have to demonstrate that you are willing to ease the burden of your own difference.

Doing Diversity

When women of colour enter the institutions of whiteness we become symbols of diversity. And we have to do diversity as well as be diversity. Sometimes we do diversity because we are expected to do so, as I suggested in my introduction; as if doing follows being. But we also do diversity because of our commitments to gender equality and race equality. We do diversity, because we experience the gap between symbolic commitments to diversity and what is going on. We come up against walls. Diversity work could be described as a 'banging your head against a brick wall job,' to quote from one practitioner I interviewed. To those who don't come up against it, a wall does not appear: a university might be experienced as happy as its mission statement, as willing as its equality statement. If a wall does not appear, but we talk about walls, it can appear that we are making it up; as if the barriers we come up against are just a fault of our own perception, as if we are the ones who are in the way of our own inclusion. To talk about walls in this way is to refuse to be diversity in the right way; it is to refuse to become happy symbols of inclusion.

You can rock the boat by talking about how you can rock the boat. Even talking about power within organisations means you are encountered as difficult, willful and obtrusive. Black feminism and feminism of colour involves, for me, a certain kind of stance: we are willing to rock the boat. Being willing to rock the boat means being willing to be willful. Willfulness becomes a collective psychic and political resource. Alice Walker describes a 'womanist' in the following way: 'A black feminist or feminist of color... Usually referring to outrageous, audacious, courageous or *willful* behavior. Wanting to know more and in greater depth than is considered 'good' for one... Responsible. In charge. *Serious*' (2005: xi, emphases in original). Alice Walker suggests here that the word *willful* conveys what being a Black feminist or feminist of colour is all about. As Black feminists and feminists of colour we might acquire certain qualities because of what we have to fight against. The very behaviours that are dismissed as weakness or immaturity become not only strengths but signs of not being willing to be subordinate. We are willing to rock the boat, that boat is whiteness: reproduced by being held steady.

Trying to steady a ship, to stop a rocky motion, can be how so much is concealed about the institutions that employ us. More recently I have been involved in a project of trying to challenge sexual harassment as an institutional problem. I supported students in testifying in multiple enquiries into sexual harassment at the college at which I worked. Eventually this work led to my own resignation: I became exhausted by how much it had taken not to get very far. I shared the reasons for my resignation on my blog, which was effectively the first time anyone had referred in public to what had been going on.[2] I will address the significance of being the 'leak' in due course. But note that as a woman of colour professor I have now unbecome a professor. Maybe stories of women of colour becoming professors need to be supplemented by unbecoming stories!

I would argue that how I ended up doing this work was a consequence of my position and stance as a feminist of colour. As women academics we often end up being the ones who listen to students especially when they come to our offices with stories of harassment and abuse; pastoral care is more often relegated to women. We are willing to hear. But while white feminism might prioritise the issue of sexual harassment at the level of supporting students with pastoral care, given the emphasis on women's career progression, other issues such as the complicity of an organisation in enabling harassment are less likely to be dealt with. White feminism as an approach seemed to be about working within the framework offered by the organisation; with an emphasis on dealing with the problem 'in house,' and with a concern about protecting the organisation's reputation from potential or anticipated damage. This is another version of 'not rocking the boat'.

It is important for me to qualify here what I mean by 'white feminism.' I do not mean simply the feminism produced by white women, though 'white feminism' does refer to the feminism which assumes white women's experiences as the norm (see Lorde 1984). I am trying to suggest that 'white feminism' can also summarise a relation *to* an organisation. Whiteness itself could be understood here as an aspirational; as what you are supposed to aspire to be, as how you would move up the organisation. So 'white feminism' is a way of thinking about how liberal

---

[2]In May 2016, I wrote a blog explaining the reasons for my resignation (https://feministkilljoys.com/2016/05/30/resignation/). The story was then picked up by the mainstream press. The college's initial response was damage limitation. I would argue that diversity often takes form as damage limitation. The response made reference to events we had organised under the auspices of the Centre of Feminist Research because they were not addressing the problem as evidence that it was addressing the problem.

feminism has a racial dynamic: how an emphasis on being included in existing structures, on being promoted within those structures, leaves the structures in place, including whiteness itself as a structure. Moving up becomes not only a vertical promise, but a system that reinforces existing ideas of agency: Black and brown women become the ones who are 'helped up' the ladder by white women. Advancement of individual women also becomes understood as the advancement of gender equality.[3] Many of the barriers faced by women of colour are racial barriers: this is the point of the intersection (Crenshaw 1989). White feminism might also refer to the technologies which transform 'gender equality,' into something that an organisation can be judged as doing well. At the same time that we were campaigning to get the college to take sexual harassment and sexual misconduct more seriously, members of the college were applying for an ATHENA Swan award. We need to learn from the fact that it is possible to have an institutional problem with sexual harassment and sexual misconduct and receive an award for gender equality.

I am not dismissing this kind of feminist work as mere institutional complicity by any means. There can be strategic benefits to working in such a way: you are more likely to sit on meetings which influence the direction of policy if you talk about gender equality as an organisational achievement. But there are risks: you are also less likely to speak out about what is deemed potentially damaging to the organisation's reputation. Indeed I learnt from the fact that some of the most critical responses to my act of speaking out came from white feminists. I was called by one 'unprofessional,' and my actions 'rash.' I think it is worth noting here how professional norms of conduct are so often about 'keeping a lid on it'. Silence becomes loyalty. Sexual harassment is treated even by professional feminists as dirty laundry: what should not be aired in public. We might need to become unprofessional feminists and let it all out.

On reflection it was my own experience of diversity work that led to me to realise that working 'in house' would not transform the master's house. The research I had previously done on racism and diversity

---

[3]See http://www.ecu.ac.uk/equality-charters/athena-swan/.

within universities became home work for what was to come. It allowed me to be more attuned to the students' experience of the role of the organisation (and not just individuals) in perpetuating a culture of harassment; and it allowed me to diagnose and challenge the institutional response as a means by which the institution was being reproduced. In *On Being Included*, I discuss how 'she becomes a problem because she keeps exposing a problem' (2012: 63). I also discussed how the work we did to address race inequality was used as evidence of race equality. In trying to address the problem of sexual harassment as an institutional problem, we became a problem all over again. And the work we did to challenge the problem of how the organisation was not addressing the problem was used by the organisation as evidence they were addressing the problem.

When you speak out about harassment publicly which I eventually did, you are treated as a leak: drip, drip. The organisational response is to treat you as the cause of the damage. They try to mop up the spillage, and make use of happy diversity to do so; they put shiny new policies in place; fill holes left by departures without any reference to what went on before; they talk of their commitment, how they do not 'tolerate' the kind of behaviour even when it has been revealed as having gone on for years. Non performativity functions as a mechanism, again.

Doing this work on sexual harassment has led me to a new project that I have only just begun on complaint. I am interested in exploring how those who make complaints, or try to make complaints, about racism, sexual harassment and bullying within institutions are treated. Complaint is another form of diversity work. The very first testimony I collected made use of the expression 'rocking the boat,' that had come up so much earlier in my research into racism and diversity. Let me share with you how this expression came up:

> I was repeatedly told that 'rocking the boat' or 'making waves' would affect my career in the future and that I would ruin the department for everyone else. I was told if I did put in a complaint I would never be able to work in the university and that is was likely I wouldn't get a job elsewhere.

Here complaining becomes a form of self-damage as well as damage to others, ruining a department no less. This student goes onto to describe how the pressure not to complain is exerted: 'In just one day I was subjected to eight hours of gruelling meetings and questioning, almost designed to break me and stop me from taking the complaint any further. We were subjected to an aggressive two hour long meeting with the head of department who repeatedly told us we needed to laugh it off'. The suggestion to 'laugh it off' is a call for the very compliance that enables the harassment to be reproduced. If diversity work is a banging your head against a brick wall job, then a wall can be what comes down on you like a ton of bricks. The word harass derives from the French *harasser* 'tire out, vex'. Those who complain about harassment are harassed. Harassment is how someone is stopped or almost stopped by being worn down. This is how power often works: you don't have to stop people from doing something; you just make it harder for them to do something.

We can place these two uses of the expression 'rocking the boat,' alongside each other. They throw light on each other. Sometimes you rock the boat just because of how you are perceived to be; any difference is registered as trying to destabilise things, to stop things from being as they are. Not rocking the boat is about minimising the signs of difference, that labour I referred to earlier as institutional passing. Complaints about harassment are also registered as 'rocking the boat.' These uses can be related. Difference from something is heard as a complaint about something whether or not it is. We can summarise this as a finding: *difference as complaint*. And then making a complaint is framed as a failure of integration: as not being willing to put aside your differences, as a failure to love, a professor say, or a centre, or a college, who are aligned as the ones who are hurt.

The ones who are hurt: we are learning here about how injury is deflected by being seen as directed. In *On Being Included* (2012) I noted how racism is often treated as an injury to an organisation's reputation for being diverse. Racism even becomes an injury to whiteness. Sexism is often framed as an injury to an organisation's reputation for being good at gender equality. Sexism becomes an injury to men.

For women of colour, racism and sexism intersect in our everyday experiences, as well as our experiences of institutional life. The point of this intersection matters. By pointing racism and sexism out, we become the source of injury at least twice; double the trouble. If speaking about racism and sexism damages the institution, we need to cause damage. And the institutional response takes the form of damage limitation. I would argue that this is how diversity often takes institutional form: *damage limitation.*

We are also learning how integration, that heavy word, so often raised up as a national ideal, is lived as a requirement to steady the ship, to smooth things out, to cover things over; it is about what you cannot say, do, be in order to stay put. The expression 'rocking the boat,' refers not only to those who cause disruption, but implies those who cause disruption are doing so with malicious intent, as if you are just trying to make things harder for others. Speaking of racism is often heard as making things harder for others.

I am speaking of racism in a seminar. A white woman comes up to me afterwards and puts her arm next to mine. We are almost the same colour, she says. No difference, no difference. You wouldn't really know you were any different to me, she says. The very talk about racism becomes a fantasy that invents difference. She smiles, as if the proximity of our arms was evidence that the racism of which I was speaking was an invention, as if our arms told another story. She smiles, as if our arms are in a smooth seamless sympathy. I say nothing. Perhaps my arm speaks by withdrawing.

We can rock the boat by turning up. We can rock the boat by speaking up. I am speaking to one of my interviewees—a woman of colour—about racism. It is the only such discussion I had in my formal interviews, although it took place after the interview. We are talking of those little encounters, and their very big effects. It is 'off tape', we are just talking, recognising each other, as you do, in how we recognise racism in those everyday encounters you have with people who can't handle it, the idea of it. She says, 'They always say to me that you reduce everything to racism.' This has been implied to me, and said to me, many times. Racism becomes your paranoia. Of course, it's a way of saying that racism doesn't really exist in the way you say it does.

As if we had to invent racism to explain our own feeling of exclusion, as if racism was our way of not being responsible for the places we do not or cannot go. It is a form of racism to say that racism does not exist. I think we know this.

But we keep on going on, we keep doing the work, using the word racism; we get so used to rocking the boat that we have learned to keep ourselves steady. And we collect more and more data. We collect responses, often visceral alarmed responses to our bodies, our work. One time quite a while back in 1999 I was presenting a paper 'Embodying Strangers,' in which I referred to Audre Lorde's (1984) description, her quite extraordinary description, of racism on a New York subway. One white woman spoke in the question time with anger about how I hadn't considered the white woman's feelings as if this was some sort of neutral situation and that to account for it we have to give an account from each point of view. Racism becomes the requirement to think of racism with sympathy, racism as just another view; the racist as the one with feelings, too. I think she spoke with anger because she heard my speech as anger.

Pointing out racism within feminist spaces causes a special kind of difficulty, as if you are being mean or unkind; or as if you are depriving others of solidarity and connection. Another time, much later in 2011, I drew on bell hooks' description of how feminists of colour seem to cause tension without saying anything. She gives us a scenario. I suspect she has been here many times, I have been there too, so I will share it again: 'a group of white feminist activists who do not know one another may be present at a meeting to discuss feminist theory. They may feel bonded on the basis of shared womanhood, but the atmosphere will noticeably change when a woman of colour enters the room. The white women will become tense, no longer relaxed, no longer celebratory' (hooks 2000: 56). It is not just that feelings are 'in tension', but that the tension is located somewhere: in being felt by some bodies, it is attributed as caused by another, who comes to be felt as apart from the group, as getting in the way of its organic enjoyment and solidarity. The woman of colour is attributed as the cause of becoming tense, which is also the loss of a shared atmosphere (or we could say sharing the experience of loss is how the atmosphere is shared). As a woman of colour you do not have to say anything to cause tension. When I drew on this quote from bell hooks more recently a white woman came up to me afterwards expressing not so much anger but hurt at hooks' description, and at my uncritical use of hook's description, for the implication that all white women make women of colour 'the problem'. There was no 'all' used in the example, but this does not mean someone cannot hear the example as *all*. When that is all they can hear, they hear you as saying all. And in being heard as saying all, whatever you say, you became a problem, *all over again*.

When racism is understood as our creation, *we become responsible for not bringing it into existence*. The idea that race equality is a positive duty can thus translate very quickly into an institutional duty for Black and Minority Ethnic staff not to dwell on the 'negative experiences' of racism. The institutional duty is also what I have called a 'happiness duty' (Ahmed 2010, 2017). To use the language of racism is to risk not being heard. We do keep using the language of racism, whatever they so or they do. But keeping on using the language does not mean you can get the message through. As I pointed out one diversity workers talk about their institutional work is through the metaphor of the brick wall. Anti-racist work can feel like banging your head against the brick wall. The wall keeps its place, so it is you that gets sore. Being and doing diversity can mean becoming a sore point, but the soreness of that point is either hidden from their view (if we go along with the happiness of the image, which sometimes we 'do do') or attributed to us (as if we talk about walls *because* we are sore).

Conclusion: Support Systems

It can be difficult to rock the boat, however much we become used to steadying ourselves, or however much we become used to living with a rocky motion. And feminism of colour matters within higher education as a resource to draw upon, so that when we do rock the boat, we do not feel all alone. I still remember when I first met Heidi Mirza and became part of a collection, *Black British Feminism*, published 20 years ago in 1997. Becoming part of that collection was a life-line. It helped us to find each other. Sometimes we can miss each other in the sea of whiteness, despite how it might appear that we stand out. Once we find each other so much else becomes possible. You get to share wall stories. It is so important to share these stories, of coming up against the same things. Our frustration is a historical record. To share your experience of walls does not bring the wall down, but it does help you to keep going. We need to become each other's support system. There is so much assistance given to those who residence is assumed, as I have noted. We have to work with each other to navigate institutions whose hostility is masked by diversity: who want our smiling faces rather than our beings, who want us only insofar as we are accommodating. We cite each other; we bring each other into existence.[4]

Just by refusing to be quite so accommodating we are rocking the boat. We can turn how we are perceived as being into what we are committed to doing. If you think we rock the boat, we rock the boat. Who knows what we might yet throw up!

References

Ahmed, S. (2000). *Strange Encounters: Embodied Others in Post-coloniality.* London: Routledge.

Ahmed, S. (2010). *The Promise of Happiness.* Durham: Duke University Life.

Ahmed, S. (2012). *On Being Included: Racism and Diversity in Institutional Life.* Durham: Duke University Press.

Ahmed, S. (2017). *Living a Feminist Life.* Durham: Duke University Press.

Alexander, M. J. (2006). *Pedagogies of Crossing: Meditations on Feminism, Sexual Politics, Memory, and the Sacred.* Durham, NC: Duke University Press.

Crenshaw, K. (1989). Demarginalizing the Intersection of Race and Sex: A Black Feminist Politics of Antidiscrimination Doctrine, Feminist Theory and Anti-racist Politics. *University of Chicago Legal Forum, 1989*(1), 139–167.

hooks, b. (2000). *Feminist Theory: From Margin to Centre.* London: Pluto Press.

---

[4]In this chapter I have only cited Black feminists and feminists of colour.

Lorde, A. (1984). *Sister Outsider: Essays and Speeches*. Trumansburg: The Crossing Press.

Mirza, H. (Ed.). (1997). *Black British Feminism*. London: Routledge.

Mirza, H. (2015). Decolonizing Higher Education: Black Feminism and the Intersectionality of Race and Gender. *Journal of a Feminist Scholarship, 7–8*, 1–12.

Mirza, H. (2017). 'One in a Million': A Journey of a Post-colonial Woman of Colour in the White Academy. In D. Gabriel & S. A. Tate (Eds.), *Inside the Ivory Tower: Narratives of Women of Colour Surviving and Thriving in Academia*. Stoke-On-Trent: Trentham.

Mohanty, C. T. (2003). *Feminism Without Borders: Decolonizing Theory, Practicing Solidarity*. Durham: Duke University Press.

Muhs, G. G. y., Niemann, Y. F., González, C. G., & Harris, A. P. (Eds.). (2012). *Presumed Incompetent: The Intersections of Race and Class for Women in Academia*. Boulder: University Press of Colorado.

Puwar, N. (2004). *Space Invaders: Race, Gender and Bodies Out of Place*. Oxford: Berg.

Walker, A. (2005). *In Search of Our Mothers Gardens*. Phoenix: New Edition.

20

Leadership for Race and Social Justice in Higher Education

Uvanney Maylor

Introduction

The UK Equality Act[1] (2010) stipulates that education institutions should take account of race equality in their employment procedures and processes. I was prompted to explore the Equality Act as an instrument of employment in terms of how it influences and/or assists higher education institutions in promoting race equality in university academic leadership positions by a comment I received from a White governor of a higher education institution, who in questioning my job title and role at a university graduation said: 'You do not look like a professor'. In return I asked the governor: 'What does a professor look like?'

---

[1] The 2010 Equality Act brought together under one act previous equality legislation namely: Race Relations Act, 1968, 1975; Sex Discrimination Act, 1975; Disability Discrimination Act, 1995; Race Relations (Amendment) Act 2000 and public sector duties. Its purpose is to reduce/challenge inequalities and increase equality of opportunity for all groups.

U. Maylor (✉)
University of Bedfordshire, Bedford, Bedfordshire, UK
e-mail: Uvanney.Maylor@beds.ac.uk

© The Author(s) 2018
J. Arday and H. S. Mirza (eds.), *Dismantling Race in Higher Education*,
https://doi.org/10.1007/978-3-319-60261-5_20

To which he laughingly replied: 'White, middle class and male'. Though the governor was laughing, he was serious that his perception of a professor was a White male, as he went on to describe the White male professor he had in mind, which also included age and the type of clothing he envisioned the professor wearing. The governor's comments led me to question how often he voiced such views, in what contexts, why did he not find his views problematic and had he participated in race equality training? I was further concerned as to whether this governor had ever considered the organisational consequences of Black staff being absent from leadership positions in higher education.

Singh and Kwhali (2015) question whether the colour of staff in leadership positions matters and who decides whether it is important or not. My encounter with the university governor referred to above would suggest that the colour of staff in leadership positions matters greatly to university governors. The governor's expressed colour-conscious leadership behaviour echoed in his preference for a White male professor could have been articulated owing to a fear of change of the status quo. In that moment I was viewed as a threat and if I was not cut down through verbal comment, the potential was there for others like me to become entrenched in senior positions and ultimately dismantle the White leadership hierarchy this governor was so content with. Arguably, maintaining the status quo is easier because this means that institutions and leadership teams do not have to make adjustments in their thinking as to who or what constitutes an ideal leader. Moreover when ethnicity is factored in:

> Whites often attempt to determine what kind of Blackness and other forms of difference are acceptable, how that Blackness and difference should be expressed, and how one's differences get one disqualified or excluded from Whiteness. (Dixson and Fasching-Varner 2009, cited by Hayes and Juárez 2012: 9)

In my exchange with the university governor, it was made clear that my Blackness (and gender) represented in the role of a professor was unacceptable in higher education. As university governors are part of university decision making processes one can surmise that governors such as the one I encountered play an influential role in maintaining a White staffing profile (certainly with regard to appointing a vice-chancellor) and which is more reflective of the society in which they prefer to co-exist. What is disconcerting about my exchange with the university governor is the silence from White academic staff who heard his remarks. None commented on the governor's racism despite their familiarisation with the Equality 2010 Act through their own roles on appointment panels. Perhaps through their own racialisation and mis-education they did not understand that the governor's words could be construed as racism because the comments were not overtly racist. Therefore they determined that they heard nothing they felt they could challenge. Osler (2015) argues that "if the word racism is reserved for expressions of hate speech or physical violence, but institutional or structural racism and processes of racialisation remain hidden, racism itself goes unchallenged" (p. 258; see also Pilkington 2013). One of the reasons such racism is not challenged by White educators is the act of 'dysconscious racism' which is:

> a form of racism that tacitly accepts White norms and privileges. It is … an impaired consciousness or distorted way of thinking about race as compared to, for example, critical consciousness. Uncritical ways of thinking about racial inequity accept certain culturally sanctioned assumptions, myths and beliefs that justify the social and economic advantages White people have as a result of subordinating diverse others. (King 2007: 73)

I experienced the exchange with the university governor as one of dysconscious racism, but should I have been surprised by his response and attempt to hide his disdain through laughter? After all, his description of a university professor is largely accurate. The majority (12,420 or 69.2%) of professors are White males compared with 345 (or 1.7%) BME (Black and Minority Ethnic) female professors (ECU 2016). When the BME figure is disaggregated Black women account for just 18 professorial posts in English higher education. Across the university sector there is "no … unanimity on what a professor is, should be, does, or should do, nor on what degree of experience or what level or equality of achievement the role or grade requires or demands" (Evans 2015: 682). So it could be asked, what is wrong with the governor's assumption? The problem is that research consistently suggests that BME staff experience difficulties in being promoted to leadership positions in academia (Leathwood et al. 2009; ECU 2011; Bhopal 2014; Singh and Kwahli 2015). The appointment in 2015 of the first and only Black woman (Baronness Valerie Amos)[2] to lead a university underscores both the lack of recognition of Black leadership potential in English higher education, and the uniqueness of this achievement, as only 22% of Vice Chancellors at English higher education institutions are female (Jarboe 2016). While the appointment of Valerie Amos should be applauded it is worth noting that in contrast to the USA (even with the persistence of racism and sexism) the UK is years behind in appointing a Black woman to lead a university (see Jean-Marie et al. 2009b; Jones et al. 2012). Drucker (2005) contends that "the spirit of an organisation is created from the top" (3). As there is only one Black female university Vice Chancellor in the UK, what does this say about the spirit of English higher education institutions? That they are devoid of Black spirit?

Racism has been shown to persistently impact on the positioning and employment experiences of Black staff (EHRC 2016; Ashe and Nazroo 2016), but rather than racism (UCU 2016) accounting for the disparity in Black leadership appointments in higher education, Jarboe (2016) blames 'unconscious bias' and observes that, "few people set out to consciously discriminate but all of us have unconscious biases that influence our decisions. This often results in people appointing and promoting others like themselves" (24). The problem with such a view is that entrenched conscious biases among decision makers and/or preference for a White male leadership hierarchy in higher education go unchallenged, and therefore remain perpetual and steadfast because they are considered unconscious and at the same time biases held by everyone. Further the attribution of unconscious bias for the under-representation of Black leadership staff is particularly problematic as it accounts for the lack of challenge and therefore removal of negative perceptions about the leadership abilities of Black people, which are to a large extent

---

[2]Baroness Valerie Amos was appointed Director (Vice Chancellor equivalent) of the School of African and Oriental Studies, University of London in September 2015. http://www.independent.co.uk/news/uk/home-news/uk-gains-its-first-ever-female-black-university-leader-10352821.html.

informed by Bourdieu's (2010; Bourdieu and Passeron 1994) cultural capital theses and stereotyped views of Black people as uneducatable, not having leadership abilities and consequently not being construed as 'authentic' leaders (Walumbwa et al. 2008) as informed by long discredited racist scientific theorists such as Jensen (1969; see particularly Miele 2004 and Flynn 2012 who dedicated his book to Jensen). I have lost count of the number of times when I have been in staff meetings and the excuse of Black people lacking cultural capital has been used to justify a White leadership hierarchy.

It could be argued that the underrepresentation of Black women in senior positions reproduces assumptions of limited competence (Leadership Foundation 2015) and if this is an overarching thought, it can produce a vicious circle of being overlooked for senior positions, or being misrecognised as a junior despite being in a senior position. While attention has been given to the under-representation of women leaders in universities (Jarobe 2016) and the need for womens' academic leadership potential to be developed (Gallant 2014; see also Dopson et al.'s 2016 literature review concerning gender and diversity in higher education leadership development programmes in the UK, Australia, the USA, South Africa and New Zealand), evidence suggests that there is less emphasis in UK higher education institutions with regard to ethnicity and leadership including an understanding of factors undermining progression (Bhopal and Jackson 2013; Miller 2016), strategies for success (Bhopal and Brown 2016) and/or the value of ethnically diverse leadership in universities (Walumbwa et al. 2008). This is despite the fact that higher education institutions in England have been required since 2013 (as part of the funding they receive from the Higher Education Funding Council for England -HEFCE) to address the lack of diversity in their leadership teams and governing bodies (discussed in detail in Jarobe 2016).

Whiteness and Social Justice for Leadership

As an ideology social justice seeks to challenge the status quo and create a new hierarchy (Smith 2012). Striving for social justice in leadership positions requires a "paradigmatic shift from indifference or ignorance … to an embracement of said issues" (Jean-Marie et al. 2009a: 5). For such a shift to occur Whiteness as power needs to be interrogated because as Kilomba observes:

> Academia is not a neutral location. It is a white space where black people have been denied the privilege to speak. Historically it is a white space where we have been voiceless and where white scholars have developed theoretical discourses that formally constructed us [Black people] as the inferior 'Other', placing Africans in absolute subordination to the white subject. (Kilomba 2010: 27, author emphasis)

Ahmed (2012) contends within academia "institutional Whiteness describes an institutional habitat, [where] Whiteness recedes into the background" (39). In the university this means Whiteness and the reproduction of White privilege becomes commonplace and unnoticeable (Leonardo 2004; Murji and Solomos 2016; Bhopal 2018). This also speaks to contentions of authenticity in academia which is associated with Whiteness (Archer 2008). Social justice is considered necessary if education institutions are to recognise and respect diverse leaders (McKinsey 2014; Alexander and Arday 2015) and the intercultural knowledge which they bring to their leadership teams (Gay 2010). Social justice practice seeks to address issues of marginalisation which are reproduced through the education process (Osler 2016). A social justice perspective provides a useful analytical framework for exploring educational leadership challenges in higher education. Social justice and equality are human rights principles (Osler 2015).

Educational social justice speaks to issues of fairness and representativeness which requires higher education leaders to be representative of the national population. As the UK is ethnically diverse (ONS 2018) students in higher education should be able to see themselves in their higher education leaders, but all too often the opposite is true. Yet McKinsey (2014) maintains that leadership teams that take time to reflect on their ethnic make-up are more likely to adopt solutions to address racial inequality and which will assist in promoting racial equality at senior levels (see also Singh and Kwhali 2015). There is more at stake here than just promoting racial equality at senior levels. A social justice perspective emphasises the need for higher education institutions to consider how leadership inequalities are maintained through the ideology of meritocracy (that is leadership positions are awarded according to merit and have to be earned rather than taken as a given). There is a need to critically examine the omnipresent nature of Whiteness, how it is operationalised (including values, expectations, practices) by White bodies in academia and the role that higher education institutions play in this normalisation, reproduction and legitimation process by for example, utilising HEFCE and institutional data to infer that there are insufficient numbers of Black people with the requisite qualifications and/or experience to apply for senior posts and/or to be promoted. Alongside this it is imperative that notions of meritocracy are juxtaposed with notions of (White) entitlement (Bourdieu 2001) and being more suitable and deserving of senior academic positions.

In advocating a social justice framework in higher education employment, it is recognised that the term social justice is not unproblematic either in education or political terms. According to Reay (2012) the term social justice has been used "ideologically by the Right to both countermand and undermine the equalities agenda and by governments and policymakers to sanitise and sweeten neoliberal policies" (ix). Furthermore a commitment to social justice has not created more equal power structures (Biesta 2012). Instead a power imbalance remains with the scales of leadership firmly tilted towards White leaders (Jarboe 2016) and begs questions such as, how many Black staff are part of their university executive decision-making group, and what credentials are needed for entry? If social justice exists in higher education acquiring a leadership position should be informed by a level playing field. The process should not just be considered fair on paper, but experienced as such.

Clearly, purely in terms of numbers, we will never get to a position where Black staff are as commonplace as White staff in higher education because of their numbers in the population as a whole (ONS 2018). However, if social justice is enacted in higher education one would expect to get to a stage where at all levels of higher education institutions from the very top to middle and junior levels of leadership Black staff occupy important leadership positions such that no heads are turned when a Black staff member occupies a leadership position, and equally important, that they are not deemed to be an 'imposter' (Trotman 2009). For this to happen it is not just an understanding of how dominant racial ideologies (Picower 2009) are rationalised and maintained which is necessary, but also a commitment to unlearning deficit notions about Black people.

Re-thinking Black Educational Leadership

In re-thinking Black academic/senior leadership I draw here on Portelli and Campell-Stephens (2009) African-centred concept of 'servant leadership' which puts "service before leadership" and prioritises the people/community and their needs that the leader aims to serve (47). In this respect the leader becomes "both leader and servant at the same time" (47). Briefly:

> Servant leadership is … much more about collegiate ways of working, much more about building [communal] capacity, much more about distributive leadership in its true sense, and also much more about seeing yourself as a leader within the community as opposed to a leader in one unit of that community. (49)

Moreover 'servant leadership' is "service without the servitude" and is considered "an empowering and ennobling position for both leader and those who are served" (52). 'Servant leadership' is underpinned by a commitment to pursuing/achieving equity and to creating "space for human beings to be human, in the spirit of Ubuntu" (54). It is argued that Black and global majority people are predisposed to 'servant leadership' because of their cultural backgrounds/upbringing and experiences of racial domination (namely slavery, colonialism and imperialism). Thus emphasis is placed on shared leadership rather than domination. Certainly it is important for me as part of my commitment to working with and giving back to the community (students and educators), to support and invite the views of others, rather than dictate or exclude. If university leadership positions are to become more diverse this requires an understanding of "servant leadership qualities and styles" and what it means for Black people to "lead authentically" (49) and how this is enacted in practice (see Avolio et al. 2009). Equally important, university recruitment teams and human resource management departments would need opportunities to become critically conscious of the ways in which Black people have historically been (e.g. through slavery, colonisation) and continue to be oppressed (e.g. through lower paid, more part-time employment—ECU 2015; under valuing of their qualifications—UK NARIC,[3] n.d. online). It is also necessary for recruitment teams to analyse, reflect on and to challenge their taken for granted knowledge about Black people, as well as understanding how negative perceptions of leadership ability is reproduced through the education process and perceptions of Black cultural capital. Re-thinking of Black staff as education leaders also requires a state of mind and practice where Black staff in leadership positions is considered normal and Black leadership abilities/skills are not questioned to the detriment of the employment of Black staff in leadership roles. Moreover, a reassessment of effective leadership would warrant recognition of a diverse leadership workforce as being compatible with delivering education.

There is no time like the present where such considerations are more salient. Higher education institutions in the UK do not exist in a vacuum. They exist in a neo-liberal marketisation climate of profitability, student fees and student/consumer choice. With the government lifting the cap on the number of UK and EU domiciled undergraduate students universities can recruit, English universities are experiencing greater student choice as to which universities will benefit from their student fee income (Adams and Weale 2015). More registered and retained students' means more income for universities. With greater availability of university places, there was a government expectation that this would lead to greater student social mobility (Johnson 2015), however, universities would seem to be more concerned about student experience as reflected in national student survey (NSS[4]) scores as this, impacts on national assessments of higher education institutions. Institutions worry about negative NSS assessments for fear that such

---

[3]UK NARIC 'is the designated United Kingdom national agency for the recognition and comparison of international qualifications and skills. It performs this official function on behalf of the UK Government' for individuals and employers (UK NARIC online).

[4]NSS—The national student survey is a census of all undergraduate students in English universities in their third year of study. It is commissioned by the Higher Education Funding Council in England (more information is available at http://www.thestudentsurvey.com/about.php).

assessments will have a direct correlation on recruiting new students. However, a key consideration for many students in their recruitment and retention is not just university location or the course studied, but who is teaching their chosen course, and also the ideologies that persist within the university. Hence many Black students are not just questioning why is my curriculum White (Peters 2015) and my professor not Black? (Black 2014), but demanding that higher education institutions become decolonised education spaces with protests such as Rhodes must fall (relates to calls for the removal of the statue of Cecil Rhodes from the University of Cape Town, which occurred in 2015). If a change to the underrepresentation of Black professorial staff and/or Black staff in senior executive positions does not occur, universities may very well find that the Black student income they rely on to function effectively becomes depleted, if non-existent.

Changing the Status Quo

Shifting race norms and challenging structural exclusion at the same time as trying to remove attitudinal barriers which are preventing the employment of Black staff in professorial positions and other senior leadership roles remains problematic in the UK. Are there insights which can be drawn from the United States? While not specifically related to the employment of Black staff in academia, Banks (2016) offers a perspective as to how the leadership of an organisation can change from being always White to having a more ethnically diverse leadership. Reviewing the factors that enabled nine People of Colour to become president of the American Educational Research Association[5] (AERA—a predominantly White organisation[6]) between 1995 and 2016/2017 and the establishment of special interest groups with a focus on diversity, Banks (2016:

---

[5]The American Educational Research Association is the largest national interdisciplinary research association devoted to the scientific study of education and learning.

[6]The Banks (2016: 156) article referred to in this chapter includes AERA membership figures by ethnicity, which shows that, in 2015, 64.2% of the membership of AERA was recorded as White, non Hispanic.

155) associated this achievement and "institutionalisation of diversity within AERA" to "historic (e.g. desegregation and civil rights movements) demographic changes within American society". Changes which also enabled other scholars of Colour to attain "structural inclusion into predominantly White mainstream research and scholarly organisations and societies" as "members of committees and governing boards, publishing in the official journals and books, participating in conference sessions, and being elected to the presidency of these organisations" (Banks 2016: 150). Following a lecture at the UCL Institute of Education, University of London in May 2016 (which I attended), Professor Banks advocated this strategy (of joining special interest groups, committees) as a way of non-American minority ethnic scholars acquiring leadership positions in the AERA, and making the AERA leadership more ethnically diverse from an international perspective.

Returning to the changes made to the AERA leadership it can be concluded that over a 21 year period (1995–2016), having nine out of 21 presidents being represented by eight African Americans and one Latina is testament to the changing inclusion within the AERA and accepted scholarship and diverse epistemological knowledge of People of Colour by White academia. That said, it is evident that ethnicity changes in the presidential leadership of a once all-White institution have coincided with the AERA membership becoming more ethnically diverse from 7% in 1975 to approx 31% in 2015 (calculated from AERA membership figures in Banks 2016).

Drawing attention to the presidential leadership of the AERA might be considered unfair especially when the British equivalent to the AERA, BERA (British Educational Research Association) has never had a president at the helm from a minority ethnic background, and AERA presidents are voted for/elected by the AERA membership; it is not an appointed role. However, what the focus on the AERA demonstrates quite clearly is how it is possible (albeit over a prolonged period of time) to challenge stereotypes about Black leadership potential and transform the leadership of an organisation from all-White to ethnically diverse, and for such diversity to become accepted as normal practice. This is what needs to happen in UK higher education. Social justice in leadership requires more than a policy/institutional commitment to diversity.

It must be reflected in practice and should not just be viewed in terms of paper exercises such as carrying out equality impact assessments.[7] The recently introduced Race Equality Charter (ECU online) which higher education institutions are going to have to demonstrate they meet the criteria for if they are to be awarded race equality status, means that institutions will have to consider where there are gaps in their minority ethnic staff and student representation and progression and identify strategies for overcoming challenges and addressing areas of weakness. But given that many institutions do not have Athena SWAN status, which requires institutions for example, to "recognise a solid foundation for eliminating gender bias and developing an inclusive culture that values all staff" to achieve the bronze award,[8] and this one might argue is more easily achieveable, why would they take time to apply for the Race Equality Charter award which has a specific remit in addressing racial inequality in employment? However, such time and effort is necessary if the leadership capabilities of Black staff are to be valued such that they become "part of the fabric" (Garces and Cogburn 2015: 848) of what higher education institutions do.

To conclude, we have reached a stage in 2018 whereby excuses cannot continue to be made for the underrepresentation of Black staff in leadership positions. To address this problem it should be a compulsory requirement for staff at all levels (including recruitment and promotion panels) and university governors to participate in dysconscious racism and Whiteness as power training, and for their knowledge and understanding and how they employ race equality in practice to be regularly tested and updated to ensure that race equality becomes embedded and embodied throughout academia. Ultimately, this will assist in the appointment, progression and retention of Black staff in senior positions who are able to share their "skills, knowledge and experience" (Valerie Amos, online) to the advantage of staff and students alike.

---

[7]Equality impact assessments are an established tool for demonstrating due regard to the public sector equality duty which is required by law but EIA is not a legal requirement in England (ECU online, accessed 1 July 2016); available at http://www.ecu.ac.uk/guidance-resources/governance-and-policies/equality-impact-assessment/.

[8]There are three awards (bronze, silver and gold) which apply to the Athena SWAN and each stage has more enhanced requirements in order to achieve the specific stage award.

References

Adams, R., & Weale, S. (2015). *Record Number of University Admissions After Cap Lifted.* https://www.theguardian.com/education/2015/aug/13/record-number-university-admissions-cap-a-levels. Accessed 1 July 2015.

Ahmed, S. (2012). *On Being Included: Racism & Diversity in Institutional Life.* London: Duke University Press.

Alexander, C., & Arday, J. (Eds.). (2015). *Aiming Higher: Race, Inequality and Diversity in the Academy.* London: Runnymede Trust.

Archer, L. (2008). The New Neoliberal Subjects? Young/er Academics' Constructions of Professional Identity. *Journal of Education Policy, 23*(3), 265–285.

Ashe, S., & Nazroo, J. (2016). *Equality, Diversity and Racism in the Workplace: A Qualitative Analysis of the 2015 Race at Work Survey.* Manchester: Centre on Dynamics of Ethnicity, University of Manchester.

Avolio, B., Walumbwa, F., & Weber, T. (2009). Leadership, Current Theories, Research and Future Directions. *Annual Review of Psychology, 60*, 421–449.

Banks, J. A. (2016). Expanding the Epistemological Terrain: Increasing Equity and Diversity Within the American Educational Research Association. *Educational Researcher, 45*(2), 149–158.

Bhopal, K. (2014). *The Experience of BME Academics in Higher Education: Aspirations in the Face of Inequality.* Stimulus Paper. London: Leadership Foundation for Higher Education.

Bhopal, K. (2018). *White Privilege: The Myth of a Post-Racial Society.* Bristol: Policy Press.

Bhopal, K., & Brown, H. (2016). *Black and Minority Ethnic Leaders: Support Networks and Strategies for Success in Higher Education.* London: Leadership Foundation.

Bhopal, K., & Jackson, J. (2013). *The Experiences of Black and Minority Ethnic Academics: Multiple Identities and Career Progression.* Southampton: University of Southampton.

Biesta, G. J. (2012). The Educational Significance of the Experience of Resistance: Schooling and the Dialogue Between Child and World. *Other Education: The Journal of Educational Alternatives, 1*(1), 92–103.

Black, L. (2014, December 8). Why Isn't My Professor Black? *On Reflection.* Available at http://www.dtmh.ucl.ac.uk/isnt-professor-black-reflection/. Accessed July 2016.

Bourdieu, P. (2001). *Homo Academicus.* Cambridge: Polity Press.

Bourdieu, P. (2010). *Distinction: A Social Critique of the Judgement of Taste.* London: Routledge.

Bourdieu, P., & Passeron, J.-C. (1994). *Reproduction in Education, Society and Culture* (2nd ed.). London: Sage.

Dopson, S., Ferlie, E., McGivern, G., Fischer, M., Ledger, J., Behrens, S., et al. (2016). *The Impact of Leadership and Leadership Development in Higher Education: A Review of the Literature and Evidence.* London: Leadership Foundation for Higher Education.

Drucker, P. (2005). *The Daily Drucker: 366 Days of Insight and Motivation for Getting the Right Things Done.* New York: Harper Business.

Equality Act. (2010). London: HMI.

ECU (Equality Challenge Unit). (2011). *The Experience of Black and Minority Ethnic Staff in Higher Education in England.* London: ECU.

ECU (Equality Challenge Unit). (2015). *Equality in Higher Education: Statistical Report.* London: ECU.

ECU (Equality Challenge Unit). (2016). *Equality in Higher Education: Statistical Report Staff.* London: ECU.

ECU (online). *Race Equality Charter.* Available at http://www.ecu.ac.uk/equality-charters/race-equality-charter/. Accessed 1 July 2016.

EHRC (Equality and Human Rights Commission). (2016). *Healing a Divided Nation: The Need for a Comprehensive Race Equality Strategy Report.* London: EHRC.

Evans, L. (2015). A Changing Role for University Professors? Professorial Academic Leadership as It Is Perceived by the 'Led'. *British Educational Research Journal, 41*(4), 666–685.

Flynn, J. (2012). *Are We Getting Smarter? Rising IQ in the Twenty-First Century.* Cambridge: Cambridge University Press.

Gallant, A. (2014). Symbolic Interactions and the Development of Women Leaders in Higher Education. *Gender, Work and Organisation, 21*(3), 203–216.

Garces, L., & Cogburn, C. (2015). Beyond Declines in Student Body Diversity: How Campus-Level Administrators Understand a Prohibition on Race-Conscious Post-secondary Admissions Policies. *American Educational Research Journal, 52*(5), 828–860.

Gay, G. (2010). *Culturally Responsive Teaching: Theory, Research, and Practice.* New York: Teachers College Press.

Hayes, C., & Juárez, B. (2012). There Is No Culturally Responsive Teaching Spoken Here: A Critical Race Perspective. *Democracy & Education, 20*(1), Article 1. Available at http://democracyeducationjournal.org/home/vol20/iss1/1/. Accessed 10 Mar 2016.

Jarboe, N. (2016). *WomenCount Leaders in Higher Education 2016*. London: WomenCount.

Jean-Marie, G., Normore, A., & Brooks, J. (2009a). For Social Justice: Preparing 21st Century School Leaders for a New Social Order. *Journal of Research on Leadership Education, 4*(1), 1–30.

Jean-Marie, G., Williams, V., & Sherman, S. (2009b). Black Women's Leadership Experiences: Examining the Intersectionality of Race and Gender. *Advances in Developing Human Resources, 11*(5), 562–581.

Jensen, A. (1969). *Environment, Heredity and Intelligence*. Cambridge, MA: Harvard Educational Review.

Johnson, J. (2015, August 27). *Lifting the Cap on Student Numbers Will Drive Social Mobility*. http://www.standard.co.uk/comment/comment/jo-johnson-lifting-the-cap-on-student-numbers-will-drive-social-mobility-a2922356.html. Accessed 1 July 2016.

Jones, T. B., Dawkins, L. S., McClinton, M. M., & Glover, M. H. (Eds.). (2012). *Pathways to Higher Education Administration for African American Women*. Sterling, VA: Stylus.

Kilomba, G. (2010). *Plantation Memories: Episodes of Everyday Racism*. UNRAST: Verlag Münster.

King, J. (2007). Dysconscious Racism: Ideology, Identity and the Miseducation of Teachers. In G. Ladson-Billings & D. Gillborn (Eds.), *The RoutledgeFalmer Reader in Multicultural Education* (pp. 71–83). London: RoutledgeFalmer.

Leadership Foundation. (2015). *Why Does Ethnicity Matter in Higher Education Leadership? Leadership Insights*. London: Leadership Foundation in Higher Education.

Leathwood, C., Maylor, U., & Moreau, M. (2009). *The Experience of Black and Minority Ethnic Staff Working in Higher Education. Literature Review*. London: Equality Challenge Unit.

Leonardo, A. (2004). The Color of Supremacy: Beyond the Discourse of White Privilege. *Educational Philosophy and Theory, 36*(2), 137–152.

McKinsey, J. (2014). *Diversity Matters*. London: McKinsey.

Miele, F. (2004). *Intelligence, Race, and Genetics: Conversations with Arthur R. Jensen*. Cambridge, MA: Westview Press.

Miller, P. (2016). White Sanction, Institutional, Group and Individual Interaction in the Promotion and Progression of Black and Minority Ethnic Academics and Teachers in England. *Power and Education, 8*(3), 205–221.

Murji, K., & Solomos, J. (Eds.). (2016). *Theories of Race and Ethnicity: Contemporary Debates and Perspectives*. Cambridge: Cambridge University Press.

ONS (Office for National Statistics). (2018). Annual population survey data for England, 19th January. Ethnicity and religion broken by country using both the Annual Population Survey (JD07 to JD16) and Labour Force Survey (AJ07 to AJ16) Reference 007975. https://www.ons.gov. uk/employmentandlabourmarket/peopleinwork/labourproductivity/ adhocs/007975tablesproducedusingtheannualpopulationsurveyandthelabourforcesurveyethnicityandreligionbrokendownbycountry. Accessed 21 January 2018.

Osler, A. (2015). Human Rights Education, Postcolonial Scholarship and Action for Social Justice. *Theory and Research in Social Education, 43*(2), 244–274.

Osler, A. (2016). *Human Rights and Schooling: An Ethical Framework for Teaching for Social Justice.* New York: Teachers College Press.

Peters, M. (2015). Editorial: Why Is My Curriculum White? *Educational Philosophy and Theory, 47*(7), 641–646.

Picower, B. (2009). The Unexamined Whiteness of Teaching: How White Teachers Maintain and Enact Dominant Racial Ideologies. *Race Ethnicity and Education, 12*(2), 197–215.

Pilkington, A. 2013. The Interacting Dynamics of Institutional Racism in Higher Education. *Race, Ethnicity and Education, 16*(2), 225–245.

Portelli, J. P., & Campbell-Stephens, R. (2009). *Leading for Equity: The Investing in Diversity Approach.* Halifax, NS: Edphil Books.

Reay, D. (2012). Foreword. In Y. Taylor (Ed.), *Educational Diversity: The Subject of Difference and Different Subjects.* London: Palgrave Macmillan.

Singh, G., & Kwhali, J. (2015). *How Can We Make Not Break Black and Minority Ethnic Leaders in Higher Education?* Stimulus Paper. London: Leadership Foundation for Higher Education.

Smith, E. (2012). *Key Issues in Social Justice and Education.* London: Sage.

Trotman, F. (2009). The Imposter Phenomenon Among African American Women in U.S. Institutions of Higher Education: Implications for Counselling. In G. Watz, J. Bleuer, & R. Yep (Eds.), *Compelling Counselling Interventions: VISTAS* (pp. 77–87). Alexandria, VA: American Counselling Association.

UCU (University College Union). (2016). *The Experiences of Black and Minority Ethnic Staff in Further and Higher Education.* London: University College Union.

UK NARIC. (n.d.) http://ecctis.co.uk/naric/Default.aspx. Accessed 16 Dec 2016.

Walumbwa, F., Avolio, B., Gardner, W., Wernsing, T., & Peterson, S. (2008). Authentic Leadership: Development and Validation of a Theory-Based Measure. *Journal of Management, 34*(1), 89–126.

21

Trans/Forming Pedagogical Spaces: Race, Belonging and Recognition in Higher Education

Penny Jane Burke

Reconceptualising Belonging and Inclusion: Social Justice Frameworks

'Belonging' and 'inclusion' have become hegemonic discourses in higher education, in relation to equity and widening participation policy and practice and concerns to address the diversity of student communities. However, discourses of 'belonging' and 'inclusion' tend to be atheoretical, decontextualised and disembodied, and this often unwittingly contributes to the perpetuation of racialised inequalities. Struggles over the right to higher education pose serious challenges for equity policy and practice because such struggles are bound up with long-standing historical inequalities. Close attention must thus be paid to the different practices and contexts in which inequalities of race, ethnicity and difference are formed and reformed. Such formations are deeply connected to the politics of mis/recognition within

P. J. Burke (✉)
Centre of Excellence for Equity in Higher Education,
University of Newcastle, Newcastle, Australia
e-mail: pennyjane.burke@newcastle.edu.au

© The Author(s) 2018
J. Arday and H. S. Mirza (eds.), *Dismantling Race in Higher Education*,
https://doi.org/10.1007/978-3-319-60261-5_21

the highly stratified and selective spaces of higher education. Working towards greater equity in higher education involves holding together three interconnected social justice dimensions of redistribution, recognition and representation (Fraser 2008), with close attention paid to embodied subjectivities (McNay 2008) and the politics of emotion (Ahmed 2004).

Attention to the methods by which resources and opportunities might be redistributed to those groups who have suffered long-standing forms of social, educational and economic inequalities is also imperative. In order to develop strategies for redistribution, it is important to identify structural inequalities, which are tied in with relations of power and difference, such as race and ethnicity. This must be nuanced however to address the intricate ways that structures of inequality are always intersecting, embodied formations that operate at systemic, cultural, symbolic and affective levels. Therefore, in order to make sense of inequalities of race, it is important to analyse the intimate relationship of race to other structural inequalities, such as class, ethnicity and gender.

In such an analysis, nuanced attention to the processes of misrecognition is vital. Misrecognition is a form of symbolic violence that operates at the level of feeling, emotion, subjective construction and embodiment in relation to wider social structures and power formations, producing subtle and insidious inequalities in, through and beyond higher education. Misrecognition creates ways of imagining the kinds of persons who are identified, or not, as 'worthy' university participants. The processes of being recognised as a 'worthy' or authentic university student are deeply contextualised so that participation is differently conceptualised across (and within) different HE fields and disciplines. Misrecognitions are difficult to capture because they work at the level of everyday, taken for granted practices within heterogeneous, disciplinary communities of practice. Admissions, selection, teaching, assessment, and so forth, are social practices in which recognitions and subjectivities are produced. The practices that perpetuate histories of misrecognition take place within and across different institutional contexts, as well as within particular disciplinary fields such as Arts, Medicine, Law, Philosophy and so forth. Through taken-for-granted academic practices, constructions of difference are formed, often in problematic ways that deepen misrecognitions and inequalities. The tendency is to project a pathologising gaze on racialised bodies that have historically been constructed as a problem for education, and as suffering from a range of deficit disorders (e.g. lack of aspiration, lack of motivation, lack of confidence, lack of resilience and so on). The educational practices and systems that have perpetuated and produced enduring racialised inequalities tend to be ignored. The intersection of race with gender and class often exacerbates processes of misrecognition for certain persons and groups (Mirza 2009).

Fraser (2008) argues that social justice requires attention to 'redistribution', 'recognition' and 'representation' with a focus on enabling parity of participation. Understanding these three dimensions of social justice as interwoven is crucial for reconceptualising 'inclusion' and 'belonging' in higher education spaces, challenging hegemonic discourses. Following Fraser (1997, 2003, 2008), it is important to shift attention away from deficit discourses to attention on transforming institutional spaces, systems and practices which are implicated in reproducing exclusions and inequalities at cultural, symbolic and structural levels. Fraser explains:

> When misrecognition is identified with internal distortions in the structure of the self-conscious of the oppressed, it is but a short step to blaming the victim (…) Misrecognition is a matter of externally manifest and publicly verifiable impediments to some people's standing as full members of society. To redress it, means to overcome subordination. *This in turn means changing institutions and social practices.* (Fraser 2003: 31, emphasis added)

Such a framework illuminates that transforming higher education spaces for social justice relies on equitable distributive, recognition and representation processes that work with and through difference (Burke 2015). This challenges conceptualisations of equity that rest on over-simplified notions of treating everyone the same. Rather it is important to *redistribute* resources to those groups and communities who have experienced material and structural disadvantages, whilst simultaneously *valuing the different* experiences, histories, values and cultural practices of those heterogeneous groups and communities.

It is vital to challenge constructions of 'equity groups' as homogenous rather than recognising differences within and across groups and the intricate ways that differences intersect in identity-formations and embodied subjectivities.

It is therefore crucial to create institutional mechanisms of representation *across* different groups and communities, whilst recognising differences *within* those groups and communities. For example, it is important to redistribute resources and opportunities to those communities who have been denied such opportunities through forms of institutionalised racism (Gillborn 2008) at play in schools and higher education. It is also important to recognise and value the different perspectives and knowledges those communities bring to higher education and to provide genuine opportunities for representation of their different experiences, histories and knowleges. However, homogenising those communities (for example through policy categorisations such as 'Black and Minority Ethnic') often perpetuates a pathologising neocolonial gaze whilst ignoring differences *within* communities. Thus policy and practice must be highly sensitive and fine-tuned to the formations of difference within and across different communities and to understand this in relation to the complex intersectionalities that form subjectivities, ontologies and epistemologies. Although there are important differences between groups targeted by higher education policies to widen participation, these principles are important across different groups; so these principles apply not only to policy categorisations such as 'Black and Minority Ethnic', but also to 'Low Socioeconomic Groups', 'Mature' and 'Part-time', 'Students with Disabilities' and other such 'equity groups' targeted by HE policy and practice.

Parity of participation in higher education depends on having the means and resources to develop participation in ways that a person might be recognised as a legitimate participant within particular disciplinary contexts. Becoming a participant requires representation within that space. Having access to certain material and economic resources such as a computer, internet, transportation and books are also important in developing the forms of 'participation' that might be recognised by university lecturers and that enable representation of different student perspectives, histories and values.

Participation is more complex than simply having access to financial and material resources or cultural and social capitals, as important as this is. Nancy Fraser (2008) sheds light on the ways that misrecognition and misrepresentation deeply undermine parity of participation within social institutions such as higher education. Fraser's social justice framework (1997, 2008) is generative for questions of widening participation through the insight that the processes of misrecognition are about the institutional values and judgments that are imposed on the misrecognised person in ways that effectively exclude her/him from parity of participation. In order to have parity of participation, the person must be *recognised* and have *access to representation* as a fully valued member of the community.

However, it is also important to capture the affective, emotional, subjective and lived experiences of misrecognition and misrepresentation, that are felt in and through the body as forms of symbolic violence and injury on the self (McNay 2008: 150). This often leads to feelings of shame and fear (Ahmed 2004). Institutional fields such as schools and higher education are sites in which subjectivity is formed and personhood is constituted. Recognition is formed through the dual processes of mastery and submission of the discourses at play within a particular field (such as higher education) (Davies 2006). The discourse of 'participation', which is multiple and contested, itself formed through the social practices and values at play within a subject field, constitutes the student in particular ways through the politics of (mis)recognition and (mis)representation. The concept of 'performativity' (Butler 1993) sheds light on the ways that subjectivity is formed not through who we *are* but through what we *do*; through social and cultural practices.

In my recent research in Australia on capabilities and belonging (Burke et al. 2016), we argue that the politics of 'belonging' are deeply entwined with such questions of recognition and representation:

to be seen as a 'capable' student in higher education, the student must act in certain ways. For example, being recognised as 'academically capable' depends on performing 'academic capability' through body language, literacy and communication practices, analytical and critical practices (which might differ across and within disciplines), demonstrating certain skills in particular ways (such as time management and organisation skills) and so forth. Each of these aspects of capability are shifting discursive practices. (Burke et al. 2016)

Gaining access to higher education depends on demonstrating particular attributes and dispositions. These are embedded in a highly esoteric framework, requiring that the student decode forms of academic practice that are granted legitimacy through disciplinary technologies of assessment, ranking and measurement. Students from socially privileged backgrounds often have access to a range of resources that enable them to decode how to demonstrate academic potential and capability in increasingly stratified and stratifying pedagogical contexts (Stevenson et al. 2014). For example, to achieve in higher education, the 'successful' student must first understand how to write, speak and read in ways that is recognised as legitimate forms of practice within higher education. These academic practices of writing, speaking and reading are highly contextual and subjected to discursive performativities, profoundly constraining possibilities for developing a sense of belonging in higher education. Students from under-represented backgrounds often experience feelings of individual unworthiness or shame, which are related to, often invisible, social and cultural processes of misrecognition. Academic practices tend to be misrepresented as neutral, decontextualised sets of technical skills and literacy that students associated with racialised differences are seen to lack (Lillis 2001).

Becoming a university student demands developing a particular form of voice within the boundaries of the discipline, course or subject being studied. Ways of writing in Sociology will be different from ways of writing in Psychology or Physics and this is not just simply about learning sets of skills but learning very particular ways of thinking, arguing, being critical, analytical and so forth. These are *methodologies* rather than technical skills. Furthermore, White, Eurocentric and masculine perspectives and orientations have historically formed assumptions about who has the right to higher education (Burke 2012). Indeed, 'inclusion' tends to be more about fitting into the dominant culture than about interrogating that culture for the ways that it is complicit in the social and cultural reproduction of racialised exclusion, misrecognition and inequality.

Discourses of 'inclusion' often work as a form of symbolic violence, coercing those seen as 'excluded' to conform to hegemonic conventions, expectations and values and to participate in a process of *individual* 'transformation' into normalised personhoods. This includes for example becoming 'flexible' and 'adaptable' to volatile market conditions and thus being recognised as an appropriately 'resilient' participant. The discourses of 'resilience' however are also individualised, so that the social structures and cultural misrecognitions that undermine a person's recognition as 'resilient' are concealed from view. Thus, inclusion often perpetuates problematic deficit perspectives that place the responsibility on those individuals who are identified as at risk of exclusion through their 'lack' of aspiration, confidence, adaptability or resilience. Inclusion might also be seen as a discursive space in which the politics of shame play out in ways that are experienced as personal failure and simply not being the 'right' kind of person and worthy enough for participation in higher education (Raphael Reed et al. 2007: 19).

Therefore, it is my position that it is imperative to reconfigure 'inclusion' and 'belonging' in higher education as a broader project of transforming higher education, with a focus on redistributing opportunities to access esoteric academic practices but also to challenge misrecognition of the experiences, histories and knowledges of those communities who have been systematically marginalised. This includes creating pedagogical spaces for the representation of those marginalised experiences, histories and knowledges that challenge the re-privileging of hegemonic White Anglocentric values and perspectives (although also recognising that there are differences and contestations within communities as well as across them).

Pedagogical 'space' is an important concept in thinking through struggles for the right to higher education in all of its complexities and intricacies. Space plays a key role in structuring student experience and research reveals that belonging and inclusion are closely related to spatial relations and structures (Souter et al. 2011; Radcliffe et al. 2008; Neary et al. 2010; Ahlefeld 2009). 'Space' helps to consider how the architectural or the technological make possible certain forms of practice in relation to questions of space/time. Physical and virtual spaces in higher education generate complex pedagogical relations that are related to formations of difference and power in space/time. For example, Munoz sheds light on the ways that campus planning and campus buildings and landscapes have a critical role in perpetuating racism in the US (Munoz 2015).

Developing inclusive HE spaces involves attention to the ways that participants take up, embody and move through the different spaces in higher education that produce unequal and racialised relations; for example, the ways a lecturer might position himself in the lecture hall and the ways different students might participate (differently) in seminar discussions. The physical spaces in which our bodies are re-positioned profoundly shape our practices, experiences and emotions within that space. We might be able to subvert those spaces but this is constrained by the physicality and/or technology of those spaces. Space therefore is not only about the objective physical, technological and/or architectural 'reality' of universities but is also about our embodied, lived and emotional experiences of those spaces—how we feel in and about those spaces, how those spaces position our embodied selves, how mis/recognitions play out within those spaces and how we might reconfigure those spaces in ways that contribute to practices for social justice. The spaces are also discursively constituted and open to refashioning; we can find possibilities for articulating difference and different ways of being and knowing across and between hegemonic HE spaces. Spaces are also deeply tied in with temporalities; the ways that time is structured within and across those spaces as well as our different relationalities to time across structural and symbolic inequalities.

Gender, Race and Misrecognitions

Mathia Diawara (1998) argues that Black working class masculinity has become coded as 'cool' through representations produced across a range of popular culture, including film and music. Although attached to Black bodies signifying 'cool', this signifier can be 'transported through white bodies' (Diawara 1998: 52, cited in Skeggs 2004: 1) in particular moments in space and time. However, Skeggs points out that such signifiers become fixed on Black bodies whilst Black racialised persons are 'excluded symbolically from performing 'whiteness''. Skeggs explores the ways that 'some cultural characteristics fix some groups and enable others to be mobile' (Skeggs 2004: 1). Jackie McManus and I have drawn on such insights (Burke and McManus 2009) to illustrate the way that Black working-class applicants of Art and Design courses in higher education are marked and coded through misrecognition, and are constrained by citations of music, fashion and art (such as hip-hop) also fixed by codes associated with 'blackness'. In the research, we gained access to selection interviews with candidates of Art and Design courses and were able to observe almost 80 selection interviews across five English higher education institutions.

Our analysis of our observation data found that selection interviews in the admissions process operate as a profound space of exclusion, where knowing how to perform potential is deeply but insidiously connected to social privilege, cultural capital and the embodiment and enactment of 'appropriate' forms of personhood. This was most explicitly shown through the case of Nina (pseudonym), a young Black woman from an inner city area in England and applying for a BA Fashion course.

All the candidates were asked about their influences at the start of the selection interview, and Nina explained that she was influenced by hip-hop. Nina's interview was cut short, and she was also denied the opportunity to complete her admissions test. After the interview, we observed the admissions tutors discussing how they would formally record their decision. They decided to claim that Nina's portfolio was weak. However, we had also observed the assessment of her portfolio before the interview and it had not been judged as weak. They additionally claimed that Nina lacked 'fashion flair' although she was dressed almost identically to the other white female candidates we had observed being interviewed earlier. They were also disappointed with her desire to stay home while at university, claiming that this reflected her lack of maturity.

Yet the male, white, middle class candidate interviewed immediately after Nina was accepted. He cited famous contemporary artists as his influences, was expensively dressed and said he would 'definitely be leaving home as it's all part of the university experience'. Despite having significantly poorer qualifications than Nina, including having failed

GCSE Art, he was offered a place. The research revealed that the shared perspectives, values and assumptions of admissions tutors within their subject-based communities strongly influence their selection practices when they are caught up in identifying potential in ways that misrecognise and thus exclude young Black women such as Nina. The research points to the imperative that all those with institutional positions of authority and responsibility in making judgements about others must interrogate the taken-for-granted values, perspectives and judgements in selection and assessment processes. Discriminatory processes are not necessarily explicit and intentional; they are often subtle, subjective and almost invisible. Those with the authority to judge and assess are often deeply entrenched in the taken-for-granted constructions of potential within their related disciplinary communities of practice.

Misrecognitions in Pedagogical Spaces: Voice, Race and Gender

Voice and silence pose particular challenges for teachers and students in relation to expectation around 'participation'. This was illustrated in research on Formations of Gender and Higher Education Pedagogies (GaP) (Burke et al. 2013), a qualitative study about HE teachers' and students' experiences and perspectives of pedagogies (through in-depth and detailed interviews and focus groups) and of their practices (through observations of classroom practice). The data suggested that 'participation' is conceptualised by university lecturers in relation to 'voice' and 'silence' and tied to embodied intersections of gender and race.

Student voice has often been related to notions of student empowerment and representation. However, Batchelor (2006) points to vulnerabilities in relation to student voice arguing that we need to pay closer attention to the 'vulnerability of certain modes of voice' (787). The data from the GaP study expose the ways that students' different voices are interconnected with gendered, classed and racialised misrecognitions, reinforcing Batchelor's important insight about vulnerabilities in relation to (judgments about) different student voices. Although voice is often associated with student 'empowerment', only particular forms of 'voice' have the potential to be validated through racialised and gendered pedagogical relations. It was clear from the data for example that some voices cause quite significant levels of discomfort and disapproval, including those voices associated with Black and working-class masculinities that were repeatedly constructed as noisy and disruptive. Student voices perceived as unruly were connected to constructions of Black racialised hyper-masculinity and this is linked to pejorative discourses of 'Other' students associated with widening participation, diversity and difference.

The following exchange between two (White, male) Business Studies lecturers participating in a focus group discussion, exposes the tensions they experience in relation to student voice, race and gender:

Lecturer 1: I can hear blokes. Again I can usually hear their chatter let's say more acutely more than I can hear some female chatter simply because of the difference in pitch.

Lecturer 2: I really can't tolerate talking. It really drives me nuts and I will stop a lecture and they know. Whereas in the old days I used to just get louder and louder and they got louder and it got out of control. But I think you learn as a lecturer how to control a group.

The lecturers are particularly concerned about changes in the student constituencies they are teaching and how this raises particular challenges in terms of regulating student behaviour. The neoliberal reframing of higher education tends to reposition students as educational consumers, arguably challenging the traditional forms of authority of the university lecturer. This sometimes raised the question of how students have the potential to exercise their rights as a consumer, and to what extent teachers could or should control students. Such accounts seemed to be connected to an implicit fear of the 'Other' in the classroom; those 'new' groups of students who occupy a different and unfamiliar subject position. This was implicitly tied to classed and racialised forms of masculinity, and to narratives of those Other students who are seen as not fitting into expectations of how university student should behave. In such instances, the intersections of working class, Black young masculinities are posed as undermining the authoritative position of the (White, middle-class) university lecturer. Anxiety about the risk of contamination of the (pure/legitimate) HE pedagogical context is suggested, raising questions about the complex dynamics of changing pedagogical relations.

The lecturer below implies the personal anxiety connected with students exercising rights as a consumer of higher education. In some disciplinary fields, university teachers expressed their concern over the lack of control they had over Black and working-class male student groups who were constructed as having the 'wrong' kinds of attitudes and behaviours. The students thus were constructed as not belonging or fitting into the academic environment and as a problem linked to a perceived lowering of standards:

> …they are the same group who's actually been making noises—so affecting the students' hearing, and the problem, sometimes, you find it's the same group time and time again. When you warn the first time, come the following week, and exactly the same. So the question we raised as well, before, how far you can go to say OK, enough is enough…. I mean I've done it, I think, twice or three times, and one of them is going and complain to the boss, you know. But I mean I have nothing to hide, you know. (White, male Sports Science Lecturer)

The above account is grounded in a wider set of assumptions about the teacher's role in regulating, disciplining and containing student behaviour (see also Nicoll and Harrison 2003; Llamas 2006). However such accounts tend to ignore deeper pedagogical questions about processes of engaging diverse groups of students in ways that facilitate a sense of belonging and participation in the context of widening participation, changing student populations and trans/forming pedagogical cultures. Such questions demand deeper engagement of universities about the intersections between teaching, learning, equity and racialised, classed and gendered inequalities.

The micro-politics of voice and silence play out in complex ways in the higher education classroom in relation to formations of difference. Confidence is seen as a signifier of potential and capability.

Students constructed as 'lacking confidence' are also connected to anxieties about lowering of standards. This is linked to contemporary discourses of teaching that emphasise 'student engagement' and 'student voice' as an indication of participation. Yet, speaking out in pedagogical spaces has been identified in the wider literature as a significant source of anxiety for many students associated with equity and difference in higher education (McLeod 2011; Sellar and Gale 2011; Batchelor 2006). Test and Egan (2014) explain that:

> The social structures of race, class, and age remain a feature of the higher education sector to the detriment of all students, especially those from non-traditional backgrounds. Most participants reported that earlier in the course, they have been afraid to speak. (232)

Confidence becomes a signifier of the 'proper' university student and yet is often framed as a neutral, decontextualised and disembodied trait that 'non-traditional' students lack. The wider patriarchal and neocolonial structures and discourses that might work on the student associated with widening participation to recast them as lacking in confidence are hidden, while the individual becomes the focus of the need for remedial forms of support. Such forms of support are in turn attached to anxieties about lowering of standards and an assumed 'feminisation of higher education' (Leathwood and Read 2009), connected to anxieties about 'spoon feeding' students. The student constructed as 'non-traditional' often reproduces the narrative of lack of self-confidence and is thus repositioned as the weak, needy and passive student at the centre of derogatory discourses of widening participation. A vicious cycle of misrecognition is put into place, subtly reasserting the dominance of certain forms of White, hegemonic masculinity in universities.

Creating Inclusive Spaces in Higher Education

Students are socially situated and this is deeply embedded in racialised relations and through the discourses, formations of difference and institutional practices that name and make us; the politics of 'recognition' and 'misrecognition'. If a student is continually recognised as having 'potential', this becomes a way of understanding himself, just as being identified as 'lacking potential' profoundly shapes a student's self-understanding, feelings of worthiness, inclusion and belonging. However, in order to be recognised as 'having potential', a person must first decode the practices that will allow them recognition as an appropriate, legitimate or authentic university student. For those from under-represented backgrounds, it might take time to develop an understanding of the ways that 'potential' is constructed and recognised within particular disciplinary fields. This is exacerbated by institutional racism and forms of neocolonialism, in which the 'Other' must not only perform those attributes that might afford recognition and representation but must do this in conditions in which the embodiment of racialisation requires continual struggle against the denigrating and marginalising discourses and practices that reposition those embodying racialised subjectivities as outside, excluded, abject and 'Other'. This is felt in and through the body, as 'technologies of affect':

> rethinking race and racism as technologies of affect, a vision of anti-racist politics and practice in education can be formed in ways that go beyond recognition or resistance (Lim 2010), but rather attend to the production of pedagogical spaces and practices that create ways of living differently, that is, ways that do not repeat expected (i.e. normalized) racialized affects. These kinds of pedagogical spaces and practices would have to attend very carefully how 'race is necessarily a matter of affect and affect does not walk innocently of race' (Crang and Tolia 2010). (Zembylas 2015: 147)

An ethical and anti-racist framework for access and equity in higher education requires universities to provide the resources and opportunities for students from under-represented backgrounds to develop their understanding of ways of writing, reading, speaking and learning that will facilitate their access to privileged forms of being and knowing, whilst at the same time encouraging spaces of change and transformation at the wider institutional, cultural and social levels. This is different from providing study skills support that tends to reduce complex sets of literacy practice to remedial support for skills acquisition (Lea and Street 2000). This requires a shift in the gaze—away from identifying individual students 'with problems' and towards developing sophisticated pedagogical interventions that support students' access to meaning-making processes. This also shifts our orientation away from instrumentalised frameworks of teaching and learning and towards transformative pedagogical approaches that engage students as participants in the development, and critique, of knowledge and meaning. This extends thinking beyond formal teaching to consider the range of pedagogical relations we engage, including in the processes of recruitment and admissions and the ways students are selected in relation to judgments about potential and capability.

Strategies for equity in higher education must not only attend to objective forms of institutional discrimination but also to the symbolic violence of being misrecognised. The injuries of misrecognition are embodied, through the internalisation of shame, and are tied to the emotional level of experience, felt in and through the body. The GaP research reveals the intensive forms of anxiety many students experience, even after they successfully gain access to higher education, and this is connected to the residual memory of shame from earlier educational experiences as well as the ongoing fear of being shamed again. We need to engage in pedagogical strategies that rethink questions of race and racism as technologies of affect and the ways that affective racisms are embedded in classrooms.

We must therefore question and challenge deficit constructions associated with equity and widening participation categorisations, such as 'Black and Minority Ethnic'. Yet simultaneously, we must be accountable for ensuring that scarce resources are targeted towards those social groups who have experienced social disadvantage and structural inequality. This is a tension we are compelled to address in policy and practice; categorisations help us to decide how to redistribute resources whilst simultaneously categorisations require interrogation of the ways they become mechanisms to homogenise, standardise and pathologise. The category of 'Black and Minority Ethnic' is both a useful device to identify an appropriate target group for the redistribution of resources but it also contributes to the perpetuation of social divisions and hierarchies through reducing that person or group to one aspect of identity. We must make visible the ways such constructions are entangled in cycles of exclusion, misrecognition and unequal power relations and instead devise ethical, reflexive and participatory frameworks that challenge racialised and gendered misrecognitions and misrepresentations.

References

Ahlefeld, H. (2009). *Evaluating Quality in Educational Spaces: OECD/CELE Pilot Project.* OECD. http://www.oecd.org/education/innovation-education/centreforeffectivelearningenvironmentscele/43904538.pdf. Accessed 20 July 2015.

Ahmed, S. (2004). *The Cultural Politics of Emotion.* New York: Routledge.

Batchelor, D. C. (2006). Vulnerable Voices: An Examination of the Concept of Vulnerability in Relation to the Student Voice. *Educational Philosophy and Theory, 38*(6), 787–800.

Burke, P. J. (2012). *The Right to Higher Education: Beyond Widening Participation.* London and New York: Routledge.

Burke, P. J. (2015). Re/Imagining Higher Education Pedagogies: Gender, Emotion and Difference. *Teaching in Higher Education, 20*(4), 388–401.

Burke, P. J., & McManus, J. (2009). *Art for a Few: Exclusions and Misrecognitions in Art and Design.* London: National Arts Learning Network and HEFCE.

Burke, P. J., Bennett, A., Burgess, C., Gray, K., & Southgate, E. (2016). *Capabilities, Belonging and Equity in Higher Education* (Report to the NCSEHE). Perth: National Centre for Student Equity in Higher Education.

Burke, P. J., Crozier, G., Read, B., Hall, J., Peat, J., & Francis, B. (2013). *Formations of Gender and Higher Education Pedagogies Final Report (GaP).* York: Higher Education Academy.

Butler, J. (1993). *Bodies that Matter: On the Discursive Limits of 'Sex'.* London: Routledge.

Crang, M., & Tolia-Kelly, D. P. (2010). Nation, race, and affect: Senses and sensibilities at national heritage sites. *Environment and planning A, 42*(10), 2315–2331.

Davies, B. (2006). Subjectification: The Relevance of Butler's Analysis for Education. *British Journal of Sociology of Education, 27*(4), 425–438.

Diawara, M. (1998). Homeboy Cosmopolitan: Manthia Diawara Interviewed by Silvia Kolbowski. October, 83(Winter), 51–70.

Fraser, N. (1997). *Justice Interruptus: Critical Reflections on the 'Postsocialist' Condition*. London and New York: Routledge.

Fraser, N. (2003). Social Justice in the Age of Identity Politics: Redistribution, Recognition and Participation. In N. Fraser & A. Honneth (Eds.), *Redistribution or Recognition? A Political-Philosophical Exchange*. London and New York: Verso.

Fraser, N. (2008). *Scales of Justice: Reimagining Political Space in a Globalizing World*. Cambridge and Malden, MA: Polity Press.

Gillborn, D. (2008). *Racism and Education: Coincidence or Conspiracy?* London and New York: Routledge.

Lea, M. R., & Street, B. (2000). Student Writing and Staff Feedback in Higher Education: An Academic Literacies Approach. In M. Lea & B. Stierer (Eds.), *Student Writing in Higher Education: New Contexts*. Buckingham: The Society for Research into Higher Education and Open University Press.

Leathwood, C., & Read, B. (2009). *Gender and the Changing Face of Higher Education: A Feminized Future?* Berkshire: Open University Press.

Lillis, T. (2001). *Student Writing: Access, Regulation, Desire*. London: Routledge.

Llamas, J. (2006). Technologies of Disciplinary Power in Action: The Norm of the 'Good Student'. *Higher Education, 52,* 665–686.

McLeod, J. (2011). Student Voice and the Politics of Listening in Higher Education. *Critical Studies in Education, 52*(2), 179–189.

McNay, L. (2008). *Against Recognition*. Cambridge: Polity Press.

Mirza, H. S. (2009). *Race, Gender and Educational Desire*. London and New York: Routledge.

Munoz, F. M. (2015). Critical Race Theory and the Landscapes of Higher Education. *The Vermont Connection, 30*(6), 53–62.

Neary, M., Harrison, A., Crellin G., Parkeh, N., Saunders G., Duggan, F., Williams, S., & Austin, S. (2010). *Learning Landscapes in Higher Education*. http://learninglandscapes.blogs.lincoln.ac.uk/files/2010/04/FinalReport.pdf Accessed 28 Sept 2015.

Nicoll, K., & Harrison, R. (2003). Constructing the Good Teacher in Higher Education: The Discursive Work of Standards. *Studies in Continuing Education, 25*(1), 23–35.

Radcliffe, D., Wilson, H., Powell, D., & Tibbetts, B. (2008). *Designing Next Generation Spaces of Learning: Collaboration at the Pedagogy-Space-Technology Nexus*. The University of Queensland: Australian Learning and

Teaching Council Report. http://documents.skgproject.com/skg-final-report.pdf. Accessed 28 Sept 2015.

Raphael Reed, L., Croudace, C., Harrison, N., Baxter, A., & Last, K. (2007). *Young Participation in Higher Education: A Sociocultural Study of Educational Engagement* in Bristol South Parliamentary Constituency. Research Summary; a HEFCE-funded Study. Bristol: The University of the West of England.

Sellar, S., & Gale, T. (2011). Mobility, Aspiration, Voice: A New Structure of Feeling for Student Equity in Higher Education. *Critical Studies in Education, 52*(2), 115–134.

Skeggs, B. (2004). *Class, Self, Culture.* London and New York: Routledge.

Souter, K., Riddle, M., Sellers, W., & Keppell, M. (2011). *Spaces for Knowledge Generation.* Final Report: Australian Learning and Teaching Council. http://documents.skgproject.com/skg-final-report.pdf. Accessed 28 Sept 2015.

Stevenson, J., Burke, P. J., & Whelan, P. (2014). *Pedagogic Stratification and the Shifting Landscape of Higher Education.* York: Higher Education Academy.

Testa, D., & Egan, R. (2014). Finding a Voice: The Higher Education Experiences of Students from Diverse Backgrounds. *Teaching in Higher Education, 19*(3), 229–241.

Zembylas, M. (2015). Rethinking Race and Racism as Technologies of Affect: Theorizing the Implications for Anti-racism Politics and Practice in Education. *Race, Ethnicity, and Education, 18*(2), 145–162.

22

So What Next? A Policy Response

Gary Loke

What is common throughout the chapters in this book is the paucity of BME people at senior levels, in some subject areas and the lack of belonging that many BME people in higher education face, whether they are students or staff. These issues are well rehearsed (see for example Runnymede 2015) and this book adds to the growing evidence of inequality.

The perspectives in the different chapters are varied, for example exploring issues from different ethnic and religious experiences, issues of curriculum and how the lack of an inclusive/liberated curriculum exacerbate the sense of otherness, the shifting national policy landscape and the discomfort addressing issues of race. The myriad of experiences come together, setting out the challenges that need addressing.

Before I discuss ideas on how these challenges might be addressed, let me first address an issue with the term 'BME' and the interplay with identity. It was refreshing to see D'Arcy and Galloway

G. Loke (✉)
Equality Challenge Unit, London, UK
e-mail: Gary.Loke@ecu.ac.uk

© The Author(s) 2018
J. Arday and H. S. Mirza (eds.), *Dismantling Race in Higher Education*,
https://doi.org/10.1007/978-3-319-60261-5_22

explore the issues of Gypsy and Traveller peoples' participation in higher education as there is limited research in this area. This did give rise however to the question of whether Gypsies and Travellers see themselves as BME people, or are they a white minority that often gets forgotten. The term 'BME' is a useful collective one that helps us see commonalities of inequality. However we must not forget a white minority who also face inequality especially given the current political landscape, in the wake of the vote to leave the European Union. BME people are of course not homogenous, and as Maylor notes, her experience as a Black woman will be because of that intersection, and the intersection of other characteristics that form her identity. Similarly, the cross-over with religion in Saeed's chapter and with generational and family class groups in Li's chapter remind us of the complexity of these intersections and identities. ECU's annual statistical reports explore these intersections—in 2013/2014, 7.1% of professors were BME men, compared to 1.8%, who were BME women (ECU 2015: 278). This 5.3 percentage point difference illustrates the compounded nature of inequality. If another dimension of nationality is added, of all UK-national professors, 1.5% were BME women, compared to 3.1% of all non-UK national professors (ibid: 278). These figures illustrate the complexity of the issues.

So what is the starting point to addressing the number of complex issues? Setting aside intersectionality for the moment, I would begin by attempting to get more collective buy-in on addressing racial inequality. I suggest this because there is a risk that over analysis using Crenshaw's (1989) theory of intersectionality means that we think of individuals rather that the collective, and therefore it becomes easier to dismiss race inequality. I am not arguing that intersectionality is not important, it is important to understand that identity is complex and attitudes towards those identities are complex, however as I mention above, the collective term of BME is useful both to see commonalities and also as a political collective to press for change.

Looking back at the collection, the data for example shows the lack to BME people in senior roles (ECU 2015) as well as underrepresentation of BME people in some disciplines (for example the dearth of Black people in PE teaching as highlighted in Hobson and Whigham).

It is very easy for some to dismiss the data by contextualising it, arguing for example that there are geographical issues as to why an institution is unable to, or finds it unnecessary to address the numbers or that they are doing well benchmarked to other universities (scenario 2 in Rollock's chapter). Therefore, it is important that we argue the need to address the equal distribution of the problem, as opposed to the unequal distribution of the numbers. By this, I mean that it is clear that racism exists in society at a macro-level and so by logical application, it must exist in each institution to some degree—no university is immune from the society in which it is located.

To construct some solutions, I draw on Schiebinger's (1999, in Morley 2013) work on gender equality. She highlights that solutions have focussed on three areas: the individual, the organisation/institution and the knowledge. They are interlinked, and I would argue that work must be done to address all three areas.

Addressing the Individual

Regarding the individual, it is important not to treat BME people as deficient, i.e. that they need fixing in order to belong or to succeed. Traditional interventions in this area are things like mentoring, additional individual support and leadership development. While these may continue to be useful, they must be co-created with BME people and consider the complexity of different identities, so that they don't treat BME people as the problem. Solutions need to address all individuals, and this includes the white majority too. For example, in leadership or teaching skills development, how is white privilege explored, how are new lecturers equipped to discuss issues of race or challenge racist behaviour? How is race constructed in mentoring relationships and would sponsorship as noted in Rollock's chapter be a better model? Addressing all individuals would address in part, the dilemma Hobson and Whigham raise in their chapter.

Of course Hobson and Whigham delve much deeper into whether people can ever fully empathise with the experience of racism. It is of course a complex dilemma, but I would argue for the need to include more white-allies, drawing on the work of straight-allies in the LGBT equality movement (Stonewall 2011). This will gradually change the culture of higher education and it is this culture change that is much needed.

Addressing the Institution

Schiebinger's second area is the institution/organisation and focusing on this will help address the culture. It is also the area that the ECU Race Charter Mark focuses on. One intervention already noted in this book by Bhopal, Brown and Jackson is unconscious bias training, including being an active bystander. I would concur with that, and if this had been in place for Maylor's experience, maybe an active bystander who overheard the conversation would have openly challenged the notion of not looking like a governor, or in D'Arcy and Galloway's chapter, perhaps there would have been more critical reflection around Gypsies' and Travellers' prior education experience. The assumption of whiteness as the norm needs to be challenged, much like what Arday discusses in his chapter.

Unconscious bias training has become increasingly popular over the last few years and I consider that to be a good thing, as it may mitigate the misrecognition that Burke describes. The training must however be done carefully and in a nuanced way, so that those being trained slowly understand that everyone is biased and they are not being blamed or being told they are racist. That only creates a defensive environment which will hinder the self-reflection needed to mitigate unconscious bias. It is especially important that any training for an academic audience should be grounded in the evidence (see ECU 2013a) and the trainer is well-versed in the numerous and ever growing body of work in this area. Equally vital is that unconscious bias cannot be seen as the panacea to the issue of race inequality, there remains of course conscious bias and a myriad of other issues that BME people face, such as our sense of belonging in the academy.

Reay notes BME students feeling outside when inside elite institutions, and Joseph-Salisbury and Johnson discuss the macroaggressions that result from being outsiders in academia. For students, the link between academic success and sense of belonging is well documented (see for example Cousin and Cureton 2012; Thomas 2012) so if we want to see better degree attainment and success, tackling belonging in an institution/organisation is required. The degree attainment gap between BME and white graduates is well documented (ECU 2015) as Richardson notes in his chapter. Getting a lower class degree also affects whether one gets onto a post graduate research course, usually an important stepping stone to an academic career. If this issue is not addressed we will continue to see low numbers of BME academics and professors. The low numbers means there continues to be few role models; these role models can be important for students to get a sense of belonging in their university (see for example NUS, accessed 2016) and they can also be the sponsor some BME people need to provide strategic help to navigate the barriers to progression. Of course, nobody should be made to be a role model just because of their ethnicity, and universities must be cautious not to overburden senior BME academics with the responsibility for dealing with race issues just because of their colour.

It is crucial that a sense of belonging is built, especially given the current political context. Universities have a duty to promote good relations between different groups which will help with belonging. However the duty to promote good relations can sometimes come into conflict with other duties, like the counter-terrorism duty. Saeed explores the experiences of Muslim staff and students, and there is increasing scrutiny on Muslim people because of the counter-terrorism duty. Universities would do well to carefully consider their responsibilities on managing competing duties and follow guidance (ECU 2013b) on managing good relations so that those who feel vulnerable on campus are not made to feel even more so, and that they don't belong.

What happens when someone feels they don't belong? Institutions need to give people more opportunities and ways to raise their issues and concerns. Saeed discusses how there can be a reluctance to raise issues to do with race and if the issues are raised, whether anything will be done about it. Higher education institutions must have clear ways to allow disclosure of such issues, as noted in the Universities UK Changing the Culture report (UUK 2016) and crucially, they must also equip their staff to deal with those disclosures. The constantly changing student cohort and the changing use of technology means the institution must also ensure they repeat communicating disclosure routes in a variety of media, working with students' unions to co-communicate.

Addressing the Knowledge

Schiebinger's third area of addressing the knowledge gives rise to BME people being included and supports that sense of being. One area the National Union of Student's campaign 'Liberate my degree'[1] addresses is curriculum which is not reflective of BME people's lives, experiences and knowledge. Andrews' chapter explores the Black studies movement and his institution, Birmingham City University will be the first university in Europe to offer a degree in Black Studies. This is of course a step in the right direction, but it is also a reflection of how much more needs to be done to address decolonising knowledge of the academy.

There needs to be a paradigm shift that considers how our research, teaching and knowledge-exchange includes BME people and their experiences. We need more co-creation with students, as Burke suggests, to ensure the curriculum is reflective of their lives. To ensure that this is taken into consideration, one way of doing this is to ensure that at programme approval stage, there are robust questions asked about whether the curriculum reflects race diversity in its knowledge as a criteria to gain programme approval. There is a growing awareness of this in terms of gender, for example the gendered innovations project[2] at Stanford University, and we would do well to consider how including race diversity makes for better research and knowledge.

---

[1]http://www.nusconnect.org.uk/winning-for-students/campaigns/liberatemydegree, accessed 2016.
[2]https://genderedinnovations.stanford.edu/.

The ECU Race Equality Charter Mark

Many chapters in this collection mention the ECU Race Equality Charter Mark as a framework for actions and I would of course agree. The basis of the charter mark is collecting good data and evidence and devising an action plan to meet targets and objectives—this for me is 'doing the doing' which Pilkington mentions in his chapter.

Given the political context in which the Prime Minister Theresa May commissioned the recent government audit on race,[3] universities would be wise to take action on race inequality now. The audit is a data stocktake and focuses on government data across the public sector, publishing what data the government has on a digital platform. While it shows great disparities and growing racial inequalities, some argue that this will result in no real change and just more data. However, if we consider that the Prime Minister, in her previous role as Home Secretary did a similar exercise on police stop and search by looking at the data from individual constabularies and in finding disproportionate stopping of Black people pushed for reform of such powers, it may be that data will lead her to push for reform in a range of public services.

If universities were to be examined, the ECU Race Charter Mark could be a useful way for universities to demonstrate what they are doing to address race inequality. Of course the ECU Race Charter Mark is not a panacea, it is merely a framework for action. The end goal is not about achieving an award, it is about continuous progression to advance race equality, and this is the critical point—many universities are slowly starting that journey, and we all need to push a bit harder to accelerate that pace of change.

---

[3]https://www.theguardian.com/uk-news/2017/oct/09/audit-lays-bare-racial-disparities-in-uk-schools-courts-and-workplaces.

References

Cousin, G., & Cureton, D. (2012). *Disparities in Student Attainment (DiSA)*. York: Higher Education Academy.

Crenshaw, K. (1989). Demarginalizing the Intersection of Race and Sex: A Black Feminist Critique of Antidiscrimination Doctrine. *Feminist Theory and Antiracist Politics, The University of Chicago Legal Forum, 140*, 139–167.

ECU. (2013a). *Unconscious Bias in Higher Education: Literature Review*. London: ECU.

ECU. (2013b). *Promoting Good Relations on Campus: A Guide for Higher and Further Education*. London: ECU.

ECU. (2015). *Equality in Higher Education: Statistical Report 2015*. London: ECU.

Morley, L. (2013). *Women and Higher Education Leadership: Absences and Aspirations*. London: Leadership Foundation for Higher Education.

NUS (undated). *Race for Equality: A Report on the Experiences of Black Students in Further and Higher Education*. London: NUS

Runnymede. (2015). *Aiming Higher Race, Inequality and Diversity in the Academy*. London: Runnymede.

Stonewall. (2011). *Straight Allies: How They Help Create Gay-Friendly Workplaces*. London: Stonewall.

Thomas, L. (2012). *Building Student Engagement and Belonging in a Time of Change in Higher Education*. London: Paul Hamlyn Foundation.

UUK. (2016). *Changing the Culture: Report of the Universities UK Taskforce Examining Violence Against Women, Harassment and Hate Crime Affecting University Students*. London: UUK.

Index

© The Editor(s) (if applicable) and The Author(s) 2018
J. Arday and H. S. Mirza (eds.), *Dismantling Race in Higher Education*,
https://doi.org/10.1007/978-3-319-60261-5